This highly original study of the "manic style" in enthusiastic writing of the seventeenth and eighteenth centuries identifies a literary tradition and line of influence running from the radical visionary and prophetic writing of the Ranters and their fellow enthusiasts to the work of Jonathan Swift and Christopher Smart. Clement Hawes offers a counterweight to recent work which has addressed the subject of literature and madness from the viewpoint of contemporary psychological medicine, putting forward instead a stylistic and rhetorical analysis. He argues that the writings of dissident "enthusiastic" groups are based in social antagonisms; and his account of the dominant culture's ridicule of enthusiastic writing (an attitude which persists in twentieth-century literary history and criticism) provides a powerful and daring critique of pervasive assumptions about madness and sanity in literature.

CAMBRIDGE STUDIES IN EIGHTEENTH-CENTURY
ENGLISH LITERATURE AND THOUGHT 29

Mania and Literary Style

Some recent titles

21 *Writing and the Rise of Finance: Capital Satires of the Early Eighteenth Century*
by Colin Nicholson

22 *Locke, Literary Criticism, and Philosophy*
by William Walker

23 *Poetry and Jacobite Politics in Eighteenth-Century Britain and Ireland*
by Murray G. H. Pittock

24 *The Story of the Voyage in Eighteenth-Century England*
by Philip Edwards

25 *Edmond Malone: A Literary Biography*
by Peter Martin

26 *Swift's Parody*
by Robert Phiddian

27 *Rural Life in Eighteenth-Century English Poetry*
by John Goodridge

28 *The English Fable: Aesop and Literary Culture, 1651–1740*
by Jayne Elizabeth Lewis

29 *Mania and Literary Style*
The Rhetoric of Enthusiasm from the Ranters to Christopher Smart
by Clement Hawes

A complete list of books in this series is given at the end of the volume.

Mania and Literary Style

The Rhetoric of Enthusiasm
from the Ranters to Christopher Smart

CLEMENT HAWES

Southern Illinois University

CAMBRIDGE
UNIVERSITY PRESS

Published by the Press Syndicate of the University of Cambridge
The Pitt Building, Trumpington Street, Cambridge CB2 1RP
40 West 20th Street, New York, NY 10011–4211, USA
10 Stamford Road, Oakleigh, Melbourne 3166, Australia

© Cambridge University Press 1996

First published 1996

Printed in Great Britain at the University Press, Cambridge

A catalogue record for this book is available from the British Library

Library of Congress cataloguing in publication data

Hawes, Clement.
Mania and literary style: the rhetoric of enthusiasm from the Ranters to
Christopher Smart / Clement Hawes.
p.   cm. – (Cambridge studies in eighteenth-century English literature and thought: 29)
ISBN 0 521 55022 X (hardback)
1. English literature – 18th century – History and criticism.
2. Enthusiasm in literature. 3. Literature and mental illness – England – History.
4. Smart, Christopher, 1722–1771. Jubilate agno.
5. Literature and society – England – History.
6. English language – 18th century – Style. 7. Rhetoric – 1500–1800.
8. Levellers. 9. Ranters.I. Title. II. Series.
PR448.E57H39 1996
820.9'005–dc20   95–13569 CIP

ISBN 0 521 55022 X hardback

For my parents,
William H. Hawes and
Carolyn C. Hawes

I don't want to bore God. God is an artist.

Orson Welles, upon being asked if he prays, *Life* 6:1 (1983), p. 106

Let Huz bless with the Polypus – a lively
subtlety is acceptable to the Lord.

Christopher Smart, *Jubilate Agno*, A 84

Contents

Acknowledgments

This book has been long in the making, and has accumulated a proportionately large number of debts. It began as a Yale dissertation. In this embryonic phase, Geoffrey H. Hartman and Patricia M. Spacks supplied just the right amount of guidance of every kind. I continue to be inspired by the example of their work. They were, and remain, my teachers. Alan Liu's generously engaged early reading during this phase helped me to glimpse what the book could and should be.

I have been lucky in my friends. Among those who have patiently read most or all of this manuscript are Amittai F. Aviram, Susan L. Meyer, Charles T. Hatten, Tamar Heller, and Susan M. Schweik. They have helped me to improve this book in countless ways – not least, indeed, by the refining influence of their intellectual companionship.

As the project began to take shape, I benefited immensely from the editors and readers for Cambridge University Press. To a person I know only as the second reader, in particular, I am indebted for the single most exacting, shrewd, and helpful reading of *Mania and Literary Style*. Josie Dixon was unfailingly lucid and considerate throughout the process of editorial honing. The book is better for her numerous interventions, both large and small. I am likewise grateful to Linda Bree for congenial and expert assistance on many different fronts and to Audrey Cotterell for her sensitive and meticulous copy-editing.

I received invaluable comments on individual chapters from Paula A. Bennett, James Holstun, Sandra L. Moreland, Leslie Moore, Donna Heiland, and John T. Blair. From Manuel Schonhorn, my eighteenth-century comrade-in-arms at SIU, I received gifts that I can only hope to pass on, in my own way, to the next generation: not only bracing suggestions about what was on the page, but also a daily flow of warm mentoring, skeptical hectoring, cheerful nagging, and whole-hearted support. For intellectual stimulation, practical advice, and good times, I am likewise grateful to many other SIU colleagues, including Robert E. Fox, Jane Adams, Clarisse Zimra, James Allen, Ed Brunner, Mary E. Lamb, Scott McEathron, Kathy Ward, Tony Williams, John McCall, Ron Rich, and Srimati Basu.

I have received generous cooperation from the librarians who staff Yale's Sterling and Beinecke, Harvard's Widener and Houghton, Boston College's O'Neill, and Southern Illinois University's Morris. I would like to give special thanks to SIU's Angela Rubin for the heroic efforts that enabled me to set eyes on some of the more offbeat texts discussed in this book.

Some debts are so large that they can only be falsified by being named. Such is my debt to Mrinalini Sinha. On a daily basis, she makes and remakes me, and – at least to some extent, I hope – saves me from myself. To the extent that she has succeeded, this book is hers.

I am acutely aware that problems and perplexities remain. These I claim as my own.

I am grateful to Oxford University Press for permission to quote from *The Poetical Works of Christopher Smart*, eds. Karina Williamson and Marcus Walsh (Oxford: Clarendon Press, 1980–1987), and to Doubleday for the following: excerpt from "The Dark Angel," from *Straw for the Fire: from the Notebooks of . . .* by Theodore Roethke, selected and arranged by David Wagener, copyright © 1972 by Beatrice Roethke; and excerpt from "Heard in a Violent Ward," copyright © 1984 by Beatrice Roethke, administratrix of the estate of Theodore Roethke, from *The Collected Poems of Theodore Roethke* by Theodore Roethke. Both extracts used by permission of Doubleday, a division of Bantam Doubleday Dell Publishing Group, Inc.

Introduction

Mania as rhetoric

Christopher, help me love this loose thing.
I think of you now, kneeling in London muck,
Praying for grace to descend.
                    Theodore Roethke, "The Dark Angel," from
                    Straw for the Fire: from the Notebooks of . . .

This book concerns three moments of what I shall call a "manic" rhetoric. It explores the evolution of that rhetoric as represented in texts by Ranter Abiezer Coppe during the Interregnum, Jonathan Swift in the late seventeenth century, and Christopher Smart in the mid-eighteenth century. Above all, it concerns the manic as a specifically rhetorical phenomenon. It attempts a break from the inherited language for discussing a certain kind of centrally eccentric text – not so much a clean break as a sort of knight's move, a strategic reorientation of the older terms. I hope to rethink the "manic," a term for individual pathology, from a transindividual and historical perspective. A certain kind of textual mania, as I shall demonstrate, can only be fully understood in connection with the prophetic and oracular religious rhetoric surrounding the English Revolution.

I contend, indeed, that the English Civil War must be seen as the wellspring of the manic rhetorical style in British letters. This is not to say that one cannot find prior texts with manic tendencies,[1] but, rather, that later cultural memory has designated manic enthusiasm as the very sign of that ill-digested revolutionary trauma. The enthusiastic rhetoric that continues to concern and influence us most is indelibly marked, and hence,

---

[1] The sixteenth-century Martin Marprelate polemics, for example, use many forms of rhetorical inversion common to the manic mode. The seventeenth-century Leveller Richard Overton, moreover, deliberately evokes the memory of that earlier controversy. See Nigel Smith, "Richard Overton's Marpriest tracts: towards a history of Leveller style," *Prose Studies* 9:2 (1986), pp. 39–66. Christopher Hill suggests that some very general geographical and doctrinal continuities, though difficult to document, can be tentatively traced from the seventeenth-century radical separatists all the way back to the Lollards. See Christopher Hill, "From Lollards to Levellers," in *The Collected Essays of Christopher Hill*, 2 vols. (Amherst: The University of Massachusetts Press, 1986), II: *Religion and Politics in 17th-Century England*, pp. 89–116.

retroactively given its primary cultural meaning, by that seventeenth-century revolution.[2] "Enthusiasm," in this sense, is the profoundly ambivalent signifier of two revolutions: the bourgeois revolution that did occur and the far more democratic and egalitarian revolution whose possibility was tantalizingly glimpsed and then suppressed.

The texts that I call "manic" all share the key element of enthusiasm: a claim, that is, to supernatural authority. This is the infamous "grandiosity" or "omnipotence" described in all the psychoanalytic literature on mania. My use of the term "manic," however, entails a revision of such notions by also invoking, through the key theme of divine election, a historical arena of ideological and political struggle. Given that Biblical authority was the outermost horizon of seventeenth-century British thought – a shared master code, as it were, even among the warring factions[3] – it is deeply unhistorical to read pathology back into such enthusiastic rhetorical strategies.

The manic rhetorical style is constituted, above all, by its rebellious stance toward traditional hierarchies of socio-economic privilege and their related hierarchies of discourse. It is thus a crucial and telling instance of "class struggle without class," in E. P. Thompson's phrase.[4] Despite the fact, that is to say, that a politically mature, self-aware, and horizontally constituted working class did not exist as such prior to the industrial revolution[5]; that socio-economic stratification was mainly described and understood throughout the seventeenth century and much of the eighteenth century not in terms of "class," but, rather, in the quasi-feudal terms of "rank" and "order"[6] – despite these well-known facts, the notion of class struggle is an indispensable heuristic device for rendering the manic

2   Because some historians prefer labels that do not maximize the implied level of change – "The Great Rebellion," for instance – the term itself is in dispute. See Barry Coward, "Was there an English Revolution in the middle of the seventeenth century?" in *Politics and People in Revolutionary England: Essays in Honor of Ivan Roots*, ed. Colin Jones *et al.* (Oxford: Basil Blackwell, 1986), pp. 9–40. The interpretative struggle over the meaning of this event has gone on, as R. C. Richardson demonstrates, for some three centuries. See R. C. Richardson, *The Debate on the English Revolution Revisited*, 2nd ed. (New York: Routledge, 1988).

3   Fredric Jameson, "Religion and ideology: a political reading of *Paradise Lost*," in *Literature, Politics, Theory: Papers from the Essex Conference 1976–1984*, eds. Francis Barker, Peter Hulme *et al.* (London: Methuen, 1986), pp. 37–39.

4   See E. P. Thompson, "Patrician society, plebeian culture," *Journal of Social History* 7 (Summer 1974), pp. 382–405, and "Eighteenth-century English society: class struggle without class?", *Social History* 3 (May, 1978), pp. 133–165. For a helpful discussion of the place and significance of eighteenth-century studies in the trajectory of Thompson's intellectual career, see Harvey J. Kaye, *The British Marxist Historians: An Introductory Analysis* (Cambridge: Polity Press, 1984), pp. 189–203.

5   See E. P. Thompson, *The Making of the English Working Class* (New York: Vintage Books, 1966).

6   See Steven Wallech, "Class versus rank: the transformation of eighteenth-century social terms and theories of production," *Journal of the History of Ideas* 47:3 (1986), pp. 409–431; and Penelope J. Cornfield, "Class by name and number in eighteenth-century Britain," in *Language, History, and Class* (Oxford: Basil Blackwell, 1991), pp. 101–130. Wallech emphasizes the lingering power of the residual feudal model, which gradually begins to be displaced only when political economists such as Ricardo and Smith bring the process of production (and the roles therein of "class") to the center of their analyses. Cornfield demonstrates, however, that an emergent language of class

style even minimally intelligible. As Christopher Hill's work on the seventeenth century and Thompson's work on the eighteenth century demonstrate, it is only by means of a class-struggle analysis of pre-industrial English society that one can explain much about either the various modes of patrician hegemony, or (granting the well-defined limits of that order of struggle) the manifold modes of plebeian resistance to such domination and exploitation. The precise forms taken by enthusiastic resistance, as we shall see, are determined by particular historical moments and their circumstances.

Thompson's emphasis on the constitutive process of socio-economic struggle in class formation preserves a meaningful role, long before an English proletariat exists as such, for the historical agency of class. At the same time, it deftly avoids two fallacies: it avoids, on the one hand, the anachronism of treating "class" as a static category, and thus reading back into history some supposedly timeless horizontal opposition between agonistic classes. On the other hand, it refuses an anthropomorphic reduction of classes to character-like collective "subjects." Manic rhetoric, with its roots in the English Revolution, is important evidence for the validity of this approach.

A seventeenth-century Puritan text, John Bunyan's *Pilgrim's Progress* is, according to Thompson, "one of the two foundation texts of the working-class movement": itself an important agency of class consciousness, and hence something of a political success in terms of nineteenth-century counter-hegemonic class formation. However, *Pilgrim's Progress*, though in dialogue with more radical views, is neither revolutionary nor very enthusiastic. By way of contrast, then, the texts of the more radical enthusiastic style can be seen as illustrating a premature emergence of revolutionary consciousness. They do of course speak to the revolutionary conflict as it was actually resolved. Yet they speak also in a different, more wishful register, to, and for, far more egalitarian social orders that could have emerged – but did not – from the revolution. To quote Christopher Hill:

---

was already being more widely disseminated by the middle of the eighteenth century. Fielding's *Jonathan Wild* (1743), as Cornfield observes, divides the world starkly into "those that use their own hands, and those that use the hands of others." Hogarth's contrast between "Beer Street" and "Gin Lane" points to a similarly Manichaean polarization. For an analysis of the latter, which also accounts for the commercialized and consumption-oriented dimensions of plebeian culture, see Hans Medick, "Plebeian culture in the transition to capitalism," in *Culture, Ideology, and Politics: Essays for Eric Hobsbawm*, eds. Raphael Samuel and Gareth Stedman Jones (London: Routledge & Kegan Paul, 1982), pp. 84–112. A broader historical and geographic perspective on these issues can be found in Peter Burke, "The language of orders in early modern Europe," in *Social Orders and Social Classes in Europe since 1500: Studies in Social Stratification*, ed. M. L. Bush (London: Longman, 1992), pp. 1–12. I hope in the course of this book to contribute further to the development of a flexible analytic use of "class" as one among several interactive social identities. See *Rethinking Class: Literary Studies and Social Formations*, eds. Wai Chee Dimock and Michael T. Gilmore, The Social Foundations of Aesthetic Forms Series (New York: Columbia University Press, 1994).

There were, we may oversimplify, two revolutions in mid-seventeenth-century England. The one which succeeded established the sacred rights of property (abolition of feudal tenures, no arbitrary taxation), gave political power to the propertied (sovereignty of Parliament and common law, abolition of prerogative courts), and removed all impediments to the ideology of the men of property – the protestant ethic. There was, however, another revolution which never happened, though from time to time it threatened. This might have established communal property, a far wider democracy in political and legal institutions, might have disestablished the state church and rejected the protestant ethic.[7]

Both the manic mode and many aspects of its reception stem from this moment of containment or failed emergence. "Milton's nation of prophets," as Hill says, "became a nation of shopkeepers,"[8] and the most subversive separatists were seemingly forced into a lengthy retrenchment, introspection, and quiescence. Thompson describes the trajectory of this big chill as follows: "*Puritanism – Dissent – Nonconformity*: the decline collapses into a surrender. *Dissent* still carries the sound of resistance to Apollyon and the Whore of Babylon, *Nonconformity* is self-effacing and apologetic: it asks to be left alone."[9] Despite this obvious political failure, however, the impact of the manic mode persists, as a subterranean factor in the cultural life of Britain, much longer and more impressively than its fringe-group origins or brief heyday in the Interregnum might suggest. In terms of literary history, there is something to be said for N. H. Keeble's argument that "it was not Civil War, nor regicide, nor Cromwell which released the Puritan imagination, but nonconformity."[10] I would add to this, however, that the millennial promise of the revolutionary moment – adapted to, reconfigured for, and transformed by changing circumstances – is itself a crucial part of what gets handed down. As such, enthusiasm is a vivid and enduring presence in Britain's literary landscape.

It is crucial, in studying the "manic," to keep its social dimension steadily in view. For it can hardly be sufficiently stressed that the translation of religious enthusiasm into a matter of *private* pathology has a generally reactionary pedigree in the history of ideas. Henry More's *Enthusiasmus Triumphatus* (1656), indeed, marks a turning point in this regard. After its publication, according to historian Michael MacDonald, Anglican pamphleteers began to rework Robert Burton's famous argument about religious pathology in *The Anatomy of Melancholy* into a

[7]   Christopher Hill, *The World Turned Upside Down: Radical Ideas During the English Revolution* (New York: Penguin Books, 1972) , p. 15.

[8]   *Ibid.*, p. 379.

[9]   Thompson, *Making*, p. 350.

[10] N. H. Keeble, *The Literary Culture of Nonconformity in Later Seventeenth-Century England* (Athens: The University of Georgia Press, 1987), p. 24.

"ruling-class shibboleth."[11] Burton's argument was, of course, that a religious faction quite recognizable as Puritans – a giddy company of "precisians" – were both the victims and the carriers of mental disease. In Burton's words: "Wee may say of these peculiar sects, their Religion takes away not spirits only, but wit and judgement, and deprives them of all understanding: for some of them are so farre gone with their private Enthusiasmes, and revelations, that they are quite madde, out of their wits."[12] It must be added, however, that this elite equation of enthusiasm with madness soon infiltrated circles well beyond the drawing rooms of the indisputably privileged. The pathologizing of enthusiasm thus became part of a broader elite hegemony. It is obvious enough that the pathologizing of manic rhetoric served to denigrate it and eventually to justify "shutting up," in all possible senses, its users. The label of madness, retroactively buttressed by medical authority, then served to naturalize and universalize this persecution, concealing its basis in historical conflict. Roy Porter observes that the sequestration of lunatics, as a matter of civil policy initiated more by magistrates and philanthropists than doctors, in some sense preceded the psychiatric rationalization of the practice: "Psychiatry could flourish once, but not before, large numbers of inmates had been crowded into asylums."[13] Precisely because of its privatizing character, moreover, the label of madness has excluded rival forms of explanation for the manic. This exclusion of more collective and historical ways of seeing the manic has long functioned to distort our reception of manic texts.[14]

The cultural fate of the manic, in this sense, is linked to the broader history of "madness" itself. I refer now not to the history of a disease, a supposedly timeless psychiatric entity, but to the history of a signifier, a meaning. For "madness" was not always the special province of an authoritative professional elite. Prior to its medicalization, the "madness" of Stuart England belonged simultaneously to a great variety of traditions, from the clinical to the moral to the astrological to the demonological. Such traditions of magic and occult knowledge, though denounced by Calvinist theologians of the period, were not distinct as such from science nor denounced by scientific practitioners.[15] Thus

---

[11] See Michael MacDonald, *Mystical Bedlam: Madness, Anxiety, and Healing in Seventeenth-Century England*, Cambridge History of Medicine Series (Cambridge: Cambridge University Press, 1981), p. 225. For a review of scholarship pertaining to the historical reaction against enthusiasm, see Michael Heyd, "The reaction to enthusiasm in the seventeenth century: towards an integrative approach," *Journal of Modern History* 53 (1981), pp. 258–280.

[12] Robert Burton, *The Anatomy of Melancholy*, 5 vols., eds. Thomas C. Faulkner, Nicolas K. Kiessling, and Rhonda L. Blair (Oxford: Clarendon Press, 1994), III, p. 387.

[13] Roy Porter, *A Social History of Madness: The World through the Eyes of the Insane* (New York: E. P. Dutton, 1989), p. 17.

[14] The concept of "mania" thus performs most of the legitimating and delegitimating strategies that have been ascribed to ideology. See Terry Eagleton, *Ideology: An Introduction* (London: Verso, 1991), pp. 5–6.

[15] Christopher Hill, "Science and magic in seventeenth-century England," in *Culture, Ideology and Politics: Essays for Eric Hobsbawm* (London: Routledge & Kegan Paul, 1982), pp. 176–193.

the prestigious seventeenth-century physician Richard Napier – who between 1597 and 1634 treated over 2000 patients for mental illness with an eclectic combination of magic, science, and religion – was probably not atypical for his time. As MacDonald's *Mystical Bedlam* shows, Napier assumed the need to negotiate with a cosmos teeming with supernatural beings. His eclectic treatments included charms, amulets, exorcisms, astrological diagnosis, phlebotomies, and various emetics. The "madness" treated thus by Napier seems quite discontinuous with that medicalized "madness" – functionally opposed to "reason" – whose subsequent career in the *âge classique* Michel Foucault attempts to trace in his *Histoire de la folie à l'âge classique.*[16] We can have no excuse, moreover, in the wake of Foucault's work, for failing to reckon the extent to which a label of individual madness may have participated in a repressive history of segregating, confining, and silencing the "mad," along with vagrants, beggars, debtors, and other stigmatized social nuisances.

To be sure, Foucault's well-known thesis that the European "Great Confinement" of the seventeenth and eighteenth centuries was a novel form of oppression has required considerable refinement and qualification, not to mention outright revision. Empirical research has nibbled away at both ends of Foucault's historical periodization. The practice of confining the mad, for example, can be traced back as far as fifteenth-century Spain, from where it spread across Europe during the sixteenth and seventeenth centuries: an origin neither bourgeois nor absolutist.[17] To recognize this origin for the incarceration of "madness" does not preclude our understanding its later efflorescence in the specific contexts of bourgeois or absolutist social control; it does, however, undercut Foucault's overly idyllic presentation of the Renaissance as the one era in which madness, benignly neglected, wandered free and easy.

Regional variations and time-lags, moreover, appear in comparative studies of psychiatric confinement in England, France, and Germany. In England, for example, private charity, in the soft name of "benevolence," rather than the policy of an absolutist state, sponsored much of the segregated housing for the incurably insane.[18] According to Roy Porter, moreover, sequestration in the eighteenth century was very unevenly developed – by no means the full-fledged bureaucratic system that arrived in the nineteenth century – and hence relatively eclectic and *ad hoc* in its improvisations. It was

[16]   Michel Foucault, *Histoire de la folie à l'âge classique* (Paris: Gallimard, 1972). Trans. into English by Richard Howard as *Madness and Civilization: A History of Insanity in the Age of Reason* (New York: Vintage Books, 1965).

[17]   See H. C. Erik Midelfort, "Madness and civilization: a reappraisal of Michel Foucault," in *After the Reformation: Essays in Honor of J. H. Exter,* ed. Barbara C. Malament (Philadelphia: University of Pennsylvania Press, 1980), p. 253.

[18]   Jonathan Andrews, "The lot of the 'incurably' insane in enlightenment England," *Eighteenth Century Life,* vol. 12, n.s., 1 (1988), p. 4.

also relatively modest in scale: "the age of the 'great confinement' in England was," as he writes, "not the Georgian era but its successor."[19] The making of British psychiatry, in this view, was less the achievement of a centralized disciplinary power than the cumulative effort of various "mental entrepreneurs" or "captains of confinement": a self-empowering professional elite who astutely capitalized on the demand for their services.[20] The Georgian era, then, is better seen as a period when the formal administrative segregation of the "mad," operating alongside the many informal means of coping with them, was gradually emerging. Granting this refinement, however, Porter otherwise recapitulates much of Foucault's argument: "All over Europe the eighteenth and nineteenth centuries witnessed a proliferation of schools, prisons, houses of industry, houses of correction, workhouses and, not least, madhouses to deal with the menace of unreason."[21] Porter attempts, with limited success, two further qualifications of Foucault. Though he concedes that some of the unreformed madhouses of the eighteenth century were indeed the benighted gothic dungeons described in reformist propaganda, he makes the rather modest point that others were somewhat more humane. He also argues against what appears to be a straw man: the hypothesis that the formal institutional confinement of the "mad" is best understood as an exercise of "naked class power."[22] Because people of all ranks were confined in madhouses, he contends that psychiatry, in his words, "was not just – probably not even primarily – a discipline for controlling the rabble."[23] Porter does concede, however, that the majority of the confined were paupers; and, moreover, that such laws as the English Vagrancy Act of 1714 did indeed link the confinement of so-called madness to broader concepts of domestic order.[24] The Vagrancy Act empowered Justices of the Peace to confine, as generic disturbers of the peace, lunatics, rogues, vagabonds, and beggars. He acknowledges, moreover, that "public opinion from the age of the Enlightenment onwards readily identified the attitudes and behaviour of marginal social elements – criminals, vagrants, the religious 'lunatic fringe' – with false consciousness and madness."[25]

Such concessions seem so far-reaching as essentially to reconfirm the Foucauldian view that eighteenth-century psychiatric confinement was indeed – if not a "naked" exercise of class power – a powerful technique of

---

[19] Roy Porter, *Mind-Forg'd Manacles: A History of Madness in England from the Restoration to the Regency* (London: The Athlone Press, 1987), p. 8.

[20] Porter, *Manacles*, pp. 166–167. More details about the "mad business" of the time can be found in Ida Macalpine and Richard Hunter's *George III and the Mad Business* (New York: Pantheon Books, 1969).

[21] Porter, *Social*, p. 16.

[22] *Ibid.*

[23] Porter, *Manacles*, p. 9.

[24] *Ibid.*, p. 7.

[25] Porter, *Social*, p. 16.

bourgeois social control: a "chose de 'police' " or "police matter," as Foucault puts it.[26] Further empirical research, moreover, has confirmed that across Europe involuntary confinement was aimed, above all, at the poor. As H. C. Erik Midelfort observes, "It was only the poor-mad, the poor-deviant, the poor-criminal, and the just plain poor who were sent to the general hospitals in Germany and France."[27] Such practices, as Midelfort points out, were often justified by an appeal to "traditional" monastic and ecclesiastical values.[28] Such apparent continuities with the past, however, in no way preclude the view that psychiatric incarceration was being adapted and expanded by a new order.

Early psychiatry was mediated by the category of the individual and articulated in the language of neutral expertise. It was exactly these depoliticizing features, indeed, that made it an effective instrument for civic administrators, religious magistrates, and their like – a class whose voice is especially audible in the following passage from Dr. J. Aiken's *Thoughts on Hospitals* (1771):

By placing a number of them [lunatics] in a common receptacle, they may be taken care of by a much smaller number of attendants; at the same time, they are removed from the public eye to which they are multiplied objects of alarm, and the mischiefs they are liable to do to themselves and others, are with much greater certainty prevented. [Public institutions] instead of being a burthen ... would be a saving to the community, not only from the relief of private families, but that of parishes.[29]

The confinement and psychiatric excommunication of the "mad" remains a significant episode in the history of English class struggle. And it is precisely the dawning of the "Great Confinement" that best serves here to distinguish Smart's moment on the manic continuum from Abiezer Coppe's. Although Coppe, like Smart, was incarcerated, his confinement was understood as punishment for blasphemy and sedition rather than as the segregation of irrationality. Jonathan Swift's *A Tale of a Tub*, which parodies enthusiasm precisely in order to reinforce its reputation for mental pathology, marks a significant transitional moment in this larger process.

In this prolegomenon, I hope to establish a framework that permits the linking of Smart back to such seventeenth-century enthusiasts as Coppe. They are linked, in my view, by a common rhetorical practice with certain salient modes of addressing social divisions between those constituted as central and those pushed to the peripheries. As I intend the term, "rhetoric"

[26] Foucault, *Histoire*, p. 75; *Madness*, p. 46. Here the term "police" anticipates everything Foucault would later mean by "discipline."
[27] Midelfort, "Reappraisal," p. 255.
[28] *Ibid.*, p. 256.
[29] J. Aiken, *Thoughts on Hospitals* (London, 1771), pp. 65 ff. Cited in Klaus Doerner, *Madmen and the Bourgeoisie: A Social History of Insanity and Psychiatry*, trans. Joachim Neugroschel and Jean Steinberg (Oxford: Basil Blackwell, 1981), p. 70.

encompasses everything implicated in notions of the verbal, the textual, the persuasive, the performative. Highly deviant behavior, such as Ranter Abiezer Coppe's prophetic "pranks" – the term itself became a crucial manic *topos* – also has its rhetorical genres: it is the head-shaving, dung-eating Biblical prophet Ezekiel to whom Coppe refers as the precedent for his own strange gestures and postures.

A *rhetoric of mania* is and has been accessible to individual authors such as Smart – even by choice – within a specific historical matrix of radical Protestant religious discourse. As with any mode, the manic mode can be appropriated for particular purposes by particular authors. As with any mode, the history of such appropriations itself operates as a dimension of its meaning. And, as with any historically cumulative practice, the mode constitutes itself both by continuities and transformations: the manic mode exists not as a timeless essence, but an evolving pattern of family resemblances. It is obvious, to be sure, that the subterranean nature of manic rhetoric makes the tracing of direct continuities – direct lines of descent from one text to another – virtually impossible: for much of its transmission, after all, may have been oral.[30] Even so, the purely textual impact of the manic style testifies both to its cultural significance and to the contours of a certain historical development.

Seen thus, then, as rhetorically constituted by the process of plebeian struggle at different historical moments, the manic mode can nevertheless be anatomized as consistently exhibiting the following features: (1) a preoccupation with themes of socio-economic resentment; (2) a "levelling" use of lists and catalogues; (3) an excessive, often blasphemous wordplay; (4) a tendency to blend and thus level incongruous genres; (5) a justification of symbolic transgression, especially in the context of lay preaching, as prophetic behavior; and (7) imagery of self-fortification against persecution and martyrdom. The latter, all too often, is related to actual or threatened incarceration: for the likes of John Bunyan, Anna Trapnel, and George Fox – to name only three of the hundreds of radical Puritans who suffered political imprisonment – prison is thus often both a *topos* of martyrdom and an actual place.[31]

It should not be surprising, given that class formation has much to do with identity, that the manic mode attempts to reconfigure subjectivity itself. I propose, by way of contextual reframing, then, a historical study of the manic "I" as a transindividual site of political and ideological contestation. The many theorists concerned with the problematic of the discursive subject have encouraged me to see that manic texts, as a particular mode of signifying

---

[30] For a broader consideration of this historiographical issue – how to trace continuities in submerged patterns of popular heresy – see Hill, "From Lollards," pp. 89–116.

[31] See John R. Knott, *Discourses of Martyrdom in English Literature, 1563–1694* (Cambridge: Cambridge University Press, 1993).

subjectivity, cannot logically be detached from the specific fields of symbolic practices that surround them at a given historical moment.[32] Thus I shall argue that the mode of subjectivity inscribed in manic texts must be understood as overdetermined by the conflicts surrounding seventeenth-century radical religious politics.

The rhetorical mode I propose to call "manic" also invariably evinces, moreover, a tendency toward fusion with the reader addressed or the thing described: thus mania has its own *rhetoric of enunciation*. This is how the manic mode intersects with certain dynamics of the sublime. Rhetorical sublimity, according to the treatise on the sublime that tradition attributes to Longinus, can be achieved by sudden changes in the number and person of pronouns: from "I" to "we," for instance, or from "I" to "you."[33] The implications of such peculiar pronominalization, moreover, go beyond the domain of mere technique. Longinus' approach to the sublime, as is well known, emphasizes the reader's emotional response of ecstatic transport. But it is less a theory of actual readers and listeners, as Suzanne Guerlac demonstrates, than a rhetoric of enunciation.[34] The Longinian sublime has to do, that is to say, with the transgression of pronominal positions of speaker/writer and addressee in the event – the actual process – of spoken utterance or written enunciation. "The transport of the sublime," to paraphrase Guerlac, includes "a slippage among the positions of enunciation": as a result, the writing "I" gets "transported" into the message and the implied interlocutor achieves a fictive identification with the written "I."[35]

So much more than aesthetic sublimity depends on pronouns. It is no longer news that pronouns are heavily laden with history, politics, and metaphysics. A conversational "we" may constitute a false consensus, a club of insiders luxuriating in their "innocently" unmarked and supposedly unsituated power to speak for others.[36] The so-called generic "he" evidently functions, by synecdoche, to universalize and normalize, as unmarked by gender specificity, the politically dominant sex. The apostrophe to a "thou", whether to a heavenly father or a wild west wind, can position one as the specially elected invoker of a sacred presence. Such a "thou" makes presentational claims – one speaks to an unseen presence – and can serve equally well, as Jonathan Culler points out, as the vocational trademark of

---

[32]   Kaja Silverman provides an elegant mapping of the converging "subjects" theorized in ethnology, semiotics, and psychoanalysis. See her *The Subject of Semiotics* (New York: Oxford University Press, 1983).

[33]   Longinus, *On the Sublime*, trans. James A. Arieti and John M. Crossett (New York: The Edwin Mellen Press, 1985), pp. 128–139.

[34]   This terminology invokes the distinction made by linguist Emile Benvéniste between the *énoncé* (the statement uttered) and *énonciation* (the act of uttering).

[35]   Suzanne Guerlac, "Longinus and the subject of the sublime," *New Literary History* 16:2 (1985), p. 275.

[36]   See Marianna Torgovnick, "The politics of the 'we,'" *South Atlantic Quarterly* 91:1 (1992), pp. 43–63.

poet or prophet: "One who successfully invokes nature is one to whom nature might, in its turn, speak. He makes himself poet, visionary. Thus, invocation is a figure of vocation."[37] Similarly, the word "I" evidently entails a staggering set of assumptions about subjective agency, unity, and presence. It is little wonder, then, that progressive and revolutionary movements frequently experiment in their rhetoric with revisionary challenges to customary modes of address.[38]

The manic first person – what linguists would call the "subject of enunciation" – belongs precisely to such a dissident rhetorical practice. It attempts to enact nothing less than a transfigured subjectivity. One notes, as a central illustration of this history, that among the earliest uses of the word "revolution" beyond its older astronomical sense – which implies not progressive change but rather the circular return to a previous position – one finds a conversion narrative by Ranter Joseph Salmon, who writes of his subjective changes as "a suddain, certain, terrible, dreadfull revolution ..."[39] And indeed, the most striking effect of the manic mode, even measured against its deliberately shocking political and sexual content, is precisely the perturbing ambiguity its form creates as to the writing "subject." Like the members of an extended family, then, texts in the manic mode also share some, but not necessarily all, of the following rhetorical features, each of which helps to enact a violent transfiguration of written subjectivity: (1) a hard-earned preoccupation with themes of praise and gratitude, often based on the Psalmic tradition; (2) an excessive use of allusion and echo; (3) hyperbole; and (4) extreme disjunctiveness.

Because gender is inevitably an important element in the process of class formation,[40] the manic style is necessarily all about gender as well. Its rebellion against the gender *status quo*, however, is quite uneven and contradictory. Indeed, though it makes space for both male and female writers, the manic mode displays a notable ambivalence toward gender hierarchy. This ambivalence is rhetorically manifested as follows: first, in a residual misogyny, often focused on the biblical "Whore-of-Babylon" *topos*;

---

[37] See Jonathan Culler, "Apostrophe," *Diacritics* 7 (1977), p. 63.

[38] Members of the Rastafarian movement, for example, often refer to themselves collectively in a doubled first person – "I and I" – that constitutes others as self. See Ernest Cashmore, *Rastaman: The Rastafarian Movement in England* (London: George Allen & Unwin, 1979), pp. 67, 135.

[39] I owe this reference to Christopher Hill, "The word 'revolution' in seventeenth-century England," in *For Veronica Wedgwood These: Studies in Seventeenth-Century History*, eds. Richard Ollard and Pamela Tudor-Craig (London: Collins, 1986), p. 141.

[40] For the role of gender in the formation of the laboring classes, see Joan Wallach Scott, "Women in *The Making of the English Working Class*," in *Gender and the Politics of History*, Gender and Culture Series (New York: Columbia University Press, 1988), pp. 68–90; for gender's role in the formation of the middle class, see Catherine Hall and Lenore Davidoff, " 'The nursery of virtue': domestic ideology and the middle class" and " 'The hidden investment': women and the enterprise," in *Family Fortunes: Men and Women of the English Middle Class 1780–1850* (Chicago: The University of Chicago Press, 1987), pp. 149–192, 272–320.

and second, in a rather more interesting preoccupation with symbolic gender-reversals that tend to dissociate identity from the physical body. In this same gender-bending spirit, authors in the enthusiastic strain sometimes evoke an androgynous or even female godhead.[41]

Ironically enough, it is precisely the relative relaxation of gender hierarchy within the enthusiastic milieu – the visibility, for example, of women who testify, minister, organize, interpret Scripture, prophesy, and write – that becomes, in the orthodox backlash against enthusiasm, an especially favored marker of its social threat and degradation. Phyllis Mack sees this subversive threat as central to the social significance of female prophecy: "In a world that seemed overrun by masterless men, the apparently masterless, untethered female visionary must have been viewed by many as the ultimate threat."[42] Hence the frequency in anti-enthusiastic invective of fiercely misogynist depictions of the female enthusiast. The "Ranter Panic" of 1650–1651, as J. C. Davis argues, frequently focused its paranoid imaginings on the inversion of traditional sexual roles.[43] A related vein of anti-enthusiastic symbolism appears in the disguise used in an especially violent attack carried out against the Diggers' communist colony in Surrey. According to Gerrard Winstanley, in June, 1649, a group of men dressed in women's clothing beat four male Diggers senseless.[44] It was an attack not only on the commune as such, as Robert A. Seaberg points out, but also "on the equality, within the Digger community, between men and women."[45] Henry More and Jonathan Swift, among other enemies of enthusiasm, followed this misogynist lead in their writings.

[41] Joseph Salmon, for instance, while discussing the trinity, refers to God both as the "Father" and the "Grandmother." See his *Heights in Depths* (1651), in *A Collection of Ranter Writings from the 17th Century*, ed. Nigel Smith (London: Junction Books, 1983), p. 222. In some enthusiastic authors, especially the women prophets, one finds the deification of a female "Wisdom" figure common to the speculative theologies of Jewish and Christian Gnostic traditions. Jacob Boehme conflated Wisdom with the figure of "The Woman Clothed with the Sun" (Rev. 22) and adapted the result to radical Protestant theology. For Jane Lead's use of this Boehmenist *topos* a generation after the English Revolution, see Catherine F. Smith, "Jane Lead's Wisdom: women and prophecy in seventeenth-century England," in *Poetic Prophecy in Western Literature*, eds. Jan Wojcyk and Raymond Jean-Frontain (London: Associated University Presses, 1984), especially pp. 60–63; and "Jane Lead: mysticism and the woman clothed with the sun," in *Shakespeare's Sisters: Feminist Essays on Woman Poets*, eds. Sandra M. Gilbert and Susan Gubar (Bloomington: Indiana University Press, 1979), especially pp. 3–15.

[42] Phyllis Mack, *Visionary Women: Ecstatic Prophecy in Seventeenth-Century England* (Berkeley: University of California Press, 1992), p. 86.

[43] J. C. Davis, *Fear, Myth, and History: The Ranters and the Historians* (Cambridge: Cambridge University Press, 1986), pp. 105–107.

[44] Gerrard Winstanley, *A Declaration of the Bloody and Unchristian Acting of William Star, and John Taylor of Walton*, in *The Works of Gerrard Winstanley*, ed. George H. Sabine (Ithaca: Cornell University Press, 1941), pp. 295–298.

[45] Robert A. Seaberg, "Ritual behavior and political solidarity: radical groups in revolutionary England," in *Persons in Groups: Social Behavior as Identity Formation in Medieval and Renaissance Europe* (Binghamton: Center for Medieval and Renaissance Studies, 1985), p. 126.

As a mode engaged in a class-conscious project of reconstructing subjectivity and gender, manic rhetoric authorized itself through certain scriptural commonplaces or *topoi*. Thus, like all Christian traditions, this one offers its own particular and selective reading of Scripture: it produced a Bible, as it were, within the Bible.[46] Manic rhetoric, though frequently millenarian, involves much more than a rewriting of Revelation and the Book of Daniel. The "pursuit of the millennium," in Norman Cohn's famous phrase, makes up only one aspect among several to consider. Other scriptural *topoi* thus deserve further emphasis: the Magnificat in Luke, for example (itself revising the "birth-of-a-hero" motif in the stories of Moses and Samson), which ultimately "magnifies" the poor over the rich; the "howling" denunciation of the rich in James 5:1–6; the warning in Isaiah 2:13–14 that God will level the high mountains and lofty cedars; the scene of King David's scandalous dancing before the Ark of the Covenant (2 Samuel 6:14–16), which vindicates ecstatically uninhibited worship; Paul's notion of the defiantly unworldly "fool for Christ" (1 Corinthians 4:10), which legitimates eccentric beliefs and behavior; his militant image of the "armour of God" (Ephesians 13:12); and the "Alpha-and-Omega" *topos* used in Revelation, which opens the door to several strains of speculative alphabetical mysticism. These latter strains touch on related notions of a divine language, from Paul's reference to "unspeakable words" heard in the "third heaven" (2 Corinthians 12:2–4) to the venerable doctrine of "divine signatures," especially as mediated by Jacob Boehme's *De Signatura Rerum* (1621).

Also among the *topoi* composing the enthusiastic Bible are the land-sharing "Jubilee" *topos* (Leviticus 25), which militates against the private monopolization of land;[47] the ubiquitous "inner light" *topos* (derived from John 1:9), which shifts spiritual authority away from all external institutions; the equally ubiquitous "book-of-nature" *topos* (derived from Psalm 19's vocal creation), which emphasizes God's immanence in the creation; and especially Paul's "two sons" allegory in Galatians 4:21–31, which deals in revisionary terms with the politics of inheriting a tradition.

What goes around comes around: thus every passage in the New Testament that authorizes its typological self-positioning as the decoding and fulfillment of the so-called Old Testament eventually comes to serve as fair game for still further sectarian development, further new testaments. There is thus a paradox inherent in tracing the history of a rhetorical mode at once so belated and yet so thoroughly saturated with repristinating manifestoes. Manic writing is a rhetorical practice that hands down claims of newness and immanence – that mediates, indeed, claims to be unmediated. It is precisely

---

[46] See Christopher Hill, *The English Bible and the Seventeenth-Century Revolution* (London: Penguin Press, 1993).

[47] See the discussion of John Bunyan's use of this *topos* in Christopher Hill's *A Tinker and a Poor Man: John Bunyan and His Church, 1628–1688* (New York: Alfred A. Knopf, 1989), p. 71.

this paradox, indeed, that best explains the popularity in millennial rhetoric of such threshold images as the "new dawn" *topos*.

Manic rhetoric, according to this definition, provides a transindividual framework for the seemingly inescapable metaphor of vision: it enables a collective way of seeing and not seeing, rather than a merely individual psychic mode. It is a crucial feature of my argument, however, that an individual author may in some important sense appropriate, by choice, the imagery, argument, and tactics of the mode. Thus, where the psycho-historian Alfred Cohen finds nothing but "real madness" amongst the female enthusiastic prophets of the English Revolution[48], I find instead a well-developed, thoroughly collective, and politically oppositional *rhetoric of madness*.

I use the term "manic" for this rhetorical matrix because, above all, it usefully acknowledges strangeness and perturbation. It would be overly fastidious to avoid the term; to use it serves to underscore the fact that manic texts present striking difficulties. These difficulties include the deliberate combination of seemingly incongruous rhetorical modes and deliberately baffling rhetorical tactics. More precisely, the term "manic" acknowledges that manic rhetoric apparently refuses to engage discursive reason within its own assumptions. Manic rhetoric thus marks a certain breakdown of dialogue. We normally view that breakdown from outside, as "reasonable" spectators of "madness," and that moment of initial strangeness and failed empathy, however redefined, must be acknowledged and incorporated into the process of critical understanding and reception. Although I intend "manic" as a sign of initial strangeness, however, the term also points to the possibility of familiarization. My project of historical analysis seeks to reframe this breakdown, this mania, as a difference constituted by history rather than by a timeless ontological gulf.[49]

Here the case of "mad" Christopher Smart – who wrote enthusiastic poetry, and who created public disturbances by praying loudly in public – exemplifies the issues at stake. It seems obvious that a critical language that labels his deviant communications as mere medical pathology forecloses the possibility of any real engagement with his *Jubilate Agno*. Such pathologizing language tends to see the text as a one-of-a-kind sport, produced as much by delusions as by an author.[50] Less obviously, perhaps, an overly cozy language

---

[48] Alfred Cohen, "Prophecy and madness: women visionaries during the Puritan Revolution," *The Journal of Psychohistory* 11:3 (1984), p. 413.

[49] In discussing the types of difficulties presented by manic rhetoric, I have relied on George Steiner's attempt to classify textual difficulties. See his "On difficulty," in *On Difficulty and Other Essays* (New York: Oxford University Press, 1978), p. 41.

[50] Elizabeth Sewell's hesitation over pronouns epitomizes this questioning of Smart's agency. She writes of "Kit Smart in a slew of drink, debt, and delusions, to whom (or should I say to which?) we owe the partly glorious and partly distracted *Jubilate Agno*." See Elizabeth Sewell, "Poetry and madness, connected or not? – and the case of Hölderlin," in *Psychiatry and Literature*, vol. IV of *Literature and Medicine*, ed. Peter W. Graham (Baltimore: The Johns Hopkins University Press, 1985), p. 43.

of normalcy may likewise betray the poem's genuinely disruptive qualities, its rough edges.[51] Almost any critical discussion of the *Jubilate*, indeed, must assume the risk of domesticating it, of assimilating it too easily to the bland and familiar.[52] Far from redeeming Smart's text, such a premature domestication of its actual strangeness in effect reduces its interest and value.

To romanticize mania as good, through a simple inversion of the negative valence attached to "madness," however, would be little better than condemning it as bad. Because much of the true scandal of the manic consists precisely in its excessive rhetoricity, the refusal to acknowledge this excess – along with its inescapable ironies – leads to equally complacent and banal clichés about persecuted individual vision. This latter emphasis, which often seeks to preserve the "private" as a realm of unconditioned genius, tends to dwell on anecdotes of amusing eccentricity. Anecdotes of wackiness, very comfortable to a certain genteel, clubbable, and gossipy mode of scholarship, thus triumph over vigorous analysis. Sentimentally developed, the madness-as-vision *topos* leads inexorably to a note of pathos and condescending pity – "poor Kit Smart," as tradition has it. Narratively developed, the "madness-as-vision" *topos* leads to mythic renderings of sudden change: the change, as Robert Browning presents Smart's career, from a pedestrian poet "before" mental illness to lightning-struck genius and culture-hero "after."[53] Allan Ingram thus repeats a very standard view in calling *Jubilate Agno* "the most eloquent of testaments to the creative potential of madness."[54] Browning's attractive myth, given that it appears on the blurb adorning the cover of the recent Penguin paperback edition of Smart's poetry, seems to be alive and well. The Penguin blurb highlights Smart's confinement for madness and then quotes Browning's claim that Smart "pierced the screen / Twixt thing and word . . ."[55]

Whether deemed good or bad, the concept of madness tends in itself to defeat certain kinds of analysis. To approach a text or an author via the notion of the "mad genius" begs a large set of questions about the role of

---

[51] I have explored this issue at more length in a book review of Harriet Guest's *A Form of Sound Words: The Religious Poetry of Christopher Smart* (Oxford: Clarendon Press, 1989). See *Criticism* 33:3 (1991), pp. 405–409.

[52] Raman Selden uses interpretation of *Jubilate Agno* as a textbook specimen of the dynamics of "naturalization": the domesticating operations, that is, of sense-making and pattern-finding by which texts are assimilated to a larger universe of meaning. Such operations ensue inevitably upon assuming the "poeticalness" of the text. See Raman Selden, *Practicing Theory and Reading Literature: An Introduction* (Lexington: University Press of Kentucky, 1989), pp. 51–54.

[53] See Robert Browning's "Parleying with Christopher Smart," in *Robert Browning: The Poems*, eds. John Pettigrew and Thomas J. Collins, 2 vols. (New Haven: Yale University Press, 1981), II: pp. 798–799; and Sir Russell Brain's "Christopher Smart: the flea that became an eagle," in his *Some Reflections on Genius* (Philadelphia: J. B. Lippincott Co., 1961), pp. 113–122.

[54] Allan Ingram, *The Madhouse of Language: Writing and Reading Madness in the Eighteenth Century* (London: Routledge, 1991), p. 168.

[55] See back cover, *Christopher Smart: Selected Poems*, eds. Karina Williamson and Marcus Walsh (Penguin Books, 1990).

social mediations in the process of literary creation, notably the irreducibly social facts of language, of discourse, and, indeed, of subjectivity itself.[56] One then treats the "psychologized" literary artifact, by over-stretched analogies, as part of a case history, or a private fantasy, or a dream.[57] Such models tend to treat the text as a quasi-autistic event, a largely involuntary secretion, as it were, of strictly private symbolism. This serves to isolate both text and author from broader contexts, minimizing all the ways any given text addresses itself rhetorically to other minds: both to an audience and to some sort of written tradition.

It makes a decisive difference to recognize that *Jubilate Agno* can be seen as engaged in a dialogue with a subterranean manic counter-discourse that reaches back to seventeenth-century enthusiastic prophecy. This frequently oppositional mode has been, even in the versions of literary history produced by the so-called New Historicism, conspicuously neglected.[58] Many apparently anomalous features of Smart's rhetoric have affiliations with a collectively created literary and religious project. Smart's text does, after all, belong to a recognizable kind of writing: a scripturally based prophetic mode that profoundly problematizes authorial agency through claims to divine inspiration.

It might be argued that I have, in referring to "manic" rhetoric, so prejudged the status of such rhetoric as to thwart its projected rehabilitation. The term "manic" would indeed seem to suggest off-putting incomprehensibility. Moreover, any linkage of religious nonconformity and madness would seem to echo the fierce attacks on enthusiasm by seventeenth- and eighteenth-century pamphleteers such as Henry More, Joseph Glanvill, Henry Hallywell, and Jonathan Swift. My point in retaining the term, however, is precisely to remember – and thus work through – the profound implication of "mania" in the ideological conflicts of English religious history. Indeed, to stress the historical dimension of manic rhetoric, I shall also refer to "enthusiastic" rhetoric, which evokes as its opposing counterpart not a universal normality, but, rather, the ruling ecclesiastical forces and their often repressive discourses. I am convinced, however, that the best way to go beyond "mania" is not to ignore the term but, rather, to use it differently.

My attempt to estrange and reappropriate the term "manic" should expose the limits of any diagnostic pronouncements that evade discussing the collective status and bitterly contested history of religion as a discourse. As a means of defamiliarizing an easily automatized term, then, my redefinition of

---

[56]   See Karen Burke LeFevre, *Invention as a Social Act* (Carbondale, Illinois: Southern Illinois University Press, 1987).

[57]   See Meredith Skura, *The Literary Use of the Psychoanalytic Process* (New Haven, Connecticut: Yale University Press, 1981).

[58]   See James Holstun, "Ranting at the New Historicism," *English Literary Renaissance* 19:2 (1980), pp. 189–225.

mania insists above all on defining the phenomenon as collective, as historically contingent, and as informed with whatever degree of agency we normally grant to individuals, and subcultural groups, as users of rhetoric.

To avoid habitually reductive responses to such textual perturbations as Smart's *Jubilate Agno*, then, one must begin instead with questions about rhetoric. "Mania" has functioned as a kind of imposed generic framework for the *Jubilate*, and yet the notion that Smart's poem belongs to a rhetorically constitutive genre or mode has never been pushed far enough – that is, to the point of enabling a true full-length interpretation of the poem. The label of "mania" has been a mere device for emphasizing the idiosyncratic and supposedly *sui generis* status of the text. I propose to investigate the "mania" not of the supposedly private author, however, but rather of a particular combination of rhetorical features. *Jubilate Agno* is in fact working within a quite specific rhetorical mode. Such modes or patterns are products of culture; they are handed down socially rather than genetically; and their analysis requires motives beyond the mere vicissitudes of neurobiological disease.

I intend my own use of the term "manic" homeopathically, as an engagement of such politicized psychiatric reductionism on its own terrain. I acknowledge by such a term that I cannot claim to speak from any position truly outside the systems of power and knowledge that twice confined Smart in a madhouse. Rather than merely avoiding the inherited term "manic," however, I prefer to reframe its narrow reference to private health and sickness.

It might be argued that to apply the term "rhetoric" to an avowedly prophetic and oracular discourse – to view it, indeed, as one rhetoric among others – can only debunk it. But whatever seems debunking about the term (which, like "ideology," may suggest the legitimation, through sophistry, of power) must apply equally to all texts whatsoever. Every discourse, and not just the rhetoric of mania, legitimates itself through rhetorical suasion.[59] This recognition certainly does not entail the position, however, that all conflicts and interests whatsoever are of equal political significance or worth.[60] Despite its current popularity, a depiction of the world as homogeneously

---

[59] Notoriously, the term "rhetoric" has now invaded the social sciences, serving there as a reminder to devotees of the quantitative that even the fiercest number-crunching is a rhetorical gesture, an appeal not to the literal, but to "authority" within the protocols of a discipline. See, for six discussions among many, Hayden White, *Tropics of Discourse: Essays in Cultural Criticism* (Baltimore: The Johns Hopkins University Press, 1978); George Lakoff and Mark Johnson, *Metaphors We Live By* (Chicago: University of Chicago Press, 1980); James M. Mellard, *Doing Tropology: Analysis of Narrative Discourse* (Urbana: University of Illinois Press, 1987); *The Legacy of Kenneth Burke*, eds. Herbert W. Simons and Trevor Melia (The University of Wisconsin Press, 1989); *The New Cultural History*, ed. Lynn Hunt (Berkeley: University of California Press, 1989), and *The Rhetorical Turn: Invention and Persuasion in the Conduct of Inquiry*, ed. Herbert W. Simons (Chicago: University of Chicago Press, 1990).

[60] Eagleton, *Ideology*, pp. 7–10.

saturated by the will to power would only serve to trivialize the antagonism I hope to analyze. As a considerably more concrete and less inflated concept of political and economic power, "class" permits us to reconceive the common history that has constituted irreconcilable rhetorical differences. On the one hand, to see the discourse of early psychiatry as affiliated to a class-bound rhetoric challenges its claim to objectivity. On the other hand, to see the manic as class-conscious rhetoric means, quite precisely, and above all, to restore its human agency.

Although this sweeping sense of rhetoric may seem anachronistic when applied to texts from the seventeenth and eighteenth centuries, there is a sense in which the contrary is true. For millennial rhetoric itself necessarily forces the issue of rhetoric into the foreground. Among such seventeenth-century enthusiasts as the Quakers, moreover, the radical purgation of received language – even down to residual "paganism" in the calendar – demonstrates a commitment to rhetorical analysis that this project can only hope to emulate.[61] As Hugh Orsmby-Lennon points out in this context, " 'waging war with the sword of the mouth' was a favourite Quaker trope."[62] Thus Friends, as Ormsby-Lennon writes, saw their own linguistic practices as part of a "great cosmic drama of language": that drama, indeed, guided by the Johannine logos, that reached from Genesis to Revelation.[63] It is no accident that their term for conversion is "convincement." As I plan to demonstrate, other enthusiasts, given a cultural climate in which millennial expectations were figured through various kinds of "signs," likewise achieved a state of acute rhetorical self-awareness.

I prefer "rhetoric" to "poetics" precisely because it provides a common denominator that permits me to discuss, along with more strictly literary phenomena, such texts as Abiezer Coppe's Ranter tracts. More crucially, I prefer "rhetoric" to "discourse" because the connotations of the latter have become, in the wake of Foucault's "the order of discourse," so heavily deterministic. I see little point in rescuing the manic subject from neurobiological determinism merely to deliver it up to a discursive one. I do not mean, however, that subjects have perfect freedom to choose the ideologies that envelop, enweb, and construct them. Far from it. Never-theless, it is crucial to my argument that subjects in general, and manic subjects in particular, exercise a certain degree of agency. Even if such agency is conceived as a resistance arising precisely from the interference among the various discourses that a person "inhabits,"[64] such agency

---

[61] See Hugh Ormsby-Lennon, "From shibboleth to apocalypse: Quaker speechways during the Puritan Revolution," in *Language, Self, and Society: A Social History of Language*, eds. Peter Burke and Roy Porter (Cambridge: Polity Press, 1991), pp. 72–112.

[62] *Ibid.*, p. 84.

[63] *Ibid.*

[64] See Paul Smith, *Discerning the Subject* (Minneapolis, Minnesota: University of Minnesota Press, 1988).

remains politically and analytically indispensable. The term "rhetoric," then, with its overtones of calculated address, is intended to emphasize the role of an agent exercising some degree of choice among possible options.

Individuals, groups, sacred texts, and entire social formations all may be said to use rhetoric, and to inhabit, in some sense, a particular rhetorical world with particular symbols of authority and particular conflicts. The rhetoric of mania, considered in precisely such a concentric series of horizons, belongs to Smart, Swift, and Coppe, among others, but not only as their rebarbative private idiolects. It belongs to them, rather, insofar as they belong to the religious and class antagonisms of their times, and to British class society during the cultural struggles that ensued during and after the English Revolution.

This book will show that the manic does indeed constitute a crucial and influential literary style. The manic constitutes a discursive practice with a typical subject matter, a traditional fabric of commonplaces, and a matrix of characteristic rhetorical forms. Both the development of the manic as a mode and its hostile critical reception, however, must be understood historically. The book's tripartite organization, therefore – its division into the three moments, roughly speaking, of Abiezer Coppe, Jonathan Swift, and Christopher Smart – focuses attention on three very different moments in the cultural life of the manic. Scrutinized in such detail, the manic style appears less as a baton passed intact from hand to hand than a series of closely related rhetorical events, each responding to a particular historical problematic.

I have deliberately chosen for my investigation a time-span that roughly correlates with Foucault's account of the "Great Confinement." The changes that Foucault describes primarily in terms of an epistemological break, however, I will analyze rather as a telling index of, and response to, particular economic and socio-political developments. As befits a historical analysis, my book is organized chronologically. This permits me, in three broad sections, to explore literary and political transformations of the "manic mode" as I define it.

The first section, focusing primarily on texts by the Ranter Coppe, describes the rhetorical construction of manic subjectivity. Politically, the manic text responds most immediately to the stunning political and military defeat in 1649 of the Levellers, whose political program had threatened, across sectarian divisions, to emulsify and unite significant sectors of the disenfranchised. It is within the wider problematic of mid-seventeenth-century plebeian struggle, however, that the Ranters' manic style must finally be situated: namely, the insubordination of a mostly urban poor – "masterless men," as their self-proclaimed betters anxiously called them. These can be arranged along a spectrum of relative disenfranchisement, as Christopher Hill demonstrates, from small craftsmen and their apprentices, to itinerant peddlers and tinkers, to the casual laborers excluded entirely from the guild system, to the chronically unemployed: beggars, vagabonds, criminals, and so on.[65]

The second section of *Mania and Literary Style* is devoted to Swift's calculated and mocking use of the manic idiom in *A Tale of a Tub*. Swift, that is to say, while using and rearticulating the mode, is not "of" the manic in the same sense as either Coppe before him or Smart after him. This section, while demonstrating the relevance to literary studies of the manic style, analyzes the wide-ranging use of the concept of "madness" for politically conservative ends. *A Tale of a Tub* derives much of its immediate anti-enthusiastic impetus from a ferocious political backlash, following the passage of the Toleration Act in 1689, against Quakers.[66] As an elite intervention in late seventeenth-century class struggle, however, *A Tale of a Tub* finds a wider significance in the context of the late seventeenth-century emergence of a plebeian culture of market-based writing. Indeed, this "revolutionary" penetration of market forces into the production of literature is what ultimately motivates Swift's ironic appropriation of the manic mode.

The third section of *Mania* argues that a further transformation of the manic mode, both renewal and revision, takes place in Christopher Smart's *Jubilate Agno*. The usual Franciscan and patristic genealogies for Smart's "covenant theology" notwithstanding, its tendencies emerge rather from Smart's dialogue with an evangelical enthusiasm. Though officially contained within Anglicanism, this ongoing enthusiasm nevertheless remains a potent and daring force. Audaciously expanding the divine covenant to include all of creation, animals no less than persons, Smart delivers in *Jubilate Agno* a violent riposte to the usual anthropocentrism of Christian humanism. What demands further analysis, of course, is the seeming belatedness of this gesture of revival: what are we to make of its post-Enlightenment gestation and birth? For Smart writes well after Locke had succeeded Habbakuk, as Marx puts it – and after Defoe, as Terry Eagleton adds, had succeeded Milton.[67]

The problematic to which *Jubilate Agno* most deeply responds is not the thwarting of revolution, as for Abiezer Coppe; nor is it, as for Jonathan Swift, the emergence of a plebeian culture of market-based writing, though Smart himself belonged in part to that culture. And though Smart's implication in the expansionist fervor of the Seven Years' War demands rigorous analysis, his poem is not mainly about the bracketing of domestic antagonisms through reference to England's imperial destiny as a Protestant nation. The problematic to which *Jubilate Agno* responds most deeply is, rather, precisely the practice of administrative incarceration. As a further escalation of

---

[65] Hill, *World*, pp. 39–50.
[66] See Hugh Ormsby-Lennon, "Swift and the Quakers," *Swift Studies* 4 (1989), pp. 34–62.
[67] See Terry Eagleton, "The God that failed," in *Re-Membering Milton: Essays on the Texts and Traditions* (New York: Methuen, 1987), p. 344.

bourgeois disciplinary control, the emergent "Great Confinement" marks a post-Enlightenment reification of social disorder and class discontent.

It is not merely that Smart protested against his own stigmatization, confinement, and isolation. The point, rather, is precisely that he responds to such control by entering into a dialogue with a marginalized language of plebeian martyrdom and revolt. It is this historical antagonism, then, that frames and encapsulates the way *Jubilate Agno* addresses all the other issues mentioned above. Although the *Jubilate* has been received primarily as a fine specimen of "madness," its peculiar rhetoric is the overdetermined product of an asymmetrical dialogue between contingent and situated socio-political forces. The reception of *Jubilate Agno*, indeed, demonstrates how a certain historically contingent definition of normalcy has been superimposed, retro-actively, upon the vicissitudes of history.

The ongoing cold war against the enthusiastic legacy illustrates a principle articulated by social anthropologists studying symbolic inversion: that which is socially peripheral is often symbolically central.[68] Culture wars are most active at the margins and borders. The meaning of the "low" and "marginal," as Peter Stallybrass and Allon White observe, is precisely what is most contested.[69] Hence the irony remarked by Shoshana Felman: that "madness" – itself the very mark of solitude – has become a rhetorical commonplace.[70] Indeed, because the significance of the manic style goes well beyond its contextual relevance to our reading of individual texts, the stakes of this struggle over cultural memory are higher than may first appear. It is not merely a question of the political left's sentimentally revisiting a romanticized past – preferring, as one historian claims, the purity of doomed fringe groups and lost causes to the greater practical achievement of, say, Cromwell.[71] For there is a very real sense in which enthusiasm constitutes a continuing presence within literary tradition. To center an account of literary history around that rhetorical constellation sheds light not only on the various texts to be discussed in what follows, but also on a much broader literary and cultural dialogue.

---

[68] See Barbara A. Babcock, "Introduction," in *The Reversible World: Symbolic Inversion in Art and Society*, ed. Barbara A. Babcock (Ithaca: Cornell University Press, 1978), p. 32. See also Peter Stallybrass and Allon White, *The Politics and Poetics of Transgression* (Ithaca: Cornell University Press, 1986), p. 5.

[69] Stallybrass and White, *Transgression*, p. 4.

[70] Shoshana Felman, *Writing and Madness: Literature/Philosophy/Psychoanalysis*, trans. Martha N. Evans *et al.* (Ithaca: Cornell University Press, 1985), p. 13.

[71] William Lamont, "The left and its past: revisiting the 1650s," *History Workshop Journal* 23 (1987), pp. 141–153.

PART I

Defiant voice

1

"Howle, you great ones": enthusiastic subjectivity as class rhetoric

as you have, & doe in greedy and unrighteous manner heape up the Treasures of the Earth in your storehouses, to the building and raysing up of high wales of pride and Arrogancy, and nurturing the lusts of your pampered flesh ... Howle, Howle & weepe, a day of Woe & misery is at hand and the Terrible Arme of the Lord is stretched foorth ...

John Perrot,
"The Lawyer's Fee" (1656)

The most interesting criticism of Christopher Hill's *The World Turned Upside Down* may be Barry Reay's observation that it never really resolves "the wider issue of rationality."[1] As Reay points out, Hill wavers between a respect for seventeenth-century radical enthusiasts as seen in their own terms and an occasional tendency to see them as blinkered by their pre-scientific, pre-secular perspective. The question of individual irrationality, moreover, is handled in a tone of quizzical ambiguity. Hill offers a number of tentative explanations for the extent to which such enthusiasts play the role of holy madman, including the following: such enthusiasts are engrossing the attention of an unwilling audience; they are using a mask to simultaneously express and disown dangerous ideas; they are reflecting the sheer strain of their radical insights; and they are, in some cases – Thomas Tany and George Foster, perhaps – suffering an authentic mental breakdown.[2] Though he drops hints that drawing a line between the rational and the mad may involve political and historical considerations, Hill leaves such hints studiously undeveloped.

While Hill offers the rather bland observation that the radicals, especially the Ranters and Quakers, "seem to have accepted the irrational element in human experience, and irrational behavior, more than most of their contemporaries," he also makes a more interesting connection, citing the Biblical authority for becoming a "fool for Christ".[3] Once again, the question

[1] Barry Reay, "The world turned upside down: a retrospect," in *Reviving the English Revolution: Reflections and Elaborations on the Work of Christopher Hill*, eds. Geoff Eley and William Hunt (London: Verso, 1988), p. 64.
[2] Christopher Hill, *The World Turned Upside Down: Radical Ideas During the English Revolution* (New York: Penguin, 1972), p. 283.
[3] *Ibid.*, pp. 280–283.

of rationality is left hanging. The "Ranter" Abiezer Coppe can serve here as a sort of test case for this apparent impasse. Hill obviously seeks balance in assessing those, such as Coppe, who – though figuring in a chapter called "The Island of Great Bedlam" – deserve credit for daring to imagine the world turned upside down: "A partial lapse from 'sanity' may have been the price for certain insights."[4] To put "sanity" in scare quotes invites us to sophisticate the view that sanity is a historically absolute condition. At the same time, however, as the word "insight" implies, Hill's judgment would seem to be little more than a tepid version, probably by way of R. D. Laing, of the "madness-as-genius" *topos*.[5]

Hill's tendency to focus on "radical ideas," in the absence of a more explicit, adequately developed, and textually attuned notion of rhetoric, proves awkward in dealing with questions about the subjectivity of those who adopted and developed a radical religious discourse in the mid-seventeenth century. Thus his reference to such *topoi* as the "fool for Christ" does not really attempt to account for the mode of their subjective appropriation. What remains to be worked out is a more nuanced and historicized account of a rhetoric of madness.

Hill's path-breaking book intersects, especially in its references to the use of Biblical commonplaces, with issues of persuasion and authority that are essentially rhetorical. As Nigel Smith puts it, "the radical religious prophets were involved in complex modes of address connected with the conviction that they spoke the words of God, or that God spoke directly through them."[6] In this sense, *The World Turned Upside Down* implies a more interesting argument about the historicity of enthusiastic "madness" than it makes explicitly. Hill's most recent book, moreover, demonstrates even more strongly the extent to which seventeenth-century English politics was mediated by a selective and polemical deployment of such Biblical *topoi*. For Hill, it is simply an inescapable historical fact that the Bible, for thinkers as diverse as Robert Filmer and Gerrard Winstanley, constituted an omnipresent intellectual climate: it was both "the source of virtually all ideas" and the idiom in which they were discussed.[7] This recognition, indispensable as it is, does not go far enough toward analyzing the very different modes or idioms in which Biblical passages were appropriated and used. The mere fact of a Bible-soaked culture does not sufficiently explain the fact that in the Ranter imagination, as

---

[4]   *Ibid.*, p. 279.
[5]   I have not engaged with Laing's existentialist critique of "normality" – largely based on issues of authenticity for the individual – because his concerns are distinct from my attempt to study a *collective rhetoric* in its historical context.
[6]   Nigel Smith, *Perfection Proclaimed: Language and Literature in English Radical Religion 1640–1660* (Oxford: Oxford University Press, 1989), p. 62.
[7]   Christopher Hill, *The English Bible in the Seventeenth Century Revolution* (London: Penguin, 1993), p. 34.

Nigel Smith points out, "the distinction between individual utterance and Scriptural authority disappears."[8]

It is indeed Nigel Smith's work that has gone furthest in analyzing the rhetoric of radical English religion in the seventeenth century. In discussing the prophetic stances assumed by George Foster, Thomas Tany, and Abiezer Coppe as rhetoric, moreover, Smith begins to address the issue of rationality: "The pose," he writes suggestively, "is of a divinely instituted madness."[9] This prophetic persona is developed, as he demonstrates, through parallels with such Biblical prophets as Daniel and Ezekiel, through elaborate devices of renaming, and through violent imagery that dramatizes the heart-piercing presence of the in-dwelling God.[10] I contend, building on the work of Hill and Smith, that the rhetoric of enthusiastic identification in the class-based rhetoric of seventeenth-century radical Puritanism produced a subculture of "manic" writing.

In describing a "manic" mode, I shall certainly not be merely echoing the long list of those who have denied all rationality (and perhaps all meaningful political agency) to the likes of Abiezer Coppe. Nor do I wish to be counted among the writers, including numerous important psychoanalytic or psychiatric authorities on mania, who have linked an entirely ahistorical concept of "mania" with certain types of religious experience.[11] Because the cultural significance of the Ranters and their fellow enthusiasts is greater than such interpretations would concede, I propose in this and the following chapters to answer that lengthy exercise in pathologizing: for psychiatry also belongs to the history of "madness."

In much radical seventeenth-century Protestant discourse one finds Bible-based claims that the author has been chosen to speak for God, or even as

---

[8] Nigel Smith, Introduction, in *A Collection of Ranter Writings from the 17th Century*, ed. Nigel Smith (London: Junction Books, 1983), p. 31.

[9] Smith, *Perfection*, p. 56.

[10] *Ibid*, pp. 56–64.

[11] The pre-Freudian taxonomist of psychiatric disorders, Emil Kraepelin, observes how frequently the ideas of his manic patients assume a "religious coloring." Emil Kraepelin, "Manic-depressive insanity," in *Manic-Depressive Illness: History of a Syndrome*, ed. Edward A. Wolpert (New York: International Universities Press, Inc., 1977), pp. 50–52. Freud's associate Karl Abraham notes that his manic-depressive patients, echoing the language of religious conversion, frequently feel "as though new-born." Karl Abraham, "Notes on the psycho-analytic investigation and treatment of manic-depressive insanity and allied conditions," (1912), reprinted in Wolpert, *Manic-Depressive Illness*, p. 124. Sandor Rado, another member of Freud's inner circle, associates religious emotions of guilt and redemption with very early frustrations, rages, and ecstasies of nursing and weaning. Sandor Rado, "The problem of melancholia," *The International Journal of Psycho-Analysis* 9 (1928), pp. 425–426. Bertram Lewin, author of a definitive psychoanalytic account of mania, devotes considerable attention to the similarities between "manic fusion" with an ideal object and the experiences of religious ecstatics such as St. Theresa. Bertram Lewin, *The Psychoanalysis of Elation* (New York: Norton, 1950), pp. 144–150. Finally, the American Psychiatric Association's *DSM-IV* mentions grandiose delusions involving a "special relationship to God" as symptomatic of a manic episode. *Diagnostic and Statistical Manual of Mental Disorders*, 4th ed. (Washington, D.C.: American Psychiatric Association, 1994), p. 328.

God. Such claims of divine election represent a mode of rhetorical self-aggrandizement perennially denigrated as "madness," and now almost always described as a neurochemical epiphenomenon. Any particular identity is of course determined at many levels, among which is a biological substrate. The enthusiast's "I" is, nevertheless, a discursive construct – a product, indeed, not only of language, but of rhetoric, and, hence, of politics and ideology. Class resentment, indeed, as I shall demonstrate, fuels manic rhetoric: it lends an irreducibly social dimension to the levelling themes, often moralized as envy, common to manic texts.

Manic enthusiasm is a particular strategy for speaking and writing with an authority otherwise unavailable to those assigned a lowly social identity. What makes manic writing deviant is not merely "pathology," as if the subjective crisis it dramatizes were finally merely a matter of individual misfortune. It is, rather, the formal projection of an oppositional, sometimes subversive ideology at the level of the subject: the ideology of the "world turned upside down." A certain rhetoric of enthusiasm, under conditions politically and ideologically determined by the turmoil of the 1640s and 1650s, constructed a subcultural ethos of manic subjectivity. Hence the "I" of manic textuality – the enthusiastic subject, as it comes down to us in British texts – must be understood as taking its modern impetus and meaning from the class-based rhetoric of seventeenth-century radical Puritan conflict.

Numerous others before me have noted the extremities of mood entailed by the ideological processes of seventeenth-century Protestantism. Hill notes a pattern of religious melancholia followed by religious conversion in about twenty mid-seventeenth-century English Protestant writers.[12] William Hunt likewise remarks that many of the Puritan preachers suffered from "chronic melancholia."[13] And, most useful for my own project, John Stachniewski analyzes a historically finite Calvinist culture of religious despair in England, from the late sixteenth century to middle of the seventeenth.[14] This culture, indeed, is the precise historical background against which manic rhetoric, as a revolutionary break, emerged in the 1640s.

Stachniewski highlights the anxiety, fatalism, and melancholia inevitably produced on a considerable scale by the Calvinist doctrine of double predestination. This doctrine he describes as God's "arbitrary" and "inscrutable" polarization of human destinies into the eternally elect – a tiny minority, by all accounts, of those who considered themselves Christians –

[12] Hill, *World*, pp. 171–173.
[13] William Hunt, *The Puritan Moment: The Coming of Revolution in an English Country* (Cambridge, Massachusetts: Harvard University Press, 1983), p. 120.
[14] John Stachniewski, *The Persecutory Imagination: English Puritanism and the Literature of Religious Despair* (Oxford: Clarendon Press, 1991).

and the eternally reprobate.[15] The starkly binary scheme of these twin paradigms constituted the bipolar frame through which a great many individuals in sixteenth- and seventeenth-century England attempted to understand the vicissitudes of their own lives. This bipolar frame produced "violent mood swings" in individuals such as John Bunyan, for example, in whom the paradigms alternately succeeded and effaced one another.[16] No more apt image could be found for this bipolarity of faith and doubt than the following image of oscillating scales from Bunyan's *Grace Abounding to the Chief of Sinners*: "for this [Biblical passage] about the sufficiency of grace, and that of Esau's parting with his Birthright, would be like a pair of scales within my mind, sometimes one end would be uppermost, and sometimes again the other, according to which would be my peace or trouble."[17]

Stachniewski makes clear that the "theological barbed wire" of Calvinism, as a mediation of economic volatility and social dislocation, served double duty.[18] Calvinism worked both as a rationalizing instrument of social discipline and as itself a theological justification for the exploitative *status quo*.[19] Above all, the Calvinist doctrine of the calling served to mediate between the secular realm of labor and its spiritual meaning as a sign of one's eternal destiny.[20] The stigma of predestined damnation inevitably fell most heavily on those who were not securely incorporated into the system of economic production and its rewards. The equivocal notion of the secular "calling," therefore, often served to dehumanize still further the "surplus" of vagrant poor. In Stachniewski's words, "The puritan preparedness to consider as rejected by God those who had no control over their circumstances is indicated in their attitude towards the city poor, a group which had greatly increased as a result of population growth, enclosures, and other effects of market forces in the agrarian economy."[21] Anxiety about individual spiritual destiny, however, was not confined to the disenfranchised only. Indeed, given that such anxiety was itself cruelly recuperated as one more signifier of eternal doom, there were many among even the respectable classes who could not entirely escape the harrowing "iron cage" of Calvinist despair.[22]

I concur with Stachniewski's emphasis on the ideological production of subjects. This approach demands, however, that we consider further the means by which individual emotions are called forth and channeled by a

---

[15] *Ibid.*, p. 33.
[16] *Ibid.*, pp. 137–138.
[17] John Bunyan, *Grace Abounding to the Chief of Sinners / The Pilgrim's Progress*, ed. Roger Sharrock (London: Oxford University Press, 1966), p. 67.
[18] Stachniewski, *Despair*, p. 89.
[19] *Ibid.*, p. 62.
[20] *Ibid.*, p. 74.
[21] *Ibid.*, p. 76.
[22] *Ibid.*, p. 20.

collective system of character-building beliefs, images, and symbols. Stachniewski invokes Foucault's account of "subjectification" for this purpose: a process he describes, in the case of Calvinism, as the "enwebbing of a hapless body and mind in a symbolic system."[23] I find Louis Althusser's concept of "interpellation" more useful, however, insofar as it retains an emphasis, crucial to my project, on both ideology and subjectivity. Interpellation, given certain refinements,[24] seems to me to permit a more successful mediation between theories of the discursively constituted subject, on the one hand, and a materialist analysis of the larger social structure, on the other. This mediating explanation need not reduce agency to a mere optical illusion of socio-political structure. In the case of enthusiastic texts, indeed, the concept of interpellation serves precisely to *restore* a sense of agency to texts and authors too often reduced to, and hence dismissed as, medical curiosities.

Interpellation is the gesture by which an ideological apparatus – a church, a school, a political organization – hails and recruits us with its address of *Hey, you!*[25] The word "you," which permits a pseudo-personal buttonholing in the name of a remote agent, permits a collective form of address to speak, in a tone of personal urgency, to individuals. A usefully obvious form of this pseudo-personal address occurs in the famous US Army recruitment poster that depicts the avuncular, finger-pointing Uncle Sam gazing directly at the viewer above the slogan "Uncle Sam wants *you*." Precisely this illusory *personalization* of a collective mode of address, according to Althusser's notion of interpellation, bespeaks the "hailing" operation of ideology on individuals and, thus, their "recruitment," as subjects, into preexisting structures seemingly oriented to them.

It seems worth noting in this context that in Bunyan's *Grace Abounding*, as Hill observes, "texts are hurled at Bunyan's head like thunderbolts of God."[26] And indeed, radical Puritan authors such as Bunyan often personify the Scriptures as acting upon them, as Nigel Smith observes, "with human force."[27] Most explanations for Bunyan's sense of being acted upon rather than acting, however, tend to be heavily pathologizing. Among the more sophisticated of these explanations is Peter J. Carlton's. Using terminology derived from a psychoanalyst's call for an action-oriented vocabulary,

23 *Ibid.*, p. 5.
24 For two useful critiques of "interpellation," see Terry Eagleton, *Ideology: An Introduction* (London: Verso, 1991), pp. 141–155; and Rosemary Hennessy, *Materialist Feminism and the Politics of Discourse* (New York: Routledge, 1993), pp. 74–79.
25 Louis Althusser, "Ideology and the state," in *Lenin and Philosophy* (London: Monthly Review Press, 1971), pp. 170–186. I also use Althusser's concept of overdetermination throughout. See Louis Althusser, "Contradiction and overdetermination," in *For Marx*, trans. Ben Brewster (New York: Vintage Books, 1970), pp. 87–128.
26 Hill, *World*, p. 95.
27 Smith, *Perfection*, p. 33.

Carlton describes such passive locutions as "disclaimed action" and "objectifications of the subjective." In Carlton's words, "when Bunyan says, 'the Scripture fell on me,' he is using a disclaiming locution to narrate something that he did as though it had happened to him."[28] Such disclaiming locutions served at once to contest ecclesiastical authority, to compensate for its absence, and to provide the alternative authority of generic convention.[29]

Alternative authority, viewed under the rubric of interpellative rhetoric, is indeed the key to interpreting such passages. For what needs even more emphasis is the extent to which the radical Puritans rearticulated the prevailing Anglican mode of Calvinistically inflected "hailing." In the very practice of lay preaching, the "mechanic preachers" such as Bunyan decentralized control over the "ideological apparatus": this begins to explain how genuinely subversive subjects could be produced. All of the radical Puritans discussed here transposed in various fashions the interpellative address of Calvinist rhetoric. Lodowick Muggleton and John Reeve, who founded the Muggletonians, performed an especially remarkable travesty of such hailing operations: claiming the power themselves to recognize the elect and the damned, they traveled around pronouncing sentence accordingly.

Many radical Protestants rejoiced in nothing so much as their own interpellation. In so doing, there is a sense in which they necessarily suppressed the contingency of the process that brought them in a position to be thus hailed. Nevertheless, the rhetoric of manic enthusiasm is not merely a random or politically meaningless claim to teleological "election." For there were, as Hill writes, "inherent contradictions in combining a theology which stressed that the elect were a minority with a moral preaching designed to reach all men."[30] The manic "I" is, quite precisely, the defiance of this prior negation: the speakers and writers of the manic mode, that is, respond to, defy, and seek to account for a prior socio-theological discourse that has positioned them as economically marginal, politically mute, and eternally damned. The great variety of ways in which they did so obviously spawned, like the proverbial dragon's teeth, a great multitude of separatist splinter-groups rather than a unified mass movement; their rhetoric, nevertheless, is fueled by the radical politicization of economic hierarchy and social rank in the 1640s.

I contend that manic rhetoric, as it has developed in various British religious and literary traditions, must ultimately be seen in the context of this particular socio-theological conflict. In the ideological struggle that immediately preceded and followed the English Revolution, divine favor was claimed

---

[28] Peter J. Carlton, "Bunyan: language, convention, authority," *English Literary History* 51:1 (1984), p. 19. The source of Carlton's approach is Roy Schafer, *A New Language for Psychoanalysis* (New Haven: Yale University Press, 1976).

[29] Carlton, "Bunyan," p. 27.

[30] Hill, *World*, p. 159.

promiscuously by all sides. Hill, indeed, discerns no fewer than three such broadly competing claims, on behalf of the competing political agendas of the Royalists, the Parliamentary Presbyterians, and the far more radical Levellers. A veritable "trinity" of Gods, in this view, was providentially working – at cross-purposes – during the English Revolution: (1) the cavalier God of Royalist propaganda, who sanctioned kings, bishops, tithes, and the established order; (2) the bourgeois God of Parliament's propaganda, who favored the justice of limited reform and an ethic of thrift, sobriety, frugality, hard work, and monogamy; and (3) the rather more unbuttoned God of some radical Puritan propaganda, who proclaimed the doom of class distinctions and (at least in the case of the Ranters) rejected a disciplinary work ethic.[31]

These conflicting articulations of God's favor illustrate a crucial point, seemingly neglected by Althusser: that individual subjects are always simultaneously addressed by, and identified with or against, competing, overlapping, and often contradictory discourses. Active resistance to the pressure of ideological scripts – the very possibility of subversive agency – can result then not from a position "outside ideology," but precisely from the immanent interference among the discourses that a person inhabits.[32] The very possibility of rearticulating Christ as the revolutionary "head Leveller"[33] or "mighty Leveller"[34] also illuminates a second point about the specific ideology of "election": the idea of a divinely ordained necessity functioned as a particularly valuable idea for the most revolutionary radicals precisely because, properly transposed, it authorized even radical change.

It is not always sufficiently stressed, moreover, that a rational hope for a much fuller revolution than in fact occurred existed for a period during the English Civil War. In their radically democratic political program, the Levellers – a primarily secular movement which threatened to create a radical coalition uniting separatist factions – circulated inflammatory mass petitions from 1646 to 1649. Their demands, reflecting a movement mainly comprising petty tradesmen and urban artisans, included a new constitution that provided the lineaments of a republican state: full religious toleration; the equality of individuals before the law (which would

---

[31] Christopher Hill, "God and the English Revolution," *History Workshop Journal*, 17 (1984), pp. 19–31. It was precisely on the issue of the work ethic (and a more general wariness of sexual hedonism) that Winstanley dissociated Diggers from what he terms the "Ranting practice." See *A Vindication of Those Whose Endeavors is Only to Make the Earth a Common Treasury, Called Diggers*, in *The Works of Gerrard Winstanley*, ed. George H. Sabine (Ithaca: Cornell University Press, 1941), pp. 397–403; see also G. E. Aylmer, "The religion of Gerrard Winstanley," in *Radical Religion in the English Revolution*, eds. J. F. McGregor and Barry Reay (Oxford: Oxford University Press, 1984), pp. 106–107.

[32] See Paul Smith, *Discerning the Subject* (Minneapolis, Minnesota: University of Minnesota Press, 1988).

[33] Gerrard Winstanley, *A New Yeer's Gift Sent to Parliament and Armie* (1650), in Sabine, *Works*, p. 390.

[34] Abiezer Coppe, *A Second Fiery Flying Roule*, in Smith, *Ranter*, p. 87.

entail the abolition of kings and lords); and the abolition of tithes, excise taxes, monopolies, and imprisonment for debt.[35] In an England where 90 percent of the men and all women were denied the vote, moreover, the Levellers argued, using the familiar terms of covenant theology, that a "new covenant" entailed a massive extension of manhood suffrage.[36] The Levellers also encouraged women to mobilize politically *en masse* – a development threatening, as Howard Shaw observes, "the very foundations of the patriarchal family."[37] After Cromwell purged the army of Levellers and then brutally crushed them at Burford in 1649, the remnants of the movement desperately called for an armed insurrection against the government, to no avail.[38]

The disappointment of the Levellers' dream (along with the defeat of the Diggers' much less influential communist project in 1650), has been seen by some as the decisive turning point in the chronology of radical religious feeling of the era. Barry Reay, however, argues persuasively for a "continual ebb and flow" of radical hopes in response to changing circumstances.[39] And Nigel Smith similarly describes the "Leveller movement and its culture" as an evolving process tied to the "very special circumstances" that had politicized the middling sort in the later 1640s.[40] "When that moment had passed," he writes, "new allegiances and ideas were entertained in an evolving process. 'Levelling' was the negotiating of rights; in the 1650s, the Levellers had become very largely either republicans, millenarians or Quakers."[41] The progress of events in the late 1640s and early 1650s thus led in the writing of certain so-called "Ranters," along with many fellow travelers in the enthusiastic constellation – some radical Quakers, Muggletonians, Fifth Monarchists, and so on – to the sense of an imminent and apocalyptic overturning of the social order. The fact that many Levellers did not become enthusiasts at this juncture is no surprise; such choices as resignation and disengagement are no less overdetermined by the coincidence of personal and social factors than is the choice of millennial thinking. For those who did embrace the desperate hope of a new age, however, a quasi-Hebraic rhetoric

---

[35] Howard Shaw, *The Levellers* (London: Longmans, Green and Co., Ltd., 1968), pp. 47–48.

[36] Historians debate ambiguities about exactly which men – the list includes servants, paupers, and possibly wage-earners – were *not* to be enfranchised by the Levellers' program. See Shaw, *Levellers*, pp. 62–66. They did not argue against private property. It was precisely these limitations to Leveller reform that provoked Winstanley's communist movement to call themselves the "True Levellers." A handy gathering of documents relevant to this debate can be found in *Puritanism and Liberty: Being the Army Debates (1747–49) from the Clarke Manuscripts*, 3rd ed., ed. A. S. P. Woodhouse (London: J. M. Dent & Sons Ltd.), 1992.

[37] Shaw, *Levellers*, p. 100.

[38] *Ibid.*, p. 87.

[39] Barry Reay, Introduction, in *Radical Religion*, p. 20.

[40] Nigel Smith, *Literature and Revolution in England 1640–1660* (New Haven: Yale University Press, 1994), p. 153.

[41] *Ibid.*

of "prophesying,"[42] combined with a special personalized and immediate understanding of "election," enabled an astonishingly radical rhetorical intervention against the institutions and beliefs that legitimated economic exploitation.

The "Ranters," so named by their enemies, constituted a radical milieu especially given to enthusiastic rhetorical modes. J. F. McGregor describes them as follows:

> Their authors were not spokesmen for a sect or movement but prophets of certain universal truths which they had come to comprehend through personal revelation ... The Ranter Prophets were mystical antinomians: mystical in their claim to have become one with God; antinomian in denying the reality of sin to the believer.[43]

As adepts of the doctrine of salvation by free grace alone, the Ranters made a point of public drinking, smoking, and blaspheming.[44] Their swearing, as Nigel Smith points out, was justified as manifesting a Ranter claim to esoteric knowledge.[45] As Coppe himself explains: "Well! one hint more; there's swearing ignorantly, i'th darke, vainely, and there's swearing i'th light, gloriously."[46] Hill has pointed out, moreover, that the swearing had a triangulated class content: "Lower class use of oaths was a proclamation of equality with the greatest, just as Puritan opposition to swearing was a criticism of aristocratic and plebeian irreligion."[47] Through such guerrilla tactics, the Ranters thus harassed established authority. These attacks on authority generally reflected their radically democratic political goals. Ranter Coppe, moreover, who claims to have delivered the matter of his pamphlets as street-sermons, produced levelling pamphlets vehemently denouncing the rich and directly voicing the simmering rage of London's poor. It is these pamphlets that best exemplify the seventeenth-century British version of the manic mode.

Abiezer Coppe was born in Warwick in 1619, to a family of middling status. He was enrolled in All Souls' College at Oxford in 1636, where he was tutored in Latin and Greek by the schoolmaster William Dugard in Warwick; at the outbreak of the Civil War, however, he left the university without having taken a degree. In the 1640s Coppe became an itinerant Baptist preacher of high reputation in the Warwickshire region. By 1649 he had

---

[42] As Kenneth Carroll points out, around this time the meaning of "prophesying" shifts among the Quakers from meaning lay Biblical exegesis, governed by the in-dwelling spirit, to something much closer to the directly inspired admonitions of the Hebraic prophets. See Kenneth Carroll, "Early Quakers and 'going naked for a sign,'" *Quaker History* 67 (1978), pp. 74–75.

[43] J. F. McGregor, "Seekers and Ranters," in *Radical Religion*, p. 129.

[44] For an analysis of Bunyan's class-based sense of language shame, and his own terrible obsession with blasphemy and swearing, see Stachniewski, *Despair*, pp. 146–151.

[45] Smith, Introduction, *Ranter*, p. 32.

[46] Coppe, *Roule*, p. 92.

[47] Hill, *World*, p. 202.

embarked on a remarkably radical political and spiritual quest. It is probably Coppe who earned the loosely defined group its hostile nickname. As McGregor writes, "Coppe resolved a common Puritan obsession with swearing by public indulgence in mildly blasphemous, ecstatic rants."[48] Coppe's two *Fiery Flying Rolls* quickly provoked hostile propaganda. Coppe was jailed in early 1650, interrogated by a Parliamentary committee, and forced to issue two recantations. His Ranter tracts were ordered burned by Parliamentary decree, and after his imprisonment, a "Blasphemy Act" was passed that resulted in his retroactive guilt. After the Restoration, Coppe changed his name to "Higham" – a subdued pun on *I am*? – practiced medicine, and died in 1672.

As a result of the consignment of such enthusiasts as Coppe to the margins of history, very few enthusiastic writers have achieved a recognition that goes beyond a small band of specialists. It is almost unnecessary to add that anti-enthusiastic views are very well represented in our current construction of British literary tradition. From direct attacks on levelling (as in Andrew Marvell) to satires against Puritan claims to inspiration (as in Samuel Butler and Jonathan Swift), the elite backlash against popular enthusiasm constitutes a well-developed strand of British literature.

Exceptions to this pattern of enthusiastic invisibility do exist. The recent inclusion of Coppe in the sixth edition of the *Norton Anthology of English Literature* may be taken to signal his advent as a canonical literary figure in his own right.[49] Coppe's inclusion in the *Norton Anthology* should ideally also mark the possibility of a less distorted dialogue between mainstream literary tradition and enthusiasm. Norton's editorial headnote, however – unlike the historical and critical work by Nigel Smith and others on which it evidently builds – treats Ranter antinomianism with a ponderous irony. A "cavalier" mode of annotation may be inferred, moreover, when we find a footnote that seems designed to reinforce Coppe's misleading image as an ignorant tub-preacher.[50] This annotation explains Coppe's reference to his own body as a "corpse" by way of his supposed ignorance of the difference between English *corpse* and Latin *corpus*.[51] In fact, however, Coppe refers to his body as a "corpse" to dramatize the "death" of his external carnal self in the violent process of awakening into a new identity animated by divine inspiration. Used thus, "corpse" is both a figure of speech and an enthusiastic

---

[48] McGregor, "Seekers and Ranters," p. 130.

[49] *The Norton Anthology of English Literature*, 6th ed., 2 vols., ed. M. H. Abrams (New York: W. W. Norton & Co., 1993), I, pp. 1744–1748.

[50] For a more balanced account of Coppe's education, including reports from Coppe's tutor of his reading Crashaw's Latin epigrams, see Nigel Smith, "The uses of Hebrew in the English Revolution," in *Language, Self, and Society: A Social History of Language*, eds. Peter Burke and Roy Porter (Cambridge: Polity Press, 1991), pp. 63–64.

[51] *Norton*, p. 1746 (note).

topos.[52] These misreadings arise precisely because Norton, in the absence of a more whole-hearted dialogue with enthusiasm as a collective and richly developed oppositional phenomenon, is simply unable to comprehend the particular contributions of enthusiasm to literary tradition.

Coppe's apparent "arrival," then, is framed with the highly ambiguous cues that often attend token inclusion. Coppe's ambivalent mode of canonization demonstrates two points simultaneously: (1) his unmistakable originality and verve; and (2) a certain lack of interest, on the part of the shapers of tradition, in venturing beyond a dismissal of enthusiasm. A canon, after all, is a version of history. If the "master narrative" of British religious and constitutional history has largely excluded enthusiastic voices, as James Holstun claims,[53] then the canon of seventeenth-century literature has come close to imposing an absolute silence on them. To understand Coppe as other than mad, or ignorant, or as both ignorant and mad, would entail a burdensome rethinking of that often anti-enthusiastic history.

As a writer, Coppe constantly makes stylistic choices that reveal his sense, necessary and enabling for his radical project, of omnipotence. His "commission to write" is attributed directly to God's intervention. His aphoristic numbered paragraphs, moreover, directly recall the typography of Scripture:

The Word of the Lord came expressely to me, saying, write, write, write.

And ONE stood by me, and pronounced all these words to me with his mouth, and I wrote them with ink in this paper.[54]

As this claim continues, Coppe attempts to forestall censorship and inevitable persecution by establishing omnipotent power over the reader:

Wherefore in the Name and Power of the eternall God, I charge thee burn it not, tear it not, for if thou dost, I will tear thee to peices [*sic*] (saith the Lord) and none shall be able to deliver thee; for (as I live) it is the day of my vengeance.[55]

A more aggressive relation with one's reader can scarcely be imagined. The patent defensiveness of "burn it not," though the recourse to divine vengeance smacks of the imaginary, recognizes a very real social threat to the text and its author.

So admirably insouciant is Coppe's willingness to speak for God that he prophesies in the first person, occasionally interjecting a parenthetical "saith the Lord." A similar internalization of the divine, specifically, the

---

[52] The Fifth Monarchist Anna Trapnel, for example, describes herself as "like a dead carcase in respect of bodily strength, but filled with the spirit" during a visionary out-of-body experience. Anna Trapnel, *A Legacy for Saints* (London, 1654), p. 27.

[53] James Holstun, "Ranting at the New Historicism," *English Literary Renaissance* 19:2 (1989), p. 208.

[54] Coppe, *Roule*, p. 99.

[55] *Ibid.*

Ark of the Testimony, occurs in a line in which Coppe refers, punning on "chest," to the "divine power which dwelleth in this Ark, or chest": a covenantal reference.[56] That Coppe had no other available language of self-authorization; that, indeed, his attempt to break the ideologically imposed silence of the British poor was in itself an unwelcome act; that he was saying precisely what England's elite least wished to hear – all of these political factors militate against a study of his rhetoric as a mere case study in psychopathology. It is crucial, therefore, not to isolate and circumscribe the "manic" text with an over-emphasis on merely individual pathology.

One simply cannot adequately describe Coppe's act of identification with God, on the one hand, or London's poor, on the other, as, say, "denial,"[57] or "projective identification," or "introjection."[58] Indeed, whatever terminology one might use to analyze such *topoi* would apply not primarily to the vicissitudes of an "individual" ego, but to the subject-positions constructed within a deliberately oppositional discourse. Such *topoi*, moreover, cannot be the product of mere "madness." For to explain away the enabling fictions of uncompromising dissent, in whatever tone, as "madness," serves precisely to contain questions about the material and ideological environment out of which the "mad" voice was produced.

The enthusiastic subject was created, first of all, from within a wider intersubjective ethos in which certain Biblical *topoi* were reworked and deployed in the context of a politicized claim to divine election. The complex transactions negotiated with Scripture and readers in the following two enthusiastic passages illustrate the collective context of their genesis. The first was published anonymously in 1648; a Digger or near-Digger pamphlet, it was produced by a local group in Buckinghamshire with probable links to the Levellers just before Gerrard Winstanley began to publish his calls for the abolition of private property.[59] The second is by Coppe, who by dint of the pamphlets he published in 1649, when he was 30, became the most celebrated Ranter. Both passages depend on the diatribe about divine justice in the Epistle of James 5:1–6, which begins, "Go to now, ye rich men, weep and howl for your miseries that shall come upon you."

The first passage begins by addressing the poor of England, rebuking those who continue to accept their own domination:

---

56 *Ibid.*, p. 103; see also Smith, *Perfection*, p. 61.
57 According to psychoanalysis, "denial" is the defense mechanism that, above all others, constitutes mania. See Helene Deutsch, "The psycho-analysis of manic-depressive states, with particular reference to chronic hypomania." Reprinted in *Neuroses and Character-Types: Clinical Psychoanalytical Studies* (New York: International Universities Press, 1965), pp. 203–217.
58 These terms, taken from the object-relations school of psychoanalysis, frame Sander Gilman's attempt to mediate between the political fact of stereotypes and their supposed roots in psychological development. See Sander L. Gilman, *Difference and Pathology: Stereotypes of Sexuality, Race, and Madness* (Ithaca: Cornell University Press, 1985).
59 See Aylmer, "Religion," p. 115; see also Hill, *World*, p. 117.

Mark this, poor people, what the Levellers would do for you. Oh why are you so mad as to cry up a King? It is he and his Court and Patentee men, as Majors, Aldermen, and such creatures, that like Cormorants devoure what you should enjoy, and set up Whipping-posts and Correcting-houses to enslave you. Tis rich men that oppresse you, saith *James*.

From there it modulates into a fierce address to the rich:

it is not lawfull nor fit for some to work, and the other to play; for it is Gods command, that all work, let all eat: and if all work alike, is it not fit that all eat alike, have alike, and enjoy alike priviledges and freedoms? And he that did not like this, is not fit to live in a Common-wealth. See *Gen.* 9. And therefore weep and howl, ye Rich men, by what vain name or title soever: God will visit you for all your oppressions; You live on other mens labours, and give them bran to eat, extorting extreme rents and taxes on your fellow-creatures. But now what will you do? for the People will no longer be enslaved by you, for the knowledge of the Lord shall enlighten them, &c.[60]

The vehemence of this passage consists precisely in its recycling of the *topos* from James. In writing thus, the anonymous author assumes something like an apostolic authority to speak for God.

The same holds true for the second passage. Coppe, like James, hears the earth testifying to the agony of the exploited and to the imminent and well-earned doom of the exploiters. Coppe's "I," as he addresses himself to the rich, incorporates the poor of England. More than that, his identification with the Jamesian *topos* permits him to speak, in the present, for God:

Thus saith the Lord, Be silent, O all flesh before the Lord; be silent; O lofty, haughty, great ones of the Earth.

There are so many Bils of Indictment preferred against thee, that both heaven and earth blush thereat.

How long shall I heare the sighs and groanes, and see the teares of poore widowes; and heare curses in every corner; and all sorts of people crying out oppression, oppression, tyranny, tyranny, the worst of tyranny, unheard of, unnatural tyranny.

– O my back, my shoulders. O Tythes, Excize, Taxes, Pollings, &c. O Lord! O Lord God almighty!

"Howle, you great ones," he concludes this chapter, and "heare your doome."[61]

The tone of Coppe's diatribe could indubitably be described as defensive, and even manic.[62] The transactions enacted in this passage, however, have only secondarily to do with the individual fantasies and illusions of Abiezer Coppe. This is not to say that Coppe did not have his

---

[60] Anonymous, *Light Shining in Buckinghamshire*, in Sabine, *Works*, p. 616.
[61] Coppe, *Roule*, p. 93.
[62] Peter Carlton does describe a similar passage from Coppe as "rather appealing in its manic way." Carlton, "Bunyan," p. 25.

own particular history, with its own rhythms and vicissitudes, and his own irreducibly particular subjectivity. My point, rather, is that to read Coppe's text through categories of individual pathology alone would amount to the highly premature reduction of what was clearly not a merely individual phenomenon. Indeed, Coppe's "divine madness" is an especially interesting example of the way, during the politicized moment of the Interregnum, that political and ideological causes fused with, catalyzed, and thus overdetermined personal ones. And indeed, very similar examples of this "howl" *topos* can be found in the writings of such levelling contemporaries as George Foster and (as in the epigraph to this chapter) the Quaker John Perrot.[63]

Coppe's identifications arise first of all from his appropriation and reapplication of Scripture. Because certain basic configurations of class exploitation inscribed in the Jamesian diatribe continue in Cromwell's England, the echo, replacing then with now, reverberates strongly. As in the earlier citation of James, the author's identification with James here serves to produce an underdog's view of history. Its apocalyptic premise, moreover – a conviction that oppression would soon end – was a common and potentially self-fulfilling "fantasy" in the highly politicized religious discourse surrounding the turmoil of the English Revolution.

A second Biblical *topos* sometimes reworked and deployed in the context of the enthusiastic claim to divine election is Paul's allegorical revision of the Biblical story of Abraham's children by Sarah and Hagar in Galatians 4:21–31. No *topos* more aptly fits the fluid situation of a sectarian revisionary process: for if a new claim of election is to succeed, a "new covenant" must be shown to have rendered obsolete the one it purports to supersede. Certain ingenious rhetorical operations are necessary for this necessarily transgressive claim to prevail, notably figurative reversals of cause and effect and of temporal sequence. Christian typology, a triumph of "mystery" over "history," is a central instance of this metaleptic strategy.[64] In Galatians 4:21–31, Paul attempts to show that the Christian covenant supersedes the old Hebraic law because Christians are figuratively in the position of Isaac, the son of the free woman, who inherits God's promise to Abraham's children. The Jews, then, are like Ishmael, child of the bondwoman, who is cast out. The story, according to Paul, represents the two covenants of the "Old" and "New" Testament. The freedom of Christianity is to the "Old

---

[63] See George Foster, *The Pouring Forth of the Seventh and Last Viall* (1650), p. 18 (cited in Smith, Introduction, *Ranter*, p. 22); and John Perrot, "The Lawyer's Fee" (1656) Swarthmore MSS 5/22 [Trans. vii, 110], cited in Kenneth L. Carroll, *John Perrot: Early Quaker Schismatic*, Supplement No. 33 to the *Journal of the Friends' Historical Society* (London: Friends' Historical Society, 1970), pp. 4–5. Foster is further discussed in Jerome Friedman's *Blasphemy, Immorality, and Anarchy: The Ranters and the English Revolution* (Athens, Ohio: Ohio University Press, 1987).

[64] See Harold Bloom, "Before Moses was, I am," in *Poetics of Influence*, ed. John Hollander (New Haven: Henry Schwab, 1988), pp. 387–403.

Law" of Judaism as free Isaac is to the exiled child of bondage. Various groups have since used this "dispensational" model to trace their claim to the "true covenant," attempting to be to Christianity as Christianity claims to be to Judaism.[65] This "two sons" *topos*, an allegorical solution to the problem of cultural belatedness, is thus inevitably a commonplace of enthusiastic discourse.[66]

Coppe's use of such conventions demonstrates to what extent his intelligibility depends on a knowledge of the enthusiastic rhetoric of millenarian "dispensations." An example appears in *Some Sweet Sips, of Some Spirituall Wine* (1649). Unattached to any fixed congregation and opposed to all external ordinances, Coppe wrote and published *Some Sweet Sips* while he still belonged to the "Seeker" milieu around Richard Coppin in the Thames Valley.[67] This was one year before he had the decisive "awakening" experience, described in his *Second Fiery Flying Roule*, which led him to become identified as a full-fledged Ranter. In *Some Sweet Sips* Coppe transposes the Pauline "two sons" allegory about Isaac and Ishmael in connection with his doctrine of perfect freedom from the law, or Libertinism:

For *Abraham had two sons*, the one by a *bond maid* (who is persecutor of all that are not *flesh* of his *flesh*, and *forme* of his *forme*;) the other by a *freewoman*, *Jerusalem* which is above, which is free; and the son of the *freewoman* is free indeed, and persecuted of all *flesh* and *forme* (for every *forme* is a persecutor) but the son of the *freewoman*, who is free, and very free too – is also free from persecuting any – so, and more then so, the son of the *freewoman* is a Libertine . . .[68]

A story about the burden of illegitimacy thus becomes, through a strenuous metalepsis, an allegory of libertinism. It already looks forward to the Ranter paradox that liberation from the "dead fleshly forms" of social convention leads, among other things, to an ostentatious erotic freedom and hostility to monogamy and marriage. The Quakers similarly denied that revelation was a "closed account," that "Scriptures were *the* Word of God, given once and

---

[65] A similar key concept is the sectarian idea of the "Everlasting Gospel," which can be traced back to the medieval mystic Joachim of Fiore. Joachim taught that the history of the world fell into three ages, corresponding to the persons of the trinity. In the coming third age, that of the Holy Ghost, both the Old and the New Testaments will be superseded by the full truth of the Everlasting Gospel. This will be revealed "not in a new sacred book, but in a completely new understanding of the meaning of the Bible, which will illuminate the hearts of men." See A. L. Morton, *The World of the Ranters* (London: Lawrence & Wishart, 1970), p. 126. Contemporary Christian fundamentalists in the US often espouse a related concept of *dispensationalism*, a periodization of Christianity into distinct ages or dispensations. One effect of this periodization is to give the texts of Paul greater authority than the teachings of Jesus. See Kathleen C. Boone, *The Bible Tells Them So: The Discourse of Protestant Fundamentalism* (Albany: State University of New York Press, 1989), pp. 50–60.

[66] Gerrard Winstanley, for instance, repeatedly uses this *topos* in *The New Law of Righteousness* (1649); see Sabine, *Works*, pp. 147–244.

[67] See Smith, "Hebrew," p. 63. For an account of the "Seeker" milieu, see McGregor, "Seekers and Ranters."

[68] Coppe (1649), *Some Sweet Sips*, in Smith, *Ranter*, p. 55.

for all."[69] They denied their own exclusion from the drama of sacred history, their marginality – as uneducated lay people – to a social and religious order supposedly sanctioned, once and for all, by divine command. In so doing, they overcame an externally imposed silence and claimed the right to narrate their own version of history.

A third Biblical *topos* through which enthusiastic subjectivity was rhetorically constructed is Luke's account of Mary's "magnification" of God. Several paradigmatic Biblical scenes prepare us for the idea that God may "elect" us, personally, as individuals for his purposes. For Christian culture, however, the most important of these "identity-imposing" stories or "scenes of nomination" is the Annunciation.[70] Moreover, the hymn ascribed to Mary upon the Annunciation, known as the "Magnificat," stresses class themes that reverberate loudly in the context of the class-based discourse of radical Protestant enthusiasm. God's "regard" for Mary, despite her poverty and gender, represents a triumph for all the lowly of the earth, and a defeat for the rich:

My soul doth magnify the Lord, and my spirit hath rejoiced in God my saviour. For he hath regarded the low estate of his handmaiden: for, behold, from henceforth all generations shall call me blessed ... He hath showed strength with his arm; he hath scattered the proud in the imagination of their hearts. He hath put down the mighty from their seats, and exalted them of low degree. He hath filled the hungry with good things; and the rich he hath sent empty away ... (Luke 1:46–53, King James Version)

In this hymn of thanksgiving, inserted into the narrative of Christ's miraculous birth in Luke, Mary praises God for reversing the hierarchical distribution of attention. His elective "regard" substitutes for the dehumanizing gaze of the rich. It is not only that Mary is elected and "magnified": more generally, the poor are likewise chosen over the rich, who are to be "sent empty away."

The Magnificat "magnifies" not only God, but also the materially and spiritually dispossessed. It is thus a scriptural passage ripe for appropriation by spokesmen for the "lower" orders. To be changed from nobody to somebody, to have a place and purpose, to be an end in oneself, rather than a means: these are the pragmatic effects of recognizing that one is personally elected. Such "magnifying" effects, indeed, can speak to the needs of various politically and economically invisible groups. The Fifth Monarchist Anna Trapnel makes various references to herself as the "handmaid" in *A Legacy for Saints* (1654), as Diane Purkiss points out: both a feminist appropriation of

[69] Richard Bauman, *Let Your Words Be Few: Symbolism of Speaking and Silence among Seventeenth-Century Quakers*, Cambridge Studies in Oral and Literate Culture (Cambridge: Cambridge University Press, 1983), p. 25.
[70] Geoffrey H. Hartman, "Psychoanalysis: the French connection," in *Psychoanalysis and the Question of the Text: Selected Papers from the English Institute, 1976–77*, ed. Geoffrey H. Hartman (Baltimore: The Johns Hopkins University Press, 1978), p. 103.

this passage and an implicit identification with the Virgin Mary.[71] Trapnel also uses "magnification" as the appropriate response to God's indifference to social stratification:

here [in God] is no respect of persons, but the poor begger that lyeth in the street, that knows not where to have a bit of bread, hath nothing but a clothing of tatters, to outward view a very miserable creature, such a one more respected than a rich *Dives* that goeth in his velvet and diadems of gold every day; oh what manner of love is this! that makes no difference between fools and learned ones, preferring ideots before the wisdom of the world, making the ignorant and erring Spirit to have the greatest understanding? Surely such must needs magnifie free grace . . .[72]

Similarly, in 1650 "Digger" or "True Leveller" Gerrard Winstanley, whose commune was itself a small-scale utopian project and model community, echoes it in the course of a radical redefinition of true magistracy:

If you would find true Majestie indeed, goe among the poore despised ones of the Earth; for there Christ dwells, and there you shall see Light and Love shine in Majestie indeed, rising up to unite the Creation indeed, into the unitie of spirit, and band of peace; the blessing of the Lord is amongst the poore, and the covetous, scoffing, covenant-breaking, thieves and murderers, that croud themselves under the name Magistracie, shall be sent empty away.[73]

To magnify the lowly, moreover, goes hand in hand with demystifying those previously "magnified" by aristocratic ideology. Coppe puts it as follows:

Hills! Mountains! Cedars! Mighty men! Your breath is in your nostrils.
   Those that have admired, adored, idolized, magnified, set you up, fought for you, ventured goods, and good name; limbe and life for you, shall cease from you.[74]

This political reversal is a commonplace feature of the "magnifications" of enthusiasm. It begins to explain why the Magnificat (and a more general preoccupation with the Psalmic "magnification" of God through the creation) became a prominent *topos* in the class-based rhetoric of mania.

The levelling theme of "magnification" also explains volumes about the insistent labeling of enthusiasm as madness by the ruling classes. If a claim to equality in things spiritual is asserted, can a levelling of things temporal be far behind? To quote Winstanley again: "this phrase of *Mine and Thine* shall be swallowed up in the law of righteous actions to one another, for they shall all live as brethren, every one doing as they would be done by; and he that sees his brother in wants, and doth not help, shall smart for his iniquity . . ."[75]

---

[71] Diane Purkiss, "Producing the voice, consuming the body: women prophets of the seventeenth century," in *Women, Writing, History 1640–1740*, eds. Isobel Grundy and Sue Wiseman (Athens: The University of Georgia Press, 1992), p. 156.
[72] Trapnel, *Legacy*, pp. 15–16.
[73] Winstanley, *Fire in the Bush*, in Sabine, *Works*, pp. 473–474.
[74] Coppe, *Roll*, p. 87.
[75] Winstanley, *The New Law of Righteousness*, in Sabine, *Works*, p. 183.

Class struggle is not merely a sociological angle imposed externally by my analysis; it is, rather, a constitutive dimension of enthusiastic rhetoric, and, hence, the very condition of its semantic intelligibility. From this perspective, Stachniewski's description of those radical Puritans who made the first sharp break with Calvinist thought-control is suggestive but inadequate:

the writings of Ranters, Quakers, and other groups almost invariably attest the experience of Calvinist despair. They confirm the extent of persecution as much as they indicate a means of escape. It was language, primarily, the Ranters realized, that oppressed them. Their exhilarated emancipation took the form of inverting and abusing the language of Calvinism in order to scramble its concepts. It was an admirable exercise in bravura.[76]

There are several problems with this summary analysis, which leads to an underestimation of the radical potential of enthusiastic rhetoric. The basic problem is that the Ranters, Quakers, and Diggers, though they demystified the prevailing religious language, were oppressed by forces beyond the merely linguistic; this they knew very well, as their consistent attention to inequalities of property demonstrates.

From this problem stem others. For it is because he neglects the enthusiastic disruption of dominant politics that Stachniewski oversimplifies the enthusiastic project as one of mere linguistic reversal. Having written so eloquently about religious despair, Stachniewski gives short shrift to what he sees, too reductively, as its mere inverted mirror-image. Some modes of enthusiastic rhetoric are indeed implicated in the trap of mere counter-hegemonic inversion; they thus produce, in James Holstun's phrase, "a vengeful double of the more staid Presbyterian or Protectorate oligarchies they attack."[77] Much enthusiastic rhetoric, however, achieves a further and more productive break: an attempt to disidentify with Calvinist subjectivity as such.[78] The selective rearticulation of Biblical *topoi*, as a prophetically licensed rhetorical mode, did indeed work out new possibilities of subjectivity. And precisely because enthusiastic subjectivity did indeed expose and threaten the limits of a merely bourgeois revolution, it cannot be adequately treated as the insignificant permutation of an all-powerful dominant discourse. Ranter rhetoric, as Holstun points out, "attempts to fabricate a new human collectivity by criticizing received oppositions between rich and poor, man and woman, the sacred and the blasphemous, the elect and the damned, God and the Devil, and ultimately, good and evil."[79]

A final problem with Stachniewski's conclusions have to do with his

---

[76] Stachniewski, *Despair*, p. 159.

[77] Holstun, "Ranting," p. 214.

[78] I have adapted for my purposes here the discussion of *disidentification* in Michel Pêchaux, *Language, Semantics, and Ideology*, trans. Harbans Nagpal (1975; New York: St. Martin's Press, 1982), pp. 158–159.

[79] Holstun, "Ranting," p. 214.

elevation of Bunyan's cultural significance at the expense of the more "manic" enthusiasts. It is perhaps fitting for a book about an insidious and claustrophobic culture of despair to offer little in the way of utopian consolations. Nevertheless, it is a serious mistake to take John Bunyan's despair as the best popular emblem of the age. Bunyan's persecutory imagination, according to Stachniewski, "responds more fully to the predicament of the lower orders than that of more radical contemporaries exactly because his estimation of the insuperable power of his worldly antagonists was, at that historical juncture, accurate."[80] Such realism in hindsight, however, fails to acknowledge what the enthusiasts did in fact achieve: a disruption of elite discourses so profound that it permanently altered the languages of religion and literature.

The enthusiasts' transgression of bourgeois limits is precisely what explains the onslaught of retroactive pathologizing with which the "winners of history" have greeted their memory. The English Revolution itself has continued to be fought and refought, through the medium of culture, for some 300 years. It is little wonder, then, that the era's most radical partisans – vivid figures of an unfinished revolution within the Revolution – continue themselves to be a site of intense cultural struggle. Indeed, the history of religious enthusiasm has thus been ceaselessly reshaped according to the political and cultural interests of one or another political agenda. For enthusiasm, more than any other single word or symbol, conjures up the stubborn memories of class polarization during the English Civil War. Even a brief analysis of the various genealogies that have been constructed for enthusiasm serves to illustrate the intensely contested status of its memory.

The most disingenuous genealogy of enthusiasm belongs largely to critics of Anglo-Catholic sympathies who, in the words of Stachniewski, "wish to assert the continuity of faith through the Christian millennia."[81] Such critics find ubiquitous evidence of patristic influences, Ignatian meditative exercises, Franciscan sensibilities, and doctrinal continuity in literary works that in fact belong to quite different historical *milieux*. Thus a certain High Church appropriation of *Paradise Lost*, for example, best represented by the criticism of C. S. Lewis, smooths over the disruption potentially represented by a full engagement with the regicidal Milton and his rebarbative zeal. Consider the following exercise in recuperation from Lewis' *A Preface to Paradise Lost*:

In so far as *Paradise Lost* is Augustinian and Hierarchical it is also Catholic in the sense of basing its poetry on conceptions that have been held "always and everywhere and by all" ... Heretical elements exist in it, but are only discoverable by search; any criticism which forces them into the foreground is mistaken ...[82]

---

[80] Stachniewski, *Despair*, pp. 166–167.
[81] *Ibid.*, p. 2.
[82] C. S. Lewis, *A Preface to Paradise Lost* (New York: Oxford University Press, 1961), p. 82.

In this world, even to recall that Milton was arrested and jailed briefly in 1660; that some of his prose works, like Coppe's pamphlets, were burned by the common hangman; and that he had reason to fear for his life,[83] feels like bad manners. To bring up Milton's mortalism or his anti-trinitarianism – much less the fact that censorship would have prevented their more direct expression – would indeed be a lapse of taste.

A second tradition of hostile pedigrees for enthusiasm, though inaugurated by such seventeenth-century heresiographies as Blome's *Fanatick History* (1660), is best represented here by Norman Cohn's *Pursuit of the Millennium*: a sweeping overview of what Cohn sees as history's lunatic fringe. Cohn begins by condemning Jewish and early Christian apocalyptic – the Book of Daniel, the Book of Revelation, the Apocalypses of Baruch and Ezra – as a form of "collective megalomania."[84] From the tainted ideas in these pathogenic books, themselves a symptom of pathology, according to Cohn, stem many of the world's ills. A lurid history ensues: a parade of crazed gnostics, bizarre self-flagellants, and nihilistic megalomaniacs. Over and over again, Cohn reduces the ideologies of popular protest to the terms of individual psychopathology. Terms like "delusional" and "markedly paranoid" are sprinkled liberally throughout the book. Cohn's panoramic view of history eventually lumps together as "remarkably uniform" the social situations that engendered the fourteenth-century English Peasants' Revolt, the sixteenth-century Bohemian *Bundschuh* and Anabaptist movements, and the seventeenth-century English Ranters, Diggers, and Quakers.[85] Although some important continuities do exist between some of the groups thus catalogued, Cohn paints with too broad a brush. Seventeenth-century English enthusiasm is thus robbed of its historical specificity and assimilated to a sort of timeless Bedlam.

These narrative strategies – essentially incompatible with one another, it is worth noting – make clear that there are always political stakes involved in tracing the pedigree of enthusiasm. A recent polemical discussion of the historiographical fortunes of the Ranters, the epitome of "enthusiasm," can serve by way of bringing this battle of the books up to the present. J. C. Davis has advanced the argument that the "Ranters" were a bogeyman hardly existing outside the fevered imagination of hostile pamphleteers and a yellow press in the mid-seventeenth century, or of leftist historians (A. L. Morton and Christopher Hill) in the mid-to-late twentieth century.[86] *Fear, Myth, and*

---

[83] See Michael Wilding, "Regaining the radical Milton," in *Dragon's Teeth: Literature in the English Revolution* (Oxford: Clarendon Press, 1987), pp. 232–258.

[84] Norman Cohn, *The Pursuit of the Millennium: Revolutionary Messianism in Medieval and Reformation Europe and Its Bearing on Modern Totalitarian Movements*, 2nd ed. (New York: Harper Torchbooks, 1961), p. 3.

[85] *Ibid.*, p. 22.

[86] J. C. Davis, *Fear, Myth, and History: The Ranters and the Historians* (Cambridge: Cambridge University Press, 1986).

History is clearly a conservative version of that current historiographic genre by which socially constructed "inventions" are deconstructed. Davis claims that the Ranters were "necessary" for a marxist version of Britain's history: "Without the Ranters there would have been no thoroughgoing popular rejection of the Protestant ethic and, therefore, no illustration of the strength and continuity of the popular tradition whereby the people sought to make their own history and throw off the hegemonic impress of those to whom they were subjected."[87] This claim, however, does not withstand scrutiny. "The idea of a radical revolution within the wider English Revolution," as Barry Reay observes, "is not affected one jot by the presence or absence of the Ranters; they are but one aspect of a wider radical constellation."[88]

What does emerge in the passage above is a genealogical motive, however misguided, for the revisionist attempt to wipe the Ranters off the historical map. The method of this revisionism is ingenious. First Davis defines "Ranter" so stringently that even Coppe, for example, is excluded from the "practical antinomian" portion of Davis' criteria on the grounds that he continues to believe in one sin: hypocrisy.[89] "One must be unhappy," as Iain Hampscher-Monk observes, "about the disposal of a historical phenomenon through the deployment of definitions."[90] Davis then demands, unrealistically, proof from the surviving archive that is at once abundant, untainted by polemical motives, and, despite a multitude of oppressive conditions, unambiguous.[91] That he does not find such evidence is little surprise. What is surprising, however, is that Davis discounts Coppe's earlier *Flying Rolls* by reading his legally coerced recantations at face value: those recantations, indeed, are almost the only evidence regarding the Ranters that he does take at face value. Finally, Davis labels Hill and Morton as leftist ideologues: insinuating, as David Underdown notes, that having named political affiliations, as opposed to unspoken political assumptions, detracts from the professional worth of their work.[92] Thus do the Ranters – even, inexplicably, those studied by various non-marxist scholars – evaporate under Davis' gaze.

Davis is saying less than first appears, however, when he roundly declares, "There was no Ranter movement, no Ranter sect, no Ranter theology."[93] For both Hill and J. F. McGregor have already provided thoughtful analyses

---

87 *Ibid.*, p. 134.
88 Reay, "The world turned upside down," p. 67.
89 See Davis, *Fear*, p. 57; for critiques of this definition of antinomianism, see Edward Thompson, "On the rant," in Eley and Hunt, *Reviving*, pp. 155–157; and G. E. Aylmer, "Review article: did the Ranters exist?" *Past and Present* 117 (Nov., 1978), pp. 215–216.
90 Iain Hampscher-Monk, review in *The History of Political Thought* 8:3 (1987), p. 575.
91 *Ibid.*
92 David Underdown, review in *Journal of Modern History* 61:3 (1980), p. 594.
93 Davis, *Fear*, p. 124.

of the many perplexities of denominational pigeonholes in this era, and of the dangers inherent in their careless or anachronistic reification.[94] Thus Davis' nominalist arguments for terminological rigor can go only so far. As Hill writes, "Professor Davis proved to his own satisfaction that the Ranters were not a sect (correct) and drew the incorrect conclusion that they were a figment of the imagination of their contemporaries and of later historians. By the same logic we could prove that Baptists, Independents and Quakers did not exist."[95] The term "Ranter" can legitimately identify those who shared, unevenly and incompletely, a certain set of family resemblances. Given that Hill has not claimed either doctrinal uniformity or organizational coherence for the Ranters, the force of Davis' critique is rather limited.[96] Hill has consistently emphasized the fluidity of religious groupings during the Cromwellian period: "Looking back," Hill writes in response to Davis, "we can see sects in process of formation."[97] Because 1660 is the point at which persecution forced informal congregations into more formally consolidated organizations, Hill now suggests that the word "sect" be prohibited for the period before 1660.[98]

Davis has also dwelled at length on the historiographic problem of relying on seventeenth-century sources, overwhelmingly abusive, for whom the Ranters are necessarily a polemical image. In the book's most valuable chapter, Davis makes clear that contemporary references to Ranters could be used for such diverse agendas as the following: (1) bashing separatists generally;[99] (2) manufacturing prurient gutter-press news; (3) defining an outer limit or uncrossable frontier in comparison with which one's own

---

[94] See Christopher Hill, "History and denominational history," in *The Collected Essays of Christopher Hill*, 2 vols. (Amherst: University of Massachusetts Press, 1986), II: *Religion and Politics in 17th Century England*, pp. 3–10; see also McGregor, "Seekers and Ranters," pp. 121–139.

[95] Hill, *Bible*, p. 35.

[96] Davis' critique does have some bearing on the work of A. L. Morton and the more recent work of Jerome Friedman. In *The Everlasting Gospel: A Study in the Sources of William Blake* (London, 1958), Morton does describe the Ranters as a "sect" (p. 41). In *The World of the Ranters*, however, Morton twice disavows inflated notions of organizational or doctrinal coherence; he describes the Ranters there as "a movement rather than a sect" (pp. 17, 93). Although Davis claims in an article that Morton relapses back into calling the Ranters a "sect" on p. 92 of *The World of the Ranters*, what Morton actually writes on p. 92 is the following: "It would probably be incorrect to speak of the Ranters as a church, or even as a sect." See J. C. Davis, "Fear, myth, and furore: reappraising the 'Ranters,'" *Past and Present* 129 (1990), p. 89. Friedman's book seems incautious in its repeated use of the word "sect" to describe the Ranters; like Cohn, moreover, Friedman assimilates the Ranters to a dualist tradition stretching back for two thousand years. See his *Blasphemy, Immorality, and Anarchy: The Ranters and the English Revolution* (Athens, Ohio: Ohio University Press, 1987).

[97] Christopher Hill, "The lost Ranters? a critique of J. C. Davis," *History Workshop Journal* 24 (1987), p. 135.

[98] Hill, *Bible*, p. 35.

[99] The extension of the term "Ranter" to cover all sectarian radicals – a form of guilt by association – repeatedly compelled Winstanley's Diggers, Fox's Quakers, and Bunyan's Baptists, for example, to dissociate themselves from the Ranters. All of these thinkers, however, also had genuine doctrinal differences with the Ranters. The Ranter Coppe, for his part, disavows association with "sword-levelling" or "digging-levelling."

grouping – the Quakers, say – appears more moderate;[100] and (4) redefining, through a "moral panic," the boundaries of normalcy and deviancy in a bewildering universe of *de facto* religious toleration. Ironically enough, however, it is the conservative historian Cohn, rather than either Morton or Hill, who seems conspicuously credulous in his reliance on even the most lurid accounts of enthusiastic transgression.[101] Some hostile sources, moreover, demonstrably describe at least some of the doctrinal deviations correctly.[102] In any case, the obvious fact that the Ranters were turned into a sensationalized scapegoat simply does not prove that Ranteresque separatists never existed. Similarly, although no one can doubt that the ideological reversals attributed to the Ranters relate to the "importance of inversions and contraries in the cognitive procedures of early modern England,"[103] that relationship does not in any way prove the nonexistence of the Ranters. The possibility of transgressive inversion is simply built into political hierarchies from the start. We can recognize that authorities have often licensed and coopted such transgressions without granting them the ability to produce and control, with invulnerable omnipotence, all subversive practices. As Nigel Smith writes, "if the Ranters were a fiction, they were one of their own as well as of others' making."[104]

Davis does not appear to have convinced many historians that the Ranters were merely a factitious myth. In the wake of *Fear, Myth, and History*, Hill himself has restated the position that the Ranters certainly did exist as a well-recognized and influential *milieu*.[105] G. E. Aylmer's final word, after a point-by-point analysis of Davis' argument, is that "the Ranters existed and did not have to be invented in 1650 – or in 1970."[106] Numerous other historians have concurred.[107] In any case, Davis has already implicitly conceded the most crucial point for my purposes: that the Ranters, ever since the "moral panic" they provoked in the 1650s, have inevitably *represented* – whether as threat or promise, as temptation or phobia – the compelling image of "the world turned upside down." Whereas Davis locates the scapegoating of the

---

[100] See McGregor, "Seekers and Ranters," pp. 135–136, for an account of how the Quakers used the "Ranter" image as an instrument of congregational discipline.

[101] See Thompson, "On the rant," p. 154.

[102] Thomas Edwards' *Gangraena*, for instance, accurately describes the ideas found in various extant pamphlets. See Reay, "The world turned upside down," pp. 67–68. See also McGregor ("Seekers and Ranters," p. 132) for the point that the provisions of the Blasphemy Act of 1650 "presented a reasonably dispassionate summary" of Ranter doctrines.

[103] Davis, "Furore," p. 86. This article contains a helpful bibliography of the "Lost Ranters" controversy.

[104] Smith, *Perfection*, p. 9 (note).

[105] Hill, "Lost Ranters," p. 135.

[106] See Aylmer, "Did the Ranters exist?" p. 219.

[107] See Underdown, review; Thompson, "On the rant"; Reay, "The world turned upside down"; Hampscher-Monk, review; Paul Slack, review in *English Historical Review* 104:413 (1989), pp. 1039–1040; and Jerome Friedman, untitled book review in *Journal of Interdisciplinary History* 19:1 (1988), pp. 115–117.

Ranters in a broad spectrum of paranoid fantasies about crypto-Royalism, feminism, and atheism, however, I insist upon refocusing on the politics of plebeian struggle. Even the paranoia provoked by reputed Ranter teachings about sexuality, and summed up in the charge that they practiced "community of women," had much to do with a brutally patriarchal definition of women as private property.[108] To delink the "Ranter" image from class politics in the seventeenth century may be the most cunning assault of all on their significance for posterity.

As a cultural memory, enthusiasm is anything but marginal; as an enduring mode, its "manic" tendencies are more than merely individual. Moreover, the defining significance for enthusiasm of a particular historical break – the revolutionary outburst of the 1640s and 50s – serves to highlight longstanding narrative strategies by which the seventeenth-century radical Puritan disruption of elite hegemony has been recuperated. Hostile pedigrees for enthusiasm, whether they minimize its historical importance, on the one hand, or its sanity, on the other, are so many strategies of containment. The "mania" of Abiezer Coppe and his fellow radicals – whatever its individual elements may be – can only be fully understood as a mode of collective opposition: the rhetorical contours, indeed, of a manic style.

[108] For Winstanley's rebuttal of this charge against his "Digger" commonwealth, see Winstanley, *Gift*, in Sabine, *Works*, pp. 366–367.

2

"A huge loud voice": levelling and the gendered body politic

and day and night with a huge loud voice proclaiming the day of the Lord throughout London and Southwark.   Abiezer Coppe, *A Second Fiery Flying Roule*

The rhetorical project of the manic mode is best defined as a politics, far-reaching but ultimately uneven, of levelling. This levelling agenda explains not only the enthusiastic propensity for catalogues and for the use of certain *topoi* from Biblical prophets, but also more blatantly "irrational" rhetorical features. These latter features include the disjunctiveness of enthusiastic rhetoric – its "stammering tongue," its deliberately fractured evocations of the ineffable – as well as its peculiarly serious playfulness with language. A certain rhetoric of bodily desire, moreover, drawing on the Song of Songs, serves as a favorite medium for a "levelling" of the mind/body hierarchy. What gives a certain unity to this constellation of rhetorical effects is a consistent collective project in which the levelling "materiality" of paralogical language figures the body.

We must not forget, however, that the body itself is a politically contested figure. For my point is precisely not to reproduce the conservative bromide that enthusiasm is merely displaced eroticism. As James Grantham Turner points out, "the secular diagnosis of 'Enthusiasm' as a genital disorder...was already strong at the time of the English Revolution."[1] Henry More's *Enthusiasmus Triumphatus* (1662), for instance, presents this familiar anti-enthusiastic *topos* in terms of humor pathology: the vapors from "lower" melancholic and sanguine humors rise up to cloud the enthusiast's "higher" faculties and thus inspire the doctrine of "community of wives."[2] Instead of such tendentious medical materialism, which in fact *literalizes* the "body-politic" *topos*, we need an account of enthusiasm that can remain rigorously faithful to rhetorical analysis while linking it to material sexual practice.

This enthusiastic rhetoric of economic and social levelling in fact knowingly

---

[1]   James Grantham Turner, *One Flesh: Paradisal Marriage and Sexual Relations in the Age of Milton* (Oxford: Clarendon Press, 1987), p. 82.
[2]   Henry More, *Enthusiasmus Triumphatus* (1662; rpt. Los Angeles: Augustan Reprint Society, 1966), p. 26.

engages, through its deliberate "irrationality," the ideology of the body politic. The *topos* of the "body politic" is perhaps most familiar to modern readers as the "fable of the belly" in Shakespeare's *Coriolanus*, in which the patrician Menenius Agrippa puts down a rebellion of the Roman plebeians by elaborating the image of a body fragmented by the mutiny of various parts against the belly. Extremely widespread in Renaissance and Restoration political and religious controversies, this *topos* harks back to classical, Biblical, and medieval antecedents.[3] Its usual function, as its use by the ruling-class Roman in *Coriolanus* demonstrates, is to validate the existing structure of superordination by analogy with the division of bodily functions in a human body: political rebellion thus can be equated with disease and "unnatural" phenomena. It is worth noting, indeed, that an important historical source for our information about the Ranters and other heretics is Thomas Edwards' *Gangraena* (1646), a vast compendium, as the subtitle has it, of the "Errours, Heresies, Blasphemies, and pernicious Practices of the Sectaries of this time, vented and acted in England in these four last years." The heresiographer's image of "gangrene" invokes the image of a diseased body politic, doubtless also implying that the cure is some sort of violent "amputation."

Enthusiasm thus interacts, as a levelling rhetoric, with an ensemble of dominant discourses that linked vertically stratified social hierarchies to vertically differentiated bodily zones. It seems clear, moreover, that enthusiastic levelling, though remarkably programmatic, meets its greatest complication in the domain of sexual hierarchy. Though the achievement of enthusiastic rhetoric in levelling the male/female hierarchy is uneven, the broader point holds: manic levelling, even as a conspicuously "carnal" rhetoric, is as concerned with the body politic as with the vagaries of the individual body. I hope to demonstrate in this chapter that Coppe's project of enthusiastic levelling remains of particular interest precisely in its visionary reinvention of the body politic. Indeed, it is above all through its revisions of the gendered body politic that enthusiastic rhetoric seeks to point toward new subjectivities and an alternative order.

The Quakers, the largest and most successful radical separatist group, illustrate the wider context of insubordination within which enthusiasm found its voice. Their practice of "plain speech" – a socio-linguistic rebellion against many of the key forms of seventeenth-century English "politeness" – justified

---

3   See Ernst H. Kantorowicz's *The King's Two Bodies: A Study in Mediaeval Political Theology* (Princeton, N.J.: Princeton University Press, 1957); David George Hale's *The Body Politic: A Political Metaphor in Renaissance English Literature* (The Hague: Mouton, 1971); and Leonard Barkan's "The human body and the commonwealth," in *Nature's Work of Art: The Human Body as Image of the World* (New Haven: Yale University Press, 1975), pp. 61–115. An anthropologist's perspective on the social implications of rituals that concern bodily boundaries can be found in Mary Douglas' "The two bodies," in *Natural Symbols: Explorations in Cosmology* (New York: Pantheon Books, 1970), pp. 65–81.

itself as a rejection of worldly social divisions. The rebellion focused on such "politeness phenomena," obviously saturated with messages about social stratification, as greetings, salutations, titles, and honorific pronouns.[4] Thus George Fox explains that he withholds "hat-honor" and other social formalities on God's command: "Moreover, when the Lord sent me forth into the world, He forbade me 'to put off my hat' to any, high or low; and I was required to thee and thou all men and women, without any respect to rich or poor, great or small."[5] One can see, in the struggles provoked by this minuscule rejection of social deference, the contention of two irreducibly conflictual visions of social reality and history. Such contentious challenges to social subordination were obviously among several aspects of Quaker provocation that aroused hostility, both by persecuting officials, by whom the "Children of Light" were "whipped, branded, dunked, put in stocks, and imprisoned,"[6] and by mobs representing a popular traditionalist backlash, as Barry Reay demonstrates.[7]

The Ranters, moreover, went beyond the rhetoric of pronominal familiarity used by the Friends. Mirroring the gaze of the rich through him, Abiezer Coppe boasts of

charging so many Coaches, so many hundreds of men and women of the greater rank, in the open streets, with my hand stretched out, my hat cock'd up, staring on them as I would look thorough [sic] them, gnashing with my teeth at some of them, and day and night with a huge loud voice proclaiming the day of the Lord throughout London and Southwark...[8]

This ranting rhetoric, whether or not it records actual events, should not be dismissed as a mere monologue. Coppe in fact simultaneously speaks within, and tries to dramatize, the grossly asymmetrical dialogue that necessarily frames his voice and its reception. His rant incorporates within itself the full knowledge of its likely reception by those who, hermetically cocooned inside the "greater ranks," will deny all mutuality and reciprocity with him. He thus attempts to proclaim, in "a huge loud voice," how much has been endured

---

[4]   Richard Bauman, *Let Your Words Be Few: Symbolism of Speaking and Silence among Seventeenth-Century Quakers*, Cambridge Studies in Oral and Literate Culture (Cambridge: Cambridge University Press, 1983), pp. 43–62.

[5]   George Fox, *The Works of George Fox*, vol. I: *A Journal or Historical Account of the Life, Travels, Sufferings, Christian Experiences, and Labour of Love in the Work of the Ministry of that Ancient, Eminent, and Faithful Servant of Jesus Christ, George Fox* (1831; rpt. New York: AMS Press, 1975), p. 91. For a discussion of the textual problems with Fox's *Journal*, see James Olney, *Metaphors of Self: The Meaning of Autobiography* (Princeton: Princeton University Press, 1972), pp. 155–156 (note).

[6]   Douglas Gwyn, *Apocalypse of the Word: The Life and Message of George Fox (1624–1691)* (Richmond, Ind.: Friends United Press, 1986), p. 41.

[7]   Barry Reay, "Popular hostility towards Quakers," in *The Quakers and the English Revolution* (London: Temple Smith, 1985), pp. 62–78.

[8]   Abiezer Coppe, *A Second Fiery Flying Roule*, in *A Collection of Ranter Writings from the 17th Century*, ed. Nigel Smith (London: Junction Books, 1983), p. 105.

by those deemed not of the same flesh and blood – not fully human – and, hence, habitually invisible and inaudible.

Enthusiastic rhetoric further extends its insubordinate response to social hierarchy through levelling enumerations. The following list, taken from Coppe's Seeker pamphlet *Some Sweet Sips, of Some Spirituall Wine* (1649), deliberately reduces the hierarchy of estates and professions to a heap of irrelevant distinctions based on outward appearance: mere clothes. In this remarkable parody of academic discourse, complete with proto-Scriblerian marginalia, Coppe explains that unlearned sectarians are the spiritual equals of their supposed betters in the university:

And it is neither Paradox, Hetrodox [*sic*], Riddle, or ridiculous to good Schollars, who know the *Lord in deed*, (though perhaps they know never a letter in the Book) to affirm that God can speak, & gloriously preach to some through Carols, Anthems, Organs; yea, all things else, &c. Through Fishers, Publicans, Tanners, Tent-makers, Leathern Aprons, as well as through University men, – Long-Gowns, Cloaks, or Cassocks; O *Strange*![9]

"The confusion of academic and sectarian trappings," as Nigel Smith observes, "both in clothing and in language, results in a comic release of laughter."[10] Because apocalyptic revelation is precisely that which strips away external pretensions, such laughter has an edge to it: for the catalogue is that rhetorical form which links up best with other social practices of stripping, levelling, and purging.

Radical separatists cultivated the strategy of stripping away all external signs of artificial distinctions: divesting themselves, in effect, of vain customs and worldly fashions. This strategy governs both linguistic and sartorial gestures. The Digger or True Leveller Gerrard Winstanley thus offers *The Law of Freedom* as "a poor man that comes cloathed to your door in a torn country garment." Hence he urges the reader to "take of [f] the clownish language, for under that you may see beauty."[11] So the "mere clothes" *topos* of levelling discourse, in such sectaries as Coppe, exposes social stratification itself as a grand masquerade – one, indeed, that can, in principle, be called off. It is not surprising that eighteenth-century authorities, still haunted by memories of the English Revolution, feared the levelling, anti-taxonomic implications of masquerades.[12]

The Quakers were especially known for their determination to divest

9 Coppe, *Some Sweet Sips*, p. 60.
10 Nigel Smith, *Perfection Proclaimed: Language and Literature in English Radical Religion 1640–1660* (Oxford: Clarendon Press, 1989), p. 291.
11 Gerrard Winstanley, *The Law of Freedom*, in *The Works of Gerrard Winstanley*, ed. George H. Sabine (Ithaca: Cornell University Press, 1941), p. 510.
12 See Terry Castle, *Masquerade and Civilization: The Carnivalesque in Eighteenth-Century Culture and Fiction* (Stanford: Stanford University Press, 1986), p. 79. Among the farther adventures of the "mere clothes" *topos*, perhaps the strangest is its appropriation and elaboration by Thomas Carlyle in *Sartor Resartus*.

themselves of vain fripperies. Given the millennial expectations of the moment, moreover, it is little wonder that some, both male and female, beginning around 1652, began going "naked for a sign."[13] This bit of millenarian popular theatre looked back to the prophetic behavior ascribed to Isaiah in Isaiah 20, and used the naked body as an emblem for an impending apocalypse. One such Quaker, William Simpson, explains, "As naked shall you be spiritually, so my body hath been temporally naked in many places in England, as a sign of the nakedness and shame that is coming upon the Church of England, who live in Oppression and Cruelty ..."[14] Like most images of the end, the practice of going naked for a sign simultaneously evoked perfectionist connotations of an prelapsarian origin: Adam and Eve, innocently undisguised in Eden.[15] The Ranters were similarly accused, albeit in propagandistic contexts, of orgiastic exercises in paradisal sexuality.

The apocalyptic stripping and purging work of enthusiastic catalogues operates as well against the appropriative mediations of names and titles. The anonymous author of the near-Digger pamphlet, *More Light Shining in Buckinghamshire*, in an extraordinary analysis of how the established system of property coerces and coopts ordinary people into working and even committing violence against their own economic and political interests, produces a fierce levelling catalogue:

the creature, man, is enslaved to his kinds, and all Monopolizings, Encroachings, Inhancings, Licenses, Patents, Grants, Prerogatives, Priviledges, unjust and unnatural, arbitrary and wicked, compacted, unreasonable, and all unjust interests are unlawful, and the Scriptures do everywhere protest against it, calling it *Oppressions*; and pronounceth Judgments against it, calling the Abettors, Promotors, and Actors of the same, though Men call them *Kings, Lords, Generals, Parliaments, Councels, Consuls, Judges*, or by what name else they are known, dignified or distinguished, as the Priests call it, to be but *Lions, Bears, Wolves, Leopards, Foxes, Bulls, Beasts, Dogs, Whelps*, from their Natures...[16]

The point is not merely to vent a litany of woes. Prophetic discourse, insofar as it requires a ritualistic renaming of social reality, naturally gravitates toward inventories and lists. Their effect is to denude the system of its cloak of respectability.

A second manner in which enthusiastic rhetoric seeks to level the hierarchical *status quo* is through a revoicing of Isaiah's prediction of a divine

---

[13] See Kenneth Carroll, "Early Quakers and 'going naked as a sign,'" *Quaker History* 67 (1978), pp. 69–87; Bauman, *Words*, pp. 84–94; and Hugh Ormsby-Lennon, "Swift and the Quakers," *Swift Studies* 4 (1989), pp. 34–62.

[14] William Simpson, *A Discovery of the Priests and Professors, And their Nakedness and Shame, which is coming upon them* (London, 1660), p. 8. Cited in Carroll, "Early Quakers," p. 79.

[15] Hugh Ormsby-Lennon, "From shibboleth to apocalypse: Quaker speechways during the Puritan Revolution," in *Language, Self, and Society: A Social History of Language*, eds. Peter Burke and Roy Porter (Cambridge: Polity Press, 1991), p. 84.

[16] Anonymous, *More Light Shining in Buckinghamshire*, in Sabine, *Works*, pp. 631–632.

levelling of high mountains and lofty cedars (Isaiah 2:13–14).[17] Coppe's version of this enthusiastic *topos* may be the passage that gives the fullest vent to popular class animus, and to the desire that the English Revolution fulfill itself in a thorough abolition of class distinctions. The verb "to level" resounds like thunder through Coppe's hyperbolic cry of wrath:

And now thus saith the Lord:
  Though you can as little endure the word LEVELLING, as could the late slaine or dead *Charles* (your forerunner, who is gone before you –) and had as live heare the Devill named, as heare of the Levellers (Men-Levellers) which is, and who (indeed) are but shadowes of most terrible, yet great and glorious good things to come.[18]

The revolutionary energy is bracing; the conflation of the recently beheaded Charles Stuart with John the Baptist, as a "forerunner" of the aristocracy's doom, wickedly amusing. What follows is an extraordinary levelling chant:

Behold, behold, behold, I the eternall God, the Lord of Hosts, who am that mighty Leveller am comming [*sic*] (yea even at the doors) to Levell in good earnest, to Levell to some purpose, to Levell with a witnesse, to Levell the Hills with the Valleyes, and to lay the Mountaines low.
  High Mountaines! lofty Cedars! its high time for you to enter into the Rocks, and to hide you in the dust, for feare of the Lord, and for the glory of his Majesty. For the lofty looks of man shall be humbled, and the haughtinesse of men shall be bowed downe, and the Lord ALONE shall be exalted in that day; For the day of the Lord of Hoasts, shall be upon everyone that is proud, and lofty, and upon everyone that is lifted up, and he shall be brought low.[19]

The impressive release of energy in this passage is directly connected to the theme of social levelling. Identifying himself with the grandeur of a wrathful God, to whom all human social distinctions are laughable, Coppe assumes the voice of apocalyptic justice. No humble plea for benevolent reform, this: what may shock here, and what is intended to shock, is precisely the sheer exuberance with which Coppe's triumphalist rant welcomes revolutionary destruction.

This passage was written soon after the Levellers were crushed at Burford; placed thus chronologically, it has been seen by A. L. Morton as marking an abandonment by embittered Levellers of rational hope.[20] "Where Levelling by sword and spade had both failed," Morton says, "what seemed called for was a Levelling by miracle, in which God himself would confound the mighty by means of the poorest, lowest, and most despised of the earth."[21] If we read

---

17 For more about this and related Biblical *topoi*, see Christopher Hill, *The English Bible and the Seventeenth Century Revolution* (London: Penguin Press, 1993), pp. 116–122.

18 Coppe, *Roule*, p. 87.

19 *Ibid.*

20 A. L. Morton, *The World of the Ranters: Religious Radicalism in the English Revolution* (London: Lawrence & Wishart, 1970), p. 18.

21 *Ibid.*, p. 71.

this prophetic ultimatum merely as a shift from the political and juridical to
the supernatural, a large element of the merely imaginary does seem visible;
and yet these domains were not, after all, so clearly distinct. Morton's view
accepts too easily the idea that millenarian sentiments, regardless of time and
place, are essentially irrational. Coppe's prophetic rhetoric, however, also
responds to historical contingencies in the realms of epistemology and
signification, namely: (1) the fact that Biblical exegesis had floated entirely
free from the social relations that had previously stabilized and guaranteed its
meaning; and (2) the related fact that the very notion of immediate
inspiration licensed a tremendous associative and incantatory play with a
Biblical text that was still lived and breathed as the horizon of all thought.
"Irrationality," in such tumultuous circumstances, is a relative rather than an
absolute term. It is only within a fully secular framework that such ways of
knowing are beyond the epistemological pale.

I contend, therefore, against premature psychologizing, that "irrationality"
is a particular register of the levelling project of manic rhetoric. No less than
in the case of Coppe's levelling lists and thundering echoes of Isaiah, his
indulgence in paralogical figures of speech deliberately exploits the resources
of a broader radical Puritan mode. The alliteration and repetition in the
following passage, for instance, center on the portentous (astrological)
significance of the letter "G":

Which was the Lords day I am sure on't, look in your Almanacks, you shall find it was
the Lords day, or els I would you could; when you must, when you see it, you will find
the Dominicall letter to be G. and there are many words that begin with G. at this
time (GIVE) begins with G. give, give, give, give up, give up your houses, horses,
goods, gold, Lands, give up, account nothing your own, have ALL THINGS common,
or els the plague of God will rot and consume all that you have.[22]

Similarly, in describing his conversion experience, in which he was "throwne
into the belly of hell" for a time and then saved, Coppe employs an
incantatory rhetoric that promotes sound over sense. Overinvesting in the
phonetic properties of words, such as rhyme and consonance, Coppe
produces a sentence that mingles ordinary syntax with a holiday logic of
association: "And under all this terrour, and amazement, there was a little
spark of transcendent, transplendent, unspeakable glory, which survived, and
sustained it self, triumphing, exulting, and exalting it self above all the
Fiends."[23] One hears something akin to "clang associations"[24] here in the

---

[22] Coppe, *Roule*, p. 101. As Nigel Smith explains in his introduction (*Ranter*, p. 32), astrologers had
calculated that each Sunday in 1649 was represented by the letter "G."
[23] Coppe, *Roll*, p. 82.
[24] "When psychic associations are the result of sounds or clangs, they are called clang associations.
Clang association is commonly observed in the manic phase of manic-depressive psychosis, and in
the schizophrenias." Leland E. Hinsie and Robert Jean Campbell, *Psychiatric Dictionary*, 3rd ed.
(New York: Oxford University Press, 1960).

conjunctions of "transcendent/transplendent" and "exulting/exalting." The same tone recurs in a letter written by Coppe from Coventry jail to his Ranter comrades Joseph Salmon and Andrew Wyke. The salutation puns elaborately on their names: "My Quintessence, my heart, and soule, my sal, and sol, my Wyke, (which being interpreted) is my soul and strongehold[.] here can I bee solitarie while sol shines upon me . . ."[25]

The psychoanalytic explanation for such rhetoric is predictably centered around, and biased toward, the individual ego as the unit of study and meaning.[26] In this view, the question of a socially constructed and contested reality, and the rhetoric appropriate to it, scarcely arises. The sole issue is the degree to which an individual's language bespeaks a loss of a "reality" that is simply given. Although there is in mania a serious loss of contact with the outside world, the "clanging" in mania is less serious than in schizophrenia: reality is never completely lost. Therefore, in the psychoanalyst Maurits Katan's formulation: "In schizophrenia the external world is restored by means of the word; in mania, contact with the world is maintained by means of the word."[27]

The repetitive, punning, and name-freighted rhetoric of Abiezer Coppe, however, is by no means wholly explicable in terms of pathological "clanging." Rather, Coppe borrows his punning language from a broad radical Puritan tradition of incantatory rhetoric, both oral and written, including especially the Quakers and the Ranters. As Nigel Smith makes clear, many other separatist authors – John Saltmarsh, John Webster, Samuel Fisher, and Thomas Tany, among others – thought, wrote, and read according to the logic, in one version or another, of this "extreme nominalism."[28] The mode, indeed, is a particular Protestant appropriation of the doctrine of "signatures," which blossoms in the Renaissance, persists into such eighteenth-century mystics as Emanuel Swedenborg, and resurfaces afterwards in authors as diverse as Ralph Waldo Emerson and Charles Baudelaire. According to this doctrine, which "reads" according to a logic of analogy, God has indicated, say, the medicinal properties of various plants through such hieroglyphics as their shape (the walnut, a cure for headache,

---

[25] Coppe, "Letter from Coppe to Salmon and Wyke," in Smith, *Ranter*, p. 117.

[26] Maurits Katan, a psychoanalyst, explains clanging in mania as a partial submission of the ego to "primary process thinking" such as Freud described in dreams. In his view, in mania the word becomes, at the expense of the object it signifies, a thing in itself: "the word has become an object...the form of the trend of thought is to the highest degree determined by the primary process, and...the pleasure principle is dominant." Maurits Katan, "The role of the word in mania," in *Manic-Depressive Illness: History of a Syndrome*, ed. Edward A. Wolpert (New York: International Universities Press, Inc., 1977), p. 211. First published in German in 1940.

[27] *Ibid.*, p. 218.

[28] See Smith, *Perfection*, pp. 274, 307. The term "nominalism" usefully reflects the way that the enthusiastic linguistic project simultaneously demystified language – subjecting it to a skeptical critique – and invested it with every sort of supernatural significance.

"resembles" the human cranium and brain).[29] This notion is sometimes linked to the equally widespread *topos* of the "book of nature": the idea, often derived from Psalm 19, that God's creation is voicing a message that complements the supernatural revelations of Scripture. Hence an extremely widespread appropriation of "creatures," and knowledge about them, as revelatory emblems of a "reality" informed by divine glory.[30] This *topos* could also be combined with an allusion to Paul's account (in 2 Corinthians 12:2–4) of one who, while transported into the "third heaven," heard the "unspeakable words" of a divine language. George Fox thus recounts the following ineffable rapture: "I was come up to the state of Adam, which he was in before he fell. The creation was open to me; and it was showed to me, how all things had their names given them, according to their nature and virtue."[31] This experience, or "opening," almost led him to practice medicine.

If the creation itself is a kind of language that must be deciphered, then language itself, or at least some languages, less corrupted by the Fall than the rest, can likewise be seen, in this radical Puritan view, as one more created phenomenon marked by divine "signatures." Such an Adamic language would thus "signify in more powerful ways than ordinary language."[32] Hence a pervasive mysticism of linguistic resemblances and similitudes: a widespread fascination with puns, homonyms, rhymes, and, in the context of a search for divine speech, even the hieroglyphic shapes of letters and words. Moreover, a popular rage for "the Hebraic" – seen by some millenarians as both the originary and the millennial language – was given an ideological charge in the Interregnum. In an atmosphere of millennial philosemitism, when even Andrew Marvell was entertaining fashionable notions about the imminent conversion of the Jews, signs of Hebraicity looked forward to the reign of the saints on earth.[33] What thus developed among the more radical enthusiasts is perhaps best described, paraphrasing Wallace Stevens, as "the Hebrew of the Imagination." Hebraicizing rhetoric became a means, as Nigel Smith shows,

---

[29] See Umberto Eco, "Overinterpreting texts," in *Interpretation and Overinterpretation*, ed. Stefan Collini (Cambridge: Cambridge University Press, 1992), pp. 45–66; Michel Foucault, "Signatures," in *The Order of Things: An Archaeology of the Human Sciences* (1970; New York: Vintage Books, 1973), pp. 25–30; Smith, *Perfection*, pp. 280–284; and Ormsby-Lennon, "Shibboleth," pp. 87–88. For a Rosicrucian version of this doctrine, see *Confessio Fraternitatis*, trans. T. Vaughan (1652), rpt. in F. A. Yates, *The Rosicrucian Enlightenment* (London: Routledge & Kegan Paul, 1972), p. 257.

[30] See N. H. Keeble, *The Literary Culture of Nonconformity in Later Seventeenth-Century England* (Leicester: Leicester University Press, 1987), pp. 255–262.

[31] Fox, *Journal*, p. 85.

[32] Smith, *Perfection*, p. 307.

[33] Christopher Hill, " 'Till the conversion of the Jews,' " in *The Collected Essays of Christopher Hill*, vol. II: *Religion and Politics in 17th Century England* (Amherst: University of Massachusetts Press, 1986), pp. 269–300.

"of imagining a converted or perfected self, or a reformed society, in which the traces of the chosen Ancient Israelites were reborn in the New Men (or 'late converted Jews') of Interregnum England."[34] Hebrew transliterations of English words and proper names, which were then retranslated back into English, appeared in the title pages and prefatory matter of such topical publications as Henry Walker's Independent newsbook, *Perfect Occurrences*. Hebraicizing authors such as Walker constructed what amounts to Hebraic folk etymologies for English words, and thus legitimated and glorified Parliamentary victories.[35] So Abiezer Coppe, calling himself a "late converted Jew," likewise signed *Some Sweet Sips* with "the original characters of his Hebrew Christian name."[36]

It was Thomas Tany (rechristened "Theauraujohn" by God in 1649) who plunged deepest into a multilingual vortex of infinite significations. Finding innumerable cross-references between the shapes, sounds, and meanings of Hebrew letters and etymons, on the one hand, and English words and syllables, on the other, Tany spins out meanings for his "translations" of Biblical texts that are, to say the least, esoteric.[37] Tany's texts, indeed, are so focused on hieroglyphic connotations that they completely fragment the verbal surface, seeming to dissolve into a private macaronic surrealism. Aside from the sheer exoticism of such titles as *Theauraujohn His Aurora in Tranlogorum in Salem Gloria* (1651) or *Thau Ram Tonjah* (1654), Tany's texts provide such bemusing declarations as this: "Take this from me that am a man unlearned in any art or tongue. *Arki, vea, arni, ophiat, al sabi, arni, ary, alpha, am, O Threarpha, alba army anat.*"[38] Such manic "nonsense" does not remain within the innocuous and recuperative paradigm found in Susan Stewart's definition of nonsense as that which "gives us a place to store any mysterious gaps in our order."[39] For opaque and baffling as Tany's text seems, it belongs to a broader subcultural context in which its own impenetrability, as a sublime gesture, figures as one more portent of sublime events. As a publishing event, such an anomalous text was of a piece with a cultural landscape saturated with news of strange and terrible prodigies: monster births, earthquakes, blazing stars, ghastly apparitions, and showers of

---

[34] Nigel Smith, "The uses of Hebrew in the English Revolution," in Burke and Porter, *Language, Self, and Society*, p. 55.

[35] *Ibid.*, p. 62. For more about Walker's allegiances to the Independents during the pamphlet wars of this moment, see Nigel Smith, *Literature and Revolution in England 1640–1660* (New Haven: Yale University Press, 1994), pp. 59–70.

[36] *Ibid.*, p. 63.

[37] Smith, *Perfection*, pp. 299–307 and "Hebrew," pp. 66–67.

[38] Thomas Tany, *Theauraujohn, His Epitah* (1653). Cited in Jerome Friedman, *Blasphemy, Immorality, and Anarchy: The Ranters and the English Revolution* (Athens, Ohio: Ohio University Press, 1987), p. 173.

[39] Susan Stewart, *Nonsense: Aspects of Intertextuality in Folklore and Literature* (Baltimore: The Johns Hopkins University Press, 1978), p. 5.

toads and frogs from the skies. A slightly later pamphlet, indeed, perhaps best captures Tany's likely effect on whatever audience he may have had: it reports the apparition in the sky of "many *Turkes* and *Greek* and *Hebrew* Letters, which none could Interpret."[40]

Enthusiasts engaging in such wordplay invoked certain Biblical *topoi* to authorize their sense of a divinity latent in language. Abiezer Coppe, in his remarkable preface to Richard Coppin's *Divine Teachings* (1649), begins as follows, rearticulating Rev. 1:8: "Thus saith the Lord, I am...Alpha and Omega, the beginning and the ending, the first and the last; and now the last is reaching the first, and the end the beginning."[41] In the elaborate hieroglyphic exercise that follows, Coppe or "ABC" makes much of the triangular, and hence trinitarian, shape of the letter "A." Lady Eleanor Davies/Douglas, whose patrician class position is exceptional in this context, discovered this same *topos* in the contrasting first vowels of her two married surnames, Davies and Douglas. In *The Appearance or Presence of the Son of Man* (1650), "alpha" and "omega" are the signs for Douglas of a female deity coeternal with God. The Greek letters become *Da.* and *Do.*, abbreviations of Davies and Douglas respectively, and Douglas herself then declares "I am A and O."[42] This same *topos*, moreover, explains why *Thau*, the final letter of the Hebrew alphabet, is, as Nigel Smith observes, prefixed as "the first letter of Tany's new names 'Theauraujohn' and 'Thau Ram Tanjah Rex Israel' & 'Anglise.'"[43]

Coppe's sense of the total immanence of God in language leads him in another passage from *Some Sweet Sips* to a rejection of mere linear reading. To be sure, certain acrostic Psalms had long established a Biblical precedent for a "cross-wording" already at odds with linear reading. Coppe, however, pushes an arresting sense of simultaneity to the limit. Having praised as "brave scholars" those that can hear God in all things, Coppe continues as follows:

but better schollers they, that have their lessons without book, and can reade God (not by roate) but plainly and perfectly, on the backside and outside of the book, as well as in the inside...that can reade him from the left hand to the right, as if they were reading *English*, or from the right to the left, as if they were reading *Hebrew*...that can read him within book, and without book, and as well without book, as within book: that can read him downwards and upwards, upwards and downwards, from left to right, from right to left...[44]

---

[40]　*A Strange and True Relation of Several Wonderful and Miraculous Sights* (London, 1661). Rpt. in *Anomalous Phenomena of the Interregnum: Horrid and Strange News from Ireland, &c., Tracts and Rants Series* (London: Aporia Press, 1991), p. 25.

[41]　Coppe, *An Additional and Preambular Hint, – As a general Epistle written by ABC*, in Smith, *Ranter*, p. 73.

[42]　Elaine Hobby, *Virtue of Necessity: English Women's Writing 1649–88* (London: Virago Press, 1988), p. 28.

[43]　Smith, "Hebrew," p. 65.

[44]　Coppe, *Sips*, p. 61.

It follows that acrostics and anagrams could be a path to divinity, or at least divine significance. Lady Douglas justified her prophetic authority because of an anagram rearranging her maiden name, Eleanor Audeley, into "Reveale O Daniel." Such logic was sufficiently widespread for the parodic proposal for a roundhead feast of "godly turnips" to be explained as follows: "for a turnip hath a *round-head*, and the anagram of a *puritan* is a TURNIP."[45] Amusing as this Cavalier deflation may be, however, the radical Puritans were engaged in a strenuous and consequential effort "to break free from received interpretive traditions," as James Holstun puts it, and "to fabricate a new way of reading."[46]

The most crucial authority for such extreme linguistic essentialism is, as Jackson I. Cope observes, the opening of the Johannine Gospel: "In the beginning was the Word, and the Word was with God, and the Word was God" (John 1:1).[47] It is a dwelling on the Word that leads Puritans to a dwelling on words and their hidden meanings, their homonyms, their roots and punning associations: it both assumes and constitutes a sacred language that claims access to essential reality. The festivity of manic speech intermittently overthrows the abstract hierarchy of syntactical relationships in favor of an investment in sound and shape. A strategically permitted process of free association, or "primary process," can thus be part of the method for seeking truth. Manic bursts of free association have, and are meant to have, specific rhetorical effects. Given that English orthography was far from fixed at this point, moreover, it may be somewhat anachronistic to view this perception of omnisignificance as the exact equivalent to modern punning on "individual" words: "then," as Peter Stallybrass says, "words bled into each other."[48]

The apparently random coincidence of meaning and sound is often recuperated by reference to the intentions of a divine author. The Quaker William Penn for instance, finds a significant pun in reference to his "principle and principal, Christ Jesus."[49] Or *spirit*, in an example cited by Nigel Smith, can be respelled as *spi-right* to bring out its putative link with the "single eye of God," the perceptive faculty that permits one to distinguish light from darkness.[50] It is interesting to note that Gerrard Winstanley,

---

[45] Anonymous. Cited in Daniel Neal, *The History of the Puritans, or Protestant Non-Conformists, from the Battle of Edge-Hill to the Death of King Charles I*, new ed., 5 vols., ed. Joshua Toulmin (Boston: Charles Ewer, 1817), III, p. 67.

[46] James Holstun, "Ranting at The New Historicism," *English Literary Renaissance* 19:2 (1989), p. 216.

[47] Jackson I. Cope, "Seventeenth-century Quaker style," *Publications of the Modern Language Association of America* 76 (1956), p. 729.

[48] Peter Stallybrass, "Shakespeare, the individual, and the text," in *Cultural Studies*, ed. Lawrence Grossberg *et al.* (New York: Routledge, 1992), p. 601.

[49] William Penn, *Rise and Progress of the Quakers* in *The Peace of Europe and Other Writings by William Penn* (Everyman's Library, London, n.d.), p. 209. Cited in Cope, "Quaker," p. 726.

[50] Smith, *Perfection*, p. 282.

seldom charged with irrationality, also picks up this punning habit. In his interpretation of Genesis, which takes the Fall of humanity to be the sin of privately enclosing the "common treasury" of the earth, Winstanley makes a truly wretched pun on Adam: "But this coming in of Bondage, is called *A-dam*, because this ruling and teaching power without [*i.e.*, socio-economic hierarchy], doth *dam* up the Spirit of Peace and Liberty."[51] Such a punning rhetoric is a way of knowing, of constructing a new and different "common sense." It is "an epistemological tool," as Cope says of Quaker punning, and it "appears when Christ is speaking within the Quaker, and showing forth the Word which is Alpha and Omega, beginning and end of understanding the runes of eternity."[52] As a method, it may deliberately fragment the surface logic of discourse: it provokes, as Cope says again, "an ever closer attention to the words' 'syllabatim' until one is drawn physically into the special literalness in which alone words can give up their secrets."[53]

Manic nonsense seeks, finally, to point toward new subjectivities and an alternative order. In Abiezer Coppe's case, the manic playfulness may be seen as the invitation to the communion he finds in the Song of Solomon.[54] Here, as elsewhere, Coppe does not simply quote the candidly erotic Biblical text, which was canonized with some difficulty, and then relentlessly allegorized in terms of the nuptial union between Christ and his church. Rather, in an elaboration characteristic of enthusiastic rhetoric, he appropriates and fully occupies its various voices. This is all the more striking because the text itself is in the form of a dialogue.

It is thus true that Coppe often speaks in the wooing voice, as Nigel Smith observes, of the Christly bridegroom:[55]

Deare hearts! Where are you, can you tell? Ho! where be you, ho? are you *within*? what, no body at *home*? Where are you? What are you? Are you asleepe? for shame rise, its break aday, the *day* breaks, the *Shaddows* flie away, the *dawning* of the *day* woes [woos] you to arise, and let him *into* your *hearts*.[56]

The subsequent sentence, however, would seem to be more precisely an *answer* to that voice – which then identifies and quotes the bridegroom's voice – from the perspective of the desiring bride. Here is the sentence: "It is the

[51] Gerrard Winstanley, *The True Levellers Standard Advanced*, in Sabine, *Works*, p. 252.

[52] Cope, "Quaker," p. 738.

[53] *Ibid.*, p. 740.

[54] For the importance of the Song of Songs to the Ranters more generally, see Noam Flinker, "Milton and the Ranters on Canticles," in *A Fine Tuning: Studies in the Religious Poetry of Herbert and Milton*, ed. Mary A. Maleski (New York: Binghamton, 1989), pp. 273–290; see also Turner, *One Flesh*, pp. 88–92. For an exploration of Ranter playfulness in light of Wittgenstein's concept of language-games, see Byron Nelson, "The Ranters and the limits of language," in *Pamphlet Wars: Prose in the English Revolution*, ed. James Holstun (London: Frank Cass, 1992), pp. 60–75.

[55] Smith, *Perfection*, p. 57.

[56] Coppe, *Sips*, p. 51.

voyce of my beloved that knocketh, saying, Open to me my *Sister*, my *love*, my *dove*, for my head is filled with dew, and my locks with the drops of night."[57] This second voice in Coppe's paragraph identifies the knocker as the bridegroom, and then quotes him as addressing her as "my *Sister*, my *love*, my *dove*." Given the implied superimposition of the author/ reader positions onto the Biblical dialogue, this voice in effect imagines a reader who responds to Coppe by quoting him. Coppe, in short, is everywhere at once: both bride and bridegroom, both reader and writer. Such comically exorbitant intimacy with the reader, who is both spoken to and for with unwonted freedom, addresses its appeal to a "species being" – anonymous and yet not depersonalized – rather than to individuals as such.[58] The "desire" it figures is not some baseline of the psycho-physical, on the order of a Freudian drive; rather, precisely because it puts into play an already allegorized text, "desire" here is visionary and collective: an allegory, strictly speaking, of a reinvented "body politic."[59]

A closely related point is made in the epistle from Mrs. T. P. of Abingdon, one of Coppe's disciples and converts, which he excerpts in *Some Sweet Sips*. In this epistle – both a Pauline genre and, as Jerome Friedman suggests, a sort of fan letter to Coppe[60] – Mrs. T. P. recounts a recent dream. Her interpretation of this dream makes a critique of erotic exclusivity: she thus decries her own possessiveness, possibly toward a husband, or possibly toward Coppe himself. In the dream, Mrs. T. P., while near a very pure and clear river, held various wild animals to her bosom, even those she had feared and loathed. One beast, however – a wild tiger – she picked out of the crowd, unsuccessfully trying to collar and domesticate it. In the course of interpreting this dream she writes as follows: "Now concerning my taking one of them from all the rest (as distinct,) and setting a collar about it – this was my weaknesse, and here comes in all our bondage, and death, by appropriating of things to our selves, and for our selves ..."[61] This dream and its interpretation would seem to be a libertine version of the *topos* used in Wyatt's rueful poem "Whoso List to Hunt," where kingly erotic possessiveness is likened to the collars, inscribed *Noli me tangere*, by which Caesar singled out as untouchable the deer he claimed as his own.

[57] *Ibid.*

[58] For erotic relations as an index of human development – of humanity's approach to its human essence as a "species being" (*Gattungwesen*) – see Karl Marx, *Economic and Philosophic Manuscripts of 1844*, in *The Marx-Engels Reader*, 2nd ed., ed. Robert C. Tucker (New York: W. W. Norton & Co., 1978), pp. 83–84.

[59] See Fredric Jameson, "Pleasure: a political issue," in *The Ideologies of Theory: Essays 1971–1986*, Theory and History of Literature Series, 2 vols. (Minneapolis: University of Minnesota Press, 1988), II: *The Syntax of History*, pp. 73–74.

[60] Friedman, *Blasphemy*, p. 81.

[61] Coppe, *Sips*, p. 65.

Coppe's own interpretation of the dream provides the climax and conclusion of *Some Sweet Sips*. In an ecstatic interpretation of the "river of life," Coppe reads it as a punning figure of the emptied out, crystalline, and hence transparent self:

We are (I say) in that *River*, and that *River in us*, when we are *besides* our selves, undone, nothing, and *Christ* all, in *all, in us*.

The *River* is as cleare as Chrystall, nothing but Christ, all Christ, Chrystall – it is as clear as Chrystall, *Christ-all*. Hallelujah.[62]

The pun on "Christ-all," it should be noted, provides a stunning one-word refutation to J. C. Davis' misguided contention that the Ranters, including Coppe, lack a truly pantheistic theology.[63] Coppe's understanding, while affirming the tentative one offered by Mrs. T. P., then develops the link between "collaring" and naming:

Let us not therefore any longer single out any appearance, and appropriate it to ourselves; no – not a *Paul*, an *Apollo*, or a *Cephas*, *&c.* – *all is yours, if you will not set a collar upon the neck of any – distinct – or beare it in your bosome, &c.* For, *while one saith I am of Paul* — (and so single him out –) and another, I am of *Apollo*, *&c.* *are ye not carnal?* — *But whether Paul, or Apollo, or Cephas*, or things present, or things to *come*, or *life*, or *death*, *&c.* all is yours (*in the Spirit*) for you are *Christs*, and *Christ is Gods*, Amen, Amen, *Hosanna* in the highest.[64]

As a mode of ideological hailing, then, the manic also interpellates us chorically and anonymously, beyond the subjecting and individuating force of proper names, as neither no one nor anyone.

Such radical unnamings, indeed, abound in the enthusiastic project of reconstituting given identities. The anonymous author of *A Justification of the Mad Crew* (1650) extends God's levelling of all names and labels even to the bitterest conflicts of the moment:

[God] loves all with an everlasting love, the theif that goes to the Gallows as well as the Judg [*sic*] that condemns him, and the Judg with a love of and from eternity as well as the theif: He loves as dearly with an infinite unchangeable love the *Cavileer* as the *Round-head*, and the *Round-head* as the *Cavileer*: the *Army* as abundantly as the *Levellers*, and the *Levellers* as the *Army*: For with him is no distinction. He pulleth down the mighty from their Throne, and sets up men of low degree.[65]

A very similar passage is found in Coppe's *Some Sweet Sips*, which is addressed not only to all the contesting factions in England, but also to "all the Saints, (of all sizes, statures, ages, and complexions, kindreds, nations, languages,

---

[62] *Ibid.*, p. 69.
[63] See J. C. Davis, *Fear, Myth, and History: The Ranters and the Historians* (Cambridge: Cambridge University Press, 1986), pp. 21–25, 57. I am grateful for this point to James Holstun (personal communication).
[64] Coppe, *Sips*, p. 72.
[65] *A Justification of the Mad Crew* (1650), rpt. in the appendix to Davis, *Fear*, p. 145.

fellowships, and *Families*, in all the Earth."[66] It is a tension intrinsic to such levelling projects that they simultaneously envision a utopian space beyond social divisions as well as a final thundering doom for the named and exposed oppressor.

The position of Mrs. T. P.'s epistle, however, framed within Coppe's text, requires us to consider more closely the extent to which enthusiastic levelling in general challenged gender hierarchy. Precarious as was the position of "mechanic preachers" such as Abiezer Coppe, George Fox, and John Bunyan, that of female prophets such as the Fifth Monarchists Anna Trapnel and Mary Cary/Rand was even more so. Given both the prevalent eroticizing of women's public speech[67] and the prevailing Pauline strictures against women's teaching and preaching, the transgression involved in female prophecy was considerably greater.[68] The doubly marginal status of the female prophet, as summed up by Phyllis Mack, was frighteningly liminal: "one end of a very slippery continuum, the other end of which was the polluted whore or witch."[69] Along with inferior education, economic dependence on men, compulsory domesticity, and the threat of the scold's bridle, the pressure of prevailing misogynist discourses compelled the authors of women's prophetic texts "to negotiate a path," as Sue Wiseman puts it, "between the speaker's femininity, prophetic authority, and any body of readers."[70]

This process of both negotiating with and bypassing earthly powers involved a great many ploys.[71] Female prophets often spoke, for example, through the reassuring frame of prefaces by male patrons, who usually affirmed their virtue and meekness.[72] Similarly, female prophets sometimes explicitly defended the very "natural order" they simultaneously claimed to be transcending.[73] They often invoked, and sometimes spoke as the incarnation of, various male prophets and sages from the Bible.[74] Finally, the female prophets made extreme disclaimers of their own agency as women.[75] Sarah Wight, for

---

[66] Coppe, *Sips*, p. 51.
[67] Mary Ellen Lamb, *Gender and Authorship in the Sidney Circle* (Madison: The University of Wisconsin Press, 1990), pp. 3–27.
[68] The Pauline interdiction, to be sure, was effectively challenged by Priscilla Cotton, Nancy Cole, George Fox, Richard Farnworth, and Margaret Fell. See Hobby, *Virtue*, p. 43; and Margaret Olofson Thickstun, "'This was a woman that taught': feminist scriptural exegesis in the seventeenth century," *Studies in Eighteenth Century Culture* 21 (1991), pp. 149–158.
[69] Phyllis Mack, *Visionary Women: Ecstatic Prophecy in Seventeenth-century England* (Berkeley: University of California Press, 1992), p. 120. The witches in *Macbeth* are an apt example of the conflation of prophecy with witchcraft.
[70] Sue Wiseman, "Unsilent instruments and the devil's cushions: authority in seventeenth century women's prophetic discourse," in *New Feminist Discourses: Critical Essays on Theories and Texts,"* ed. Isobel Armstrong (London: Routledge, 1992), p. 177.
[71] *Ibid.*, p. 194; Hobby, *Virtue*, p. 48.
[72] Mack, *Visionary*, p. 90; Wiseman, "Unsilent instruments," pp. 183–185.
[73] Mack, *Visionary*, p. 108.
[74] *Ibid.*, p. 174.
[75] *Ibid.*, p. 5; Wiseman, "Unsilent instruments," p. 186.

example, as Wiseman points out, exploits the cypher-like status of women to authorize a prophetic text from 1656: her signature reads "Sarah Wight,/an empty nothing, whose fulness is all in that Fountain that filleth all in all."[76] This denial of agency, indeed, necessarily complicates the appropriation of their texts for a genealogy of feminist resistance.[77]

This argument seems to strengthen the usual consensus that only women from the higher social strata of seventeenth-century England are candidates for a genealogy of feminist resistance: namely, those whose class politics are bourgeois, as in some Quaker women, or royalist (as in the "Tory feminism" of Mary Astell and Aphra Behn). Mack thus finds a proto-feminist consciousness – "those who were most conscious of their authority as females" – most fully developed in the seventeenth century among economically privileged women who, ironically enough, had the least interest in championing the poor.[78] The fact should be noted, however, that such relatively privileged seventeenth-century figures as Behn and Astell, now routinely canonized as "early feminists," are scarcely less ambiguous and compromised than the female prophets. Astell does *not*, in her *Some Reflections upon Marriage*, directly challenge a husband's authority in marriage; rather, she describes its effects in loathsome detail, then reminds women that the choice of *whether* to accept a domestic tyrant is highly consequential. Her proposal for women's higher education, similarly, falls back on "instrumental feminist" arguments that such education will strengthen women in their traditional roles – as mothers, for example.[79] Behn, meanwhile, blithely grounds her poetic authority on an inner "Masculine Part."[80]

A final historical point about such negotiations, moreover, compels us to rethink our underestimation of enthusiastic radicalism. Although the enthusiasts concede that all agency is "masculine," enthusiastic rhetoric nevertheless creates a context in which such terms as "masculine" and "feminine" are not naturalized as the attributes of particular sexed bodies.[81] In the mid-seventeenth century, indeed, "masculinity" and "femininity" still could be rhetorically transcended – if not through appeals to divine

[76] Sarah Wight, *A Wonderful Pleasant and Profitable Letter Written by Mrs. Sarah Wight* (London, 1656). Cited in Wiseman, "Unsilent instruments," p. 185.
[77] Wiseman, "Unsilent instruments," p. 189.
[78] Mack, *Visionary*, p. 4.
[79] See Mary Astell, *A Serious Proposal to the Ladies, for the Advancement of their True and Greatest Interest* (London, 1694) and *Some Reflections upon Marriage* (London, 1700). I am indebted for the term "instrumental feminism" to Alice Browne's *The Eighteenth Century Feminist Mind* (Detroit: Wayne State University Press, 1987), pp. 1–10.
[80] Aphra Behn, "Preface," *The Lucky Chance*, in *The Works of Aphra Behn*, 6 vols., ed. Montague Summers, (1915; rpt. New York: Benjamin Blom, 1967), III, p. 187.
[81] Thomas Laqueur observes a similar elasticity in the literature of early modern Europe more generally: "so-called biological sex," he writes of some texts from the Elizabethan era, "does not provide a solid foundation for the cultural category of gender, but constantly threatens to subvert it." See his *Making Sex: Body and Gender from the Greeks to Freud* (Cambridge, Massachusetts: Harvard University Press, 1990), p. 124.

inspiration, then to the spiritual equality of a genderless soul, both of which were accessible outside "Nature."[82] A century later, however – by the time of Mary Wollstonecraft – a far stronger articulation of biological essentialism, now framed by a certain disenchantment of the supernatural,[83] threatened to envelop female identity entirely. As Denise Riley argues, this ideological development would make appeals to a domain transcending gender anachronistic and unavailable.[84]

What is truly radical about the seventeenth-century prophets' approach to gender, then, is their *denaturalization* of sexual and gender personae. Both the "feminized male" and the "masculinized female" *topoi* deserve to be recognized as markers of an enthusiastic affiliation. While both are vehicles of transcendence, however, the latter – that of "female masculinization" – often points toward a rhetoric of disembodiment. This is precisely because women's bodies, as Diane Purkiss reminds us, were supposed to be shielded from public exposure; they were, moreover, supposedly at a further remove from the divine image than men's bodies.[85] Thus the rapturous account by the Fifth Monarchist prophet Anna Trapnel of her illuminations in jail, which was narrated in a trance state after much fasting, locates its authority outside the body. The following passage is from Trapnel's *A Legacy for Saints* (1654), published while she was incarcerated in Bridewell Prison:

oh how transcendently glorious is the true sealing of the Spirit! sure no tongue is able to speak it out, the pen of the readiest writer cannot write this, it may give some hints of this seal, but for depth, length, and breadth, who can give a full description or relation of it, it is a thing impossible to be published? Could not *Paul* tell what he saw in the third heaven?

---

[82] See Rachel Trubowitz, "Female preachers and male wives: gender and authority in Civil War England," *Pamphlet Wars: Prose in the English Revolution*, ed. James Holstun (London: Frank Cass, 1992), p. 119.

[83] I have in mind not only Wollstonecraft's general *milieu*, but also, for example, her skeptical reference to the Biblical account of Eve's creation as "Moses's poetical story." See Mary Wollstonecraft, *A Vindication of the Rights of Woman*, 2nd ed., ed. Carol H. Poston (New York: Norton, 1988), p. 26.

[84] Denise Riley, *Feminism and the Category of "Women" in History* (Minneapolis: University of Minnesota Press, 1988), pp. 42–43. It is precisely this point – that the "somatization" of women is a historical product – that weakens a recent attempt to read the female prophets through the lens of Julia Kristeva's timeless "semiotic." Kristeva's "semiotic," moreover, though suggestive in this context, inclines too much toward a literalization of the somatic; despite its well-advertised "materialism," it tends toward a certain corporeal essentialism. It threatens to reduce all levels of the "manic" – as rhetoric – to that of the somatic drive. See Christine Berg and Philippa Berry, "'Spiritual whoredom': an essay on female prophets in the seventeenth century," in *1642: Literature and Power in the Seventeenth Century*, ed. Francis Barker *et al.* (Colchester: University of Essex, 1981), pp. 37–54.

[85] Diane Purkiss, "Producing the voice, consuming the body: women prophets of the seventeenth century," in *Women, Writing, History 1640–1740*, eds. Isobel Grundy and Susan Wiseman (Athens: The University of Georgia Press, 1992), pp. 140–141.

"How then," Trapnel writes, "shall we declare our heavens glory, when we know not whether we are in the body or out?"[86] Two points emerge, then, of equal importance: (1) embodied carnality, far from marking the sonorous "potency" of women's voices, is much more an oppressive condition to be evaded; and (2) "femininity" itself, nevertheless, can after all be rhetorically transcended. So here, through the reference to Paul's unearthly and disembodied revelation, Trapnel escapes the limitations of her particular sexed body. This "unsexing" – unlike the "monstrous" androgyny of a Lady Macbeth – manages to work around a cultural logic that could sometimes celebrate male gender-bending but more often demonized female androgyny.[87]

The asymmetrical position of male and female prophets provides the context in which enthusiastic revision of the "body politic" *topos* is best understood. Coppe's complex use of gendered symbolism in a dazzling passage from his *Second Fiery Flying Roule* marks perhaps his most complex and effective blasphemy against the traditional "body politic" *topos*. Coppe draws implicitly on Solomon's reputation as a man of superhuman virility, a monarch with 700 wives and 300 concubines. Coppe's strategy is to "confound"[88] the meanings of such terms, simultaneously applicable to the body and to the class structure, as "base" and "majestic." The reader, as part of this strategy, is compelled to imagine a drastic regression: "to be plagued back into thy mothers womb, the womb of eternity: That thou maist become a little child . . ." This regression is in fact an education in the arbitrariness of sexual morality:

And to such a little child, undressing is as good as dressing, foul cloaths, as good as fair cloaths – he knows no evil, &c. – And shall see evil no more, – but he must first lose all his righteousnesse, every bit of his holinesse, and every crum of his Religion, and be plagued, and confounded (by base things) into nothing.[89]

As regards sexuality, the reader must surrender all moral prejudices. This prepares the reader for a dialectic, which Coppe goes on to describe in himself, whereby "base things" (wanton kisses, swearing, and lust) confound not only "holiness" (self- righteous and hypocritical purity) but also the very category of "baseness." The resulting "true purity," a vision of religious ecstasy, expresses itself so erotically that it suggests not so much transcendence of the flesh as transcendence of the "dead fleshly forms" of sexual guilt. To be "confounded . . .into nothing," moreover, evokes a well-known genital pun, made notorious

[86] Anna Trapnel, *A Legacy for Saints: Being Several Experiences of the Dealing of God with Anna Trapnel* (London, 1654), p. 11.

[87] See Rachel Trubowitz, " 'The single state of man': androgyny in *Macbeth* and *Paradise Lost*," *Papers on Language and Literature* 26:3 (1990), pp. 305–333.

[88] According to the OED, the historically available meanings of this term, one of Coppe's favorites, include "to mingle," "to defeat utterly," "to confute in argument," "to confuse," and "to throw into confusion."

[89] Coppe, *Roule*, pp. 107–108.

in Hamlet's bawdy repartee with Ophelia.[90] This pun suggests either that Coppe becomes a woman, or that he returns to the womb, or (somehow) both.

Having established the child as a trope of innocence, Coppe expounds the riddle of his sexual dialectic – that "by base things, base things so called have been confounded also; and thereby have I been confounded into eternall Majesty, unspeakable glory, my life, my self." By way of explication, he goes on record, in a passage that attributes the "paternity" of male desire to female beauty, as enthusiastically revering his own desire:

Again, Lust is numbered amongst transgressors – a base thing. –
    Now faire objects attract Spectators eyes.
    And beauty is the father of lust or love.
    Well! I have gone along the streets impregnant with that child (lust) which as [sic] particular beauty had begot: but coming to the place, where I expected to have been delivered, I have providentially met there a company of devills in appearance, though Angels with golden vialls, in reality, powring out full vialls, of such odious abominable words, that are not lawful to be uttered. Words enough to deafen the ears of plaguy holinesse. And such horrid abominable actions, the sight whereof were enough to put out holy mans eyes and strike him stark dead, &c.
    These base things (I say) words and actions have confounded and plagued to death, the child in the womb that I was so big of.[91]

At this point it seems, reading quite literally, that Coppe – possibly seeking "deliverance" in a brothel – has been "plagued" and "confounded" into losing his erection. As this vision continues, however, a recovery occurs: the strangely feminized Coppe is transported into the arms of his love, "which is invisible glory, eternall Majesty, purity it self, unspotted beauty, even that beauty which maketh all other beauty but meer ugliness, when set against it, &c." Through "BASE things" he is carried into the quintessence of all beauty:

Which transcendent, unspeakable, unspotted beauty, is my crown and joy, my life and love: and though I have chosen, and cannot be without BASE things, to confound some in mercy, some in judgment[.] Though also I have concubines without number, which I cannot be without, yet this is my spouse, my love, my dove, my fair one.[92]

Though this passage acknowledges (in the references to being "confounded" and "plagued to death") a struggle in overcoming shame and guilt, it nevertheless achieves an impressive release from shame, and from the binaries of "base" and "majestic." Coppe asserts that desire is innocent, like a child; that he was converted to this conviction by an experience in which he was pregnant – "big" – with desire; and that his "delivery" – playing on the multiple meanings of birth, ejaculation, literary creation, and religious

---

[90] This pun is further discussed in Chapter 4.
[91] Coppe, *Roule*, p. 108.
[92] *Ibid.*, p. 109.

salvation – produced a shocking, disorienting, and "unlawful" discourse much like his own. The child's innocence thus figures not only his desire, but also his writing. Its birth, moreover, like the birth of Christ, is attended by angels. The process is perhaps best seen as the "killing of sin by sin," as Turner puts it: the "transformation of sexuality" into a "vehicle for transcendence."[93]

The transvaluation of the 'base/majestic' binary, moreover, reverberates in all of the domains linked by the "body-politic" *topos*. Of these domains, it is the reverberation in the sex/gender system, in which the binaries of immanence and transcendence play a pivotal role, that matters for our purposes. It is in this context that Coppe's rather remarkable gender politics can best be understood.

Coppe's use of the *topos* of masculine childbirth is typical of enthusiastic gender-reversals. This *topos*, as Susan Stanford Friedman observes, is common among male authors as an organicist figuration of artistic creation.[94] Friedman goes on to argue that books are not babies; that men cannot give birth; that biological procreation, because of the traditional sexual division of labor, is culturally quite distinct from literary creation; and that such incongruous tropes, therefore, can be said to enact a subtle theft of female procreative labor.[95] One must certainly concede, as a simple fact of material sexual practice, a brutal discrepancy in male and female experience: while no seventeenth-century men ever died during "spiritual childbirth," vast numbers of seventeenth-century women succumbed to the dangers of relentless pregnancies. In the case of an author such as Coppe, however, it is crucial to avoid over-extending this historical point into a full-blown biological essentialism. Such an essentializing critique, indeed, would tend to restore and naturalize precisely those ideological scripts – those fixed positions within the gender hierarchy, those normative links between a certain sexed body and a certain gender persona – that enthusiasm loosens and unsettles.

The key point is that Coppe's rapturous gender-bending does not in this case compare word and flesh merely to remind his readers of the ultimate superiority of the patriarchal Word to flesh, of male production to female reproduction. His transgressive metaphors mark a point, rather, at which his discourse insists on the dependence of his, or any, conscious "I" on both linguistic process and desire, word and flesh. Such desire, as in the following rhapsody, is thus the vehicle for a ravishing and climactic union with God. By the "fiery chariots" of "wanton" and "external" kisses, Coppe "mounts" into the divine bosom: "Where I have been, where I have been, where I have been, hug'd, imbrac't, and kist with the kisses of his mouth, whose loves are

---

[93]   Turner, *One Flesh*, p. 90.

[94]   Susan Stanford Friedman, "Creativity and the childbirth metaphor: gender difference in literary discourse," *Feminist Studies* 13:1 (1987), pp. 49–82.

[95]   *Ibid.*, p. 56.

better then [*sic*] wine, and have been utterly overcome therewith, beyond expression, beyond admiration."[96] In thus seeking to represent a limit experience in homoerotic terms, Coppe's text converges with seventeenth-century religious lyrics on the theme of "divine penetration" by George Herbert, Richard Crashaw, Thomas Traherne, and John Donne. The latter's Holy Sonnet "Batter My Heart," which asks to be ravished by all three persons of the godhead, can indeed be read as a "queer" levelling of "top" and "bottom" sexual positions.[97] So too Coppe's enthusiastic "ravishment" *topos*, in refusing a fixed gender position, baffles the binary traps that naturalize gender identities and link them to heterosexual trajectories of desire.

To be sure, it might be argued that comparable passages exist in mystical tradition – passages, indeed, that have hitherto seldom seemed salient in discussions of gender transgression. The twelfth-century monk St. Bernard of Clairvaux, for one, wrote a well-known and lengthy series of sermons about the bride and bridegroom from Canticles: a Biblical coupling whose lively eroticism was traditionally allegorized as symbolizing either the union of God with his church or with the individual soul. Bernard writes as follows in his sermon "On the kiss":

When I reflect, as I often do, on the ardor with which the patriarchs longed for the incarnation of Christ, I am pierced with sorrow and shame...Soon now we shall be rejoicing at the celebration of his birth (Lk 1:14). But would that it were really for his birth! How I pray that that burning desire and longing in the hearts of these holy men of old may be aroused in me by these words: "Let him kiss me with the kiss of his mouth" (Sg 1:1).[98]

The parallel, however, only goes so far. For one thing, Bernard *quotes* the Song of Songs, carefully respecting the mediations between him and the sacred text. Indeed, he merely asks to be given the same zeal as the holy men of old. (The immediate context of Bernard's own zeal, it should be noted, includes the Crusades and the condemnation of Peter Abelard.) Coppe, however, as we have seen, does not quote: he simply appropriates and occupies scriptural utterance, with a rather greater effect of immediacy and ecstasy. Similarly, Coppe's claim to have been "hug'd, imbrac't, and kist with the kisses of his mouth" – as opposed to Bernard's more humble request for spiritual intensity – is daringly presented as a *fait accompli*. Finally, Coppe's "divine kiss" *topos* occurs in the context of a radical political manifesto in which lust has already been foregrounded and in which all mundane

---

[96] Coppe, *Roule*, p. 108.

[97] See Richard Rambuss, "Pleasure and devotion: the body of Jesus and seventeenth-century religious lyrics," in *Queering the Renaissance*, ed. Jonathan Goldberg (Durham, North Carolina: Duke University Press, 1994), pp. 269–274.

[98] St. Bernard of Clairvaux, "On the kiss," in *Bernard of Clairvaux: Selected Works*, trans. G. R. Evans, The Classics of Western Spirituality Series (New York: Paulist Press, 1987), p. 215.

identities and values have already been transvalued. It is above all this context that makes Coppe's language far more resonant than Bernard's in terms of stretching and loosening the bonds of gender identity.

A similar passage of subjective ravishment occurs in Coppe's *Some Sweet Sips*. It begins by echoing a familiar rhetorical question from Psalm 8: "Oh Lord, our Lord, how excellent is thy Name – Lord! What is man that thou art thus mindfull of him?" What gives energy to Coppe's unexpected reply to this query is the sudden turn it gives to the seemingly generic sense of "man":

Man is the *Woman*, and *thou* art the *Man*, the *Saints* are thy *Spouse*, our *Maker* is our *Husband*; *We* are no more *Twaine*, but *One. Hallelujah.*[99]

Although the Jewish and Christian "nuptial metaphor" is seldom taken so far, the revolutionary decades were in fact marked by a certain proliferation of such "male wife" or "feminized manhood" images among radical Puritan authors: Coppe is in that sense a representative figure.[100] It is significant, however, that Coppe's use of this enthusiastic *topos* occurs in a context in which – addressing an anxiety expressed by Mrs. T. P. – he validates female prophecy: "I know that Male and Female are all one in *Christ*, and they are all one to me. I had as live heare a daughter, as a sonne prophesie."[101] As Holstun observes, moreover, the image with which Coppe follows this is "an extraordinary inversion of the metaphors of gender hierarchy."[102] "I am your eccho," Coppe the dream-interpreter writes, "in that which followeth in your Letter."[103] And indeed, as Holstun points out, Coppe generally does elaborate rather than merely dominate Mrs. T. P.'s interpretation.[104]

Such egalitarian moments demonstrate the genuine political promise inherent in the manic *topoi* of fluid and interchangeable gender identity. Even in Coppe's boast of "concubines without number," which would seem to celebrate a grossly unilateral sexuality, he confesses that he "cannot do without" his hyperbolically numerous lovers. To the extent that bodily desire – passion – is represented as "passive," its inscription motivates tropes in which "feminine" and "masculine" positions are easily exchanged and reversed. As above, however, the exchange is ideologically ambivalent: although it reinforces an equation of passivity with "femininity," it also ecstatically surrenders the "masculine" position of conscious, self-transparent mastery.

This mapping of enthusiastic gender-bending, moreover, gives us a new perspective for considering an often-quoted passage from the Fifth Monar-

---

[99] Coppe, *Sips*, p. 69.
[100] Trubowitz, "Female preachers," pp. 121–122.
[101] Coppe, *Sips*, p. 66.
[102] Holstun, "Ranting," p. 220.
[103] Coppe, *Sips*, p. 66.
[104] Holstun, "Ranting," p. 220.

chist Mary Cary/Rand's image of her own utter passivity in the writing process:

I am a very weak and unworthy instrument, and have not done this work by any strength of my own, but have often been made sensible, that I could do no more herein (wherein any light of truth could appear) of myself, than a pencil, or pen can do, when no hand guides it.[105]

It is true enough, as many have noted, that this image utterly obliterates Cary's agency. It virtually annihilates her body, moreover, reminding us that, ironically enough, the male prophets, such as Coppe and Fox, had more comfortable access to female maternal and sexual symbolism than did the female prophets.[106] The more interesting point, however, given the traditional "pen-penis" equation, is that the particular image also crosses gender lines to claim a symbolically "male" prerogative. Like Eleanor Douglas' claim to speak in the voice of Daniel, such a claim, on the one hand, does not challenge the idea that authority is "masculine." On the other hand, it does in fact sharply disrupt the ideology that links "masculine" public authority "naturally" to biological maleness.

Coppe's gender-reversals are often linked to erotic contexts primarily because his rhetoric seeks to dramatize a levelling of the mind/body hierarchy. Whereas the transcendence of gender involves disembodiment for the women prophets, for Coppe and other male prophets such transcendence entails an intensified sense of embodiment. Coppe's "bodily" speech, paradoxically enough, transcends gender ideology precisely as a *rhetoric of heightened immanence*: thus it disrupts the position within more usual orders of discourse of the "absolute" or "transcendent" masculine subject. Such gender-reversals here, and in other male enthusiastic authors also, are thus a corollary of the rhythmic and stuttering speech of desire. "But perhaps I now speak with a stammering tongue," Coppe confesses:[107] his version of a Biblical *topos* whose career includes, as Herbert Marks notes, "the 'slow tongue' of Moses and its variations, the 'unclean lips of Isaiah,' the demur of Jeremiah, the mutism of Ezekiel."[108] It is an ecstatic language that dramatizes through rhythm and trope the sublime inexpressibility of what – in contrast, say, to a coolly self-possessed inventory of the beloved's physical attributes – cannot quite be said.

It must be conceded that enthusiastic feminist consciousness shows a markedly uneven development in relation to the Protestant heritage – everywhere visible as well in such long-canonized authors as Edmund Spenser – of demonizing enemies through misogynist imagery. A telling

[105] Mary Cary/Rand, *The Little Horns Doom and Downfall*, "To the Reader" (London, 1651).
[106] Mack, *Visionary*, p. 21.
[107] Coppe, *Sips*, p. 70.
[108] Herbert Marks, "On prophetic stammering," *Yale Journal of Criticism* 1:1 (1987), p. 5.

example appears in another passage in which Coppe evokes the symbolism of
the lower body. No respecter of persons, he insists on a perfect invulnerability
to the haughty gaze of his social superiors. His utter scorn for social
respectability is legitimated through an identification with the Biblical King
David. Through this identification Coppe assumes the royal indifference of
David to his wife Michal's scorn for his shameless dancing before the Ark of
the Covenant. Thus flaunting his own exuberant sexuality, Coppe deploys, as
another key *topos* of enthusiasm, the example of David's ecstatic and
provocative religious celebration: "I am confounding, plaguing, tormenting
nice, demure, barren *Mical*, with *Davids* unseemly carriage, by skipping,
leaping, dancing, like one of the fools; vile, base fellowes, shamelessely,
basely, and uncovered too before handmaids ..."[109] Christopher Hill,
remarking the sexual overtones and desire to shock in this passage, observes
that "the connection between sexual innuendo and class hostility is in itself
interesting."[110] That hostility, indeed – the inscription of class antagonism
toward the "respectable" – rearticulates a prevailing misogyny in the figure
of a "respectable" woman. As an attack on what Elaine Hobby terms "a
class-specific femininity," it is comparable to separatist images of the Whore
of Babylon likewise used by most women prophets of the era.[111]

We need not be surprised, moreover, to find Anna Trapnel, while
describing her ecstatic conversion experience, having recourse to the
"Michal" *topos* in *A Legacy for Saints*:

In the night before sleep had seized upon me, a bright light shined round my head
visible, and in the midst of that light stood one all in white, in the likeness of a
creature all covered with brightness...Death was still presented without a sting, and
the Law without Strength, these were now dissolved and gone, and I saw an
accomplishment of the great work of redemption by Jesus Christ; I could not but
dance before this Ark, though *Michols* mocked...[112]

The female prophets, although they deflected misogynist imagery away from
themselves, seldom challenged misogyny directly.[113] That Trapnel implicitly
claims to be the dancing David, however, shows how little she, as the author
of this experience, feels tied to a gendered identity: she speaks, to be sure, but
scarcely "as a woman."

Coppe's attacks on spiritual harlotry often use such women to represent, as
Nigel Smith writes, "the conventions of social propriety."[114] Similarly,

---

[109] Coppe, *Roule*, p. 106.
[110] Christopher Hill, *The World Turned Upside Down: Radical Ideas During the English Revolution* (New York: Penguin Books, 1972), p. 280.
[111] Elaine Hobby, "'Discourse so unsavoury': women's published writings of the 1650s," in Grundy and Wiseman, *Women, Writing, History*, p. 27.
[112] Trapnel, *Legacy*, p. 14.
[113] Mack, *Visionary*, pp. 117–119.
[114] Smith, *Perfection*, p. 243.

Coppe's frequent references to the "wel-favoured Harlot," or Whore of Babylon, represent the established and respectable strata as degraded female sexuality. The constant factor in these figurations, whether the symbolic woman has "too much" or "too little" sexuality, is a virtually universal misogyny that Coppe appropriates for his immediate purposes. "Respectable" women, as the most vulnerable fraction of their class, absorb class hostility tactically expressed through gender: a specular image, it can finally be argued, of monstrous and promiscuous female enthusiasts. So Cary and Douglas, as Mack points out, likewise promulgate images of demonized feminine decadence – whores, Jezebels, strumpet-hags, menstruous rags – and so on – for the enemies of their religious and political project.[115] It must be granted, therefore, that enthusiastic levelling continues to find some bodies "lower" than others: its critique of the "body politic" *topos*, in this sense, remains uneven. And indeed, Coppe's vague reference to the residents of Biblical Sodom as "Filthy blinde Sodomites" may suggest a further hierarchy of sexual activities.[116]

How, then, shall we evaluate the enthusiastic project of reinventing the body politic? One view that cannot be accepted without further qualification is Mack's notion that the period harbored "at least two kinds of radicalism."[117] Plebeian men, in other words, questioned class oppression, while neglecting gender; and patrician women, while overlooking class, struggled against gender oppression. Such a bifurcation of seventeenth-century radicals and feminists, however, is misleading in several respects. The appropriation of a strong individual subjectivity by a handful of privileged women – however admirable, however compromised – is not strictly parallel to the attempt in radical Puritanism to form a politicized collective consciousness. The further claim by Mack, moreover, that the two strains of radicalism were "actually at odds," seems even more problematic.[118] I remain unconvinced by the argument that, in her words, "Those sects who were most radical were least likely to be attentive to the needs and rights of oppressed people who were female."[119] The enthusiastic reworking of the body politic *topos* demonstrates something quite different. What needs comparison, rather, are the following asymmetrical alternatives: (1) the enthusiastic dissociation of biological sex differences from gender; and (2) the bourgeois formation of individualized female subjectivities, which occurred on the basis of an unquestioned and fully naturalized equation of gender with differences of sex. It is at least arguable that the former presents a more far-

---

[115] Mack, *Visionary*, pp. 117–118.
[116] Coppe, *Roule*, p. 91. One of the two "Ranter" poems unearthed and published by Anne Laurence, however, makes explicit reference to "getting" a boy in the context of the New Jerusalem. See Anne Laurence, "Two Ranter Poems," *Review of English Studies* 31 (1980), p. 59.
[117] Mack, *Visionary*, p. 5.
[118] *Ibid.*
[119] *Ibid.*

reaching challenge to patriarchal oppression than does the latter. Enthusiastic rhetoric, in any case, did in fact go a certain distance toward dismantling distinctions based on gender. If that record is uneven, it is nevertheless not easily matched anywhere among the more elite writers, male or female, now canonized as the most enlightened shapers of seventeenth-century thought.

3

Strange acts and prophetic pranks
apocalypse as process in Abiezer Coppe

I am about my act, my strange act, my worke, my strange worke, that whosoever
hears of it, both his ears shall tingle.   Abiezer Coppe, *A Second Fiery Flying Roule*

Just as the Quakers "thee'd" and "thou'd" everyone, regardless of their rank,
so Abiezer Coppe begins the preface to his *A Fiery Flying Roll* with a tone of
startling familiarity:

> My Deare One.
> All or None.
> Everyone under the Sunne.
> Mine own.
> My most Excellent Majesty (in me) hath strangely and variously transformed this
> forme.
> And behold, by mine owne Almightinesse (In me) I have been changed in a
> moment, in the twinkling of an eye, at the sound of the Trump.[1]

This amazing entrance, highly effective in its abrupt, staccato sentence
fragments, violates every "proper" form of address. Coppe begins, in a tone
of knowing and paternal benevolence, with "My Deare One." The next
address – "All or none" – implies a supreme indifference as to who in
particular might be listening. Shifting again to "Every one under the Sunne,"
Coppe in five words levels all social distinctions. His fond "Mine own," like
"My Deare One," seems to presume an almost omniscient knowledge of the
reader, a knowledge that confers possession. It is a mode of address that
seemingly incorporates its interlocutors, whether they will or no, into its own
world.

Coppe's rhetoric is more precisely seen, however, as deliberately mediating
between two apparently incommensurable worlds. One world provides the
millennial vantage point of the "end of days": the accomplished fact of an
illumination whose ineffable perfection Coppe can only intimate. The second
world is circumscribed by the horizons of historical place and time: "the

[1] Abiezer Coppe, *A Fiery Flying Roll*, in *A Collection of Ranter Writings from the 17th Century*, ed. Nigel
Smith (London: Junction Books, 1983), p. 81.

everyday and untransformed world," as Thomas N. Corns puts it, "of early Republican London."[2] So situated, the author of this more fallible vision must address a readership likewise situated within an incomplete process of illumination that, through available suasive forms, he hopes to drive forward and amplify. "The Sun begins to peep out...":[3] so Coppe uses a threshold image that aptly describes a rhetoric itself somehow poised, between past and future, in the suspended temporality of an apocalyptic now that bridges the two worlds.

This "new dawn" *topos*, indeed, with its potential pun conjoining the filial and solar, is very common among the radical millenarians. A lively instance appears in Gerrard Winstanley's *New-Yeers Gift to the Parliament and Armie* (1650):

The fall of mankind, or his darkness, is this, When that Son of universal Love, which was the seed out of which the creation sprung forth, did begin to go behind the cloud of flesh...[4]

When this Son arises in more strength, and appears to be the Saviour indeed, he will then make mankind to be all of one heart and one mind, and make the Earth to be a common treasurie...[5]

The daybreak image can also develop the political and spiritual overtones of "awakening": so Milton imagines a newly mobilized England in the following terms: "Methinks I see in my mind a noble and puissant nation rousing herself like a strong man after sleep, and shaking her invincible locks."[6] The rising sun/son *topos* can thus bring together multiple liminalities: pre-dawn radiance, pre-waking consciousness, and pre-revolutionary "rousing."

Enthusiastic rhetoric, which often begins where it hopes to end, deliberately blurs the fine line between imminence and immanence. There is thus a sense in which the remainder of Coppe's two *Fiery Flying Rolls* can be seen as further elaborating the *transformation of discursive positions* that he has already established. Coppe has already achieved, through his modes of address, a fusion of his "I" with God, who knows all, and thus with the reading "you," who is already known. "God in him" hails "God in us." And we, regardless of our social pretensions, are addressed as equals in a rhetorical cosmos where being is not vertically stratified.

Coppe's enthusiastic pronominalization can be read as an extreme instance of a much larger Christian project. As Susan A. Handelman writes, "The

2   Thomas N. Corns, *Uncloistered Virtue: English Political Literature, 1640–1660* (Oxford: Clarendon Press, 1992), p. 193.
3   Coppe, *Roule*, in Smith, *Ranter*, p. 104.
4   Gerrard Winstanley, *A New-Yeers Gift for the Parliament and Armie*, in *The Works of Gerrard Winstanley*, ed. George H. Sabine (Ithaca: Cornell University Press, 1941), p. 378.
5   *Ibid.*, p. 380.
6   John Milton, *Areopagitica*, in *John Milton: Complete Poems and Major Prose*, ed. Merritt Y. Hughes (New York: The Odyssey Press, 1957), p. 745.

Christian desire...is to escape the deferral and mediation of the text and language for a communion with pure presence."[7] Such a project of physical incarnation, as she points out, is precisely an attack on verbal representation as such: "Jesus, as the word-become-flesh, redeems language, returns substance to shadows, collapses the text, time, history, and the distance between man and God. And absolute presence means the end of language, the text, and the law."[8] It can be argued, therefore, that "while claiming to spiritualize Judaism, Christianity in effect literalized it with a vengeance."[9] Enthusiasm, in any case, is indeed impatient with mediations, which it terms "formalism." The "impossible" nature of such presentational claims will seem all the more pronounced in a critical moment such as ours, preoccupied as it has been with the critique of concepts that imply presence, immediacy, and totality.

Given the problematic of re-presenting "presence," however, it should come as little surprise that enthusiastic rhetoric cannot, after all, so easily escape the divisive implications of form. Difference, after all, is built into the most minute articulations of language. As a passage near the conclusion of Coppe's earlier Seeker pamphlet shows, there is necessarily a paradox inherent in the attempt to stage a dialogue, or to devise a mediation, between difference and nondifference. *Some Sweet Sips, of Some Spirituall Wine* (1649) demands nothing less than an overcoming of language itself, now seen in the Pauline terms of "types" and "shadows":

> O dear hearts! let us look for, and hasten to the comming of the *Day* of *God*, wherein the *Heavens* being on *fire* shall be *dissolved*, and the *Elements*, (*Rudiments, first principles*). (Imagine formall *Prayer*, formall *Baptism*, formal *Supper* – &c.) shall *melt away*, with fervent heate, *into* God; and all *Forms*, appearances, *Types, Signes, Shadows, Flesh*, do, and shall *melt away* (with fervent heate) into *power*, reallity, *Truth, the thing signified, Substance, Spirit.*[10]

Indeed, given that even such verbal forms as Coppe must use are inevitably complicitous "with the hierarchy reacted against," as Nigel Smith observes, there is a certain "embarrassment" inherent in the project of enthusiastic liberation from all "carnal" forms.[11] This paradox constitutes the basis for Coppe's rhetoric of address, which must negotiate with the very world his presupposition of nondifference preemptively disavows: a "fallen" structure of alienating forms.

The manic rhetoric of fusional identification, then, is not just a matter of a levelling "content," of radical politics and millennial dreams. It involves a

---

[7] Susan A. Handelman, *The Slayers of Moses: The Emergence of Rabbinic Interpretation in Modern Literary Theory* (Albany: State University of New York Press, 1982), p. 89.

[8] *Ibid.*

[9] *Ibid.*, p. 17.

[10] Coppe, *Some Sweet Sips*, in Smith, *Ranter*, p. 71.

[11] Smith, Introduction, *Ranter*, p. 8.

complex constellation of formal shifts as well: from serially iterated metonymies to arresting metaphors, for instance, and from paratactic catalogues to chiasmic crossings. Above all, like the Longinian sublime, the rhetoric of mania formally transgresses the relations between text and reader, intrinsic and extrinsic, producing slippages between the positions constituted by pronouns and prepositions. The manic mode thus attempts to enact the transfigured subjectivity necessary to any realization of its communitarian desires. Indeed, by building this transfiguration into the very process of its own enunciation, the rhetoric of mania figures apocalypse as an ongoing process.

Coppe understands the "you" addressed in his pamphlets as, among other things, the proprietor of a material object: the pamphlet itself. Mundane subjectivity is thus attacked first in its tendency to fetishize material possessions. In a "postscript" to his *Additional and Preambular Hint* to Richard Coppin's *Divine Teachings*, Coppe reminds us that the pamphlet, although a material object, should not be treated as private property. Coppe's scrupulous care here with prepositions foregrounds their crucial role in a rhetoric concerned with identification and division:

Do not appropriate this to thyself only; its a general Epistle: and let this *modicum* suffice thee. For should all the words, things, and thoughts, which I have, do, and will, speak of thee, to thee, in thee; act for thee, in thee and think toward thee, the whole world would be too narrow to contein [*sic*] them.
            Look into a larger volume, thy heart –
            where I am, which I am.[12]

The voice of God, speaking in and through Coppe, can likewise speak and act "in" the reader. A certain latent violence, as always in sublime rhetoric, lurks in the reference to what is withheld: an overwhelming flood of "words, things, and thoughts" so great as to exceed the containing capacity of the entire world. The final sentence then opposes the "larger volume" of the heart to both the world and the book – finite entities, both – and pointedly locates the divine "I am" there.

Central to Coppe's rhetoric of subjective transfiguration, moreover, is the emblem-like image of the heart.[13] As a locus of a potentially infinite interiority, the heart emerges in Coppe's writings as the privileged metaphor

[12] Coppe, *Additional and Preambular Hint*, in Smith, *Ranter*, p. 79.
[13] The seventeenth-century republication in England of the work of Hendrik Niclaes, the sixteenth-century prophet of the "Family of Love," invites speculative comparisons here. Familist tracts, as Nigel Smith shows, use emblematic woodcuts with a well-elaborated heart symbolism. The heart represents experiential religion and membership in the "body of love." See Nigel Smith, *Perfection Proclaimed: Language and Literature in English Radical Religion 1640–1660* (Oxford: Clarendon Press, 1989), pp. 144–184; see also Smith, Introduction, in *Ranter*, p. 35. For reproductions of the woodcuts and more details about familist theology, see Christopher W. Marsh, *The Family of Love in English Society, 1550–1630*, Cambridge Studies in Early Modern British History (Cambridge: Cambridge University Press, 1994), pp. 17–27, 254–255.

for a permeable and reciprocal identification. The climax of Coppe's conversion narrative, as recounted in his first *Fiery Flying Roll*, combines a trinitarian mystique with the image of interfused hearts:

and immediately I saw three hearts (or three appearances) in the form of hearts, of exceeding brightnesse; and immediately an innumerable company of hearts, filling each corner of the room where I was. And methought there was variety and distinction, as if there had been severall hearts, and yet most strangely and unexpressibly complicated or folded up in unity. I clearly saw distinction, diversity, variety, and as clearly saw all swallowed up into unity. And it hath been my song many times since, within and without, unity, universality, universality, unity, Eternal Majesty, &c.[14]

The figuration of fusion occurs not only in the blending of hearts, but also in the incantatory crescendo that culminates in "within and without, unity, universality, universality, unity..." The little chiasmus that repeats "unity, universality" in reverse order represents the exchangeability of inside and outside.

The heart image here retrospectively illuminates the full import of an enthusiastic rhetoric of address that can confidently hail an unknown reader as "Dear Heart." Joseph Salmon, in the prefatory matter to his *A Rout, A Rout* (1649) addresses the "Fellowship of Saints" in the New Model Army as "Dear Hearts"; when he closes, moreover, his salutation punningly alludes to the hart who represents the bridegroom in the Song of Solomon: "*Farewel my beloved*, be thou as a Roe, or a young Hart upon the mountains of Bethel."[15] The anonymous Ranter pamphlet *A Justification of the Mad Crew* (1650) similarly addresses its readers both as "Dear Hearts" and as "Sweet hearts."[16] Coppe, however, takes this rhetoric of intimate address much further. As we saw in the previous chapter, in *Some Sweet Sips* Coppe speaks in the voices of both the bridegroom and bride in the Song of Solomon, circulating freely among those erotically interconnected subject-positions, which are then superimposed on the author/reader positions. In another remarkable passage, exhorting the reader to open up to God's message, Coppe conflates the bridegroom with the apocalyptic image of the returned Christ as a "thief in the night":

O! Open ye doors, Hearts open; let the *King of glory* come *in*. Open dear hearts.
    Dear hearts, I should be loath to be arraigned for Burglary –
    The *King* himself (whose houses you all are) who can, and will, and well may break open his own houses; throw the doors off the hinges with his powerfull voyce, which rendeth the heavens, shatter these doors to shivers, and break in upon people.[17]

[14] Coppe, *Roll*, p. 82.
[15] Joseph Salmon, *A Rout, A Rout* (London, 1649), in Smith, *Ranter*, p. 191.
[16] *A Justification of the Mad Crew* (London, 1650). Rpt. in appendix to J. C. Davis, *Fear, Myth, and History: The Ranters and the Historians* (Cambridge: Cambridge University Press, 1986), pp. 144–150.
[17] Coppe, *Sips*, p. 52.

The tone here mingles comedy with an unmistakable undertone of menace toward the propertied classes. However, the contrast between heart and property remains figurative; the doors being threatened are, after all, merely gateways into compassionate emotions.

The comic "burglary" reference, however – another image of boundaries breached – bears comparison to the truly uncanny passage in the second *Fiery Flying Roll* that ventriloquizes God's voice in the raw idiom of a highwayman. This is how Coppe's God, a sort of divine Robin Hood, describes the manner of his imminent return to earth:

I will...demand all mine, and will say on this wise.

Thou hast many baggs of money, and behold now I come as a thief in the night, with my sword drawn in my hand, and like a thief as I am, – I say deliver up your purse, deliver sirrah! deliver or I'l cut thy throat!

Deliver My money to such as poor despised *Maul* of Dedington in Oxenshire...[18]

It is difficult to imagine a more pointed challenge to the legitimacy of a certain order of property relations, and thus to the subjective divisions they produce, than this. Coppe achieves a further effect of raw immediacy, moreover, by his reference to the concretely suffering Maul of Dedington.

Precisely because a certain deconstruction of the self is involved in the transfiguration Coppe demands, his rhetoric depends on figures of violence. Kenneth Burke, in the course of a general discussion of identification, provides the best approach to such imagery: "the imagery of slaying is a special case of transformation, and transformation involves the ideas and imagery of *identification*. That is: the *killing* of something is the *changing* of it, and the statement of the thing's nature before and after the change is an *identifying* of it."[19] To turn inside out, to break in, to burgle, to rob, to ravish – even these verbs scarcely do justice to the sheer violence with which Coppe attempts to express the prelude to his own ravishing illumination:

I was utterly plagued, damned, rammed and sunke into nothing, into the bowels of the still Eternity (my mothers womb) out of which I came naked, and whereto I returned again naked. And lying a while there, rapt in silence, at length (the body or outward forme being awake all this while) I heard with my outward eare (to my apprehension) a most terrible thunder-clap, and after that a second. And upon the second thunder-clap, which was exceedingly terrible, I saw a great body of light, like the light of the Sun, and red as fire, in the forme of a drum (as it were) whereupon with exceeding trembling and amazement on the flesh, and with joy unspeakable in the spirit, I clapt my hands, and cryed out, *Amen, Halelujah, Halelujah, Amen.*[20]

Coppe is silenced, denuded, infantilized, and then utterly annihilated: reduced, indeed, to that "blank page" notorious as a favorite sexist trope for

---

[18] *Roule*, p. 100.
[19] Kenneth Burke, *A Rhetoric of Motives* (1950; rpt. Berkeley: University of California Press, 1969), pp. 20–21.
[20] Coppe, *Roll*, p. 82.

the feminine.[21] "Upon this," Coppe writes, "it was thus resembled, as if a man with a great brush dipt in whiting, should with one stroke wipe out, or sweep off a picture upon a wall."[22] The ecstatic chiasmus with which Coppe breaks his silence, however – *Amen, Halelujah, Halelujah, Amen* – anticipates his final recovery, or "crossing over," into the vision of the interfused hearts discussed above.

The emblematic heart image recurs in Coppe's anti-formalistic revision of Eucharistic bread-breaking: thus a resonant symbol of ecclesiastical community gets rearticulated so as to have no "outside." Coppe's rhetoric, indeed, relentlessly points to all of those "strategies of containment" whereby exclusive and inhumane definitions of communal solidarity, in the interests of the better off, are allowed to substitute for more truly inclusive ones. Hence the following passage, an answer to the charged rhetorical question, *What is communion?*

The true Communion amongst men, is to have all things common, and to call nothing one hath, one's own.

And the true externall breaking of bread, is to eat bread together in singleness of heart, and to break thy bread to the hungry, and tell them its their own bread &c. els your Religion is in vain.[23]

This blunt redefinition of communion exposes the sanctimonious nature of any ritual that excludes hungry people from a symbolic sharing of food. "Singleness of heart," moreover, has little to do with any doctrinal uniformity. Such forced uniformity, indeed, is precisely the essence of what Coppe sees as a false communion:

Thou [the "wel-favoured Harlot"] hast come to a poor irreligious wretch, and told him he must be of the same Religion as his neighbours, he must go to Church, hear the Minister &c. and at least once a year put on his best cloaths, and receive the Comm[u]nion – he must eat a bit of bread, and drink a sip of wine – and then he hath received, &c. he hath been at the Communion.[24]

"He that hath this worlds goods, and seeth his brother in want, and shutteth up the bowels of compassion from him," Coppe concludes, "the love of God dwelleth not in him; this mans Religion is in vain."[25]

---

[21] See Susan Gubar, "'The blank page' and the issues of female creativity," *Critical Inquiry* 8:2 (1981), pp. 243–263.

[22] Coppe, *Roll*, p. 82. The Quaker Richard Farnsworth uses a similar image in a letter to George Fox to indicate his complete annihilation in the process of Quaker ministry: "I am as a white paper book without any line or sentence: but as it is revealed and written by the Spirit, the Revealer of secrets, so I administer." See Richard Farnsworth, Swarthmore MSS iii. 51, Nov. 12, 1653. Cited in William C. Braithwaite, *The Beginnings of Quakerism*, 2nd ed., rev. by Henry J. Cadbury (Cambridge: Cambridge University Press, 1955), p. 199.

[23] Coppe, *Roule*, p. 114.

[24] *Ibid.*, p. 113.

[25] *Ibid.*, p. 115.

The rhetoric of enthusiastic fusion could likewise be seen as rearticulating
in more radical terms the traditional concept of atonement. For there is a
sense in which Coppe "atones" for the profound structural aggression of a
hierarchical system of ownership and prestige by attacking the boundaries,
both internal and external, between him and the most outcast members of
English society. The following account, specifically contrasted with his
ranting insolence toward his "betters," dramatizes his crossing of a boundary
delimiting those supposedly "beneath" him. Busily subversive, Coppe has
been

clipping, hugging, imbracing, kissing a poore deformed wretch in London, who had
no more nose on his face, then [sic] I have on the back of my hand, (but only two little
holes in the place where the nose uses to stand.)

And no more eyes to be seen then on the back of my hand, and afterwards running
back to him in a strange manner, with my money giving it to him, to the joy of some,
to the afrightment and wonderment of other Spectators.

As also in falling down flat upon the ground before rogues, beggars, cripples, halt,
maimed; blind &c. kissing the feet of many, rising up againe, and giving them money
&c.[26]

William James refers to this sort of behavior, typical of saints, as "the
inhibition of instinctive repugnance."[27] There is little reason to believe,
however, that a repugnance toward severe physical deformity is merely
"instinctive"; in any case, the social barriers of rank and status are certainly
not. Coppe's gesture of at-one-ment, necessarily a self-transformation,
delegitimates the grounds from which such feelings of repugnance are
generated and naturalized.

Another dimension of the enthusiastic transfiguration of subjectivity
involves the rearticulation of humanity's supposedly unique place in, and
dominion over, the rest of the natural world. Coppe himself, it should be
noted, is merely angered that human beings are starving while oxen and
horses are well-fed: "And is not poor *Maul* of Dedington, and the worst rogue
in Newgate, or the arrantest thief or cut-purse farre better, then a 100. Oxen,
or a 1000. such horses as mine?"[28] And Winstanley, similarly, merely wants
the poor to have their fair share of "God's common treasury": the "natural
resources" over which humanity has had traditional dominion. Nevertheless,
several rearticulations of this hierarchical relationship, from pantheism to
mortalism and annihilationism, emerge among the radical enthusiasts. If
animals have some spark of the divine, or even souls, that upgrading of
animals may challenge the usual anthropocentric horizons of moral concern.
In 1646, if Edwards' *Gangraena* can be trusted, the sectary William Bowling

---

[26] *Ibid.*, p. 105.
[27] William James, *The Varieties of Religious Experience* (1902; rpt. New York: New American Library, 1958), p. 225.
[28] Coppe, *Roule*, p. 112.

argued for a universal salvation of all creatures: "Christ shed his blood for kine and horses... as well as for men."[29] The Quaker John Perrot had a similar vision just prior to his return to England in 1661 from confinement (as a madman) by the Inquisition at Rome. As paraphrased by William C. Braithwaite, Perrot wrote in a pair of mystical epistles to the effect that

the day is come which is to show if Friends bear the image of His holy spirit of humility as Jesus did: there they may know the bosom of love, from which all pure service proceeds – service to God, service to man, service to beasts, service to fowls, service to fishes, and service to worms, "all in the love, in which they were by the humble Spirit created, according to all their respective kinds." The Lord God requires of His people "rent souls, broken spirits, contrite hearts, breathing minds, fervent prayers," thus shall they enter into the deeps of the Spirit of God.[30]

As a means of transfiguring subjectivity, the humbling of human pride cannot go much further.

By the same token, the fact that human beings die, like the beasts in the field – a humbling point made by Scripture (Ecclesiastes 3:19) – can lead to a "materialist" downward levelling. According to the heresy of mortalism, the soul dies with the body; human death is thus distinct from animal death only when the soul awakens during the general resurrection. Annihilationists went still further, denying the final resurrection.[31] In his Muggletonian pamphlet, *The Lost Sheep Found*, Lawrence Clarkson retrospectively describes his earlier mortalism: "for I understood that which was life in man, went into that infinite Bulk and Bigness, so called *God*, as a drop into the Ocean, and the body rotted in the grave, and for ever so to remain."[32]

The meditative enthusiast Jacob Bauthumley develops a pantheistic tendency in a similarly mortalist direction. Early in *The Light and Dark Sides of God* (1650), Bauthumley declares his pantheism: "Nay, I see that God is in all Creatures, Man and Beast, Fish and Fowle, and every green thing, from the highest Cedar to the Ivey on the wall..."[33] Later, he cites the "death-the-leveller" *topos* from Ecclesiastes:

And further I really see that the flesh of man, and of all other creatures differ not any thing in the nature of them...and though the spirit in them, or whatsoever is God in them, return to their originall, which is God, and so lives in him again, yet the fleshly part returns to dust from whence it came: and as the man dies, so dies the beast; as dies the wise man so dies the fool, one end is to them all as *Solomon* speaks...[34]

[29] Thomas Edwards, *Gangraena* (1646), iii. 36 (also i. 27). Cited in Keith Thomas, *Man and the Natural World: A History of the Modern Sensibility* (New York: Pantheon Books, 1983), p. 139.

[30] William C. Braithwaite, *The Second Period of Quakerism*, 2nd ed. prepared by Henry J. Cadbury (Cambridge: Cambridge University Press, 1961), p. 231.

[31] Christopher Hill, "Irreligion in the 'Puritan' Revolution," in *Radical Religion in the English Revolution*, eds. J. F. McGregor and B. Reay (Oxford: Oxford University Press, 1984), p. 201.

[32] Laurence Clarkson, *The Lost Sheep Found* (London, 1660), in Smith, *Ranter*, p. 185.

[33] Jacob Bauthumley, *The Light and Dark Sides of God*, in Smith, *Ranter*, p. 232.

[34] *Ibid.*, p. 252.

This line of thought concludes with a mortalism in which "all Creatures below God perish and die" and their immaterial souls are, at the last judgment, liquified and poured into the "endlesse and infinite Ocean" of God's being.[35] Bauthumley expresses a moving humility in seeing himself as, in this sense, a perishable creature: "In the meane time I am content to be nothing that God may be all, and to let fall my thoughts of any glory or excellency hereafter, as a creature."[36] Such language deepens the transfiguring resonance of the Ranters' purported greeting of each other as "Fellow Creature."

What about the rhetoric addressed to enemies? How do the enemies *of* enthusiasm figure *in* enthusiasm? Although the projection of enemies would seem to smuggle dualism into the reformulation of enthusiastic subjectivity, such is not always the case. For even when Coppe projects a hostile "Other" in his text, he often acknowledges his own complicity, in principle, with such a demonized figure. Coppe's writings do indeed project several enemies. One such, personified at great length, and yet ultimately reclaimed as immanent to Coppe's discourse, is the "Wel-Favoured Harlot." Coppe's well-known story of his encounter with the beggar dramatizes an extended dialogue with this "Wel-Favoured Harlot," who rises up within Coppe himself to advocate a selfish prudence in alms-giving.[37] Because even the worldly "Other" turns out to be part of him, Coppe does not entirely abandon a monist ontology.

Most interesting of all, perhaps, is the figure of the "young man void of understanding," whom the "Harlot" in the second *Roll* pursues and hunts "from corner to corner and religion to religion." This figure seems to be based on the incident of the "rich young man," discussed in the synoptic gospels, who turns sorrowfully away from Jesus after the latter asks him to give all he has to the poor. This young man, who mentions his keeping of the commandments, is an appropriate symbol of religious formalism. His refusal to follow Jesus, due to the strength of his attachment to wealth, provokes Jesus to observe that it is easier for a camel to pass through the eye of a needle than for a rich man to enter into the kingdom of God (Matthew 19:16–30). In Coppe's development of this character, however, the "young man" seems to represent a sort of temptation peculiar to the antinomian tendencies of separatist religious thought: to proclaim spiritual liberty, "formally" mouthing slogans against all formalists, without any concern for practical charity. The "young man void of understanding" thus represents, in the apt phrase of J. C. Davis, "a sterile religious enthusiasm."[38] For Coppe, however, the "young man" is also, as Nigel Smith points out, "a fictional

[35] *Ibid.*, p. 258.
[36] *Ibid.*, p. 257.
[37] Coppe, *Roule*, p. 102.
[38] Davis, *Fear*, p. 51.

representation of his own experience."[39] "Here I could tell a large story," Coppe writes of the young man's spiritual trajectory, "that would reach as far as between Oxonshire and Coventry" – that is, between the geographical coordinates of his own spiritual journey.[40] Coppe's capacity for recognizing himself in the personified objects of his own critique provides a certain inoculation, however paradoxical, against ethical polarization.

It is necessary to ask when, why, and at what level a radically enthusiastic project such as Coppe's does slide back into the "formalism" that it so vehemently criticizes. One answer might be that it does so, under the pressure of post-Restoration persecution, in the very heat and dust of sectarian consolidation. This is the moment that seems to correspond, in the case of seventeenth-century English radical enthusiasm, to Weber's concept of the "routinization of charisma."[41] The Quakers, attempting in the repressive 1660s to discipline themselves into a full-fledged sect, were racked by an exemplary crisis along these lines. The "Perrotonian controversy" revolved around the question of whether witnesses to the spirit should, as a formal rule, remove their hats when testifying, or should merely follow their individual consciences. George Fox, attempting to straddle both inward spirituality and outward communal forms, held to the former position. John Perrot, however, whom Fox likened to the Ranters, saw the ceremony of doffing the hat as one more outward form; he argued that the particular decision about wearing or doffing the hat should be left to the motion of the individually inspired spirit.[42] Fox also reacted negatively to Perrot's decision to grow a beard, which seemed too reminiscent of James Nayler and the crisis his seemingly messianic entrance in Bristol had provoked in 1656.[43] The occasion for these linked controversies was a struggle for the leadership of an organization experiencing severe adversity. They illustrate both the sectaries' scrupulous interrogation of behavioral forms and the immense pressures, both internal and external, to institutionalize a consensus.

It was not only the exigencies of sectarian consolidation under pressure, however, that led to a countervailing "formalism" in even the most radical enthusiastic rhetoric. For traces of a certain hierarchy, based on degrees of illumination, can arguably be found within Coppe's own rhetoric of address. The cryptic and parabolic nature of some passages in Coppe, especially those prior to his two *Rolls*, seem to work against a rhetorical project of universal identification. Coppe refers portentously in various places to "dark hints," "mysteries," and "keys," enigmatically pointing to levels of signification – the

<hr>

[39] Smith, Introduction, in *Ranter*, p. 29.
[40] Coppe, *Roule*, p. 113.
[41] See Max Weber, *On Charisma and Institution Building: Selected Papers*, ed. S. N. Eisenstadt (Chicago: University of Chicago Press, 1968).
[42] See Kenneth Carroll, *John Perrot: Early Quaker Schismatic*, supplement to the *Journal of the Friends' Historical Society 1958–71* (London: Friends' Historical Society, 1971), pp. 51–64.
[43] *Ibid.*, pp. 59–60.

carnal versus the spiritual – differently available to more or less spiritual readers.

Indeed, Coppe even acknowledges that his writing places deliberate obstacles in the way of "spiritual" understanding: "If thou shouldest arise into the Letter of these Letters, before the Spirit of life enter into Thee, Thou would runne before the Lord, and out-runne thy selfe, and runne upon a rock, For it is set on purpose, as one, – And a stumbling-stone to some, – even those who know Christ after the Flesh (only)."[44] A Biblical "stumbling-stone" *topos* lies behind this apparent esotericism. For there is a pattern of imagery throughout the New Testament that draws on the theme in Psalms of an unjustly neglected or rejected "building stone": a rock that nevertheless becomes, or will become, the keystone or corner-stone.[45] In the Christian elaboration of this *topos*, Jesus is simultaneously seen as the foundation stone of the church and as an ongoing obstacle to the wrongheaded:

the Lord is gracious. To whom coming, as unto a living stone, disallowed indeed of men, but chosen of God, and precious, ye also, as lively stones, are built up a spiritual house, an holy priesthood, to offer up spiritual sacrifices, acceptable to God by Jesus Christ. Wherefore also it is contained in the scripture, Behold I lay in Sion a chief corner stone, elect, precious: and he that believeth on him shall not be confounded. Unto you therefore which believe he is precious: but unto them which be disobedient, the stone which the builders disallowed, the same is made the head of the corner, and a stone of stumbling, and a rock of offense, even to them which stumble at the word, being disobedient; whereunto also they were appointed. (1 Peter 2:3–8, KJV)[46]

Coppe's "stumbling-stone" imagery thus seems to follow the same disquieting logic as Mark 4:11–12, in which, as Frank Kermode points out, Jesus explains the purpose of his parables as the deliberate exclusion of outsiders.[47]

Coppe's hieratic language does indeed seem to polarize the world into "those who know" and "those who do not know":

One touch more upon one string of this instrument. Some are at *Home*, and within; Some *Abroad*, and without. They that are at *Home*, are such as know their union *in* God, and live upon, and *in*, and not upon any thing below, or beside him.

Some are abroad, and without: that is, are at a distance from God, (in their own apprehensions) and are Strangers to a powerfull and glorious manifestation of their union with God. That their being one in God, and God one in them; that Christ and they are not twaine, but *one*, is to them a Riddle.

[44] Coppe, *Sips*, p. 48.
[45] According to Psalm 118:22, "The stone which the builders refused is become the head stone of the corner" (KJV).
[46] Romans 9:33 is another important instance of this *topos*. Given the salience of architecture in the lore and mystique of such secret societies as the Freemasons, it is hardly surprising that versions of this "stone" image sometimes appear in occult and hermetic contexts.
[47] Frank Kermode, *The Genesis of Secrecy: On the Interpretation of Narrative* (Cambridge, Massachusetts: Harvard University Press, 1979), p. 2.

These are without, *Abroad*, not at *Home*, and they would fill their bellies with *Husks*, the out-sides of Graine.

That is, they cannot live without Shadows, Signs, Representations;

It is death to them, to heare of living upon a pure & naked God, and upon, and in him alone, without the use of externalls. – [48]

The explanatory idea here is the familiar doctrine of accommodation: those who still need "representations" simply cannot yet bear the immediacy of dwelling in the "home" of God's presence. In the second postscript or "after-clap" to his preamble to Coppin's *Divine Teachings*, Coppe rewrites the parable of the Prodigal Son in light of this same "homecoming" *topos*:

This is musique, WITHIN: The Father, the younger brother, and all that are within, in this house, are merry; where this is dainty, and where there are dainties, and dancing, mirth and musique.

But the serving man – the elder brother, knows not what this meaneth, but is angry, and dogged, puffs and pouts, is sullen, snuffs, swells and censures WITHOUT doors. [49]

A marginal note glosses the "elder brother" as "the zealous formal professor."[50] Rather than marking a permanent exclusion, however, both of these passages merely mark the uneven diffusion of a light – a "home-coming," available, in principle, to all.

The real tension here, in fact, may be found in the seeming incompatibility of instantaneous and gradualist visions of millennial change. Consider the following sentence from the *Additional and Preambular Hint*: "All things are returning to their Original, where all parables, dark sayings, all languages, and all hidden things, are known, unfolded, and interpreted."[51] As Corns explains, this means that "the sign system in which divinity had been encoded is superseded by the emergence of the divine in the hearts of the saints."[52] Apocalypse it may be; it is, nevertheless, clearly an ongoing process. And indeed, a more subtle approach to this problem of uneven illumination appears a bit later on. The following passage, an indirect discourse addressed to "outsiders," is at first merely "about" what should be said to those who stumble against, and therefore censure, what they are not yet ready to understand:

They are to be pathetically and most affectionately told, that our heart akes for them; we have them in our bosom: and the everlasting bonds of eternal love, that dwells in us, yearn over them, are a flame towards them, and towards Publicans and Harlots (Considering also our selves) and knowing that they dwell where we did, and in the remaining part of that old house, which hath been fired about our ears, and over our

[48] Coppe, *Sips*, p. 49.
[49] Coppe, *Hint*, p. 79.
[50] *Ibid.*
[51] *Ibid.*, p. 73.
[52] Corns, *Virtue*, p. 188.

heads, out of which in an infinite and unspeakable mercy, we were frighted into a house made without hands, the beauty whereof dazelleth the eyes of men and Angels.[53]

This indirect discourse, however, is interrupted by the sublimity of Coppe's vision of the "house made without hands": "and at this time the glory thereof amazeth me into silence, and strikes my pen out of my hand, that if I would, yet I cannot now write of its sumptuousness, beauty, and magnificence."[54] Following this "inexpressibility" *topos*, which emphasizes the sublimity of his new habitation, Coppe resumes – but now in direct address: "only, as far as we dare, we wish you were there, and you shall be, when you must be."[55] The shift here from speaking *about* "outsiders" to speaking *to* them coincides with the prediction that effectively incorporates, willy-nilly, resistant, alienated, or baffled interlocutors. As a concept of process, "homecoming" thus mediates between a state of presence and a state of alienation.

What finally seems most remarkable in the enthusiastic campaign against formalism is its rhetorical exploitation of symbolic actions, or "pranks," as emblems of both temporal and social liminality. The opening move of this exploitation is indeed to make social marginality a site where a transfigured identity may be authorized. In so authorizing themselves, the enthusiastic prophets elaborated the rhetoric of a state that is neither properly formal (in that it avoids most forms of allegiance to the prevailing symbolic order) nor formless (in that it involves the "regularity" of donning recognizable personae). This state, indeed, through the concept of transgressive "pranks," exploits precisely the ambiguity inherent in the very idea of a *symbolic* act, which Kenneth Burke usefully terms "the dancing of an attitude."[56] Such transgressive performances, though almost always pathologized, seem far better described in terms of Victor Turner's anthropological concept of liminality: a middle or threshold state, characterized by ambiguity and paradox, that ritually bridges the gulf between old and new social identities. Although much of his discussion focuses on such individual transitions as installation rites and adolescent *rites de passage*, Turner specifically mentions millenarian movements, which spring up at "liminal" historical conjunctures, in this context.[57] The liminal space of ritual – a mode of hypothetical "what if" and subjunctive "as if" – is one where cultural givens can be tested and contested playfully. So Coppe, already assigned to the social periphery, makes a rhetorical strength of his marginal position: he converts

---

53 Coppe, *Hint*, p. 77.
54 *Ibid.*
55 *Ibid.*
56 Kenneth Burke, *The Philosophy of Literary Form: Studies in Symbolic Action*, 2nd ed. (Baton Rouge: Louisiana State University Press, 1957), p. 9.
57 See Victor Turner, *The Ritual Process: Structure and Anti-Structure* (Chicago: Aldine Publishing Company, 1969), especially pp. 11–112.

it into a "liminal" site of social drama where he is licensed to assume a prophetic identity.

Because Scripture provides several models of prophetic behavior that involve charismatic deviations from normal social practice, enthusiasts can make an ethical appeal to their precedent. Hence Coppe's references to the example of the Hebrew prophet Ezekiel. Coppe, virtually reviving the genre of pseudepigrapha, "appropriates," as Nigel Smith writes, "Ezekiel's identity, rhetoric, and gestures."[58] As Coppe points out, Ezekiel performed a number of unusual symbolic actions, or "pranks," before and during his visionary prophesying:

He saw (and I in him see) various strange visions; and he was, and I am set in severall strange postures.

Amongst many of his pranks – this was one, he shaves all the hair off his head: and off his beard, then weighs them in a pair of scales; burns one part of them in the fire, another part hee smites about with a knife, another part he scatters in the wind, and a few he binds up in his skirts, &c. and this not in a corner, or in a chamber, but in the midst of the streets of the great City Hierusalem, and the man all this while neither mad nor drunke, &c.[59]

Ezekiel's other "pranks" include refusing to speak, enacting in miniature the siege of Jerusalem, lying on his side, and eating bread made from dung. Such a ritual marking of himself as different authorized his unwelcome and alarming prophetic discourse. So Coppe, who alludes in the title *A Fiery Flying Roll* to Ezekiel's vision of the fiery chariot, authorizes his forbidden message with prophetic behavior. A traditional rhetoric of "wise folly" thus allows him to make his strange physical and behavioral gestures into something like a literary mask. This "acting out" he explains as the will of an internalized deity. Thus Coppe, referring to himself as a mere outward "forme," explains, "the same most excellent Majesty (in this forme) hath set the Forme in many strange Postures lately, to the joy and refreshment of some, both acquaintances and strangers, to the wonderment and amazement of others, to the terrour and affrightment of others."[60]

In using the roguish word "prank," moreover, Coppe has evidently adopted as a badge of honor yet another term of abuse hurled at the separatist prophets. In 1650, a titillating pamphlet entitled *The Ranters Religion* promises "a true discovery of some of their late prodigious pranks, and unparalleled deportments, with a paper of the most blasphemous Verses found in one of their pockets, against the Majesty of Almighty God, and the most favored Scriptures, rendred *verbatim*."[61] The word, as Hugh Ormsby-Lennon points out, was "a far stronger word than it is today," and one often

---

58   Smith, *Perfection*, p. 55.
59   Coppe, *Roule*, p. 104.
60   *Ibid.*
61   *The Ranters Religion* (London, 1650). Rpt. in appendix to Davis, *Fear*, p. 156.

used "to describe Quaker bizarrerie."[62] Richard Blome's anti-Quaker
polemic and genealogy, *Fanatick History* (1660) promises, on its title page, to
catalogue "their [Quakers'] Mad Mimick Pranks and their ridiculous actions
and gestures, enough to amaze any sober Christian."[63] William Jones refers
in 1679 to Quaker James Nayler's notorious entrance into Bristol (1656),
which was intended to signify not messianic pretensions but "that of God in
everyone," in similar terms:

the Blasphemous *James Nailor* (one of the first Founders of that wicked Sect) rid upon
an *Ass* with naked Women to attend him, crying *Hosanna to the Son of David, blessed is he
that cometh in the Name of the Lord*; at once abusing both these holy places (*Isa.* 32.11):
Tremble, ye women, strip and make ye bare, and that other of our Saviour's riding to
Jerusalem. And many such pranks they play'd in those days.[64]

In the 1690s, Venner's armed uprising (1661) was still termed "that mad
prank of those infatuated fifth monarchy men" by the Quaker Thomas
Ellwood, who edited George Fox's journal.[65]

A *Justification of the Mad Crew* (1650) catalogues the distinguished ancestral
ethos of such strange actions:

They are named the mad crew: mad to the Heathen, mad to the Christian carnal,
and seemingly spiritual, mad to the Gentile, mad to the Jew; mad, so was *David*
accounted one of the mad men, one of the vain base fellows; so was *Lot* in his time, so
was *Paul* a mad man, one that turn'd the world up-side down, so was Christ a Devil,
yea the Prince of Devils. It is a common thing for God in the many and several
appearances of himself to be called of men, mad, a fool, a drunkard, a vain person.[66]

The anonymous author of this passage, as James Holstun observes, "seems
already to be familiar with the political uses of psychological discourse."[67]
His title, as well as his long list of scriptural precedents, serve nicely to
"inoculate," as Holstun puts it, prophetic pranksters against charges of
madness.[68] In his forced recantation, *Heights in Depths*, Joseph Salmon
similarly invokes the Pauline "fool-for-Christ" *topos*, which implies that the
worldly wise are the real fools. He then goes on to intimate that he is forced
by law and public opinion into reticence about his experience:

---

[62] Hugh Ormsby-Lennon, "Swift and the Quakers," *Swift Studies* 4 (1989), p. 40 (note).

[63] Richard Blome, *The Fanatick History: Or, an Exact Relation and Account of the Old Anabaptists and New
Quakers* (London, 1660). Cited in Ormsby-Lennon, "Swift," p. 40.

[64] William Jones, *Work for a Cooper: Being an Answer to a Libel, Written by Thomas Wynne, the Cooper, the Ale-
Man, the Quack, and the Speaking Quaker* (London, 1679), p. 11. Cited in Ormsby-Lennon, "Swift,"
p. 44.

[65] Thomas Ellwood, *The History of the Life of Thomas Ellwood*, ed. C. G. Crump (New York: G. P.
Putnam's Sons, 1900), p. 55. Ormsby-Lennon points out that Elwood's text, posthumously
published in 1714, was completed in the 1690s ("Swift," p. 40, note 14).

[66] *Mad*, in Davis, *Fear*, p. 141.

[67] James Holstun, "Ranting at the New Historicism," *English Literary Renaissance* 19:2 (1989), p. 211.

[68] *Ibid.*

I shall be esteemed a foole, by the wise world, thorough [*sic*] an over much boasting: otherwise I could tell you how I have been exalted into the bosom of the eternall Almightines, where I have seene and heard, things unlawful, (I say unlawful) to be uttered amongst men; but I shall at present spare my self the labour, and prevent the worlds inconsiderate censure.[69]

This "glorious work" as Salmon calls it, led to a subjective transformation: "a suddain, certain, terrible, dreadfull revolution, a most strange vicissitude."[70]

A "prank," most broadly, is a transgression, usually through a gestural or bodily metaphor. While some "pranks" involved iconoclastic assaults on "external" forms of worship – sacred images, musical instruments, even the Bible itself – others involved a well-developed language of bodily histrionics. George Fox interprets this latter mode as a seismic upheaval of the heart. He sees the Lord's power to "shake" worshippers as the fulfillment of a vision in which he saw a great earthquake. This vision Fox associates with Revelation 6:12–14, which describes the opening of the sixth and penultimate seal. "Fox and the early Friends," as Douglas Gwyn explains, "understand their frequent experiences of quaking in worship as this earthquake, in which the seed begins to break free of the earthly, fleshly birth."[71] Not the final seal, but the next-to-last: the sign points again to its place in a rhetoric of temporal liminality.

The bodily or gestural semiotics associated with enthusiasts more generally included not only the convulsive "quaking" itself, a trembling or even fainting in the presence of the Lord, but also humming noises, sharp changes in vocal timbre, and various other manifestations of an internal "revolution." Such much-mocked "holy rolling" phenomena belong on the same spectrum of transgressive behavior covered by "pranks." Female prophets, moreover, were perhaps even more outlandishly "prankish" than males, as Dianne Purkiss shows, in the staging of bodily theatrics that produced their prophetic voices even as they consumed, in some sense, their bodies. These latter gestural follies include spells of dumbness, prolonged fasting, and monumentally prolonged trance states, all of which served to figure a separation of prophetic voice from the world: "To be open to God, to pour forth a continuous stream of utterance," as Purkiss argues, "meant to be closed to other sensations."[72]

It might be argued that the theme of symbolic transgression developed here returns us, through the back door, to Freud's psychoanalytic understanding of mania. For the specifically social analogue of mania, according to

---

[69] Joseph Salmon, *Heights in Depths* (1651), in Smith, *Ranter*, p. 212.

[70] *Ibid.*

[71] Douglas Gwyn, *Apocalypse of the Word: The Life and Message of George Fox (1624–1691)* (Richmond, Indiana: Friends United Press, 1986), p. 187.

[72] Diane Purkiss, "Producing the voice, consuming the body: women prophets of the seventeenth century," in *Women, Writing, History 1640–1740*, eds. Isobel Grundy and Susan Wiseman (Athens: University of Georgia Press, 1992), p. 150.

Freud's *Group Psychology and the Analysis of the Ego*, is the festival or feast – that is, the periodic, institutionalized overthrow of normal prohibitions:

The Saturnalia of the Romans and our modern carnival agree in this essential feature with the festivals of primitive people, which usually end in debaucheries of every kind and the transgression of what are at other times the most sacred commandments. But the ego ideal comprises the sum of all the limitations in which the ego has to acquiesce, and for that reason the abrogation of the ideal would necessarily be a magnificent festival for the ego, which might then once again feel satisfied with itself.[73]

Freud saw the periodicity in annual festivals as evidence of a somatic factor, the social recognition of inexorable "natural" drives. Freud's view, however, ignores two fundamental points: first, the possible political and ideological functions of festivals; and second, the related possibility that exuberant transgression, as in the case of Coppe's "pranks," can belong to a political rhetoric.

What if festivals are not so much "natural" as a domain of the political? Otto Fenichel, the encyclopedic synthesizer of psychoanalytic thought, offers the standard leftist view of festivals as "channeling" devices instituted by the ruling class in a given social formation.[74] The "festive," in this latter case, would belong to an artful and persuasive presentation of a paternalistic class ideology: in short, an oppressive "bread-and-circuses" rhetoric. The seventeenth-century Royalist defense of harvest festivals and traditional Sunday pastimes, for example, would seem to fit this pattern. Even this degree of contextual understanding, moreover, puts considerable pressure on the glib pathologizing of the manic.

It would be unwise, however, to assume that all festive rituals generally serve as homeostatic channeling mechanisms. As Stallybrass and White point out, carnivalesque transgression should not be essentialized either as always revolutionary, a staging of the emergent utopia, or as always conservative and cooptational. "The most that can be said in the abstract," in their formulation, "is that for long periods carnival may be a stable and cyclical ritual with no noticeable politically transformative effects but that, given the presence of a sharpened political antagonism, it may often act as a *catalyst* and *site of actual and symbolic struggle*."[75] Whether festivals serve politically to "inoculate" or "infect," that is to say, is entirely contingent upon particular circumstances.

---

[73] See Sigmund Freud, *Group Psychology and the Analysis of the Ego*, trans. James Strachey (1921; New York: W. W. Norton & Co., 1959), p. 63.

[74] Otto Fenichel, *The Psychoanalytic Theory of Neurosis* (New York: W. W. Norton & Co., 1945), pp. 408–409.

[75] Peter Stallybrass and Allon White, *The Politics and Poetics of Transgression* (Ithaca: Cornell University Press, 1986), p. 14.

What of the manic, then, in a situation of "sharpened political antagonism"? Enthusiastic transgressions were often genuinely subversive. Such gestures, moreover, had collective significance: they were a means of affiliating themselves with oppositional political collectives, however diffuse or poorly organized, in a moment of profound class polarization. And what if transgression itself, to clinch our argument, belongs to a class-conscious rhetoric? For enthusiastic pranks were not authorized by a ruling class: they were rhetorically authorized through a certain radical reading of Scripture; and they were rhetorically addressed – both to potential allies whom the enthusiasts hoped to convert and to oppressors whom they hoped to bewilder, intimidate, demoralize, and divide. The Quakers' term for conversion, indeed, was "convincement." Coppe, it should also be noted, has constant recourse to the metaphor of "plague": not only for its obvious resonance with the punishment meted out to the oppressor in the Exodus narrative, but also as a metaphor for the "contagious" spread of radical ideas. If the manic "pranks" of the seventeenth-century enthusiasts are analogues of the festive, they clearly belong to the model of political epidemic rather than inoculation.

Freud's analogy between mania and carnivals, as so often in his work, reduces complex and historically variant social dynamics to a "natural" background that then serves as the metaphorical vehicle for illuminating the foregrounded individual. The more complex term, society – which in fact preexists and constitutes individuals – is taken as more familiar, more known. The analogy thus collapses very different levels of being without acknowledging the disjunction: as such, it is an apt emblem of psychomedical reductionism in general. Indeed, the limited ability of the psychoanalytic lexicon to articulate historical time, beyond the psychosexual development of individuals, inevitably renders it inadequate to the actual density and diversity of the boundary-crossing phenomena it claims to describe. Terms such as "manic fusion,"[76] when used to single out and pathologize collectively meaningful behavior, screen out the significance of transindividual historical events through their focus on individual prehistory. The sheer complexity in

[76] Freud describes mania as a de-differentiation or "fusion" of the ego and the superego. The explanatory concept implicit in this analogy, as Bertram Lewin notes, is "structural regression," the return of an organized system to a simpler state, a regression that permits a release of energy. The result is that the person, "in a mood of triumph and disturbed by no self-criticism, can enjoy the abolition of his inhibitions, his feelings of criticism for others, and his self-reproaches." See Freud, *Group Psychology*, pp. 61–65; and Bertram Lewin, *The Psychoanalysis of Elation* (New York: Norton, 1950), pp. 28–29. See also Sandor Rado, "The problem of melancholia," *The International Journal of Psycho-Analysis*, 9 (1928), pp. 420–438. As Patrick Brantlinger points out, Freud's reliance on the French "crowd psychologist" Gustave Le Bon places *Group Psychology* in an elitist tradition that includes Nietzsche's anti-democratic cultural polemics and, more recently (1930), *The Revolt of the Masses* by Jose Ortega y Gasset. In this view, civilization is perpetually threatened by the ignorance and *ressentiment* of the masses, who, Caliban-like, are utterly unfit for self-governance. The conceptual limitations of Freud's social psychology are precisely the limitations of this elitist subgenre. Patrick Brantlinger, *Bread and Circuses: Theories of Mass Culture as Social Decay* (Ithaca: Cornell University Press, 1983), pp. 166–171.

Coppe's work of egalitarian "fusions" simply gives the lie to any explanation that refuses to consider their social and ideological import. It seems quite telling, moreover, that such "bizarre" acts as, say, the branding of James Nayler's forehead with the letter "B" (for "blasphemy") or the Army's boring through Jacob Bauthumley's tongue with a hot iron are seldom dwelled on by conservative historians, much less scrutinized for their fair share of psychopathology.

The reactionary effects of reducing historical phenomena to the level of the individual psyche are not difficult to see. The psychohistorian Alfred Cohen, writing in particular about the female prophets of the revolutionary era, offers a convenient illustration. Cohen argues that "there was real madness involved in most of our visionaries' methods."[77] Of the Fifth Monarchist Anna Trapnel, Cohen writes as follows:

> We hear of no liason Anna had with any man, even in a passive sense. Had she suppressed all her sexual needs? During her last trance she sings any number of songs in praise of Jesus that are very sensual and suggestive. She describes herself as the Spouse of Jesus, praises his physical features, exhalts [sic] in being "ravish'd with the Eye," and compares herself and her love for Jesus to that of Sheeba's for Solomon.[78]

The masculinist and heterosexist bias of this passage makes obvious the extent to which psychomedical "normalcy," as deployed in the construction of psychohistory, can serve as a mere stalking-horse for the denunciation of ideological "deviance." Cohen's main agenda is to sponsor a counter-revolution against the notion, found in the historiography of Christopher Hill and Keith Thomas, that there is a certain method to the seeming madness of the enthusiastic prophets. "Lady Eleanor's bizarre actions," Cohen argues, "might be used to reverse the Thomas/Hill set of priorities by setting forth the counter thesis that the radicalism was a function of the madness rather than the other way around."[79] The normal is the normal: it is a powerful and self-enclosing tautology, seamlessly equating the politically dominant with the medically normal. It serves no more interesting or noble purpose here than to repeat a gesture common among conservative historians: to exclude the seventeenth-century prophets from, in James Holstun's phrase, "the master narrative of British religious and constitutional history."[80] Such a tautological construct is profoundly dehistoricizing: it short-circuits logic precisely in order to erase all forms of historical difference and change.

The task remains, then, to accommodate Coppe into our historical narrative. Corns concludes that Coppe's transgressive mode subverts his own

---

[77] Alfred Cohen, "Prophecy and madness: women visionaries during the Puritan Revolution," *The Journal of Psychohistory* 11:3 (1984), p. 413.

[78] *Ibid.*, p. 425.

[79] *Ibid.*, p. 426.

[80] Holstun, "Ranting," p. 208.

polemic. The text of Coppe's two *Flying Rolls* is, as he puts it, "persistently subverted by the intrusion of the self-image Coppe constructs and the eccentric and linguistically deviant voice he finds."[81] Corns goes on to explain that self-subversion as a mark of the irrelevance of formal coherence "while the total transformation of the spiritual consciousness of the nation seems imminent."[82] That view, however, seems to miss the inherent paradox in the rhetorical project of enthusiasm: to constitute, in one's very discourse, the relations of apocalyptic immanence. In an absolute sense, this is impossible; in a relative sense, however, Coppe certainly does achieve a remarkable effect of heightened immediacy.

Moreover, the fact that a law was passed in 1650 retrospectively criminalizing Ranteresque pamphlets as blasphemous reminds us that symbolic actions are indeed, in some sense, consequential actions. To define the precise nature of Coppe's "impossible" achievement, then, we return to the peculiar ontology or "incipient presence" of symbolic actions. Coppe's accounts of his various "pranks," passing through the relay of print into the public domain, are themselves mediated events. Indeed, whether or not a given prank ever actually occurred, the public claiming of it "repeats" the original transgression. The time-lag involved in this repetition, moreover, is peculiarly elastic, if not infinite. Consider again one of Coppe's more memorable utterances: "I am about my act, my strange act, my worke, my strange worke, that whosoever hears of it, both his ears shall tingle."[83] A certain circularity results from the temporal immediacy of Coppe's present tense: past transgressions merge in this discourse with the present of enunciation in which the reader's ears, by this very proclamation – itself a very strange "event" – are made to "tingle." A similar self-reflexivity inheres in Coppe's jocular prediction in *Some Sweet Sips* – itself a parody of academic discourse – that learned professors will bring their books together and "burne them before all men."[84] Indeed, this imaginary violence against bibliolatry is an appropriate emblem for the aspirations both of *Some Sweet Sips* and of the aptly titled *Fiery Flying Rolls*: texts that seek, as it were, to consume themselves in the very zeal and purity of their own enunciation. "Oh Spirit!" Coppe declares in *Some Sweet Sips*: "O Spirit of burning! O *consuming fire!* O God our joy!"[85] It is Coppe's historical achievement, in such an outburst, to have given full voice to a powerful collective desire for purgative change.

[81] Corns, *Virtue*, p. 192.
[82] *Ibid.*, p. 193.
[83] Coppe, *Roule*, p. 106.
[84] *Sips*, p. 61.
[85] *Ibid.*, p. 67.

PART II

Patrician diagnosis

4

Return to madness: mania as plebeian vapors in Swift

> But to return to *Madness.*
>
> Jonathan Swift, *A Tale of a Tub*

It is typical of the narrator of *A Tale of a Tub* that through a telling ambiguity he unwittingly collapses language *about* madness into language *of* madness. Thus he ends a digression with the richly ironic phrase, "But to return to *Madness.*"[1] This irony at the tale-teller's expense signals that Jonathan Swift is not "of" the manic in the same sense that Abiezer Coppe and Christopher Smart are. Nevertheless, in *A Tale of a Tub* Swift deliberately parodies, and thus reproduces, the mode I have termed a rhetoric of mania. Swift puts on a style that includes such manic features as a stance of inspired omnipotence, levelling catalogues, irreverent punning, and non-linear reading techniques. *A Tale of a Tub*, moreover – through its "stammering" quality of self-interruption and its tendency toward fusion with the reader addressed or thing described – parodies the unorthodox rhetoric of enunciation common among enthusiastic writers. The *Tale*, finally, not only echoes such enthusiastic commonplaces as the "pranks" and "incarceration" *topoi*; it in fact elaborates its entire religious allegory, dealing with the politics of inheriting a scriptural tradition, as a revision of the sectarian "two sons" *topos*.

Swift's satire mocks both radical Protestant enthusiasm and certain dynamics of literary production that he represents as novel in the 1690s. According to the logic of *A Tale of a Tub*, both enthusiasts and hacks produce a deformed discourse that can be brought by the standards of "aristocratic" reason under the rubric of madness. Thus we learn, in Section IX of the *Tale*, "A Digression Concerning Madness," that the tale-teller was once an inmate of Bedlam, and has been urged to write – "to vent his Speculations" – as a means of retaining his precarious mental health.[2] The etiology of this madness is explained as a redundancy of vapors "ascending from the lower Faculties to over-shadow the Brain."[3] This pathologizing trope crucially reframes the

---

[1] Jonathan Swift, *A Tale of a Tub*, eds. A. C. Guthkelch and D. Nichol Smith, 2nd ed. (Oxford: Clarendon Press, 1958), p. 174.

[2] *Ibid.*, p. 180.

complex literary, political, and religious significance of "inspired" or enthusiastic authors. *A Tale of a Tub* thus dramatizes the implication of modern literary production in a "manic" mode whose specific historical resonances are too often glibly reduced to an unproblematized madness. Hence this historical paradox: the manic style first achieves high visibility in the literary mainstream as a patrician critique of commercial modernity – indeed, as Swift's ironic and grotesque foil for both sanity and proper authorship.

Swift's mockery is not confined to "the Republick of *dark* Authors" parodied in Section X: that is, those esoteric Rosicrucians, Theosophists, and Paracelsians who often overlapped with the millenarians studied here.[4] The *Tale* deliberately evokes a wide range of enthusiasts: from the flamboyant enthusiasts of Cromwellian times to their somewhat quieter post-Restoration heirs, including the more domesticated Quakers. The character of Jack the enthusiast, as the list of his nicknames suggests, is meant to encompass the Dutch Anabaptists (*Dutch Jack*), the Scottish Presbyterians (*Knocking Jack of the North*), and the Huguenots (*French Hugh*).[5] The latter, already emigrating to England in significant numbers – the total may have reached 50,000 – would soon be creating a resurgence of millennial enthusiasm in England.[6] And indeed, the connection that the "French prophets" made with the millennial and theosophical "Philadel-phians" in London, an outwardly conforming millenarian group centered around John Pordage and then Jane Lead, suggests certain continuities in the development of enthusiasm.[7]

The first six sections of *A Tale of a Tub* alternate between chapters that digressively practice and celebrate "modern" learning and chapters that present installments of a parable about European religious history. By Section VII, however, this pattern begins to erode; thereafter, as several critics have noted, the two strands increasingly converge.[8] The climax of the book, then, is a sort of structural "breakdown" in Section IX, the digression

---

[3] *Ibid.*, p. 167.

[4] As Nigel Smith explains, the overlap between hermetic and radical Puritan thought lay in a shared perfectionism: the hope, that is, of returning to "the state of pristine knowledge and spiritual perfection known by Adam." See Nigel Smith, *Literature and Revolution in England 1640–1660* (New Haven: Yale University Press, 1994), p. 269.

[5] Swift, *Tub*, p. 142.

[6] John Fletcher, "The Huguenot Diaspora," *Diaspora* 2:2 (1992), pp. 251–260.

[7] See Hillel Schwartz, *The French Prophets: The History of a Millenarian Group in Eighteenth-Century England* (Berkeley: University of California Press, 1980), pp. 45–54. See also Catherine F. Smith, "Jane Lead's Wisdom: women and prophecy in seventeenth-century England," in *Poetic Prophecy in Western Literature*, eds. Jan Wojcyk and Raymond Jean-Frontain (London: Associated University Presses, 1984), pp. 55–63; and "Jane Lead: mysticism and the woman clothed with the sun," in *Shakespeare's Sisters: Feminist Essays on Woman Poets*, eds. Sandra M. Gilbert and Susan Gubar (Bloomington: Indiana University Press, 1979), pp. 3–18.

[8] See Jay Arnold Levine, "The design of *A Tale of a Tub* (with a digression on a mad modern critic)," *English Literary History* 33 (1966), p. 209; and Everett Zimmerman, *Swift's Narrative Satires: Author and Authority* (Ithaca: Cornell University Press, 1983), p. 83.

on madness. This structure points to the essential satiric strategy of the *Tale*: a constant *conflation* of the manic mode (as one mode of non-patrician discourse) with popular or "hack" writing (as another such mode).

This "breakdown," moreover, is frequently foreshadowed in the first eight chapters: for "enthusiasm" in fact constantly spills over into the "modern" sections.[9] Enthusiasm, indeed, becomes not merely one theme among others, but rather the stylistic vehicle for Swift's entire satire. I am thus doubtful whether Erasmus' amiable and genteel *The Praise of Folly* is, in more than a very broad sense, the "formal model for Swift's *Tale*."[10] To be sure, both the *Tale* and *Folly* can be seen as paradoxical mock-encomia: not only do they blame and mock by inappropriate praise, like other mock-encomia, but they both execute a paradoxical twist in which the would-be mocker is ultimately also mocked.[11] That comparison, nevertheless, conveys very little about the specific rhetorical mode used in *A Tale of a Tub*. For it is not just the allegory of the mad enthusiast Jack, but rather the inner logic of the *Tale*'s entire rhetoric, that derives specifically from the enthusiastic politics and subjectivist epistemology of the manic mode.

Swift's bequest to build a house for "fools and mad" and his own fear of madness are all well-trodden ground. What perhaps deserves more emphasis is that "madness" itself had been institutionally and ideologically reconfigured between the time of Erasmus and that of Swift. A greater sense of distance from the "mad" is apparent. The *Tale* evokes madhouse tourism, as *The Praise of Folly* could not – a social practice linked to England's more modest version of Foucault's "Great Confinement."[12] And it is interesting, in this regard, that an essay attributed to Swift by both Sir Walter Scott and Temple Scott – "A serious and useful scheme to make an hospital for incurables" (1733) – celebrates precisely such incarceration. This essay, which is excluded from Herbert Davis' well-sifted canon of Swift's works, is almost certainly merely apocrypha in the Swiftian vein; nevertheless, it reveals much about the way that madness was being seen in Swift's moment. "A serious and useful scheme" praises the "erecting and endowing" of "proper edifices for those who labour under different kinds of distress," and duly points out that such

---

[9] Zimmerman points out a number of crucial parallels between the digressions and the parable. James William Johnson argues that the commentary eventually usurps and displaces the tale. Neither of them, however, emphasizes the *Tale*'s permeation by enthusiastic modes of rhetoric. See Zimmerman, *Narrative*, p. 83; and James William Johnson, "Swift's historical outlook," *Journal of British Studies* 4:2 (1965), p. 216.

[10] Zimmerman, *Narrative*, p. 72.

[11] *Ibid.*, p. 77.

[12] For more about madhouse tourism, see Max Byrd, *Visits to Bedlam: Madness and Literature in the Eighteenth Century* (Columbia: University of South Carolina Press, 1974) and Michael V. DePorte, "Swift: madness and satire," in *Nightmares and Hobbyhorses: Swift, Sterne, and Augustan Ideas of Madness* (San Marino: The Huntington Library, 1974), pp. 55–106. The "Great Confinement" is further discussed in the Introduction.

asylums spare others "from the misery of beholding them [the diseased and unfortunate]."[13] In this essay, moreover, as Roy Porter observes, the author imagines the potential inmates as bestial: "not unlike the brutes resorting to the ark before the deluge."[14]

Indeed, in both the "Serious scheme" and *A Tale of a Tub*, the world's manifestations of "madness" – its capacities for lying, pimping, bribing, extorting, its schemes for empire-building – seem sinister rather than merely amusing. The point is not, however, as Lillian Feder would have it, merely that Swift is an old-fashioned moralist who "offers no insight into the mind of the madman."[15] It is, rather, that two histories intersect in Swift: the earliest stirrings, on the one hand, of the "Great Confinement," with its gradual medicalization of "madness"; and, on the other hand, the patrician equation of enthusiasm with "madness." This latter ideological theme, indeed, had by this time been largely consolidated. As Hillel Schwartz points out, in 1707 John Tutchin, editor of *The Observator*, "proposed the construction of a religious bedlam ... for the French Prophets and their counterparts."[16] By this time, moreover, Anglican pamphleteers, as Michael MacDonald observes, had transformed the anti-Puritan equation of enthusiasm with madness into "a ruling-class shibboleth."[17]

By assimilating various "modern" discourses to the satirical vehicle of enthusiasm, then, Swift denounces the political and cultural expressions of common people as a "madness" possibly deserving confinement. The novelty originally signified by the political and religious upheaval of the 1640s and 1650s – one thinks of pamphlet titles such as *Strange and Terrible News from Salisbury*, or *Wonderfull News from the North* – is used by Swift to figure the "modern" penetration of market relations into the production of literature. By drawing this analogy, Swift purports to describe a historical development: the revolutionary enthusiast of the mid-seventeenth century modulates, according to this view of English cultural history, into the turn-of-the-century hack.

Is there any basis for such a view? To be sure, certain "modern" writers can be seen as mediating, in various fashions, between the literary culture of

---

[13] Jonathan Swift[?], "A serious and useful scheme to make an hospital for incurables," in *The Prose Works of Jonathan Swift, D.D.*, 12 vols., ed. Temple Scott (London: G. Bell and Sons, Ltd., 1925), VII, p. 287. Sometimes attributed to Matthew Pilkington.

[14] *Ibid.*, p. 294; Roy Porter, *Mind-Forg'd Manacles: A History of Madness in England from the Restoration to the Regency* (London: The Athlone Press, 1987), p. 43.

[15] Lillian Feder, *Madness in Literature* (Princeton, New Jersey: Princeton University Press, 1980), p. 166.

[16] Hillel Schwartz, *Knaves, Fools, Madmen, and that Subtile Effluvium: A Study of the Opposition to the French Prophets in England, 1706–1710* (Gainesville: The University Presses of Florida, 1978), pp. 51–52.

[17] Michael MacDonald, *Mystical Bedlam: Madness, Anxiety, and Healing in Seventeenth-Century England* (Cambridge: Cambridge University Press, 1981), p. 225. DePorte likewise argues that "After the publication of *Enthusiasmus Triumphatus* it became more and more common to see fanatics as men fitter for Bedlam than for Bridewell ..." (DePorte, "Madness," p. 39).

nonconformity and the bustling life of Grub Street. The most distinguished example is surely the prolific Daniel Defoe.[18] Another such mediation appears in the interest of some Augustan critics in the potential of enthusiasm for literary sublimity. In the same year that *A Tale of a Tub* was published, John Dennis argued in "The Grounds of Criticism in Poetry" (1704) that if the "Moderns" would make religion their subject, they could equal the "Ancients." Because passion is his supreme test for literary power, Dennis is consistently friendly toward religious enthusiasm. Although Dennis demands sincerity, his argument seems to imply, among other things, a possible subordination of religious feeling to the poet's *literary* desire for originality and sublimity. Dennis here anticipates a later formalist stance which considers "content" instrumentally – sheerly as raw material, that is – for retroactively "motivating" the all-important form. Dennis thus attempts to show, on the authority of Longinus, "that Religious Ideas are the most proper to give Greatness and Sublimity to a Discourse."[19] In a similar context, moreover, while describing a mode of heightened passion in which the subject and object of imagination merge, Dennis produces his own celebration of manic "fusion": "For the warmer the Imagination is, the more present the things are to us, of which we draw the Images, and therefore when once the Imagination is so inflam'd as to get the better of the understanding, there is no difference between the Images and the things themselves; as we see, for example, in Fevers and Mad-men."[20] A "professional" preoccupation with sublimity can thus be said to have provided a certain link between old enthusiasm and the "modern" sublime.

Swift's historical thesis is not entirely arbitrary; however, his conflation of enthusiasm with modernity is best understood as the ferociously partisan prelude to his satirical attempt to kill two subaltern discourses with one stone. On the one hand, he rebukes the individualistic concerns of "professional" writers as mercenary, impertinent, and self-aggrandizing. The laboring or "mechanic" classes, on the other hand, he rebukes as vile and unclean, like the "lower body": its "mad" mode of speech is thus depicted as undifferentiated, excremental, and flatulent. It should never be forgotten, moreover, that the factor common to both of these satirical targets is their upstart temerity in asserting plebeian agency. The truly interesting issue,

---

[18] According to Christopher Hill, "the democratic revolution, defeated in politics, triumphed in the novel." See Christopher Hill, "Daniel Defoe and *Robinson Crusoe*," in *The Collected Essays of Christopher Hill*, 2 vols. (Brighton: Harvester Press, 1985) I: *Writing and Revolution in 17th Century England*, p. 126. A much more conservative Defoe, however, is traced in Manuel Schonhorn's *Defoe's Politics: Parliament, Power, Kingship, and Robinson Crusoe*, Cambridge Studies in Eighteenth-Century English Literature and Thought (Cambridge: Cambridge University Press, 1991).

[19] John Dennis, "The grounds of criticism in poetry," in *The Critical Works of John Dennis*, 2 vols., ed. Edward Niles Hooker (Baltimore: The Johns Hopkins Press, 1939), I, p. 357.

[20] John Dennis, *The Advancement and Reformation of Modern Poetry: A Critical Discourse* (1710; rpt. New York: Garland Publishing, Inc., 1971), pp. 32–33.

then, is how it changes our understanding of Swift to take up, as a critical problematic, the complex and historically contingent development behind what is usually called the "madness" in *A Tale of a Tub*: namely, a rhetorical mode – not "unreadable," not "unintelligible," not merely "mad" – created primarily by those forcibly excluded, because of economic and social stratification, from legitimate channels of political self-expression.

Swift's attitudes about distinctions of social class inform *A Tale of a Tub* at many levels. Irony such as Swift's is a trope, as John Traugott notes, implicitly motivated by, and appreciated through, the sort of aristocratic elitism that was cultivated in the household of Swift's complacent patron, Sir William Temple, an overly self-assured "gentleman amateur" of classical scholarship.[21] Swift lived at Moor Park for most of the decade between 1688 and 1699, translating Temple's correspondence and transcribing his memoirs: acting as, in the words of A. C. Elias, "a secretary or glorified clerk."[22] There Swift, as a man of about 30, wrote much of the *Tale*, mainly in 1696–1697; it was not published until 1704. *A Tale of a Tub* was supposedly written in allegiance to Temple's vindication (against William Wotton and Richard Bentley) of the "Ancients" over and against the "Moderns."

Elias has provided considerable biographical and literary evidence, however, for Swift's ambivalence toward Temple. He demonstrates, for instance, that the famous "Digression on Madness" – where the narrator celebrates the comforts of "the Serene Peaceful State of being a Fool among Knaves" – is a subversive travesty of Temple's gentlemanly ideals of Epicurean tranquility.[23] Traugott goes still further. According to him, a "strange metamorphosis" takes place in the process of Swift's satirical project: "[Swift's] snobbery nurtured in the school of Moor Park reinforces his talent for mimicry and parody, makes him hawk about for the grubs and busybodies who are his natural victims. At this point the worm turns, the parodied vulgarian becomes the radical individualist."[24] In sum: "The provincial Irishman in England, the psychological bastard triumphs."[25] Swift, in this view, is a subversive mocker not only of "modernity," but also of the intellectually bankrupt snobbery of dilettantes like Temple.

Although the meaning of any such subversion must surely involve class antagonisms, Traugott retreats prematurely from the "parochial quarrels of the Restoration" to the supposedly transcendent ground of "Swift's radical imagination."[26] Furthermore, his argument glosses over numerous Swiftian

---

[21] John Traugott, "*A Tale of a Tub*," in *The Character of Swift's Satire: A Revised Focus*, ed. Claude Rawson (Newark: University of Delaware Press, 1983), p. 91.

[22] A. C. Elias, *Swift at Moor Park: Problems in Biography and Criticism* (The University of Pennsylvania Press, 1982), p. 47.

[23] *Ibid.*, pp. 157–158.

[24] Traugott, "*Tale*," p. 96.

[25] *Ibid.*

[26] *Ibid.*, p. 90.

attacks on the financially marginal. One thinks, for example, of the tale-teller's puff for a forthcoming treatise entitled *A Modest Defence of the Proceedings of the Rabble in all Ages.*[27] The very title of *A Tale of a Tub*, moreover, alludes sneeringly to the practice of "tub preaching." And Swift makes the class overtones of "mechanic" perfectly clear in the following sentence: "It is therefore upon this *Mechanical Operation of the Spirit* that I mean to treat, as it is at present performed by our *British Workmen.*"[28] The fact thus remains that Swift's gesture of satirical appropriation is, among other things, an attempt to obliterate any possible dialogue between enthusiasm and the culture at large.[29] Ultimately, the very theme of class distinctions invokes a depth of historical conflict that can neither be analyzed adequately in terms of "snobbery" nor suddenly contained as a parochial quarrel.

It should not be imagined, moreover, that Swift was merely exhuming an issue that had died in the aftermath of the Glorious Revolution. As Hugh Ormsby-Lennon has demonstrated, *A Tale of a Tub* echoes and amplifies, in scores of its particular details, a ferocious new wave of anti-Quaker propaganda in the 1690s; this propaganda offensive followed the passage in 1689 of the Toleration Act, which eased the legal pressure on the Society of Friends, and the posthumous publication in 1694 of George Fox's *Journal.*[30] Swift was mocking the enthusiasts of the mid-seventeenth century, then; but he was also intervening against a currently vulnerable sect.

Swift's conception of modernity, no less elitist than his hatred of enthusiasm, likewise demands a "class-struggle analysis" by way of the history of literacy. His emphasis in the *Tale* on a sudden and quasi-revolutionary novelty in the mode of literary production, is an extreme and distorted view of a more gradual, yet genuinely radical reorganization of literary production in late seventeenth-century England. More people, a lot more, were reading and writing. Chapbooks that appealed to a semi-literate audience, from impoverished peasants to more prosperous yeomen, had been growing in popularity, as Margaret Spufford demonstrates, throughout the seventeenth century.[31] These included such genres as jest-books, song-books, news-books, romances, anti-female satires, calendars and almanacs, such prophecies as *The Strange and Wonderful History of Mother Shipton*, and godly works of popular piety. Spufford provides evidence that as early as 1642 the average rate of

---

[27] Swift, *Tub*, p. 54.

[28] Jonathan Swift, *A Discourse Concerning the Mechanical Operation of the Spirit*, in *Tub*, p. 267.

[29] Swift's parody in the *Tale* of sectarian claims to divine inspiration can thus be said to consummate an English tradition of anti-enthusiastic invective whose main authors include Robert Burton, Samuel Butler, Henry More, and Meric Casaubon. See Thomas L. Canavan, "Robert Burton, Jonathan Swift, and the tradition of anti-Puritan invective," *Journal of the History of Ideas* 34: 2 (1973), pp. 227–242.

[30] Hugh Ormsby-Lennon, "Swift and the Quakers," *Swift Studies* 4 (1989), pp. 34–62.

[31] Margaret Spufford, *Small Books and Pleasant Histories: Popular Fiction and Its Readership in Seventeenth-Century England* (Athens: The University of Georgia Press, 1981).

literacy, in addition to the small but unquantifiable female readership, was 30 percent for males.[32] From the 1690s on, according to Raymond Williams, one can also discern the rapid growth of a new kind of middle-class reading public comprising merchants, tradesmen, shopkeepers, and administrative and clerical workers.[33] This newly literate group demanded and consumed various literary ephemera – newspapers, novels, scandalous memoirs, criminal biographies – in ever-increasing quantities. Though not truly a "mass culture" such as arrived with the advent of mass circulation news-papers and penny-dreadful novels in the nineteenth century, the new public and its new values constituted what some conservative writers represent as an uprising from below that threatened aristocratic modes of literary production and reception. Thus Goldsmith eventually termed it "that fatal revolution whereby writing is converted to a mechanic trade."[34]

Marketed merchandise, moreover, must please, whether or not it instructs. Hence a lingering problem for the concept of artistic vocation under capitalism: even though commodified art must presumably seek to maximize its popularity and exposure, "excessive" popularity, as Terry Lovell points out, tends to call into question the aesthetic credentials of a work of art or literature.[35] The same literary democratization that eventually brought into being the novel and the periodical essay, among other "substandard" literary forms, seemed to threaten the mystique of elite tradition. For those fortunate enough to be part of the educated patrician elite, the late seventeenth century was, in Walter Benjamin's sense, an age of mechanical reproduction, an age in which the written text, as an object, was profaned and subjected to a new mode of critical judgment. As printed texts superseded manuscripts, author-ship – newly democratized and decentralized by the accessibility of print – likewise lost a certain aura.[36] The mystique of authorship, given such an organization of literary production and reception, began to yield to some-thing more modest, more of a piece with other commodities. The contingencies of timing, for instance, became crucial to one's marketing strategy: "I am living fast, to see the Time," the tale-teller observes, "when a *Book* that misses its tide, shall be neglected, as the *Moon* by Day, or like a *Mackerel* a Week after the Season."[37]

The response of literary patricians to this ideological threat to their

---

[32] *Ibid.*, p. 22.
[33] Raymond Williams, *The Long Revolution* (New York: Columbia University Press, 1961), p. 161.
[34] Cited in *ibid.*, p. 162.
[35] Terry Lovell, *Consuming Fiction* (London: Verso, 1987), pp. 78–83.
[36] See Marlon B. Ross, "Authority and authenticity: scribbling authors and the genius of print in eighteenth-century England," *Cardozo Arts & Entertainment Law Journal* 10:2 (1992), pp. 495–521. For an account of the reinvention of a print-based textual aura, through canonization and "authoritative editions," see Alvin Kernan, *Samuel Johnson and the Impact of Print* (Princeton: Princeton University Press, 1987), pp. 152–158.
[37] Swift, *Tub*, p. 206.

cultural dominance was to develop an elaborate demonology of Grub Street and its "hacks," complete with urban topographies, mock-heroes, and stereotyped adventures for those heroes.[38] As Kathy MacDermott has shown, this myth is articulated by such key antitheses as genius/mechanism, brain/fingers, and author/hack.[39] As she further argues, the culturally determined contradiction between patron and bookseller – full consideration of which might have made too visible the relation between cultural artifact and economic process – is thus displaced by literary myth and stripped of its antagonistic historical resonance.[40] It is the "hack," instead, who is blamed for the systematic effects of a market-based literary economy on the quality of writing. In the figure of the bodily, excremental hack, the newer, "modern" mode of literary production is seen as grotesquely material in its determinations, whereas the older, "ancient" mode is implicitly mystified as wholly spiritual "literature." The myth of Grub Street naturalizes a class-based opposition between "high" and "low" culture by representing "hack" writing as so scurrilous and formulaic as to suggest a thorough dehumaniza-tion of the writing process: a reduction, in short, of soul to body, spirit to matter, script to scribbling.

A Tale of a Tub elaborates all the distinctions described above between "high" and "low" cultural production. The *Tale*, which in fact inaugurates many features of the Grub Street myth, is obsessed with the material conditions of its own production, including paper, ink, typographical and literary conventions, commonplaces, and the author's economic status. It is anomalous precisely in the peculiar extent to which it exhibits the marks and mechanisms, like so many unraveling seams, of its own production. The tale-teller thus mentions such shortcuts to authorship as the pillaging of common-place books: "For, what tho' his *Head* be empty," the tale-teller says of a budding author, "provided his *Common-place*-Book be full."[41] The primary concerns of the *Tale* are not then so much abuses of religion (in the allegory of Martin, Peter, and Jack) and abuses of learning (in the digressions), but rather the reciprocal relations between the two in the context of a "modern," profit-driven marketplace.

Exactly how do we get from enthusiast to hack? The theme of enthusiastic claims recurs throughout *A Tale of a Tub*. The tubbian narrator several times refers to his book, as James William Johnson observes, as a "divine" or "miraculous treatise," and eventually, while parodying the Septuagint

---

[38] In his book-length study *Grub Street: Studies in a Sub-Culture* (London: Methuen & Co. Ltd., 1972), Pat Rogers maps the sociological reference points – Moorfields, Tyburn, Fleet Ditch, Bedlam, Newgate, and of course Grub Street itself – around which the "topography of dullness" is constructed, and discusses the practices of various "dunces."

[39] Kathy MacDermott, "Literature and the Grub Street myth," *Literature and History* 8:2 (1982), pp. 159–169.

[40] *Ibid.*, p. 161.

[41] Swift, *Tub*, p. 148.

legend, "explicitly presents it as a Bible."[42] It is crucial, however, that the "abuses" of religion and learning seem interchangeable. Each abuse can figure the other, as learned digression shades into sectarianism and enthusiasm shades into a manic scholarly zeal. Section V of the *Tale*, a digression in praise of modern authors, thus begins with the following grandiose and mock-enthusiastic apostrophe:

> This, *O Universe*, is the Adventurous Attempt of me thy Secretary;
> ———— *Quemvis perferre laborem*
> *Suadet, & inducit noctes vigilare serenas.*[43]

An amusingly ungrounded and omnipotent claim to authority is not far behind: "But I here think fit to lay hold on that great and honourable Privilege of being the *Last Writer*; I claim an absolute Authority in Right, as the *freshest Modern*, which gives me a Despotick Power over all authors before me."[44] Swift's tale-teller is a would-be author who intends to win the battle of the books by fiat. He makes a claim to literary authority that parodies the strategies by which belated would-be prophets, especially those from the revolutionary era, negotiated their access to public attention. The result is a rhetoric of mania: but the enthusiastic themes of divine intervention and social levelling, as illustrated in Coppe's Ranter tracts, have become a "modern" contempt for the Ancients and a triumphalist sense of fashionable virtuosity that Swift represents as a cultural revolution.

Another example of Swift's combinatory satire turns on his parody of the egalitarian rhetoric of enthusiastic fusion. Early in the *Tale*, the narrator insists that the reader can understand him only through a total identification – indeed, a sort of manic fusion – with his exact circumstances at the time of writing. He holds to an extreme version of what some have called the "biographical fallacy":

I hold fit to lay down this general Maxim. Whatever Reader desires to have a thorow Comprehension of an Author's Thoughts, cannot take a better Method, than by putting himself into the Circumstances and Postures of Life, that the Writer was in, upon every important Passage as it flow'd from his Pen; For this will induce a Parity and strict Correspondence of Idea's [*sic*] between the Reader and the Author.[45]

As the tale-teller continues, we are told not only that he sharpened his invention with hunger, but that he conceived his shrewdest passages while in bed, in a garret.[46] The "diligent Reader," according to his literal-minded

---

[42] Johnson, "Outlook," p. 208; Swift, *Tub*, pp. 124, 181–182.

[43] Swift, *Tub*, p. 123. As Guthkelch and Smith observe, this may be an echo of a Paracelsian author, John Heydon, who claimed on the title page of *The Rosie Crucian Infallible Axiomata* (1660) to be "a Servant of God, and Secretary of Nature" (*Tub*, p. 356).

[44] *Ibid.*, p. 130.

[45] *Ibid.*, p. 44.

[46] *Ibid.*

logic, must duplicate these exact circumstances: consumption must mirror production. The image of the starving writer's garret thus joins the Bedlamite's cell in a series of claustrophobic images of incarceration. Although Hopewell Selby argues that these "fictions of confinement" express Swift's anxieties about epistemological imprisonment,[47] Swift's satirical purpose is primarily to provoke a reactionary backlash – a reassertion of the social boundaries of the "gentle reader" against the likes of a Fox, a Bunyan, a Coppe, a Trapnel. Thus the tale-teller's manifestation of class-consciousness is carefully controlled by Swift so as to reduce the reader's potential for cross-class identification with certain writers and certain circumstances of deprivation and incarceration. The emptiness of the tale-telling Hack's stomach, then, is yet another emblem of his nothingness, his jejune existence as an author. Such an author, one must infer, should silence himself, should assume the burden of his public nullity. The mockery of confinement in *A Tale of a Tub* is thus linked to a more general mockery of poverty.

The satire in *A Tale of a Tub* ultimately depends on attacking the agency, as authors, of enthusiasts and hacks. The *Tale* thus gives us a sampling of something like automatic writing, but not in the honorific sense assigned to it either by inspired enthusiasts from the Cromwellian era or twentieth-century surrealists; the automatism is, rather, an exact parallel to what Swift calls the "mechanical operation of the spirit." As the self-proclaimed "secretary to the universe," Swift's Hack claims to be the amanuensis of one sort of cosmic power; as a starving hack, however, he is actually driven by the drearier reality of economic necessity. *A Tale of a Tub* seems to write itself, as if the author were the mere function of unmediated economic pressures. Having already admitted the influence of hunger on his writing, the tale-teller goes on to admit that "in general, the whole Work was begun, continued, and ended, under a long Course of Physick, and a great want of Money."[48] If this passage seems to evoke Trapnel and other female prophets who fasted during their prophetic trances, it also points forward. For *A Tale of a Tub* dramatizes the process by which a *modern* text is produced – and, indeed, specifically mass-produced – by a crass hack, whose utter lack of authorial integrity is the chief challenge to interpretation. The text seems to fall apart moment by moment as it comes under the sway of impersonal or superhuman forces. The experience of "enthusiasm" is thus translated, across class lines, and into "modern" times, as the overwhelming need to write for money.

Swift "hacks" the *topoi* of manic enthusiasm precisely by playing on its paradoxical tropes of the writer's agency. As the following two passages demonstrate, he seems well acquainted with the mode's tendency to disclaim

[47] Hopewell Selby, "The cell and the garret: fictions of confinement in Swift's satires and prose writings," in *Studies in Eighteenth-Century Culture*, vol. VI, ed. Ronald C. Rosbottom (Madison: University of Wisconsin Press, 1977), pp. 133–156.
[48] *Ibid.*

its actions. The first is Fifth Monarchist Mary Cary/Rand's well-known image describing her own utter passivity in the writing process: "I am a very weake, and unworthy instrument, and have not done this work by any strength of my owne, but have been often made sensible, that I could doe no more herein, (wherein any light, or truth could appeare) of myselfe, then a pencil, or pen can do, when no hand guides it …"[49] The second is Swift's version of such supernatural "ghost-writing." As the tale-teller boasts very near the end of the *Tale*, "I am now trying an Experiment very frequent among Modern Authors; which is to *write upon Nothing*; When the Subject is utterly exhausted, to let the Pen still move on; by some called, the Ghost of Wit, delighting to Walk after the Death of its Body."[50] The pun here on *subject* – as topic, as authorial agent – highlights the idea of a writing process that is driven by impersonal economic forces. These inhuman forces are not mere themes of the book, but, through Swift's satiric self-reduction, its very ground, the place from which it speaks.

In conflating his two main targets, Swift seizes in particular on the highly ambiguous concept of originality. Swift's attack on plebeian agency in the *Tale* thus parodies the claims to originality, as grandiose and empty, of both enthusiasm and popular writing. "Modern" writing in *A Tale of a Tub* is represented as an appropriative economic process that attempts to conceal its grotesquely derivative origins through reference to superior penetration, depth, and "originality." The hack's grandiose claim to a peculiarly "penetrating" vision unwittingly reveals nothing more than his uncontrollable envy of the classic authors. Having patronized these Ancients for various supposed defects, he goes on exultantly to steal their ideas:

> I do affirm, that having carefully cut up *Humane Nature*, I have found a very strange, new, and important Discovery; That the Public Good of Mankind is performed by two Ways, *Instruction*, and *Diversion*. And I have farther proved in my said several Readings (which, perhaps, the World may one day see, if I can prevail on any Friend to steal a Copy, or on certain Gentlemen of my Admirers, to be very Importunate) that, as Mankind is now disposed, he receives much greater Advantage by being *Diverted* than *Instructed*.[51]

The tale-teller's unblushing reproduction of even such platitudes as "divert and instruct" reduces authorship to the merest plagiarism.

Originality, in the sense of claimed proximity to an origin, is likewise a key issue in the *Tale*'s allegory of organized religion. Picking up the "two sons" *topos* so prevalent in the rhetoric of sectarian formation, Swift, while adding a third son, turns its meaning against the radical Protestants. As a figure who refuses all mediations on principle, Jack the enthusiast represents "originality"

---

[49] Mary Cary/Rand, "To the reader," in *The Little Horns Doom and Downfall* (London, 1651).
[50] Swift, *Tub*, p. 208.
[51] *Ibid.*, p. 124.

at its most garish: he is a jack-o'-lantern, fueled by candles and flaming brandy ("Snap-Dragon"), and consumed with his own inner light.[52] Jack was "wont to say," as the narrator points out, "That *a Wise Man was his own Lanthorn.*"[53]

A sartorial trope, moreover, prepares for further travesties of unmediated "originality" by way of a parodic version of the "mere clothes" *topos* found in the Ranters' levelling discourse. The religious allegory is organized around the three brothers' "inheritance," by way of the "Father's Will," of their divinely fitted coats: the narrator's trope for the gospel legacy. The "mere clothes" *topos* then reappears in *A Tale of a Tub* in the tubbian narrator's exposition of the "clothes philosophy" attributed to a sect that worshipped tailors. (This is possibly a jab at the Muggletonians, given that their prophet Lodowick Muggleton, who lived until 1698, had been a tailor.) The sect, which held the universe to be "a large *Suit of Cloaths*,"[54] allows the tale-teller to ring various absurd changes on the apocalyptic themes of investiture and unveiling: man himself is a "*Micro-Coat*," honesty is a "*Pair of Shoes*," and – most memorably – conscience is "a *Pair of Breeches*, which, tho' a Cover for Lewdness as well as Nastiness, is easily slipt down for the Service of both."[55] Even the parody, however, is not without its own levelling force:

'Tis true indeed, that these Animals, which are vulgarly called *Suits of Cloaths*, or *Dresses*, do according to certain Compositions receive different Appellations. If one of them be trimm'd up with a Gold Chain, and a red Gown, and a white Rod, and a great Horse, it is called a *Lord-Mayor*; If certain Ermins and Furs be placed in Certain Position, we stile them a *Judge*, and so an apt conjunction of Lawn and black Sattin, we intitle a *Bishop*.[56]

The satire here seems, as so often in Swift, to cut two ways – as much against the beneficiaries of sartorial distinctions as against the tailor-worshipping sect. The "worldliness" of such distinctions is of course what eventually corrupts the three brothers. Led by Peter, who represents the Catholic Church, they adorn their coats with all manner of vain fripperies.

Jack's destructive zeal, however, inevitably turns against the excessive mediations of such sartorial frippery. This zeal is described in terms highly reminiscent of such enthusiastic exhortations as Abiezer Coppe's rhetoric of apocalyptic disrobing: "Wherefore, awake, awake, and shake off thy *filthy fleshly* garments; shake off Self; cast off thy carnall clouts, and put on thy beautiful garments."[57] According to Swift's tale-teller, such transgressions are

---

[52] *Ibid.*, p. 192.
[53] *Ibid.*
[54] *Ibid.*, p. 77.
[55] *Ibid.*, p. 78.
[56] *Ibid.*, p. 79.
[57] Abiezer Coppe, *Some Sweet Sips, of Some Spirituall Wine* (1649), in *A Collection of Ranter Writings from the 17th Century*, ed. Nigel Smith (London: Junction Books, 1983), p. 56.

both a mode of indecent exposure and a destructively schismatic tearing of the social fabric: "*Zeal* is never so highly obliged, as when you set it a *Tearing*: and *Jack*, who doated on that Quality in himself, allowed it at this time its full Swinge. Thus it happened, that stripping down a Parcel of *Gold Lace*, a little too hastily, he rent the *main Body* of his *Coat* from Top to Bottom ..."[58] Later Jack tries to persuade Martin to share his folly: "*Ah, Good Brother* Martin, said he, *do as I do, for the Love of God; Strip, Tear, Pull, Rent, Flay off all* ..."[59] Such zealous revelations clearly echo the dissecting and flaying gestures of modernity. The purifying and denuding gesture, according to such logic, leads merely to the lower body in all its supposed impurity: an "origin" of sorts, to be sure, but one all too mundane in the banality of its plumbing.

The *Tale*'s religious allegory goes on to depict a fixation on spiritual immediacy as the deluded concern of mud-hurling, urine-spraying sectaries. It is far from accidental, moreover, that the term *pranks*, linked to enthusiastic prophecy and street-theatre, reappears in the tale-teller's description of Jack's strange public conduct. According to Swift, what outlandish "pranks" prefigure is not prophetic discourse, but rather a grotesquely physical sort of outpouring:

WHEN he had some Roguish Trick to play, he would down with his Knees, up with his Eyes, and fall to Prayers, tho' in the midst of the Kennel. Then it was that those who understood his Pranks, would be sure to get far enough out of his Way; And whenever Curiosity attracted Strangers to Laugh, or to Listen; he would of a sudden, with one Hand out with his *Gear*, and piss full in their Eyes, and with the other, all to-bespatter them with Mud.[60]

Waste products are neither unique nor closely linked to a pure origin. To figure a discourse as featureless excrement is thus, among other things, to deny it any capacity for originality. The typically Swiftian scatology here expresses his scathing attitude toward discourse not backed up by political and economic power, not guaranteed by its access to official channels.

Further examples of Swift's "hacking" of enthusiasts abound in *A Tale of a Tub*, sometimes in all possible senses of the word. Consider the multi-layered passage in which Swift's tale-teller trots out his favorite commonplace, the "degeneration" *topos*. This parrots a hackneyed cliché harking back to the Renaissance "decay-of-nature" controversy, which Swift spoofs throughout *A Tale of a Tub* and *Gulliver's Travels*.[61] Here he laments, with phallic innuendo and sly reference to Puritan "roundheads," a sad decline in the size of men's

58 Swift, *Tub*, p. 138.
59 *Ibid.*, p. 139.
60 *Ibid.*, pp. 194–195.
61 See Johnson, "Outlook," pp. 61–63. The Brobdingnagians in *Gulliver's Travels* seem to have declined from "giant" ancestors; the mathematicians of Laputa are concerned that the sun is growing old. See *Prose Works of Jonathan Swift*, 14 vols., ed. Herbert Davis (Oxford: Basil Blackwell, 1935–1968), XI: *Gulliver's Travels*, pp. 137, 164–165.

ears: a sample, it appears, of his forthcoming book, the *General History of Ears*, which will treat a cruel king's "bloody Persecution" of oversized ears."[62] Although this passage mocks the "hacking" grotesqueries of judicial torture in general, it also parodies three elements specific to enthusiastic rhetoric. One is the Ranteresque pursuit of a "naked" religious ecstasy, like David dancing uncovered before handmaids; the second, the stark opposition of interior grace and exterior appearance; and the third, the stance of martyrdom especially common in Quaker historiography. The special cunning of Swift's satirical strategy, then, is that it operates at the point where the documentation of pathetic sufferings and trials, as a response to state-sponsored persecution, intersects with the Hack's ludicrous musings about the decline of ears:

For, if the only slitting of one *Ear* in a Stag, hath been found sufficient to propagate the defect thro' a whole Forest; Why should we wonder at the greatest Consequences of so many Loppings and Mutilations, to which the *Ears* of our Fathers and our own have been of late so much exposed: 'Tis true, indeed, that while this *Island* of ours, was under the *Dominion of Grace*, many Endeavours were made to improve the Growth of *Ears* once more among us. The Proportion of Largeness was not only lookt upon as an Ornament of the *Outward* Man, but as a Type of Grace in the Inward. Besides, it is held by the Naturalists, that if there be a Protuberancy of Parts in the *Superior* Region of the Body, as in the *Ears* and the *Nose*, there must be a Parity also in the *Inferior*. And therefore in that truly pious Age, the *Males* in every Assembly, according as they were gifted, appeared very forward in exposing their *Ears* to view, and the Regions about them.[63]

"Such was the progress of the *Saints*," the tale-teller concludes, after several more phallic innuendos, "for advancing the Size of that Member."[64]

The aim of the passage above is to ridicule, by desublimation, ascetic Puritan haircuts, exposing a supposed sexual displacement.[65] Swift's allusion here, in addition to the Biblical *topos* of the "uncircumcised ear,"[66] and to the fallacy that acquired characteristics can be genetically transmitted, is to the slitting of ears as a legal punishment for convicted libellers. This punishment was often used against Puritans in the mid-seventeenth century, sometimes more than once.[67] As the tale-teller cheerfully puts it, "some were slit, others

---

[62] Swift, *Tub*, p. 202.

[63] *Ibid.*, p. 201.

[64] *Ibid.*, p. 202.

[65] For the parallels between Swift's thought and the psychoanalytic concept of sublimation, see Norman O. Brown, "The excremental vision," rpt. in *Swift: A Collection of Critical Essays*, ed. Ernest Tuveson (Englewood Cliffs: Prentice Hall, 1964), pp. 31–54.

[66] In Jer. 6:10, the prophet rebukes those of his people who refuse to hearken to God's word for having "uncircumcised ears."

[67] Benjamin Brook recounts, for example, the redundant torture of the unfortunate Puritan polemicist William Prynne. Prynne, who had already had his ears cut off, was sentenced by the Star Chamber in 1637 to have the remainder of the stumps sawed off. In the words of Brook, "When he was delivered out of the pillory, and again brought upon the scaffold, the executioner cut off his ears in a most barbarous manner; during which, and while the blood was streaming in

cropt, and a great Number sliced off to the Stumps."[68] By his mock-praise of the Puritans for having cultivated large ears, Swift's narrator implies that they lack "circumcised ears" and that they have the ears of asses: in short, and in a sense that the book overdetermines, he *hacks* them.[69]

This passage about the over-developed "members" of Puritans looks back to an earlier one in which the tale-teller celebrates "modern" writing for its inventiveness on a single low topic:

What I mean, is that highly celebrated Talent among the *Modern* Wits, of deducing Similitudes, Allusions, and Applications, very Surprizing, Agreeable, and Apposite, from the *Pudenda* of either Sex, together with *their proper Uses*. And truly, having observed how little Invention bears any Vogue, besides what is derived into these *Channels*, I have sometimes had a Thought, That the happy Genius of our Age and Country, was prophetically held forth by that antient typical Description of the *Indian* Pygmies; whose Stature did not exceed above two Foot; *Sed quorum pudenda crassa*, & *ad talos usque pertingentia.*[70]

The use of "pygmies" here, as figures of grotesque smallness, shows that the young Swift was not above a cheap laugh. Figured thus, with oversized genitals supposedly reaching to their ankles, modern wits are represented as tiny, inferior, and unable either to conceal or to sublimate their over-whelming physicality.

Swift likewise implies a parallel between the enthusiastic project of non-linear reading of Biblical texts, sometimes by analogy with the right-to-left orientation of Hebrew writings,[71] and the easy "modern" way of acquiring knowledge "without the Fatigue of *Reading* or *Thinking*": that is, by "reading backward" from indexes.[72] Two modes of reading are thus linked as self-serving and arbitrary. The first hint of such interpretative aggression appears in the religious allegory, where the allegorical reading of scriptural passages entails a shattering of the textual surface into a veritable alphabet soup.[73] Such interpretation is performed merely in order to rationalize behavior clearly forbidden by the "Father's Will." Hence the anagram-matic scrabbling that permits the trio of brothers, plucking the individual

every direction, he manifested the greatest constancy and composure of mind." Benjamin Brook, *The Lives of the Puritans*, 3 vols. (London: 1813), III, p. 54.

[68] Swift, *Tub*, p. 202.

[69] The *Dictionary of Cant* (1699) demonstrates the semantic drift of this term into the literary arena, listing as possible eighteenth-century meanings of *Hacks* the following: *Hackney-whores*, "Common Prostitutes"; *Hackney-Horses*, "to be let to any body"; *Hackney-Scriblers*, "Poor Hireling Mercenary Writers." Cited in MacDermott, "Grub," p. 160.

[70] Swift, *Tub*, p. 147.

[71] This same analogy is made explicit in *A Discourse Concerning the Mechanical Operation of the Spirit*, in Swift, *Tub*, p. 283.

[72] Swift, *Tub*, p. 145.

[73] For a broader discussion of Swift's deconstructive wordplay, see Deborah Baker Wyrick, *Jonathan Swift and the Vested Word* (Chapel Hill: The University of North Carolina Press, 1988), ch. 3.

letters S-H-O-U-L-D-E-R from their surrounding words, to justify putting shoulder-knots on their coats.[74] Lord Peter's fragmenting interpretations clearly parody Catholic casuistry; but they are reminiscent as well of the strategies of, to name only a few anagrammatic enthusiasts, Thomas Tany, Lady Eleanor Davies/Douglas, and Abiezer Coppe. Such violence eventually modulates, according to the combinatory logic of Swift's satirical device, into the "modern" practice of knowing a book only by its index, "by which the whole Book is governed and turned, like *Fishes* by the *Tail.*"[75] What follows is a manic catalogue of far-fetched analogies for this backward practice:

Thus Physicians discover the State of the whole Body, by consulting only what comes from *Behind*. Thus Men catch Knowledge by throwing their *Wit* on the *Posteriors* of a book, as Boys do Sparrows with flinging *Salt* upon their *Tails*. Thus Human Life is best understood by the wise man's Rule of *Regarding the End*. Thus are the Sciences found like *Hercules*'s Oxen, by *tracing them Backwards*.[76]

As a parable about hermeneutic aggression toward malleable texts, Swift's satire seems definitive. As Carole Fabricant points out, Swift's exploration of hermeneutic ambiguity is not primarily about the fear of indeterminacy; rather, it points to the techniques by which arbitrary authority can intervene to fix, appropriate, and prematurely close the meaning of a text for its own purposes.[77] What one must register, nevertheless, is the fact that in the case of Swift's "materialist analysis" of enthusiastic exegesis, he generally takes aim against the groups most exploited by the material conditions of the economic *status quo*.

Swift's appropriation of the disjunctive "stammering tongue" of enthusiastic prophecy affords him still further ammunition with which to mock "modern" literary production. The conspicuous "absence" of the writing subject is an ambiguous sign. Swift seizes upon the ambiguity for his satiric purpose, which is to merge, and thus mutually discredit, two popular discourses that disrupt traditional notions about the autonomy of authorship. For the portentous breaking of discursive form, according to Swift, often masquerades as a disguise for social ambition and change that he deems illegitimate. If form implies a certain commitment through time, and thus is a fiction of duration and tradition, then the absence or breaking of form can be used to signify the presence of originality. Such transgressions themselves, in a familiar paradox, can be codified as a rhetoric of originary presence: hence the pentecostal practice of glossolalia, and hence the self-interrupting style of enthusiasm.

---

[74] Swift, *Tub*, p. 85.
[75] *Ibid.*, p. 145.
[76] *Ibid.*
[77] Carole Fabricant, "The battle of the ancients and (post)moderns: rethinking Swift through contemporary perspectives," *The Eighteenth Century: Theory and Interpretation* 32:3 (1991), p. 269.

It is precisely in these terms, the claim that a formal absence bespeaks a numinous presence, that Swift's satire uses literary form to attack contemporary writing. More specifically, *A Tale of a Tub* parodies the rhetorical machinery of the literary sublime, and above all, of the modern or belated sublime. The symbol for both factionalism and poetry in a sublime mode is the wooden ladder, because, in the Hack's words, "Orators do *perorare* with a Song; and because climbing up by slow Degrees, Fate is sure to turn them off before they can reach within many Steps of the Top: And because it is a Preferment attained by transferring of Propriety, and a confounding of *Meum* and *Tuum*."[78] Something like textbook sublimity is mocked here, both in its methodical elaboration of rules for "ascending the sky" and in its goal of imposing on the reader a rhapsodic identification with the self-elevating text. This gallows ladder, this worm-eaten wooden "oratorical machine," represents *both* Poetry and Faction, moreover, because Swift insistently conflates modern literature with mid-century enthusiasm. Indeed, embedded in this passage is a mini-narrative about the social climbing of the "monied interest," its transfer of property/propriety, and its confounding of mine and thine. The latter point, of course, is the charge constantly hurled at Quakers for their pronominal levelling. The "Battle of the Books" that Swift wages here makes visible precisely "the fatal revolution" bemoaned by Goldsmith: a bourgeois revolution won militarily in 1649, consolidated politically in 1688, and continuing – as market forces redefined the social relations of literary production – on the cultural level.

That revolution Swift represents as an all-pervasive desublimation in which the material and bodily stratum of things insists on emerging into the foreground. Swift finally literalizes this desublimation as nothing more than the portentous absence of text:

The present Argument is the most abstracted that ever I engaged in, it strains my Faculties to their highest Stretch; and I desire the Reader to attend with the utmost Perpensity; For, I now proceed to unravel this knotty Point. There is in Mankind a certain   *   *   *   *   *   *   *   *   *   *   *   *

*   *   *   *   *   *   *   *   *   *   *   *   *   *

*   *   *   *   *   *   *   *   *   *   *   *   *   *

*   *   *   *   *   *   *   *   *   *   *   *   *   *

*   *   *   *   *   *   *   *   *   *   *   *   *   *

*   *   *   *   *   *   *   *   *   *   *   *   *   *

After many more asterisks, this passage concludes, "And this I take to be a clear Solution of the Matter."[79] The mock note in the margin of this passage, *Hic multa desiderantur* ("Here many words are wanting"), is of course double-edged.

---

[78] Swift, *Tub*, pp. 62–63.
[79] *Ibid.*, p. 170.

Modernity ultimately appears in *A Tale of a Tub* as a metalanguage that cannot keep a proper distance from its object language. Thus the passages in the *Tale* "about" enthusiasm invariably collapse, through Swift's device of satirical conflation, "into" enthusiasm. Swift's narrator proves to be a "modern" scholar of enthusiasm; like Longinus, who was supposed to have achieved sublimity in the very act of describing it, he becomes the thing he describes. Analyzing Jack's raging enthusiasm, he fuses with it:

However, for this Meddly of Humor, [Jack] made a Shift to find a very plausible Name, honoring it with the title of *Zeal*; which is, perhaps, the most significant Word that hath been ever yet produced in any Language; As, I think, I have proved in my excellent *Analytical* Discourse upon that Subject; wherein I have deduced a *Histori-theo-physi-logical* Account of *Zeal*, shewing how it first proceeded from a *Notion* into a *Word*, and from thence in a hot Summer, ripened into a *tangible* Substance. This Work containing three large Volumes in Folio, I design very shortly to publish by the *Modern* way of *Subscription*, not doubting but the Nobility and Gentry of the Land will give me all possible Encouragement, having already had such a Taste of what I am able to perform.[80]

On the one hand, we have *zeal*, the author's enthusiasm; on the other, his self-important advertisement for the book's subscribers. Enthusiasm thus modulates into a "modern" combination of arrogance, maniacal pedantry, and naked material interest. It is a satire specifically aimed at, and constituted by, the paradoxical rhetoric of enunciation common among enthusiasts.

Given Swift's customary contempt for *idées reçues*, it is rather disappointing to recognize that the lens through which he produces his debased view of the enthusiastic style is, finally, nothing more profound than the old *topos* of the "body politic."[81] This tired commonplace, indeed, almost certainly borrowed in the version expounded in More's *Enthusiasmus Triumphatus*, is what ultimately holds together the disparate objects of satire in *A Tale of a Tub*. The motifs of bodily exposure simultaneously figure degraded literary production and elaborate the class politics of the "organic" but hierarchically stratified body politic, threatened with an "epidemic" of vapors issuing up from the lower faculties. Mutilation and excrement – implicitly opposed to a supposedly lost or vanishing wholeness and purity – are thus the key images in Swift for "explaining" plebeian alienation, on the one hand, and, on the other, for attacking the reduction of high-culture artifacts to commodities with exchange value.

---

[80] *Ibid.*, p. 137.

[81] The "body-politic" *topos* is further discussed in Chapter 2. For Swift's lifelong use of the body – state analogy, see Johnson, "Outlook," p. 73. It is worth noting that Swift eventually came to mock some features of this rhetoric. In Book III of *Gulliver's Travels* (1726), we find a "political projector" in the Academy of Lagado whose particular intellectual dysfunction is an overly literal interpretation of the "body-politic" analogy. Thus he proposes to cure political disorders by treating "Senates and great Councils" with a lengthy and highly emetic catalogue of emetics. See *Gulliver's Travels*, in Davis, *Prose Works*, XI, pp. 187–188.

A Tale of a Tub thus enacts stylistically the equation Swift would later make, as the chief author of *The Examiner* in 1710–1711, between revolution and physiological madness. Having devoted himself to putting out the party line of Queen Anne's Tory ministry on a weekly basis,[82] Swift uses a typical variant of the "body politic" *topos* in *The Examiner* No. 24 to equate revolution with the displacement upward of bodily "humours":

> Besides, all great Changes have the same Effect upon Commonwealths that Thunder hath upon Liquors; making the *Dregs* fly up to the Top: The Lowest *Plebeians* rise to the Head of Affairs, and there preserve themselves by representing the Nobles and other Friends to the Old Government, as Enemies to the Publick ... By these and the like Arts, in Conjunction with a great Depravity of Manners and a weak or corrupt Administration, the Madness of the People hath risen to such a Height, as to break in Pieces the whole Frame of the best instituted Governments ... In our own Island we had a great Example of a long Madness in the People, kept up by a thousand Artifices like intoxicating Medicines, until the Constitution was destroyed; yet the Malignity being spent, and the Humour exhausted that served to foment it; before the Usurpers could fix upon a new Scheme, the People suddenly recovered, and peaceably restored the old Constitution.[83]

From microcosm to macrocosm, everything has its established place in a natural, divinely ordained hierarchy, which can only be upset by artificially induced madness, by a subjective "revolution" in which diseased plebeian vapors overthrow aristocratic "reason." It is indeed a very different appropriation of madness than the amiable reversals explored in Erasmus and Shakespeare, whereby "folly" eventually demonstrates its own antithetical wisdom.

It must be conceded that the sheer instability of Swift's irony in *A Tale of a Tub* does permit occasional glimpses of a more authentically subversive textual politics. The satiric gesture of appropriation – by which one creates a hybrid discourse, a negation that also incorporates its low "Others" – is necessarily fraught with certain ambiguities.[84] Indeed, in a text that seems to dramatize its own abandonment to something akin to possession, the question of Swift's own authorial control, emanating from a stable ideological position, must inevitably arise. An unforgettable example of this unstable irony is found in the tale-teller's praise of delusion and self-deception as a defense against the levelling tendency of "modern" rationalism: "How shrunk is every Thing, as it appears in the Glass of Nature? So, that if it were not for the Assistance of Artificial *Mediums*, false

---

[82] For a detailed account of this era, see F. P. Lock, *Swift's Tory Politics* (Newark: University of Delaware Press, 1983).

[83] Jonathan Swift, *The Examiner* 24 (1710), in Davis, *Prose Works*, III, p. 65.

[84] For a treatment of such discursive hybridity as a generic feature of the grotesque in Augustan satire, see Peter Stallybrass and Allon White, *The Politics and Poetics of Transgression* (Ithaca: Cornell University Press, 1986), pp. 105–118.

Lights, refracted Angles, Varnish, and Tinsel; there would be a mighty Level in the Felicity and Enjoyments of Mortal Men."[85] The irony of praising delusion seems obvious enough; yet the reference to the levelling effect of mere nature suggests the further and more perplexing irony that unvarnished truth may in fact be undesirable. "If this were seriously considered by the World," the tale-teller solemnly continues, "as I have a certain Reason to suspect it hardly will; Men would no longer reckon among their high Points of Wisdom, the Art of exposing weak Sides, and publishing Infirmities; an Employment in my Opinion, neither better nor worse than that of *Unmasking*, which I think, has never been allowed fair Usage, either in the *World* or the *Play-House*."[86] This is the uncanny irony of a skepticism that is having it both ways.[87] On the one hand, the cutting and mangling effects of "officious" reason[88] are linked to the violent stripping activities of enthusiastic purification. Hence the justly famous line, "Last Week I saw a Woman *flay'd*, and you will hardly believe, how much it altered her Person for the worse."[89] This remarkably grotesque image – a cruel literalization of the enthusiastic exhortation to "shed one's fleshly garments" – is influenced by the anatomical imagery of "modern" surgeons, who were busily dissecting human cadavers and vivisecting various animals. It goes a long way toward discouraging all forms of "unmasking." On the other hand, however, this voice goes on to recommend, as an antidote to such overly rational demystifications, an impossible choice: "The Serene Peaceful State of being a Fool among Knaves."[90]

Further memorable moments in which *A Tale of a Tub* seems to cross over into something like enthusiasm appear in the book's risky punning. An extended example figures in the early pages of Swift's religious allegory. How should we read the outburst of manic clanging that accompanies the story of Lord Peter's roaring, pissing, farting bulls? Relentlessly recycling his favorite "degeneration" *topos*, Swift's tale-teller first tells us that the bulls' feet – "extreamely vitiated by the Rust of Time" – have declined from brass to lead.[91] Attempting then for the sake of his allegory to focus on Papal Bulls, the tale-teller moves associatively from the mythic bulls who guarded the Golden Fleece to Papal Bulls to hobgoblins known as "Bull-Beggars" to

---

[85] Swift, *Tub*, p. 172.

[86] *Ibid.*, pp. 172–173.

[87] Michael McKeon situates Swift within a broader historical dialectic of "double negation" that renders his politics strangely ambiguous. See Michael McKeon, *The Origins of the English Novel 1600–1740* (Baltimore: The Johns Hopkins University Press, 1987), p. 61. Such extreme skepticism, though analogous to conservative ideology, nevertheless may finally undermine it by pointing to "the unavailability of narrative truth as such" (p. 119).

[88] Swift, *Tub*, p. 173.

[89] *Ibid.*

[90] *Ibid.*, p. 174.

[91] *Ibid.*, p. 111.

English Bulldogs – the morpheme "bull" providing the only link.[92] Swift intends us to think as well of the meaning of "bull" as nonsense.[93]

Most manic of all, however, is the later pun-by-Biblical-quotation by which the mad Hack indicates that a hypothetical inmate of Bedlam is a cuckold: "like *Moses, Ecce cornuta erat ejus facies*" (Behold, his face was horned).[94] This alludes to the "horned Moses" tradition, itself based on Jerome's mistranslation of the Hebrew for "shining." The flirtation with blasphemy in such wildly associational punning positions the author perilously close to a Ranteresque practice of giddy wordplay. This latter passage, indeed, is attacked by William Wotton;[95] it is doubtless among those that finally compelled Swift to write a prefatory apology admitting to several youthful sallies "which from the Grave and the Wise may deserve a Rebuke."[96]

Swift's lifelong enjoyment of puns and similar verbal games is well known. Both his "Pun-ic Wars" with Thomas Sheridan and his affectionately smutty punning in the *Journal to Stella* (1710–1713) might invite comparison with such passages as this.[97] In the context of his private correspondence with Esther Johnson, however, the use of "manic" wordplay signifies intimacy. It is a lover's coded babble, a deliberately regressive "little language" that constitutes a shared private world – oddly mediated in this case, to be sure, because "Presto" (Italian for "swift") nevertheless insists on invoking a second reader, the chaperone-like presence of Rebecca Dingley. In the public world of the *Tale*, however, such associational logic is intended to signify idiosyncrasy in its most negative connotations: privacy as deprivation, as the glaring solitude of madness. The density, allusiveness, and indeterminacy of such disinhibited wordplay are, in the public arena, intended as further signs of a strangely fragmented and "modern" sensibility.

Such density, allusiveness, and indeterminacy are of course no longer so odd to the postmodern reader, and it thus becomes arguable, to some extent, that, in Ellen Pollak's words, "the very violence of Swift's resistance to transition becomes a form of capitulation in his work." In this view, Swift "managed to mourn the passing of a culture in the very act of becoming a modern writer."[98]

---

[92] *Ibid.*, pp. 110–113.

[93] According to the OED ("bull", sb., 4), the word meant a nonsensical jest or a self-contradiction as early as 1630. The etymology of this meaning is unknown. Although this word seems obsolete, it has been fortuitously replaced, or perhaps combined with, the twentieth-century American usage that equates worthless verbiage with bullshit.

[94] Swift, *Tub*, p. 177.

[95] William Wotton, "Observations upon *The [sic] Tale of a Tub*," in Swift, *Tub*, pp. 322–323.

[96] Swift, *Tub*, p. 4.

[97] See David Nokes, *Jonathan Swift, A Hypocrite Reversed* (Oxford: Oxford University Press, 1985), pp. 49–51, 60, 117–118. See also Susan L. Manning, "Mirth and melancholy: the generative language of fantasy in Swift and Smart," *Swift Studies* 7 (1992), pp. 54–68.

[98] Ellen Pollak, *The Poetics of Sexual Myth: Gender and Ideology in the Verse of Swift and Pope* (Chicago: The University of Chicago Press, 1985), p. 172.

Traugott similarly argues that the so-called Hack, considered as a locus of exuberant energy, really is Swift, or at least Swift minus his superego: "Though speaking in tongues, though playing the fool, the author of the *Tale* is always Swift, but Swift relieved of responsibility and its decorums and hence liberated and energized."[99] The Hack persona, in this view, is not only a satiric target, but also a fool's license to transgress, an alibi for Swift's imagination.

Such interpretations suggest above all the extent to which the gesture of violent discursive appropriation, a key weapon in Augustan satire generally, can itself, in the end, tend to reappropriate the "author." The very mechanisms of projection and identification that permit one to ventriloquize as the "Other" bespeak complicity. It is the stylistic metaphor of "madness" that enables Swift's ironic gesture, his supposed demonstration that popular culture is pathological. And it is the rhetorical inventiveness, energy, and demonic vehemence of the manic mode that finally begins to produce him – the author whose signature is above all a certain *negative excess* – even as he reproduces it. A more adequate knowledge of the manic mode thus provides a more nuanced perspective for describing the complex affiliations and commitments of Swift's socio-political location.

Can Swift then be celebrated as a "manic" author? Although it is crucial to honor the "negative excess" in Swift's appropriation of the manic, an interpretation committed to even a minimal respect for the historical reality behind the "madness" in *A Tale of a Tub* cannot conclude on so entirely conciliatory a note. Because Swift's critics tend to overlook or play down the class dimension of the manic style, a language of pathology has often been allowed to substitute, beyond a certain limit, for political analysis.[100] Edward Said, in his otherwise valuable analysis of Swift's *oeuvre* as the work of an opportunistic and meddling local agitator, thus refers to the Swiftian tale-teller as "manic": a term which in fact serves to mark a limit beyond which his analysis cannot go.[101] So too with the attempt in Traugott's otherwise sensitive criticism of the *Tale* to trace a path from snobbery to subversion. If such a path exists, one can never find it merely by extracting from the *Tale* an ahistorical concept of "madness" as, in Traugott's phrase, "the rock-bottom, universal, and irreducible

---

[99] Traugott, "*Tale*," p. 88.
[100] Frederik N. Smith thus makes an elaborately unhistorical comparison between *A Tale of a Tub* and twentieth-century theories about the language of schizophrenia. See Frederik N. Smith, *Language and Reality in Swift's A Tale of a Tub* (Columbus: Ohio State University Press, 1979), pp. 93–124.
[101] Edward Said, "Swift's Tory anarchy," in *The World, the Text, and the Critic* (Cambridge, Mass.: Harvard University Press, 1983), p. 56. Said's seeming indifference toward class oppression is scrutinized in Aijaz Ahmad, "*Orientalism* and after: ambivalence and metropolitan location in Edward Said," in *In Theory: Classes, Nations, Literatures* (London: Verso, 1992), pp. 159–220.

narcissism and aggression of all men."[102] All of these critics lose sight of the text's use of "madness" as stylistic metaphor and rhetorical weapon in the British class struggle.

It is understandable that Said, an admirably engaged public intellectual, expresses admiration for Swift's excruciating awareness of the temporal ironies to which his own time-bound and contingent interventions were necessarily subject.[103] He wraps up this theme as follows: "Ahead of his critics, Swift is always aware – and troubles the reader with the awareness – that what he is doing above all is *writing* in a world of power."[104] Swift's undeniable brilliance notwithstanding, however, this latter point should not be reduced to an abstract question of "awareness." For Swift is himself the supreme master of the intellectual cooptation of topics and ideas. The contextual and contingent nature of written texts; their situatedness in, and by, and with, and against economic and political power: it is precisely this abstract "truth" that Swift coopts in *A Tale of a Tub* for largely reactionary purposes. Indeed, Swift's satire should warn against assuming that a contextual approach – or any particular approach – is essentially progressive. For *A Tale of a Tub* demonstrates that an analysis *selectively* exposing material determinations can be coopted for a fiercely elitist political agenda.

Although I agree that "Tory" is often a reductive label for Swift's views, especially with regard to his later critiques of imperialism, it is crucial to keep the class animosity that fuels *A Tale of a Tub* steadily in view. Such a focus makes one skeptical that *A Tale of a Tub* is sufficiently subversive in its particular effects to counterbalance the global impact of Swift's pathologizing strategy. Swift does reproduce the disjunctive and destabilizing manic style; but the point is that he does so while simultaneously elaborating on several fronts the venerable *topos* of the "body politic." This is how *A Tale of a Tub* does its intended cultural work of establishing an influential set of terms, a pathologizing framework, within which enthusiastic rhetoric will be misread, misinterpreted, and misremembered.

As we refine our sense of Swift's literary career, it may seem increasingly crucial, as Fabricant argues, to mark a decisive break between the politics promoted by Swift before and after 1715: a break that marks, as she persuasively argues, "a general movement from a hegemonic to a counter-hegemonic outlook."[105] *Gulliver's Travels*, the greatest satire of the eighteenth century, is the masterwork of an engaged anti-colonial

---

[102] Traugott, "*Tale*," p. 122.
[103] Said, "Tory," p. 63.
[104] Edward Said, "Swift as intellectual," in *World*, p. 87.
[105] Fabricant, "Battle," p. 259.

activist.[106] *A Tale of a Tub*, however, written while Swift was at Moor Park, is another matter. In perfecting a strategy of pathologizing enthusiasm, the *Tale* contributes to that very mode of resolute patrician deafness that the "loud voice" of mania was designed to overcome.

[106] For detailed discussion of the progressive features of Swift's critiques of imperialism, see Laura Brown, "Reading race and gender: Jonathan Swift," *Eighteenth Century Studies* 23:4 (1990), pp. 425–443; Clement Hawes, "Three times round the globe: Gulliver and colonial discourse," *Cultural Critique* 18 (1991), pp. 187–214; and Wolfgang Zach, "Jonathan Swift and colonialism," in *Reading Swift: Papers from the Second Münster Symposium in Jonathan Swift*, eds. Richard H. Rodino and Hermann J. Real (Munich: Wilhelm Fink Verlag, 1993), pp. 91–99.

PART III

Challenging liminality

5

Scribe-evangelist: popular writing and enthusiasm in Smart's *Jubilate Agno*

For I am the Lord's News-Writer – the scribe-evangelist...

Christopher Smart, *Jubilate Agno*, B 327

Eighteenth-century enthusiasm has provided the terrain for a classic debate among historiographers: namely, whether or not the Methodist revival somehow inhibited a second English revolution on the French model. Historians thus disagree as to the extent to which Methodism can be understood as the containment of an older and more radical tradition. As is well known, the eulogy delivered at John Wesley's funeral "stressed the leavening influence of Methodism in a politically restive situation,"[1] implying that Wesley had helped to prevent revolution. Methodism can thus be seen as little more than a massive cooptation of plebeian energy for conservative and disciplinary purposes.[2] A usefully nuanced contribution to this debate emerges in the historiography of Bernard Semmel, who emphasizes the ways in which Methodism did nevertheless produce significant popular reforms. What Semmel stresses is, above all, the supple and fence-straddling nature of mid-Georgian evangelical enthusiasm:

The Methodists saw themselves not as a danger to the established order, but as a catalyst for evangelizing and revitalizing what was widely regarded as a sluggish church, more and more given to the preaching of a flat "enlightened" religion, while at the same time shielding the state from the unsettling effects emanating from the preaching of religious Enthusiasm. That they were largely successful in this was in a

[1] Frank Whaling, Introduction, in *John and Charles Wesley: Selected Prayers, Hymns, Journal Notes, Sermons, Letters and Treatises*, The Classics of Western Spirituality Series (New York: Paulist Press, 1981), p. 57. For more particulars about John Wesley's politics, see Anthony Armstrong, *The Church of England, the Methodists and Society 1700–1850* (Totowa, New Jersey: Rowman and Littlefield, 1973), pp. 72–102; and Henry Abelove, *The Evangelist of Desire: John Wesley and the Methodists* (Stanford, California: Stanford University Press, 1990).

[2] See Eric Hobsbawm, "Methodism and the threat of revolution in Britain," rpt. in *Labouring Men: Studies in the History of Labour* (London: Weidenfeld and Nicolson, 1968), pp. 22–33. See also E. P. Thompson, *The Making of the English Working Class* (New York: Vintage Books, 1966), pp. 41–46, 53–54, 350–394. This debate revisits issues originally raised in 1906 by Elie Halévy's monograph "La naissance du Méthodisme en Angleterre." See Elie Halévy, *The Birth of Methodism in England*, trans. and ed. Bernard Semmel (Chicago: The University of Chicago Press, 1971).

good part a consequence of their ability to make the appeal and wield the discipline of both sect and church.[3]

Much of the evangelical revival, even as it created separate organizations and distinct theological emphases, remained officially within the Church of England. Operating inside the belly of a more powerful beast – a thoroughly consolidated and self-consciously "enlightened" Anglican hegemony – mid-century enthusiasm was thus, out of historical necessity, a more equivocal phenomenon than the radical Puritanism of Cromwell's era: rife at its very heart, as Semmel says, with "real ambiguities and contradictions."[4]

It is clear that the Methodist revivals of the mid-Georgian period did renew certain oppositional themes. For such enthusiasm not only recalled the millenarian "French prophets" of the recent past, but also awakened unwelcome cultural memories of the more overtly oppositional seventeenth-century separatists.[5] The intense emotionalism, the convulsionary paroxysms, the large crowds, the practice of lay ministry (including preaching by women up until 1803), the field-preaching in defiance of the Anglican parish system – these aspects of Methodism released strong popular fervor, and aroused corresponding anxieties among the elite. An unsigned contribution to *The Connoisseur* in 1755 lightly voices such patrician unease about plebeian religious practices: "It is observed by the French, that a cat, a priest, and an old woman, are sufficient to constitute a religious sect in England."[6] The author continues in a straightforwardly patrician vein, complaining about "plebeian" pretensions to religious knowledge:

So universally, it seems, are learning and genius diffused through this island, that the lowest plebeians are deep casuists in matters of faith as well as politics; and so many and wonderful are the new lights continually breaking in among us, that we daily make fresh discoveries, and strike out unbeaten paths to future happiness...The most extraordinary tenets of religion are very successfully propagated under the sanction of the leathern apron instead of the cassock; every corner of the town has a barber,

---

3   Bernard Semmel, *The Methodist Revolution* (New York: Basic Books, Inc., 1973), p. 21. In the same vein, Harriet Guest usefully describes Wesleyan Methodism as an "unstable dialectic." Harriet Guest, *A Form of Sound Words: The Religious Poetry of Christopher Smart* (Oxford: Clarendon Press, 1989), p. 99.

4   Semmel, *Methodist*, p. 4.

5   For some of the links between the French Prophets and the Methodist Awakening, see Hillel Schwartz, *The French Prophets: The History of a Millenarian Group in Eighteenth-Century England* (Berkeley: University of California Press, 1980), especially pp. 202–210. For some of the links between Methodism and radical Puritanism, see Dean Freiday, "The relationship of Quakerism to Methodism," in *Barclays's Apology in Modern English* (Elberon, New Jersey, 1967), pp. xxxiv-xli. George Whitefield, as Freiday points out (p. xxxvi), returned to Methodism after having been a Quaker for a while.

6   Unsigned essay, *The Connoisseur* 61 (1755), in *The British Essayists*, XXV, ed. Alexander Chalmers (Boston: Little, Brown, and Company, 1856), p. 339.

mason, bricklayer, or some other handicraft teacher; and there are almost as many sects in this metropolis, as there are parish churches.[7]

The author's sarcastic allusion to the irruption of many and wonderful "new lights" probably refers specifically to the newest generation of enthusiasts, the Methodists.[8] The same author, in a final flourish of patrician indignation, goes on to accuse domestic servants of using Methodist piety as a cloak for laziness: "neglecting their common business," in his words, "under the pretext of performing acts of supererogation."[9] It is some measure of the social and psychic distance that Smart was shortly to travel in *Jubilate Agno* that the editors and chief writers of *The Connoisseur* were Smart's literary cronies Bonnell Thornton and George Colman.[10]

The ambiguities of the Methodist project – Elie Halévy calls eighteenth-century Methodism "the High Church of Nonconformity"[11] – provide a useful backdrop against which to set Christopher Smart's particular negotiations with the enthusiastic mode. Smart was not, lest I be misunderstood, a sectarian. He does not voice a fully coherent system of alternative doctrines that broke self-consciously with those of the Church. The point, rather, is that Smart, in the context of a growing evangelical revival,[12] eclectically adopted many elements of an available and durable enthusiastic rhetoric. And though Smart did not intend to stray from the Church of England, he nevertheless belonged to a social and doxological borderland. His plans for radical liturgical reform, based on his own translation of the Psalter; his celebration of street-preaching; his interest in congregational hymn-singing; his evangelical emphasis on free grace, experiential zeal, and national purification; his belief in witchcraft; his "Bibliolatry"; his fascination with ecstatic dancing; and even his outbursts of indignation at social stratification: all of these elements point to a rhetorical ethos far more affiliated with evangelical enthusiasm – far more vitalized and shaped "from below" – than is commonly recognized.

---

[7] *Ibid.*

[8] According to the OED, *New Light* became a term for novel theological doctrines as early as 1650. It has long been current in Scotland, as opposed to *Auld Licht*, to mark various divisions among the Presbyterians. (OED, "Light," 6.d.) It was also current in mid-eighteenth-century America. After Whitefield, Jonathan Edwards, and others had sparked a "Great Awakening" in New England, the enthusiastic Methodists there were called the "New Lights" as opposed to the anti-enthusiastic "Old Lights" of the established Congregational and Presbyterian churches. In Connecticut, legal suppression of the "New Lights" led briefly to the organization of "Old Light" and "New Light" political parties. See Alan Heimert and Perry Miller, *The Great Awakening: Documents Illustrating the Crisis and Its Consequences* (Indianapolis: Bobbs-Merrill Company, Inc., 1967), pp. 305–307.

[9] *Connoisseur*, p. 392.

[10] See Lance Bertelsen, "Taste and *The Connoisseur*," in *The Nonsense Club: Literature and Popular Culture, 1749–1764* (Oxford: Clarendon Press, 1986), pp. 32–61.

[11] Halévy, *Birth*, p. 51.

[12] Methodism, as David Hempton points out, was but the largest and most influential element in a much wider evangelical constituency. See David Hempton, *Methodism and Politics in British Society 1750–1850* (London: Hutchinson & Co., 1984), p. 12.

Above all, Smart makes in *Jubilate Agno* the fundamentally enthusiastic move of claiming to be a private channel of grace, bypassing all priestly offices: "For by the grace of God I am the Reviver of ADORATION amongst ENGLISH-MEN."[13] In being divinely commissioned, as he claims, to give voice to "adoration," he revives in the *Jubilate* an orientation to inspiration whose very survival as a literary possibility was being anxiously questioned elsewhere. The Pindaric odes of Thomas Gray and William Collins, for example, had looked in vain for a daring bard to reawaken the somnolent harp of lyric poetry.[14] Daring bard though he was, Smart's peculiar achievement in *Jubilate Agno* is yet more specific: to reopen a dialogue with a subterranean "manic" counter-discourse that reaches back to seventeenth-century enthusiastic prophecy. Such a dialogue, however, given its particular historical moment in the evolution of British enthusiasm, was necessarily marked by profound ambiguities.

There are several reasons why it is important to understand Smart's enthusiastic claim, and the *Jubilate* as a whole, in the context of an evolving style of British enthusiasm. First of all, such an approach prevents the facile dismissal of whatever seems unpalatable in Smart as merely the product of his private pathology. At the same time, however, and even more crucially, such an emphasis also prevents a premature "normalization" of Smart in terms of a high-church tradition: a tradition that nevertheless remains embarrassed by certain aspects of his devotional poetry. Such a recuperation of Smart, indeed, no less than the application of psychiatric labels, threatens to diminish his achievement in renewing and rearticulating the manic style.

It must be conceded from the outset that the *Jubilate* is simultaneously a refinement, a sophistication – even a gentrification – of that more plebeian millennial mode. *Jubilate Agno* is profoundly marked by Smart's superb education, by his years of work as a sophisticated neoclassical poet and translator, by his innumerable ties to the artistic traditions of high culture.[15] Yet the fact remains that a countervailing emphasis is long overdue. Literary historians, to the extent that they have even acknowledged Smart's affiliations with enthusiasm, have seldom gone beyond a casual remark here and there.

---

[13] Christopher Smart, *The Poetical Works of Christopher Smart*, 4 vols., eds. Karina Williamson and Marcus Walsh (Oxford: Clarendon Press, 1980–1987), I: *Jubilate Agno*, B 332.

[14] Collins, of course, refers in his "Ode on the Poetical Character" (1746) to Fancy as the "loved Enthusiast." See William Collins, "Ode on the Poetical Character," in *The Poems of Thomas Gray, William Collins, Oliver Goldsmith*, ed. Roger Lonsdale (London: Longmans, Green and Co. Ltd., 1969), p. 431.

[15] Donald Davie, indeed, has recently attempted to describe Smart's lyric poetry more generally in terms of an aesthetics of rococo. See Davie, "Christopher Smart and English rococo," *The Eighteenth Century Hymn in England*, Cambridge Studies in Eighteenth-Century English Literature and Thought (Cambridge: Cambridge University Press, 1993), pp. 95–106. And Robert Brittain long ago described Smart's poetic art as "baroque." See Robert Brittain, Introduction, *Poems by Christopher Smart*, ed. Robert Brittain (Princeton, New Jersey: Princeton University Press, 1950), p. 74.

The context for a crucial dimension of Smart's complexities has thus been largely neglected. For *Jubilate Agno*, beautifully liminal as it is, does produce a return to an enthusiastic ethos that ultimately tends to subvert even its own professions of orthodoxy.

It is an index of *Jubilate Agno*'s liminality that the critical reception of Smart has so often been able to ignore his enthusiastic affiliations. The tendency has been to see the poem in terms of a contrast between high-church "normalcy" and sectarian "pathology." Many of Smart's critics, indeed, have not been eager to spell out the ambiguous and hybrid affiliations of his religious project. In particular, there is a pattern of Anglo-Catholic high-church recuperation of Smart that, while celebrating him as one of their own, tends to play down, or label as "pathological," his enthusiastic strains: a misreading strikingly similar to the critical domestication of Milton by C. S. Lewis. Thus Father Christopher Devlin, explicitly affiliated with the Roman Catholic Church, attempts to claim Smart as a fellow Anglo-Catholic high churchman. Devlin's interpretation of *Jubilate Agno*, therefore, gives us a quasi-monastic Smart whose intellectual and spiritual debts are all to the Church Fathers. Stumbling against Smart's anti-papism and other problems, he describes Smart's "eccentric theology" in terms reminiscent of earlier Anglican attacks on enthusiasm: "a fatal pit of delusion" and "a most revealing symptom of his mental disorder."[16]

Given the Church's snubbing of Smart in his own time, it seems late in the game to claim Smart now as the favorite son of Anglo-Catholic tradition. Can "belligerently Anglican"[17] really be the most precise way to locate such a fraught and ambiguous project as Smart's? In the case of Smart's translation of the Psalms, Marcus Walsh seems more accurate, concluding that Smart "implicitly associated himself with tendencies within the Church some of which were, to more conservative men, at best suspicious, at worst positively dangerous."[18] Thus Smart, had he been more realistic, "must have realized that the Anglican establishment would not welcome, still less formally accept and authorize, his *Translation*."[19] I would further argue that there could be no more powerful device of domestication than to sanitize, retrospectively, such tensions in Smart's spiritual project.

It is true enough that Smart always considered himself a staunch Anglican, and always maintained close ties to Anglican institutions. Yet such an emphasis can too easily miss the full import of his remarkable religious and literary project. Thus the anomaly of Smart's writing in the largely evangelical genre of hymns has often been addressed with a certain diffidence.

[16]   Christopher Devlin, *Poor Kit Smart*, (London: Rupert Hart-Davis, 1961), pp. 160–161.
[17]   This is Donald Davie's description of Smart's hymns. Davie, *Hymn*, p. 79.
[18]   Walsh, Introduction, in *Smart*, III: *A Translation of the Psalms of David*, p. xxxviii.
[19]   *Ibid.*, p. xxxix.

Karina Williamson, while noting that Smart was "the only Anglican hymn-writer of this period who was neither a Methodist nor an Evangelical," emphasizes that his hymns remain strongly connected to the liturgy and church calendar.[20] Her understated remark – that such high-church hymns would have seemed strange *both* to orthodox churchmen *and* to Methodists and evangelicals[21] – is the real heart of the matter. And indeed, the historical force of Smart's flirtation with evangelical affiliations emerges most fully in the context of new research about the hymn's origins. For it was Dissent during the English Revolution that provided the historical context for the hymn's emergence, from a merely private and unperformed mode of devotion, into the collective space of the gathered church. The English Revolution, as Nigel Smith summarizes this finding, "produced the English hymn as we know it, many decades before it is usually assumed to have emerged."[22] Although Smith does unearth evidence of hymn-singing among a few Anglicans in the 1640s and 1650s, such practices were not officially condoned. It was, rather, precisely the separatists – notably including such radical groups as the Fifth Monarchists and the Seventh Day Baptists – who proved to be most responsive to the opportunities for devotional inventiveness afforded by the political crisis.[23]

As Walsh points out, Smart's heavily Christianized Psalms, which insistently intrude the concept of *free grace*, are even more evangelical than his hymns.[24] Walsh, who introduces Smart's *Translation of the Psalms of David*, fruitfully captures the ambiguities, even in this relatively orthodox work, of Smart's subtle cross-breeding: "when he wrote his *Translation*, Smart was a loyal Anglican of an Evangelical persuasion."[25] It is precisely this threshold status – typical as well of many dimensions of eighteenth-century Methodism – that provides the necessary context for rethinking the depth of Smart's subversions in *Jubilate Agno*.

A compelling indication of Smart's affiliations with an ethos of popular enthusiasm lies in his strongly revisionist rewriting of the Augustan literary assault on popular writing. As we have seen, the essential strategy of that patrician attack was to equate popular writing with enthusiasm. Smart, however – as the self-proclaimed "Lord's news-writer" and "scribe-evange-list"[26] – intervenes in *Jubilate Agno* against the Augustan imagery for popular

[20] Williamson, Introduction, in *Smart*, II: *Religious Poetry 1763–1771*, pp. 11–14.
[21] *Ibid.*
[22] Nigel Smith, *Literature and Revolution in England 1640–1660* (New Haven: Yale University Press, 1994), p. 260.
[23] *Ibid.*, pp. 260–275.
[24] Walsh, Introduction in *Smart*, III, p. xxxii. I am not convinced by Davie's argument that Smart's use of the term *grace* in the Psalms overlaps with a more secular sense of elegance and refinement. See Davie, *Hymn*, p. 116.
[25] *Smart*, III, p. xxx.
[26] Smart, *Jubilate*, B 327.

writers, redeeming the reputation of "news-writing" from the perspective of a
defiant literary populism. Smart deliberately glosses the Greek roots of
"evangelism" as a kind of journalism: the subliterary task of news-writing is
thus assimilated to the divine task of spreading the "good news" of the gospel.
The buried allusion to Psalm 19, in which the creation's praise of God is
daily published and diffused to the ends of the world, works to reinforce
Smart's rearticulation of such Augustan mockery in very different terms.
Rather than pitting the demons of satire against the spirits of local and
vernacular energies, Smart seeks to make room for such energies: to
accommodate, to celebrate, and, more subversively, even to amplify them.[27]

It seems likely, moreover, that in calling himself a "scribe" Smart
compares himself to Ezra the scribe, who claimed to have rediscovered and
transcribed the lost Torah, and who thus instituted sweeping religious
reforms.[28] However, the term also seems to recall "scribblers," a favorite
synonym for "hacks" among the patrician "Scriblerians." "Scribblers" is a
term, as Marlon B. Ross points out, that emphasizes individual eccentricity,
waywardness, and self-delusion: the individual's hyperactive deviance, by way
of a supposed unreadability, from "the sane consensus of externally vested
authorities."[29] Defined thus, a scribbler would seem to be the very opposite
of the scribe: for the scribe, as Ross points out, is "merely a vehicular
authority, a translator or medium of authority."[30] Smart's "scribe-evange-
list," however, is put in apposition with news-writing: apparently a
quintessentially "scribbling" role. "Scribe-evangelism" is thus a trope that
mediates between popular and elite concepts of cultural authority: it claims
the alternate authority of divine inspiration for something relegated to the
cultural margins.

Smart, indeed, could be said to recover an older unity prior to any
differentiation of prophecy from "news." For when the weekly newsbook first
emerged in England, prophecy and journalism were scarcely so distinct. First
appearing in the war decade of the 1640s – during the highest pitch of
millennial hopes and apocalyptic fears – regular newsbooks about domestic
affairs created a crucial new vehicle for the public discourse of the day. They
served, in Smith's words, as "a highly important counter in politics" and "a
channel of democracy."[31] Joad Raymond likewise sees seventeenth-century

---

[27] For a related argument about the domesticating strategies of post-Augustan poetry more
      generally, see Geoffrey Hartman, "Romantic poetry and the genius loci," in *Beyond Formalism*
      (New Haven: Yale University Press, 1970), pp. 311–336.
[28] Some modern scholars believe Ezra is such a crucial redactor that he can be said, in some sense,
      to have "written" the Bible. See Richard Elliott Friedman, *Who Wrote the Bible?* (New York:
      Summit Books, 1987), pp. 219–233.
[29] Marlon B. Ross, "Authority and authenticity: scribbling authors and the genius of print in
      eighteenth-century England," *Cardozo Arts & Entertainment Law Journal* 10:2 (1992), p. 501.
[30] *Ibid.*, p. 497.
[31] Smith, *Revolution*, p. 54.

newsbooks – emerging in a world "where some men and women were treated as if they were born for others to ride" – as a means of "inventing the future."[32] Popular prophecy, moreover, continued thereafter to produce pamphlets with titles featuring the word "news," as in the case of a pamphlet from 1694 that was seminal for the "Philadelphians": *Strange News from Bishop's Stafford near Buckingham.*[33]

The personal and professional roots of Smart's sympathy for scribbling scribes are not far to seek. For the details of Smart's biography during the 1750s clearly show how his practice of mingling popular and elite discourses developed into a characteristic habit. This straddling of cultural divides, indeed, correlates closely with the wider tensions that shaped his own professional trajectory: above all, the precarious situation of professional writers in a moment when, as Charles Ryskamp puts it, "the old rewards of patronage were rapidly declining, when subscription might still prove successful, but when proper payments and something like royalties would only occasionally happen."[34]

Beginning in 1749, when he left an academic life at Cambridge for London, Smart subsisted in this world as a member of publisher John Newbery's hard-driven stable of writers. Smart became a supremely versatile editor, journalist, flatterer of patrons, burlesque actor (cross-dressing as "Mother Midnight"), Grub-Street mud-slinger, occasional versifier, and agile self-promoter: in short, an overworked hack. He shored up this subliterary professional identity by writing religious poetry that won five annual prizes at Cambridge between 1750 and 1755. As Moira Dearnley observes, the contrasts in Smart's life during the early 1750s are initially striking: "One would not expect that an ugly little man, who had taken on the literary persona of that pantomime-dame character, Mother Midnight, was at the same time writing Miltonic verse-essays on the Eternity, Immensity, Omniscience, Power, and Goodness of the Supreme Being – which he was."[35]

An illustration of Smart's frenetic life during this period appears in the sheer thoroughness with which he exploited an epilogue written for a production of *The Conscious Lovers*. This epilogue managed simultaneously to wrap up the play, to flatter a potential patron, and (by recasting one of the play's characters as a man-midwife) to publicize Smart's own work.[36] Smart similarly capitalized on *The Midwife* as both as commodity in itself and as a

[32] Joad Raymond, Introduction, in *Making the News: An Anthology of the Newsbooks of Revolutionary England 1641–1660*, ed. Joad Raymond (New York: St. Martin's Press, 1993), p. 25.
[33] Schwartz, *Prophets*, p. 44.
[34] Charles Ryskamp, "Christopher Smart and the Earl of Northumberland," in *The Augustan Milieu: Essays Presented to Louis A. Landa*, eds. Henry Knight Miller *et al.* (Oxford: Clarendon Press, 1970), p. 320.
[35] Moira Dearnley, *The Poetry of Christopher Smart* (London: Routledge & Kegan Paul, 1968), p. 7.
[36] Ryskamp, "Northumberland," pp. 323–327.

print vehicle for plugging another of Newbery's ventures: the "Old Woman's Oratory." The latter was a burlesque theatrical performance – a spin-off from *The Midwife* – that featured, in addition to Mother Midnight's parodic orations, a concert orchestrating such instruments as the salt-box, the hurdy-gurdy, the jew's harp, and the marrow bones and cleaver.[37] To the music of this madcap ensemble danced "great Timbertoe": a wooden-legged dancer celebrated in a bit of verse likely written by Smart.[38]

The personal crisis that led Smart to move toward enthusiasm began in the mid-1750s. The economic pressure that provoked such a carnivalesque creation as Mother Midnight had indeed been relentless. Smart had married Newbery's stepdaughter in 1752, and by 1754 the couple had two daughters. He was notoriously improvident; moreover, squeezed as he was by Newbery, he was experiencing intermittent bouts of a debilitating fever. By the autumn of 1755, an especially unsuccessful year for Smart, exploitation by Newbery had become galling enough to force a financial break.[39] In attempting this break, however, Smart seems merely to have traded one exploiter for another: he felt sufficiently strapped, at any rate, to sign a 99-year contract with the publisher of the *Universal Visiter*.[40] A decisive turning point then arrived in 1756: Smart suffered a serious illness, including an episode of delirium, that prevented him from doing more than intermittent work for the *Visiter*. Upon regaining his health, he wrote his "Hymn to the Supreme Being, on Recovery from a Dangerous Fit of Illness." Smart announced in this poem, once again published by Newbery, both a renewed spiritual zeal and his signature theme of gratitude: "Brisk leaps the heart, the mind's at large once more, / To love, to praise, to bless, to wonder and adore."[41] The continuing interpenetration of the economic and the sacred, however, is marked by the dedicatory letter affixed to this poem, which advertises a patent medicine vended by Smart's always enterprising father-in-law: Doctor James's Fever Powder.[42]

In 1757 Smart adopted the manic religiosity that led his in-laws to have him put away. It is worth remembering again that Samuel Johnson, who met

---

[37] Lance Bertelsen, "Journalism, carnival, and *Jubilate Agno*," *English Literary History* 59 (1992), pp. 368–396.

[38] Smart, "Mons. Timbertoe," in *Smart*, IV: *Miscellaneous Poems, English and Latin*, p. 393. Williamson includes this poem, published anonymously in *The Midwife*, among poems of uncertain authorship.

[39] Brittain, Introduction, in *Poems*, p. 33.

[40] Details of this contract are reprinted in Stuart Piggott's "New light on Christopher Smart," *Times Literary Supplement*, 13 June 1929, p. 474; for the desperation of 1755, see Ryskamp, "Northumberland," p. 322; and Arthur Sherbo, *Christopher Smart: Scholar of the University* (East Lansing: Michigan State University Press, 1967), pp. 105–107.

[41] Christopher Smart, "Hymn to the Supreme Being, on Recovery from a Dangerous Fit of Illness," in *Smart*, IV, p. 321.

[42] See Christopher Smart, "To Doctor James," Letter XIII, in *The Annotated Letters of Christopher Smart*, eds. Betty Rizzo and Robert Mahoney (Carbondale: Southern Illinois University, 1991), pp. 67–68. See also Devlin, *Kit*, pp. 76–79; and Sherbo, *Scholar*, p. 108.

some of his incapacitated friend's obligations to the *Universal Visiter*, did not think Smart needed to be locked up. After a year-long stay in St. Luke's Hospital, he was discharged "uncured"; sometime between May 1758 and January 1759, he entered a private madhouse in Bethnal Green run by Mr. Potter.[43] Smart seems to have begun the *Jubilate* in mid-March of 1759. He was indeed marking time with a ritual, a daily act of worship that produced the fragmentary poem at a rate of two or three verse-pairs per day. Nearly four more years of confinement, of which the *Jubilate* is a sort of chronological record, passed in this way. During these years Smart lost his physical autonomy; he lost the affection of his wife Anna Maria and his two young daughters, who moved to Dublin; and he lost his reputation as an "ingenious" man of letters. His sense of desertion appears acutely in a line that attempts to make a virtue of his poverty: "For the purse is for me because I have neither money nor human friends."[44] As Arthur Sherbo remarks, the qualifier "human" appears here in deference to his cat Jeoffry, first mentioned in line B 68: "For I am possessed of a cat, surpassing in beauty, from whom I take occasion to bless Almighty God."[45]

It could be argued that Smart's development into an enthusiast merely reaffirms the equation, given maximum force by the Augustans, of popular writing with enthusiasm. As Lance Bertelsen puts it, "the commonplace Augustan linkage of religious enthusiasm and Grub Street wackiness achieves serious textualization in Smart's 'mad' poem."[46] *Jubilate Agno* can in this view be seen as exemplifying the very historical development – the transgression by a commercial literary marketplace of patrician generic, cultural, and social boundaries – that provoked Pope's nightmarish vision of the omnipotent Goddess Dulness.[47] An even more apt comparison can be made to Swift's *A Tale of a Tub*, which unleashes its satirical "mania" by way of dramatizing the modulation of mad enthusiasts into modern popular writers. And indeed, Swift's attack on dark authors in the *Tale* evokes both the "Mother Midnight" and the midwifery images:

'TIS true, indeed, the Republick of *dark* Authors, after they once found out this excellent Expedient of *Dying*, have been peculiarly happy in the Variety, as well as the Extent of their Reputation. For, *Night* being the universal Mother of Things, wise Philosophers hold all writings to be *fruitful* in the Proportion they are *dark*; And therefore, the *true illuminated* (that is to say, the *Darkest* of all) have met with such numberless commentators, whose *Scholiastick* Midwifry have deliver'd them of Meanings, that the Authors themselves, perhaps, never conceived, and yet may very justly

---

[43]   I have closely paraphrased Karina Williamson's summary of these events. See her introduction to
        the *Jubilate*, p. xix. For more about Smart's confinement, see also Sherbo, *Scholar*, pp. 122–123.
[44]   Smart, *Jubilate*, B 283.
[45]   Sherbo, *Scholar*, p. 130.
[46]   Bertelsen, "Journalism," p. 369.
[47]   *Ibid.*, p. 357.

be allowed the Lawful Parents of them: The Words of such Writers being like Seed, which, however scattered at random, when they light upon a fruitful Ground, will multiply far beyond either the Hopes or Imagination of the Sower.[48]

Nothing could be more reductive, however, than to depict Smart as the literal realization of such reductive patrician tropes. And indeed, Bertelsen himself offers a long overdue rethinking, through the category of carnival, of the Augustan denigration of dunces and hacks. In this vein, he especially emphasizes Smart's creation of the carnivalesque persona of Mother Mary Midnight:[49] "A lowly and disreputable midwife, she is also the writer and editor of her own subversive, irreverent journal: a journal filled with wild transformations, parodic history, mad schemes, and paradoxical commentary on the plight of the oppressed."[50] Through his exuberant description of the cultural hybridity of Grub Street, Bertelsen goes a long way toward redeeming the sheer energy involved in such profit-driven writing as Smart's work in *The Midwife*. Smart's "manic energy," as Bertelsen puts it, got channeled into a frantic race against deadlines and creditors.[51]

Despite Smart's isolation, moreover, his crisis was not merely personal. Indeed, his development into an enthusiast during this period represents precisely an ongoing engagement with the social and ideological tensions inherent during this mid-century moment in the "vocation" of writing. Far from seeing himself as the *Dunciad* or *A Tale of a Tub* come to life – the "mother," as it were, of all midnights[52] – Smart instead provocatively celebrates a popular milieu whose energies he had long been tapping. His shift toward an evangelical strain of popular feeling, though marking a well-defined break in his literary career, also marks ongoing continuities in his habitual cross-breeding of elite and popular discourses. For it is in straddling a religiously defined fault-line of social tensions that Smart's later devotional poetry, and especially his *Jubilate*, finds its deepest historical resonance. What deserves far more recognition, therefore, is the sheer audacity of his dialogue with enthusiasm.

One enthusiastic *topos* with which *Jubilate Agno* repeatedly conjures is that of inner illumination. This *topos*, indeed, also appears in Smart's heavily evangelical translation of Psalm XXXIV:

---

[48] Jonathan Swift, *A Tale of a Tub*, eds. A. C. Guthkelch and D. Nichol Smith, 2nd ed. (Oxford: Clarendon Press, 1958), p. 186.

[49] A further strength of Bertelsen's article is the good use to which it puts Robert Erickson's quasi-anthropological work on the figure of the midwife/cunning woman in eighteenth-century Britain. See Robert A. Erickson, *Mother Midnight: Birth, Sex, and Fate in Eighteenth-Century Fiction* (New York: AMS Press, 1986).

[50] Bertelsen, "Journalism," p. 361.

[51] *Ibid.*, p. 362.

[52] See Devlin, *Kit*, p. 55, for the suggestion that Smart derived the name Mother Midnight at least partially from the apocalyptic conclusion of Pope's *Dunciad*, when all the lights of art go out. To that suggestion, I would only add that Smart's appropriation may well be tinged with a defiant irony.

> Illumination beams on all
>   That to the Lord aspire:
> And, when they to the godhead call,
> Nought can abash them, or appal
>   In such a duty and desire.[53]

Twice in the *Jubilate* Smart likewise insists on the centrality of unmediated revelation, affirming that "ignorance is a sin because illumination is to be had by prayer."[54] What underscores the historical liminality of Smart's enthusiasm, however, is the way this *topos* often appears in a slightly more tempered guise. This is true even when, as in the verse-pair below, Smart evokes a Manichean struggle between "light" and "darkness." This struggle is his way of recording the treatment given to the inmates by the wardens or keepers of the asylum:

> Let Elkanah rejoice with Cymindis the Lord illuminate us
>   against the powers of darkness
> For the officers of the peace are at variance with me, and
>   the watchman smites me with his staff.[55]

Cymindis, according to Smart's editors, is the night hawk; Elkanah, a door-keeper of the Ark. Against the "powers of darkness," personified by the brutal watchman and the ironically named "officers of the peace," Smart asks for a power of illumination, a "night vision" such as might belong to the night hawk. Elkanah is compared to the asylum's watchman; and Cymindis, to Smart. One thus has a pairing, and perhaps an implied reconciliation, of enemies. What marks the lines as liminal is their indirection: overtly, Smart merely asks for illumination; less directly, in the guise of "Cymindis," he claims it.

The literary process by which Smart accommodates and refines the idea of "illumination" appears again in an intricate cluster of lines that revolve, as Francis D. Adams points out, around a voyage motif.[56] The lines in this cluster ask God to keep the adversary "at bay,"[57] request divine aid to make it to the "shore,"[58] and celebrate the building of harbors and a pier.[59] In this context Smart goes on to pray "for all light-houses, beacons, and buoys."[60] What is much less obvious, however, is that the verse-pair just prior to Smart's prayer for lighthouses uses a subdued pun to bridge the gap between "inner" and "outer" illumination:

[53] Smart, Psalm XXXIV, *Smart*, III, p. 78.
[54] Smart, *Jubilate*, B 421; C 570.
[55] *Ibid.*, B 90.
[56] Francis D. Adams, "*Jubilate Agno* and the theme of gratitude," *Papers on Language and Literature* 3:3 (1967), p. 198.
[57] Smart, *Jubilate*, B 141.
[58] *Ibid.*, B 142.
[59] *Ibid.*, B 143.
[60] *Ibid.*, B 146.

> Let Eliakim rejoice with the Shad, who is contemned in his
> abundance.
> For I pray for R and his family, I pray for Mr Becher, and I
> bean for the Lord JESUS.[61]

Mr. Becher obviously appears here as a link to "beach." More intriguing, however, is the phrase "I bean for the Lord JESUS." Here Smart has revived *bene*, an obsolete noun meaning "prayer," and used it as a verb.[62] "Bean" also suggests "beam", as Adams points out, implying that Smart himself, like the lighthouses he wishes to bless, is a "spiritual beacon."[63]

A further celebration of light in the subsequent verse-pair again seems to filter the *topos* through a screen of indirection. This time the motif is made to speak to the context of Smart's confinement. Even in such bleak conditions as a madhouse – etymologically, "bleak" means "shining" – Smart finds small mercies to praise:

> Let Sadoc rejoice with the Bleak, who playeth upon the
> surface in the Sun.
> For I bless God that I am not in a dungeon, but am allowed
> the light of the Sun.[64]

Sadoc, whose name in Hebrew connotes "justice," is briefly mentioned in the Bible as one of David's priests; the Bleak is a silvery-scaled European freshwater fish of the genus *Alburnus*, presumably named for its shininess. The line's literal meaning, that Smart has access to sunlight, provides a point of departure for an enthusiastic figuration of Smart himself, a just man, as "in" and "of" the sun.

This latter reading is all the more likely in that evangelical authors often vary the "inner light" *topos* so as to exploit the possibility in English of a pun on "sun" and "son." George Fox, for example, refers to "the Lord, who hath sent His beloved son to be their [the people's] saviour, and caused his heavenly sun to shine upon all the world, and through them all; and His heavenly rain to fall upon the just and the unjust, (as his outward rain doth fall, and his outward sun doth shine on all,) which is God's unspeakable love to the world."[65] And among Smart's contemporaries, Charles Wesley provides in his Methodist "Morning Hymn" a useful instance of this *topos*, nicely praying for an internalization of the sun/son of righteousness:

[61] *Ibid.*, B 145.
[62] Susie Tucker, "Christopher Smart and the English language," *Notes and Queries* 203 (1958), p. 469.
[63] Adams, "Gratitude," p. 198.
[64] Smart, *Jubilate*, B 147.
[65] George Fox, *The Works of George Fox*, 8 vols. (1831; rpt. New York: AMS Press, 1975), I: *A Journal or Historical Account of the Life, Travels, Sufferings, Christian Experiences, and Labour of Love in the Work of the Ministry of that Ancient, Eminent, and Faithful Servant of Jesus Christ, George Fox*, p. 91.

> Christ, whose glory fills the skies,
> Christ, the true, the only Light,
> Sun of righteousness, arise,
> Triumph o'er the shades of night;
> Day-spring from on high, be near;
> Day-star, in my heart appear![66]

As these examples are meant to suggest, Smart's leavening of the sun/son *topos* marks both continuities and differences in the evolution of enthusiasm. One is struck, above all, by the happy immediacy with which Smart celebrates his sun-struck cat Jeoffry: "For in his morning orisons he loves the sun and the sun loves him."[67] This tonal register seems to emphasize an easy, concrete availability of light, with no burdensome gap between inner and outer. Jeoffry loves the sun, and, in a lovely mutual relation, the sun/son loves him. Given a common enthusiastic *topos*, Smart finds here a finer tone for its expression.

That Smart was willing to push the "inner light" *topos* to scandalous extremes, however, is proven in another passage dealing with Jeoffry. Well charged with static electricity, Jeoffry emerges as a distinguished member of the new illuminati:

> For when his day's work is done his [Jeoffry's] business more
>   properly begins.
> For he keeps the Lord's watch in the night against the
>   adversary.
> For he counteracts the powers of darkness by his electrical
>   skin and glaring eyes.[68]

Moreover, Smart's celebration of electricity as a heaven-sent fire[69] and as a quickening remedy for paralytic cases[70] converges unexpectedly with an aspect of Methodism's mass-based healing practice: the immensely cheap and easy "electrical cure" for various ailments, including such "nervous" diseases as melancholia. As Henry Abelove points out, through John Wesley's fascination with the electrical cure, mild shock-treatment devices were gradually spread from London to Methodist societies throughout Britain.[71]

A second enthusiastic commonplace that Smart rearticulates is "magnification": that paradigmatic act of thanksgiving by which Mary celebrated the annunciation of her destiny. As used by the likes of Anna Trapnel (who refers to herself in Marian terms as the humble "handmaid") or Gerrard

---

[66] Charles Wesley, "Morning Hymn," in *John and Charles Wesley*, p. 293.
[67] Smart, *Jubilate*, C 721.
[68] *Ibid.*, B 717–719.
[69] *Ibid.*, B 762.
[70] *Ibid.*, B 267.
[71] Abelove, *Desire*, pp. 27–29; see also Roy Porter, *Mind-Forg'd Manacles: A History of Madness in England from the Restoration to the Regency* (London: The Athlone Press, 1987), p. 185.

Winstanley (who emphasizes, against the "murderous" magistrates, that the blessing of the Lord is only amongst the poor), the *topos* signifies a reversal in which the lowly are raised and the rich sent empty away. The Magnificat thus serves to "magnify" not only God, but also, and above all, the dispossessed. As context, the cultural memory of this more radical reading of the Magnificat serves to restore an edge to the potent, possibly blasphemous pun by which Smart names his poem – among other things, a tribute to his feline companion Jeoffry – a "Magnifi-cat":[72]

> Let Jubal rejoice with Cæcilia, the woman and the slow-
> worm praise the name of the Lord.
> For I pray the Lord Jesus to translate my MAGNIFICAT into
> verse and represent it.[73]

Both the wordplay and the levelling sense of magnification put Smart into dialogue with an older enthusiastic constellation. To be sure, the unobtrusive nature of Smart's pun marks the lines as a domestication of Fifth Monarchist or Digger energies. Nevertheless, Smart's self-described "Magnifi-cat" does subtly exalt even the lowest orders of the chain of being. Smart goes on to identify his cat Jeoffry with the oppressed, and suggests that by virtue of this position, Jeoffry is called perpetually by God's benevolence:

> For he is of the Lord's poor and so indeed is he called by
> benevolence perpetually – Poor Jeoffry! poor Jeoffry! the
> rat has bit thy throat.[74]

This model of God's "calling" suggests, in a stark form, the dynamics of poverty and obscurity that lie behind Smart's own sense of vocation.

Smart's enthusiastic resolution of his vocational dilemma opens his poem to "magnifying" *topoi* dealing with more general inequalities of wealth, power, and status. The theme of the humble overcoming the great, indeed, is quite common in Smart's later works: a point that has led Morris Golden to describe Smart as "the learned son of a steward" with – shades of Malvolio! – "a resentful upper servant's view of society."[75] The more important point is that Smart's insubordinate "magnifications" in *Jubilate Agno* derive from a well-developed enthusiastic mode. Early in the *Jubilate* he links Huldah, a minor Biblical character whose husband kept the royal wardrobe, with the silkworm, in a line that openly reverses the class hierarchy: "Let Huldah bless with the Silkworm – the ornaments of the

[72] For the best discussion of this crucial pun, see Geoffrey H. Hartman, "Christopher Smart's Magnificat: toward a theory of representation," in *The Fate of Reading* (Chicago: University of Chicago Press, 1975), pp. 74–100.
[73] Smart, *Jubilate*, B 43–44.
[74] *Ibid.*, C 740.
[75] Morris Golden, *The Self Observed: Swift, Johnson, Wordsworth* (Baltimore: The Johns Hopkins Press, 1972), p. 25.

Proud are from the bowells of their Betters."[76] Moreover, a number of verse-pairs in *Jubilate Agno* involve the act of reimagining oneself as the object of another's gaze. Smart insists, over and against the gaze of those who would see him merely as an impoverished madman, on his own "election." His spiritual ambitions, mediated by an identification with a great text (and the poet-monarch David), thus serve his own need for "magnification." A playful and yet plaintive expression of this need appears toward the arbitrary "end" of the fragmentary *Jubilate*:

> Let Fig, house of Fig rejoice with Fleawort. The Lord magnify
>   the idea of Smart singing hymns on this day in the eyes of
>   the whole university of Cambridge. Novr 5th 1762. N.S.[77]

This was written, as Williamson points out, during a period in which Smart was busily composing his cycle of hymns.[78] This formulation – that Smart's identification with the lofty defends against his feeling lowly and "flea-like" in human society – gains additional plausibility from an earlier line about the flea's lack of visibility: "Let Ethan praise with the Flea, his coat of mail, his piercer, and his vigour, which wisdom and providence have contrived to attract observation and to escape it."[79] While expressing ambivalence about the consequences of being observed, Smart's praise of the flea clearly reinforces a more general theme of the guerrilla warfare of the small against the great.

Such dynamics, indeed – what E. P. Thompson has termed "class struggle without class"[80] – are at the center of Smart's most poignant lines. These lines, which wrestle with the enormous gap between Smart's degraded social position and his aspirations, attempt to mediate class tensions through a process of symbolic inversion:

> Let Hushim rejoice with the King's Fisher, who is of royal
>   beauty, tho' plebeian size.
> For in my nature I quested for beauty, but God, God hath
>   sent me to sea for pearls.[81]

Smart finds an apt emblem for social contradictions in the tiny King's Fisher who is nevertheless of "royal beauty." Hushim, little more than a name in various Biblical genealogies, is listed in 1 Chronicles 7:12 among "mighty men of valour." One chain of associations links royalty and Smart's "natural"

---

76   Smart, *Jubilate*, A 91.
77   *Ibid.*, D 148.
78   Williamson, Introduction, in *Smart*, II, p. 4.
79   Smart, *Jubilate*, A 36.
80   E. P. Thompson, "Eighteenth-century English society: class struggle without class?", *Social History* 3 (1978), pp. 133–165. For more about the numerous riots that erupted in mid-century Britain, mostly in rural areas, see Tony Hayter, *The Army and the Crowd in Mid-Georgian England* (London: Macmillan Press, 1978).
81   Smart, *Jubilate*, B 30.

quest for beauty, implying that Smart has suffered an "unnatural" social degradation. God, for his own mysterious reasons, has degraded Smart totally, has sent him out "to sea."

A second axis of associations crosses the first, however, recuperating Smart's degradation and social insignificance in the name of a valorous quest for the pearls of spiritual grace. This second axis of meaning, connecting small size with a "plebeian" social position, compares the magnitude of God and the sea with the smallness of the tiny King's Fisher and of Smart: for like the young warrior David, Smart was a short man. As if ennobled by the very magnitude of his adversities, Smart contrasts his "plebeian size" with the awful sublimity of his quest for pearls: a quest that, as in the parable of the merchant in Matthew 13: 45–46, has cost him everything. Small "plebeian" stature, by means of this reversal, is revealed as a sublime calling: the poet, though seemingly degraded, is in reality magnified by his divinely enforced quest for the pearl of great price. The terror of unrelatedness, moreover, captured here in images of solitude and sphericity, suggest that for Smart the horizon of the human world is dangerously remote. Because of this acknowledgment, indeed, the lines about Smart's quest for the pearl of great price produce the poem's most convincing image of Smart's "election."[82]

Although he uses social class as a means of figuring his paradoxically elevated status, Smart clearly does so in the hopes of finding a symbolic means of bridging social alienation. Not only does Smart claim a kind of "royalty" for his apparently "plebeian" self, but he also invokes, as another image of himself, the King's Fisher, a water bird whose name combines both aristocratic and peasant associations. He figures his "election," then, both as a sort of plebeian "fishing" and as a noble quest even more severe than the quest for beauty. The meaning of the distinction, the alienating unrelatedness, is thus sublimated into a realm of spiritual values where the real King is Christ and the real fishers are disciples, "fishers of men."

A similarly keen pathos of social distance appears in another of Smart's verse-pairs. This one deals with social heights and depths by identifying with a place beyond and above them:

> Let Jemuel rejoice with Charadrius, who is from the HEIGHT
> and the sight of him is good for the jaundice.
> For I look up to heaven which is my prospect to escape envy
> by surmounting it.[83]

Charadrius is the golden plover: a bird, according to folklore, which upon being seen by a person ill with jaundice would itself absorb the disease,

[82] See Guest, *Form*, pp. 147–148, for an argument that the "pearl" image resonates also with the formal property of the *Jubilate* as a "loose string" of aphoristic lines.

[83] Smart, *Jubilate*, B 26.

leaving the person cured.[84] "Jaundice," which makes one turn yellow, here stands metonymically for envy. The proud gaze of social superiority generates the complementary gaze of jaundiced resentment from the oppressed underdog – and then a hope of triumphant transcendence through looking forwards, through curative "prospects." Smart links these prospects to the meaning in Hebrew of *Jemuel*, which is "day of God."

Still another passage in which Smart leavens a "magnifying" enthusiasm in accordance with the temper of his times appears in B 10. This verse-pair reworks, with considerable levity, a familiar enthusiastic *topos*. In B 193 Smart calls the lamprey "an eel with a title," and it is in that parodic vein that another of his class-conscious verse-pairs uses code words for the social elite – "the right sort of people" – in a transfer of such diction to the kingdom of birds:

> Let Hagar rejoice with Gnesion, who is the right sort of
> eagle, and towers the highest.
> For I bless God in the rising generation, which is on my
> side.[85]

These lines, in fact, are Smart's rather amusing version of the Pauline "two sons" *topos*: an indispensable commonplace for the sectarian rhetoric of successive "dispensations." It is worth noting that the verse-pair occurs in the same general region of the poem as the lines that describe his renunciation of his own inheritance.[86] Hagar, Abraham's dispossessed maidservant, gave birth to Ishmael, an archetype of resentment ("his hand will be against every man, and every man's hand against him") and eponymous ancestor of all the "unchosen" in the covenant between God and Abraham. Her pairing with the "right sort of eagle" and the "rising generation" suggests, at the least, a revisionary expansion of the old covenant to include the disenfranchised. As W. M. Merchant observes,

Hagar may mean 'flight,' initiating a series: 'Eagle – towers the highest – rising generation,' in which 'flight' gathers the meanings 'fly' and 'flee.' Hagar's offspring (the 'rising generation') is thus protected by the eagle-flight of the bondwoman. Further, Gnesion may be equated with the Greek 'lawfully begotten, legitimate, genuine,' which corresponds to 'the right sort of eagle,' in opposition to Hagar, whose offspring is at first outcast.[87]

The "rising generation" may refer to Smart's young daughters, anticipated allies in a family schism. It could also be read, a bit more edgily, as the

[84]   Albert J. Kuhn, "Christopher Smart: the poet as patriot of the Lord," *English Literary History* 30 (1963), p. 133.
[85]   Smart, *Jubilate*, B 10.
[86]   *Ibid.*, B 46–51.
[87]   W. M. Merchant, "Patterns of reference in Smart's *Jubilate Agno*," *Harvard Library Bulletin*, 14 (1960), p. 25.

uprising generation: this very ambiguity, however, is what often defines Smart's project.

Such intermittent flickerings of a "magnifying" social resentment are common in *Jubilate Agno*. Some passages, however, seem to escalate this motif toward something rather more akin to the confrontational tactics of Ranter plebeian hostility. Like Abiezer Coppe, charging the coaches of the aristocracy, "staring on them as [he] would look thorough them," and proclaiming the day of the Lord with "a huge loud voice,"[88] Smart boasts of rudely affronting the great with his sonorous evangelism:

> Let Shobi rejoice with the Kastrel – blessed be the name
>   Jesus in falconry and in the MALL
> For I blessed God in St. James's Park till I routed all the
>   company.[89]

Falconry, an aristocratic pursuit, appears here as a mode of religious power that Smart appropriates and uses against the rich.[90] St. James's Park was a fashionable area of London where the wealthy took leisurely walks and carriage rides. Adjoined by the tree-lined Mall, which leads up to Buckingham Palace, the park was indeed an apt stage for the strong-lunged dramatization, through street-preaching, of class resentment. As recalled in these lines, at least, the purpose of Smart's public prayers is to discharge social aggression. It was precisely for such behavior – loud prayer in public places – that Smart was confined. And Smart, indeed, gives his own version of the ranting "loud voice" *topos* in the following outburst: "For the AIR is purified by prayer which is made aloud and with all our might."[91] Such precedents for Smart's "prank," as Coppe would have said, invite us to read it not as madness, but as the convention – the subversive moral weapon – of a plebeian religious discourse.

Another *outré* moment appears in the following line: "For to worship naked in the rain is the bravest thing for the refreshing and purifying [of] the body."[92] It is not entirely clear what relevance the "Adamites" – second-century Christian nudists mentioned in Williamson's annotation to this line – have to Smart. Similar groups were rumored to exist among the seventeenth-century English sectarians; but to what extent such "Adamites"

88 Abiezer Coppe, *A Second Fiery Flying Roule*, in *A Collection of Ranter Writings from the 17th Century*, ed. Nigel Smith (London: Junction Books, 1983), p. 105.

89 Smart, *Jubilate*, B 89.

90 Andrew Marvell's "An Horatian Ode," in its surprising comparison of the regicide Cromwell to an obedient falcon, provides a precedent for precisely this sort of symbolic theft. Michael Wilding argues that this charged comparison, though it is an appropriation, also stresses "Cromwell's suitability as a continuer of the ruling-élite role." See Michael Wilding, *Dragon's Teeth: Literature in the English Revolution* (Oxford: Clarendon Press, 1987), pp. 133–134.

91 Smart, *Jubilate*, B 224.

92 *Ibid.*, B 384.

actually existed outside the fevered imaginations of hostile propagandists is difficult to know.[93] It seems fair to say, nevertheless, that the line evokes a context of religious perfectionism that repeatedly drew on the Adamic resonance of the unclothed body, the stripping and unveiling imagery of the Apocalypse, and so on.

Given the enthusiastic *topos* of David's dancing before the Ark, uncovered before handmaids, Smart's recommendation of nude worship may be connected to his praise of dancing "for the glory of God."[94] And indeed, a celebration of uninhibited dancing appears in a line that follows mention of the tarantula,[95] a creature whose name connotes tarantism, history's most famous epidemic of ecstatic dancing. Smart invokes Jakim with the Satyr to "bless God in the dance."[96] Isaiah, as Williamson points out, uses satyrs in his apocalyptic prophecy of doom, foretelling that they will dance in the desolate ruins of Babylon (Isaiah 13:21). Smart is doubtless punning on the Hebrew meaning of "Jakim," which Charles Parish translates as "a setter" or a "setter-up."[97] In context, furthermore, the setter/satyr pun also seems to evoke the strongly phallic orientation of Bacchanalian satyrs as depicted in Greek mythology and art.

Yet another enthusiastic outburst appears in Smart's declaration, repeated more than once, that "Saturday is the Sabbath for the mouth of God hath spoken it."[98] Indeed, Smart's emphasis on *Saturday* as the proper and God-given Sabbath, in complete contradiction to the Anglican establishment, harks back to a lively controversy that extended from the late sixteenth century into the Cromwellian era. It was in this connection, for his fourth-commandment zeal, that the seventeenth-century Puritan John Trask was tried by the Star Chamber in 1618 and sentenced to life imprisonment.[99] Such returns to the letter of Scripture often involved, in connection with the

---

[93] Paranoid descriptions of Ranting Adamites can be found in the anti-sectarian propaganda reprinted in the appendix to J. C. Davis, *Fear, Myth, and History: The Ranters and the Historians* (Cambridge: Cambridge University Press, 1986). For a broader discussion of the ethos of paradisal sexuality surrounding seventeenth-century perfectionism, see James Grantham Turner, *One Flesh: Paradisal Marriage and Sexual Relations in the Age of Milton* (Oxford: Clarendon Press, 1987, especially pp. 38–95.

[94] Smart, *Jubilate*, C 94.

[95] *Ibid.*, A 66.

[96] *Ibid.*, A 67.

[97] Charles Parish, "Christopher Smart's knowledge of Hebrew," *Studies in Philology* 54 (1961), p. 528.

[98] Smart, *Jubilate*, B 212.

[99] See T. L. Underwood, "The seventh day sabbath controversy," in *The Miscellaneous Works of John Bunyan* (Oxford: Clarendon Press, 1989), IV: *A Defence of the Doctrine of Justification by Faith*, pp. xlv–lv. See also Christopher Hill, "The uses of Sabbatarianism," in *Society and Puritanism in Pre-Revolutionary England*, 2nd ed. (New York: Schocken Books, 1967), pp. 145–218. Trask also appears in Benjamin Brook's martyrological work, *The Lives of the Puritans*, 5 vols. (London: James Black, 1813), III, pp. 521–522. For the analysis of Sabbatarianism in the New England context, see James Holstun, *A Rational Millenium: Puritan Utopias of Seventeenth Century England and America* (Oxford: Oxford University Press, 1987), pp. 124–126.

expected millennial conversion of the Jews, a "philosemitic" spirituality. Among those who advocated the Seventh-Day Sabbath, for example, Francis Bampfield also urged the adoption of Hebrew as a universal language and Peter Chamberlen visited synagogues in Europe.[100] Trask, though eventually released, was also sentenced to be branded with a "J" for "Jew".[101] By the middle of the seventeenth century, a continuous movement had developed, mostly among Baptists. Some Seventh-Day Sabbatarians, however, such as Thomas Tillam, were Fifth Monarchists; and indeed, a fierce controversy arose among the Fifth Monarchists over this very issue.[102]

The "prophetic prank" *topos*, moreover, is itself another subversive feature of enthusiasm that Smart revisits. Indeed, Smart uses the word "prank" in something like the same special sense – at once festive, ornery, and yet spiritually self-authorizing – as did Abiezer Coppe. One such usage, apparently referring to a brief passage in the apocryphal book of Baruch,[103] celebrates the prankishness of the iconoclastic cat in terms that link it with grace:

> Let Anna bless God with the cat, who is worthy to be
> presented before the throne of grace, when he has
> trampled upon the idol in his prank.[104]

Anna is most likely the aged prophetess (Luke 2:36–39) who, having fasted and prayed constantly – a "prank" itself reminiscent of seventeenth-century women prophets – recognizes the infant Jesus as the Messiah. A similar line celebrates the prankishness of the Sea-Bear, or fur-seal, pairing it with Chuza, one of Herod's stewards: "Let Chuza rejoice with the Sea-Bear, who is full of sagacity and prank."[105] Chuza's wife Joanna ministers unto Jesus (Luke 8:3), which may have suggested both "sagacity" and "prank" (insofar as it is an implied rebellion against Herod) to Smart, and hence a version of the "wise folly" *topos*. And, finally, a pair of consecutive "For" lines use the term "prank" as a verb that suggests the eighteenth-century meaning of "showing off,"[106] but in a more positive sense:

> For the RAIN WATER is kept in a reservoir at any altitude,
> suppose of a thousand feet, will make a fountain from a
> spout of ten feet of the same height.

---

[100] Underwood, "Sabbath," p. lxviii.

[101] *Ibid.*, p. xlvii.

[102] *Ibid.*, pp. xlviii-l; see also B. S. Capp, *The Fifth Monarchy Men: A Study in Seventeenth-century English Millenarianism* (Totowa, New Jersey: Rowman and Littlefield, 1972), pp. 178–194.

[103] Devlin, *Kit*, p. 110.

[104] Smart, *Jubilate*, A 57.

[105] *Ibid.*, B 192.

[106] Samuel Johnson defines the noun "prank" as "A frolick; a wild flight; a ludicrous trick; a mischievous act. A word of levity." As a verb, he defines "to prank" as "to decorate; to dress or adjust to ostentation." Samuel Johnson, *A Dictionary of the English Language* (London: John Jarvis, 1786).

> For it will ascend in a stream two thirds of the way and
> afterwards prank itself into ten thousand agreeable forms.[107]

This image, perhaps, is meant to suggest something about the overflowing exuberance of Smart's own prancing and prankish art.

Smart's idol-smashing views, moreover, mark a theme in *Jubilate Agno* that seems to erupt into a truly uncompromising enthusiasm. They include what many would see as the most destructive aspect of radical Puritan "pranks": a violence toward iconic representations so severe that the visual arts become vulnerable to condemnation as so many graven images. Hence this attack on painting and sculpture:

> For the blessing of God unto perfection in all bloom and fruit is by coloring.
> For from hence something in the spirit may be taken off by painters.
> For Painting is a species of idolatry, tho' not so gross as statuary.
> For it is not good to look with earning [yearning] upon any dead work.
> For by so doing something is lost in the spirit and given from life to death.[108]

Despite his long association with the stage, Smart now takes up the traditional Puritan anti-theatrical diatribe: "For all STAGE-playing is Hypocrisy and the Devil is the master of their revels."[109] And indeed, Smart's several puritanical attacks on the stage in *Jubilate Agno*[110] warn against following Bertelsen too far in equating the *Jubilate* with "Mother Midnight's Oratory." Most severely iconoclastic for Smart – translator of Horace, self-proclaimed "scholar of the university," and praiser in B 79 of libraries and booksellers – is the following celebration of Gothic assaults on classical libraries:

> For the Germans and the Dutch are the children of the
> Goth and Vandals who did a good in destruction of
> books written by heathen Free-Thinkers against God.[111]

Although it is unsurprising that such painful lines are seldom quoted, they provide a necessary context for understanding the historical wellsprings of Smart's zeal. Coppe, it will be recalled, likewise fantasized that learned professors would bring their books together and "burne them before all men."[112]

The subtly dialogical mode of Smart's engagement with enthusiasm, however, is aptly illustrated in a verse-pair that seems to accommodate a militant iconoclasm to Smart's reverence for music. Line D 217, referring to his translation of the Psalms, can be read as a gentle rebuke to the infamous Quaker iconoclast and "prankster," Solomon Eccles:

---

[107] Smart, *Jubilate*, B 209–210.
[108] *Ibid.*, B 669–673.
[109] *Ibid.*, B 345.
[110] *Ibid.*, C 68, C 93.
[111] *Ibid.*, B 459.
[112] Coppe, *Some Sweet Sips*, in Smith, *Ranter*, p. 61.

> Let Eccles, house of Eccles rejoice with Heptapleuros a kind
> of Plantain. I pray for a musician or musicians to set the
> new psalms.

Eccles was a recently converted Quaker and anti-musical zealot of the Restoration era who abandoned his practice as a music teacher to take up tailoring. He responded to the massive persecution of Quakers with a notorious series of apocalyptic "pranks," including the public burning of his own musical instruments.[113] Although Eccles may be "corrected" here by Smart, however, he is not mocked in the brutal fashion of a Swift: merely quietly subsumed, with no overt irony, into Smart's all-inclusive chorus of praise.

Smart's 100–line millennial "prophecy" in Fragment C (57–162) further serves to confirm the liminal status, both socially and historically, of *Jubilate Agno*'s rearticulated enthusiasm. Such prophecies, as a subgenre, straddled class boundaries in Smart's moment: for covenant theology, as A. D. Hope has usefully demonstrated, including learned speculations about the timing of the millennium, was a "respectable" topic for university intellectuals.[114] It is imperative, nevertheless, to understand the ongoing centrality of prophecy in chapbooks and other forms of popular culture in Smart's era. The immense popularity of chapbooks with prophetic and apocalyptic themes shows that prophecy was at this time "a household word in the commoner's vocabulary."[115] These illustrated chapbooks typically featured natural prodigies, such as monstrous births, ambiguous predictions about current and future events (especially natural calamities), puffs for patent medicines, anti-clericalism, and a preoccupation with miraculous coincidences.[116] Some, such as *The Christian's Diary* (1776) predicted a day of vengeance against exploiters – here including beggars – of the working poor.[117] The chapbook concludes, as Valenze says, on a levelling note, predicting that "a cobler and Caesar shall stand at equal terms."[118] Millennialism, and a stress on the imminence of the Day of Judgment, were especially popular themes. The research of Smart's editors, moreover, reveals that his millennialism, as in the following line, can sometimes be traced to the expectations of contemporary pamphleteers as regards the significance of England's military victories during the Seven Years' War over Roman Catholic France: "For this is the

---

[113] See William C. Braithwaite, *The Second Period of Quakerism*, 2nd. ed. prepared Henry J. Cadbury (Cambridge: Cambridge University Press, 1961), p. 25; and Hugh Ormsby-Lennon, "Swift and the Quakers," *Swift Studies* 4 (1989), p. 45.

[114] A. D. Hope, "The apocalypse of Christopher Smart," *Studies in the Eighteenth Century*, ed. R. F. Brissenden (Toronto: University of Toronto Press, 1967), pp. 269–284.

[115] Deborah M. Valenze, "Prophecy and popular literature in eighteenth-century England," *Journal of Ecclesiastical History* 29, No. 1 (1978), p. 78.

[116] *Ibid.*, pp. 78–81.

[117] *Ibid.*, p. 80.

[118] Cited in *ibid.*, p. 80.

twelfth day of the MILLENNIUM of the MILLENNIUM foretold by the prophets –
give the glory to God ONE THOUSAND SEVEN HUNDRED AND SIXTY – ."[119]

To prophesy an *imminent* millennium was to embrace, with very little
ambiguity, a popular enthusiasm. A certain process of give and take,
however, continues to mark Smart's engagement with the *topoi* of radical
Puritan prophecy. Among Smart's major prophetic themes is the prediction
that immediate revelation – through what Quakers and other enthusiasts call
"the motion of the spirit" – will be generally diffused and amplified by a
process of spiritual contagion:

> For it will be better for England and all the world in a
> season, as I prophecy this day.
> For I prophecy that they will obey the motion of the spirit
> descended upon them as at this day.[120]

Smart's own experience and attitude, therefore, will become epidemic:

> For I prophecy that the praise of God will be in every man's
> mouth in the Publick streets.
> For I prophecy that there will be Publick worship in the
> cross ways and fields.[121]

This would seem to go a long way toward subverting Anglican control over
religious functions and services. At the same time, however, Smart foresees
that days of fasting and abstinence on the Anglican calendar will be
observed,[122] and explicitly prophesies against "schismaticks" and "meeting-
houses."[123]

Many passages in *Jubilate Agno*, indeed, are marked by this supple sort of
negotiations with enthusiasm. Smart does embrace the Quaker project to
eliminate vestigial paganism from English names for the days of the week and
the names of the months:

> For the Names of the DAYS, as they now stand, are foolish
> and abominable.
> For the Days are the First, Second, Third, Fourth, Fifth,
> Sixth, and Seventh.
> For the names of the months are false – the Hebrew
> appellatives are of God.[124]

This should be the less surprising in view of Smart's praise in 1752 for a

---

[119] Smart, *Jubilate*, C 382. In this case, Karina Williamson cites as a possible source a pamphlet
appearing in 1759 entitled: *A Short Explication of the Apocalypse of St. John...wherein is shewn that the
present war may probably terminate in the restoration of the Jews, and in the millennium.*
[120] Smart, *Jubilate*, C 58–59.
[121] *Ibid.*, C 62–63.
[122] *Ibid.*, C 70.
[123] *Ibid.*, C 106–107.
[124] *Ibid.*, B 406–408.

Quaker friend's garden as exemplifying, "like friendly *Yea* and *Nay*," an admirable simplicity.[125] At the same time, however, he condemns hats such as Quakers wear as "an abomination of the heathen."[126] Is this then an orthodox repudiation of Quaker spirituality? Or could it be argued that the very vehemence of Smart's reasoning on this issue – "a man should put no obstacle between his head and the blessing of Almighty God"[127] – seems reminiscent in spirit of the Perrotonian "Hat" schism?[128] It is certain that the subsequent line, at any rate, does not clinch a safe return to orthodoxy: "For the ceiling of the house is an obstacle and therefore we pray on the house-top."[129]

How, then, to assess *Jubilate Agno*? It should be acknowledged that Smart often voices sentiments in the poem that express a quite orthodox political and religious affiliation. What also needs to be acknowledged is the extent to which Smart's enthusiasm, often sifted out and sidelined as mere pathology, serves to place the whole of Smart's religious vision in a new and more complex context. Both orthodoxy and enthusiasm are simultaneously and inseparably present in *Jubilate Agno*: precisely that dialogism, indeed, marks Smart's "mania" as a historically situated attempt to renew an earlier style of enthusiasm. There is an unacceptably high cost, however, in continuing to ignore the extent to which *Jubilate Agno*, while indubitably informed by Anglican orthodoxy, is simultaneously inspired and shaped by a very different and far more subversive mode. Moreover, to read Smart along with the likes of Abiezer Coppe, George Fox, Gerrard Winstanley, and Anna Trapnel is to know a rather different Smart than we have hitherto been given: more home-grown, more daringly rambunctious, and perhaps more comprehensible. For it is the obliteration of affiliations and continuities that makes his "manic" rhetoric seem a merely individual phenomenon, merely the regrettable but isolated wackiness of an otherwise staunch Anglican.

It must be also said, furthermore, that the fraught critical reception of *Jubilate Agno* is merely a signal instance of a much more pervasive critical bias against enthusiasm. Geoffrey Hartman has suggested, indeed, that the

---

[125] Smart, "To my worthy Friend, Mr. T.B. one of the People called Quakers" (*Smart*, IV, p. 200); see p. 440 for Williamson's identification of T. B. as Timothy Bevan.

[126] Smart, *Jubilate*, C 135.

[127] *Ibid.*, C 134.

[128] George Fox, after all, in the face of Perrot's challenge, condemned the refusal to doff hats during meetings in no uncertain terms. In one of his pastoral letters Fox writes that he would as soon see "a priest stand up in a Meeting, as one of these dark, earthly spirits with their hats on their heads, when that Friends pray." See George Fox, Epistle 214 (1661), in *The Works of George Fox* VII: *A Collection of Many Select and Christian Epistles*, p. 213. For more about this controversy, see Kenneth L. Carroll, *John Perrot: Early Quaker Schismatic*, in Supplement No. 33 to the *Journal of the Friends' Historical Society* (London: Friends' Historical Society, 1971), p. 57; and William C. Braithwaite, *The Beginnings of Quakerism*, 2nd ed. revised by Henry J. Cadbury (Cambridge: Cambridge University Press, 1955), pp. 228–250.

[129] Smart, *Jubilate*, C 136.

dominant style of critical prose in English developed precisely as a civil and cultural antidote to enthusiasm. Such prose makes up a tradition that has, in his words, "created a middle style avoiding both carnival and apocalypse, both slanderous rage and idealistic mania, in short, those political and religious enthusiasms which had contributed to civil war in the sixteenth and seventeenth centuries."[130] The value of such a "civilized" public sphere is too obvious to require elaboration. The many questionable exclusions by which that sphere has hitherto been constituted, however, are perhaps somewhat less obvious. Under such circumstances, literary historiography itself tends to be one more episode in an unequal and asymmetrical struggle between competing narratives of the past.

[130] Geoffrey Hartman, "Literary criticism and the future," in *Minor Prophecies: The Literary Essay in the Culture Wars* (Cambridge, Mass.: Harvard University Press, 1991), p. 205.

6

Double jeopardy: the provenance and reception of *Jubilate Agno*

For I am not without authority in my jeopardy, which I derive inevitably from the name of the Lord.   Christopher Smart, *Jubilate Agno*, B 1

In being confined to an asylum, Christopher Smart suffered a dramatic shrinking of his own prospects – indeed, something akin to homelessness. Like homeless people, at any rate, he had to endure a peculiar limbo, typical of homelessness,[1] between public and private space. Smart was at once confined to a quasi-public space – one where, indeed, madhouse tourists apparently passed by him "on their tour,"[2] as he bitterly writes – and yet largely excluded from the public sphere of communication.[3] Stigmatized as mad for praying loudly in public, Smart had lost much of his own privacy and his status as a public man of letters.[4]

The history of such confinement and stigmatization offers an essential context for understanding Smart's rhetorical strategies in *Jubilate Agno*. By Smart's time, a profound privatization and medicalization of madness was well underway. Much of *Jubilate Agno*, indeed, may be seen as a response precisely to the new understanding of "madness." I refer not to the history of a disease, a timeless psychiatric entity, but to the history of a label, a reified category: that "madness," strategically opposed to "reason," whose career Michel Foucault traces in *Histoire de*

[1]   See Neil Smith, "Contours of a spatialized politics: homeless vehicles and the production of geographic scale," *Social Text* 33 (1992), p. 59.
[2]   Christopher Smart, *The Poetical Works of Christopher Smart*, 4 vols., eds. Karina Williamson and Marcus Walsh (Oxford: Clarendon Press, 1980–1987), I: *Jubilate Agno*, B 63.
[3]   For more about madhouse tourism, see Max Byrd, *Visits to Bedlam: Madness and Literature in the 18th Century* (Columbia: University of South Carolina Press, 1974). Smart was first confined in St. Luke's asylum, a slightly more enlightened public asylum than Bedlam, and then Mr. Potter's private madhouse in Bethnal Green. Although St. Luke's apparently did not permit casual madhouse tourism, it did expose its inmates to the clinical gaze of medical students. See Roy Porter, *Mind-Forg'd Manacles: A History of Madness in England from the Restoration to the Regency* (London: The Athlone Press, 1987), p. 130.
[4]   For the contemporary rumor that Smart had died, see Arthur Sherbo's *Christopher Smart: Scholar of the University* (East Lansing: Michigan State University Press, 1967), p. 119.

la folie à l'âge classique.[5] This is a "madness" that haunts the poem not only as an external label for later commentators, but also constitutively, as a profoundly stigmatized *position* from which the poem attempts to speak.

The eighteenth-century confinement of "madness" thus provides a context both for mapping the contours of public and private within *Jubilate Agno* itself and for linking those contours to issues of broader political import. Literary criticism has tended to overlook the redrawing of public/private boundaries to which *Jubilate Agno* responds. The provocation of confinement, however, is the context that best makes sense of Smart's peculiar combination of two seemingly disparate discourses: the languages, in Harriet Guest's words, of "retired devotion" and "congregational praise."[6] As interpretative frames, confinement and stigmatization may also help to resolve a certain impasse in Smart studies: namely, the fact that generic appraisal of *Jubilate Agno* has been largely divided between, rather than integrative of, the twin poles of private devotion and liturgical praise.

It is an indication of how strongly *Jubilate Agno* seems oriented to the private sphere that so many critics have seen it primarily in terms of a private ritual function. Arthur Sherbo stresses the text's function as a time-marker. Because Smart composed *Jubilate Agno* by writing two or three verses every day during several years of confinement, Sherbo sees it as a calendar.[7] *Jubilate Agno* has been seen by W. K. Wimsatt as an "antiphonal logbook," a term that emphasizes its formal use of alternating voices.[8] It has been called a "private spiritual diary" by Christopher Devlin, who stresses that it was not intended for publication,[9] and a "meditation upon the creatures" by Geoffrey H. Hartman, who suggests that it revises the meditative genre of spiritual exercises.[10]

To explain *Jubilate Agno* as a private devotional tool serves to accentuate, as its ultimate meaning, only the particular process, religious and psychological, by which the poem took shape. Mark Booth, who terms the form of the *Jubilate* a "heuristic of inspiration," provides the most sophisticated version of this critical emphasis on the ritualized generation of Smart's lines: "The regular isolation of each day's writing (perhaps one pair of lines, perhaps more) from all else, in a setting of great physical and social isolation, radically

---

[5] Michel Foucault, *Histoire de la folie à l'âge classique* (Paris: Gallimard, 1972). Trans. into English by Richard Howard as *Madness and Civilization: A History of Insanity in the Age of Reason* (New York: Vintage Books, 1965).

[6] Harriet Guest, *A Form of Sound Words: The Religious Poetry of Christopher Smart* (Oxford: Clarendon Press, 1989), p. 67.

[7] Arthur Sherbo, "The dating and order of the fragments of Christopher Smart's *Jubilate Agno*," *Harvard Library Bulletin* 10 (1956), pp. 210–205.

[8] W. K. Wimsatt, "Imitation as freedom," in *Day of the Leopards: Essays in Defense of Poems* (New Haven: Yale University Press, 1976), p. 128.

[9] Christopher Devlin, *Poor Kit Smart* (London: Rupert Hart-Davis, 1961), p. 100.

[10] Geoffrey H. Hartman, "Christopher Smart's Magnificat: toward a theory of representation," in *The Fate of Reading* (Chicago: University of Chicago Press, 1975), pp. 84–85.

enforces 'writing to the moment' ..."[11] The ritual, in this view, achieves sacredness by isolating it from the worldly. Helpful as these tentative suggestions may be, they reduce the text too immediately to a private function. They ultimately fail to help us grasp, as a source of meaning, the poem's undeniable links to a larger world of public discourse and its genres.

The epitome of the public/private crux in Smart studies can be seen in the explanations surrounding the "Let:For" pattern in *Jubilate Agno*. W. H. Bond's edition of *Jubilate Agno*, in which he makes the case for the poem as an experiment in Hebraic antiphony, inaugurated exploration of the poem's liturgical form. Nothing, as the very title of the Book of Common Prayer makes clear, could be more public in its aims.[12] According to Bond, the *Jubilate*'s "Let" and "For" lines, though physically distinct in the manuscript, nevertheless correspond due to a call-and-response structure: a given "For" line thus answers to a "Let" line with which it has been paired. Bond also suggests that Smart, if he envisioned a liturgical performance of *Jubilate Agno*, may have imagined himself as the second reader or responder.[13]

Critics after Bond have emphasized certain limits in this explanation, focusing their attention on the strain with which Smart's binary antiphons are sometimes conjoined. This sense of strain, described as follows by Robert Folkenflik, is felt as a public/private split: "there is a distinct break between the 'Let' passages, which deal with the world, and the 'For' passages, which deal with the self. The two halves make up a choral whole ... but they are so discontinuous that they can only come together through the contiguities of prayer and association."[14] Fredric Bogel, who sees the *Jubilate* as exemplifying "a distinctly late-eighteenth-century form of binary mania," likewise suggests that Smart's binary "Let:For" conjunctions are a precarious affair: "Such structures may intimate connection, but they insist at least as much on the gulf dividing the two terms and on the precariousness or absence of the center that might have joined them."[15]

Guest has made an especially ingenious attempt to advance beyond the

[11] Mark Booth, "Song form and the mind in Christopher Smart's later poetry," *Studies in Eighteenth-Century Culture* 15 (1986), p. 220.

[12] It is some measure of the public orientation of *Jubilate Agno* that the Bible figures large in most of the other literary genres proposed by critics for Smart's text: psalm, prophetic poetry, and apocalypse. See Jeanne Murray Walker, "*Jubilate Agno* as psalm," *Studies in English Literature* 20:3 (1980), pp. 449–459; Francis D. Adams, "*Jubilate Agno* and the theme of gratitude," *Papers on Language and Literature* 3:3 (1967), p. 197; and A. D. Hope, "The apocalypse of Christopher Smart," in *Studies in the Eighteenth Century*, ed. R. F. Brissenden (Toronto: University of Toronto Press, 1967), pp. 269–284.

[13] W. H. Bond, Introduction, in Christopher Smart's *Jubilate Agno* (London: Rupert Hart-Davis, 1954), p. 20.

[14] Robert Folkenflik, "The artist as hero in the eighteenth century," *The Yearbook of English Studies* 12, special number: *Heroes and the Heroic*, eds. G. K. Hunter and C. J. Rawson (London: The Modern Humanities Research Association, 1981), p. 106.

[15] Fredric V. Bogel, *Literature and Insubstantiality in Later Eighteenth-Century England* (Princeton: Princeton University Press, 1984), p. 38.

limits of Bond's dialogical model. Swerving from his influential suggestion, Guest denies that the "Let" and "For" verses constitute a consistent, line-by-line "antiphonal" dialogue. She argues, rather, that the "For" lines are a strictly private and relatively autonomous commentary (meant to be read in silence) on the public and liturgical "Let" verses (meant to be performed).[16] The "Let" verses, in this view, do not require, or formally depend on, the "For" verses. This compartmentalizing solution, however, still does not offer a persuasive framework within which the public and private strands of the poem can be fully integrated.

It casts a good deal of light on this generic impasse to reconsider *Jubilate Agno* as a critique of its own marginalization in the terrain of public discourse. It is by seeking affiliation with a collective and oppositional rhetoric of enthusiasm that Smart is able to politicize anew the privatized conditions of his confinement. Enthusiasm, rather than mere retired devotion, thus allows him better to come to terms with private obscurity and public defamation. Indeed, it is precisely by bringing a dialogue between liturgical and enthusiastic genres into the very structure of his poem that Smart recasts his dilemma as more than merely personal. What Smart achieves in *Jubilate Agno*, then, is an enthusiasm that is reforged as a tool with which to complicate boundaries between private and public: an enthusiasm that challenges, above all, the eighteenth-century privatization of "madness."

It is in order to renegotiate the definition of his situation as strictly private that Smart interprets his confinement in light of the *topoi* of an older enthusiastic language of martyrdom. Smart attempts to redefine his own incarceration – his experience of the early phases of Foucault's "Great Confinement," as that confinement had evolved in England – as political imprisonment.[17] Puritan martyrology documented and thus turned to rhetorical advantage such anti-Puritan spectacles as the public amputation of William Prynne's ears. As John R. Knott shows, Prynne capitalized on his being branded with the letters "SL" (for "Seditious Libeller") by translating them as "Stigmata Laudis."[18] Thus, in Knott's words, "Prynne cast Laud as torturer and himself as Christ-like victim, making his mutilated body the sign of his spiritual victory."[19] Some martyrs were more extravagant still in dramatizing the paradoxical logic of their sweet suffering. Henry Burton, a preacher who was imprisoned after being mutilated along with Prynne, felt in prison the joy of King David: "my

---

[16] Guest, *Form*, pp. 142–145.
[17] For qualifications and refinements of Foucault's account of that evolution, see the Introduction.
[18] John R. Knott, *Discourses of Martyrdom in English Literature, 1563–1694* (Cambridge: Cambridge University Press, 1993), pp. 142–143.
[19] *Ibid.*, p. 143.

heart leaped for joy, and I could not contain my selfe, but that my body also sprang and jumped in my chamber ... as David danced before the Arke."[20] Swift mocked precisely this language of martyrdom in enthusiasm through his references in *A Tale of a Tub* to a forthcoming work entitled *The General History of Ears*.

Knott demonstrates that the stance of Protestant martyrdom, which ultimately harks back to John Foxe's influential *Acts and Monuments* (1571), was reappropriated in the seventeenth-century context by such leading Puritans as John Bunyan and George Fox. Bunyan, who composed his *Grace Abounding to the Chief of Sinners* and part of *The Pilgrim's Progress* in prison, was jailed for unlicensed preaching. Fox, as his journal records, was imprisoned on eight distinct occasions, usually for refusing to take legal oaths; he was also stoned and repeatedly beaten. Innumerable other enthusiasts were likewise persecuted: among those already mentioned in this book, Jacob Bauthumley was bored through the tongue; James Nayler was branded on the forehead, repeatedly flogged, jailed, and bored through the tongue; and Anna Trapnel and Abiezer Coppe were jailed. Coppe was eventually coerced into writing recantations of his two *Fiery Rolls*, which were also publicly burned. It was Fox and the Quakers, however, who perfected this discourse of martyrdom: for the wider context for these seventeenth-century incidents was a legal and political persecution that fell heaviest on them.[21] In a pastoral letter written in 1657, Fox lays out this strategy of documentary witnessing: "All Friends every where, that are in any sufferings, let your sufferings be gathered up together in every county, ye that have suffered by justices, or constables, or bailiffs; let your names be set to your sufferings, and the names of them that caused you to suffer."[22]

It is thus from within the terms of incarceration and censorship that we may begin to appreciate a crucial dimension of Smart's links to earlier radical Protestant authors. Acknowledging his disgraceful confinement, or "jeopardy," Smart construes it in his own terms almost as another confirmation of his election. Smart, like a caged bird, will "sing" his prophecies in captivity:

[20] Henry Burton, *A Narration of the Life of Mr. Henry Burton* (1643), p. 20. Cited in Knott, *Martyrdom*, p. 144.

[21] It has been estimated that "some three thousand Quakers suffered various forms of persecutions during the Commonwealth period." Douglas Gwyn, *Apocalypse of the Word: The Life and Message of George Fox (1624–1691)* (Richmond, Indiana: Friends United Press, 1986), p. 42. Things got even worse between 1660 and 1689: "In the first five years of Charles II's reign," according to Hugh Ormsby-Lennon, "8,600 Friends were gaoled; thereafter, 3,400 were behind bars at a time." Some 500, according to his estimate, perished due to terrible prison conditions. Hugh Ormsby-Lennon, "Swift and the Quakers (I)," *Swift Studies* 4 (1989), p. 46.

[22] George Fox, Epistle 141, *The Works of George Fox*, 8 vols. (1831; rpt. New York: AMS Press, 1975), VII: *A Collection of Many Select and Christian Epistles*, p. 135.

> Let Elizur rejoice with the Partridge, who is a prisoner of
> state and is proud of his keepers
> For I am not without authority in my jeopardy, which I
> derive inevitably from the name of the Lord.[23]

The reference to "jeopardy" recurs in B 560, where Smart prays for direction "in the better way of going on in the Fifth year of my jeopardy ..."[24] These "jeopardy" passages in the *Jubilate* are illuminated by comparison with the following passage from one of Fox's pastoral epistles, written in 1674 when Fox was ill in Worcester prison, where he had been imprisoned under the Conventicle Act:[25]

> my travels have been great, in hunger and colds, when there were few [Quakers], for the first six or seven years, that I often lay in woods and commons in the night; that many times it was a by-word, that I would not come into houses, and lie in their beds. And the prisons have been made my home a great part of the time, and in danger of my life, and in jeopardy daily.[26]

It is precisely in renewing this older discourse that Smart rhetorically converts his own "jeopardy" into a mode of triumphant authority.

It is of obvious interest, moreover, that Christopher Smart's own great-great-uncle Peter Smart, prebendary of Durham Cathedral, was for some eleven or twelve years imprisoned in King's Bench Prison after preaching in 1628 a sermon entitled "The vanitie and downefall of superstitious popish ceremonies."[27] This sermon, an attack on the "idolatrous" innovations introduced at Durham by the Laudian John Cosin,[28] uses a standard Puritan misogynist imagery against creeping "popery" in the Anglican church: "The whore of Babylon's bastardly brood, doating upon their mother's beauty, that painted harlot, the church of Rome, has laboured to restore all her robes and jewels again, especially her looking-glass, the mass, in which she may behold all her bravery."[29] By 1640, the political climate had entirely changed:

---

[23] Smart, *Jubilate*, B 1.

[24] A similar use of "jeopardy" appears as well in Smart's translation of Psalm 18. See *Smart*, III: *A Translation of the Psalms of David*, p. 36.

[25] For more about this grim period in Fox's life, see William C. Braithwaite, *The Second Period of Quakerism*, 2nd ed., prepared by Henry J. Cadbury (Cambridge: Cambridge University Press, 1961), pp. 427–428. See also Gwyn, *Apocalypse*, p. 51.

[26] George Fox, Epistle 308, *The Works of George Fox*, VIII: *A Collection of Many Select and Christian Epistles*, p. 61. There is some reason to believe that "jeopardy" had become a sort of cant term for religious persecution. The Quaker William Penn, who wrote a preface to the first edition of Smart's journal, uses "jeopardy" in a similar way, referring to "mockings, contradictions, confiscations, beatings, prisons, and many other jeopardies" suffered by the early Quakers. See William Penn, "Preface," in *The Works of George Fox*, I: *A Journal or Historical Account* ..., p. xi.

[27] Devlin, *Kit*, p. 23; Sherbo, *Scholar*, p. 3.

[28] For more about Smart and Cosin, see John Morrill, "The attack on the Church of England in the Long Parliament," in *The Nature of the English Revolution* (London: Longman, 1993), pp. 74, 79, 81, 86.

[29] Peter Smart, "The vanitie and downefall of superstitious popish ceremonies" (1628). Cited in Benjamin Brook, *The Lives of the Puritans*, 3 vols. (London: James Black, 1813), III, p. 91.

members of parliament had begun to refer to Peter Smart as "the proto-
martyr"; he was released from prison; and he lived to testify, in 1644, against
Archbishop Laud, his main persecutor.[30] Christopher Smart thus views
himself as joining a line of persecuted prophets that includes his eminent
relative, the Puritan proto-martyr. Like Peter Smart – and like the infinitely
less privileged George Fox and John Bunyan – he too is a "prisoner of state."

It is as a second countering gesture – a second means by which to attack
the contemporary privatization of madness – that Smart assumes in *Jubilate
Agno* an extraordinary identification with animals. Interpretation of Smart's
parade of animals should explore the likelihood that he is responding to the
age's bestial imagery for madness. As Foucault demonstrates, the eighteenth-
century image of madness bore, and organized anew, many social and moral
connotations, including unproductive idleness, libertinism, and animality.[31]
Indeed, the "animality" of madness in this period, according to Foucault,
inherits the iconographic forms by which European culture has understood
the relation of humankind to animals: the supposed animality of the insane
thus joins, rather than the laws of nature, "les milles formes d'un Bestiaire"
["the thousand forms of a bestiary"].[32] As we have seen, an anonymous
satirical projector of the Swiftian school provides a British version of this
imagery, imagining the potential inmates of a proposed asylum in Dublin as
"not unlike the brutes resorting to the ark before the deluge."[33]

The provocation of medical stigmatization thus provides a context in
which to rethink a conspicuous feature of *Jubilate Agno*: Smart's apparent
interest in giving voice to every one of God's creatures. It is as if the attitude
that produced the bestial imagery also provided Smart with his point of
departure. In a very early line of the poem, Smart telescopes the Ark of the
Covenant with Noah's Ark, and implies thereby that his poem is to instate a
new, all-inclusive covenant.[34] Radically altering the covenant of coupling
within species that the myth of Adam and Eve assumes and the myth of Noah
validates once more, Smart instead pairs human beings with animals. It is a
pairing that is based on, as Robert P. Fitzgerald points out, the "transcen-
dental pair, God and the Lamb."[35] Two by two they are invoked to rejoice,
and two by two they enter the all-inclusive covenant of the *Jubilate*.

What is extraordinary about this procession is that Smart does not respond

[30] *Ibid.*, p. 95.
[31] I am indebted for this summary of Foucault's work to Roland Barthes' "Taking sides," in *Critical
Essays*, trans. Richard Howard (Evanston: Northwestern University Press, 1972), pp. 163–170.
[32] Foucault, *Histoire*, p. 168; *Madness*, p. 76.
[33] Jonathan Swift[?], "A serious and useful scheme to make an hospital for incurables," in *The Prose
Works of Jonathan Swift, D.D.*, 12 vols., ed. Temple Scott (London: G. Bell and Sons, Ltd., 1925),
VII, p. 287. See Ch. 4, p. 103, for doubt about the attribution of this essay to Swift.
[34] Devlin, *Kit*, p. 107; Guest, *Form*, p. 139.
[35] Robert P. Fitzgerald, "The form of Christopher Smart's *Jubilate Agno*," *Studies in English Literature*
8:3 (1968), p. 497.

to the double negation of animals and human madmen by the more obvious
strategy of reasserting his humanity; rather, he abandons, in effect, the core
of Christian humanism: a supposed moral hierarchy – usually based on the
supposedly unique possession of God-given souls – that insists on humanity's
unique status as lord of creation. It is thus not only that Smart includes
animals within the world of moral concern, as elsewhere throughout his
poetry.[36] And it is not only that *Jubilate Agno*, like William Cowper's snail
poem, Robert Burns' "To a Mouse," and William Blake's "Auguries of
Innocence," shares a feature – "a curiously intense awareness of the animal
world" – described by Northrop Frye as peculiar to Smart's literary
generation.[37] It is, rather, that Smart makes common cause with animals as
fellow sufferers and celebrants. It is as if Smart said, implicitly, "You say I'm
an animal? Very well, then – I'm an animal: and I will write a poem from
that point of view." His gesture serves to remind us as well that the torture of
animals – and especially of cats – was, as Robert Darnton points out, "a
popular amusement throughout early modern Europe."[38]

In thus reshuffling the commonplaces and structural elements of
enthusiasm, moreover, Smart extends the rhetoric of persecution and
struggle to the domain of creatures in general. It is this feature of *Jubilate
Agno*, more than any other, that opens the poem to a dramatically "levelling"
discourse. Smart's juxtapositions of, say Moses with a lizard,[39] Cornelius
with the Swine,[40] Mary with the Carp,[41] and Rehob with Caucalis Bastard
Parsley[42] seem subversive and levelling in the extreme. Such hierarchical
distinctions as popular wisdom had imposed on the world of creatures,
moreover, are given no weight. The preference for tame over wild, for
handsome over ugly, for mammals over amphibians, reptiles, and insects:
such early modern prejudices as these[43] are systematically transgressed in
Jubilate Agno. The *Jubilate*, indeed, deliberately extends attention to such
"low" creatures as the Toad,[44] the Rat,[45] the Spider,[46] the Beetle,[47] the

---

[36] In this respect, Smart's general attitudes, though advanced, are in tune with a shift toward the
benevolent treatment of animals that acquires a notable momentum in the 1740s. See Keith
Thomas, *Man and the Natural World: A History of the Modern Sensibility* (New York: Pantheon Books,
1983), pp. 149, 173–191.

[37] Northrop Frye, "Towards defining an Age of Sensibility," in *Fables of Identity: Studies in Poetic
Mythology* (New York: Harcourt Brace Jovanovich, 1963), p. 135.

[38] Robert Darnton, *The Great Cat Massacre and Other Episodes from French Cultural History* (New York:
Basic Books, Inc., Publishers, 1984), p. 90.

[39] Smart, *Jubilate*, A 25.

[40] *Ibid.*, A 63.

[41] *Ibid.*, B 168.

[42] *Ibid.*, C 152.

[43] Thomas, *Natural*, p. 53.

[44] Smart, *Jubilate*, A 29.

[45] *Ibid.*, A 33.

[46] *Ibid.*, A 37.

[47] *Ibid.*, A 38.

Weasel,[48] the Moth,[49] the Canker-Worm,[50] and even the Gnat.[51] It is not quite right, therefore, to see a grim joke in Smart's pairing of Nebuchadnezzar with the Grasshopper in A 69.[52] It is true that Nebuchadnezzar, punished by God with insanity, ate grass in the field like an ox (Daniel 4:25). But it is precisely this sort of bestial icon of the madman – William Blake depicts Nebuchadnezzar as walking on all fours[53] – that Smart subverts through his drastic exercise in levelling. The real joke, indeed, is that in the world of *Jubilate Agno*, Nebuchadnezzar and his insectile partner are scarcely a conspicuous pairing.

In Smart's own time, John Wesley's dictum that the Golden Rule applies also to creatures[54] seems within hailing distance of the ethos of *Jubilate Agno*. Certain related tendencies can arguably be found in earlier challenges to the human/animal hierarchy, from pantheism to mortalism and annihilationism. As noted above, the Quaker schismatic John Perrot demanded human service to all creatures, down to the lowest worm; and another separatist of the same era, William Bowling, reputedly argued for a universal salvation of all creatures.[55] Smart's revisionary covenant with God, however – both enabled and incited by a shared position of exclusion from the human world – seems to take even this radical logic a step further.

Smart's attempt to imagine a new covenant embracing all creation begins with a sense that he shares a common oppression, and a common silence, with animals. "Let Levi rejoice with the Pike – God be merciful to all dumb creatures in respect of pain."[56] And more poignant even than the image of the caged partridge is the imagery in the following passage, which hints that Smart was physically "worked over" in the madhouse:

> Let Andrew rejoice with the Whale, who is array'd in
> beauteous blue and is a combination of bulk and activity.
> For they work me with their harping irons, which is a
> barbarous instrument, because I am more unguarded
> than the others.[57]

Andrew, the brother of Simon Peter, was one of the disciples converted by Jesus from a fisherman to a "fisher of men." It may also be relevant that, according to Apocryphal traditions, Andrew was crucified. The "fisher of

48 *Ibid.*, A 50.
49 *Ibid.*, A 68.
50 *Ibid.*, A 70.
51 *Ibid.*, A 96.
52 See W. Moelwyn Merchant, "Patterns of reference in Smart's *Jubilate Agno*," *Harvard Library Bulletin* 14 (1960), p. 21.
53 See Sander L. Gilman, *Seeing the Insane* (New York: John Wiley & Sons, 1982), pp. 120–121.
54 Thomas, *Natural*, p. 173.
55 See Chapter 3 for more about John Perrot and William Bowling.
56 Smart, *Jubilate*, B 183.
57 *Ibid.*, B 124.

men" thus joins both the piercing fate of harpooned whales and of Christ, whom early Christians symbolized, from a Greek acronym spelling "Ichthus," as a fish.[58] In any case, the sudden transfer of the bulky, active, beauteous whale's shocking *vulnerability* to Smart, suffering some sort of abuse in the madhouse, gives these lines remarkable pathos.

Above all, this solidarity with animals explains why Smart extends the Pauline "soldier-of-faith" *topos* in celebration of a militant defensiveness throughout the animal world. The following verse-pair makes this link explicit, and may be considered one of the nodal centers of the poem:

> Let Abiezer, the Anethothite, rejoice with Phrynos who is
>   the scaled frog.
> For I am like a frog in the brambles, but the Lord hath put
>   his whole armour on me.[59]

(Abiezer the Anethothite is an eminent captain in David's army mentioned in 1 Chronicles 11:18; 27:12.) The image of an embattled and vulnerable animal is transformed by its conflation with the militant Christian's armor of faith; and, conversely, the Pauline *topos* is irrevocably altered by Smart's extraordinary expansion of the Christian covenant.

Smart's marked fascination with zoological "defense mechanisms," moreover, resonates in a far wider context of militant Puritan language about the warfaring Christian. Hartman, who has usefully called our attention to this feature of the poem, intends to suggest the term's resonance in psychoanalytic discourse.[60] To avoid such an immediate reduction to the domain of the private case history, however, it should be noted that the enthusiastic mode veritably bristles with martial images of Protestants deploying "spiritual" weapons, as distinct from merely "carnal" ones. George Fox, for example, elaborates a crucial dimension of Quaker millenarianism in discourse about what early Friends liked to call "The Lamb's War."[61] Similarly, John Bunyan's *The Holy War* elaborates images of the soul's apocalyptic battle on an epic scale.[62]

The author of *Jubilate Agno* writes as a man acutely vulnerable to the slanderers, scorners, and accusers that constitute, as he fears, what remains of his social world. An accusing gaze and slandering voice – the Greek word *diabolos* means "the accuser" – both threaten the entire cosmos and animate its struggles. Smart praises and rejoices with a deep sense that he himself has been wounded by the stigma of "madness." "For I am under the same

---

[58] Spelled out, the acronym reads "Iesous CHristos THeou Uios Soter," meaning "Jesus Christ, Son of God, Saviour."

[59] Smart, *Jubilate*, B 95.

[60] Hartman, "Magnificat," p. 90.

[61] Gwyn, *Apocalypse*, pp. 179–207.

[62] See John R. Knott, Jr., *The Sword of the Spirit: Puritan Responses to the Bible* (Chicago: The University of Chicago Press, 1980), p. 154.

accusation with my Saviour," Smart writes − "for they said, he is besides himself."[63] Another verse-pair, punning on Bukki/book-y,[64] answers accusations of folly with an implicit assertion of his own bookish cleverness:

> Let Bukki rejoice with the Buzzard, who is clever, with the
>   reputation of a silly fellow.
> For silly fellow! silly fellow! is against me and belongeth
>   neither to me nor my family.[65]

Extending his battle with the "Adversary" to cosmic dimensions, Smart thus views the entire creation as engaged in battle against the principle of slander.

The need to fortify oneself against the "Adversary" is mentioned very early in the poem: "Let Jehoida bless God with an Hare, whose mazes are determined for the health of the body and to parry the adversary."[66] Even the flower, as a line about its medicinal value suggests, is a more militant creature than one might think: "For the flower glorifies God and the root parries the adversary."[67] Finally, Smart directly links zoological defenses to his own practice as a writer, invoking James, author of a Biblical epistle, to rejoice with the cuttle- fish, "who foils his foe by the effusion of his ink."[68]

Like warfaring Christians, Smart and his creatures do put on the whole armor of the Lord, and that armor turns out to be a prickly shell of parabolic language: "Let Jotham praise with the Urchin," Smart writes early in *Jubilate Agno*, "who took up his parable and provided himself for the adversary to kick against the pricks."[69] Language is a spiritual weapon − "For the word of God," Smart thunders, "is a sword on my side"[70] − because it mediates a sacred discourse. But it is also crucial that the medium of language, as a field of polysemous symbols, constitutes a terrain ideal for a certain sort of imaginary guerrilla warfare: hidden contestations, unexpected reversals, surprising appropriations. Smart makes a revealing play on words in another line that repeats the old fallacy that birthmarks were imprinted on fetuses by things the mother saw or imagined: "For the marking of their [women's] children," he proclaims, "is from the same cause [the Devil] both of which are to be parried by prayer."[71] P-r-a-y-e-r, as Smart's anagrammatic transformation instructs us, can turn inside out and become the name for the need to p-a-r-r-y. Thus Smart writes, in his own words, "to parry the Adversary." Defense mechanisms and vigilance are everywhere to be celebrated: "Let Samuel, the Minister from a Child, without ceasing praise

---

63 Smart, *Jubilate*, B 151.
64 Guest, *Form*, p. 153.
65 Smart, *Jubilate*, B 60.
66 *Ibid.*, A 22.
67 *Ibid.*, B 499.
68 *Ibid.*, B 125.
69 *Ibid.*, A 32.
70 *Ibid.*, B 20.
71 *Ibid.*, C 298.

with the Porcupine, which is a creature of defense and stands upon his arms continually."[72] Even Jeoffry the cat is likewise celebrated: "For the dexterity of his defense is an instance of the love of God to him exceedingly."[73]

Very early in the *Jubilate*, Smart – celebrating another zoological defense mechanism – writes, "Let Nathan rejoice with the Badger – bless God for his retired fame, and privacy inaccessible to slander."[74] The juxtaposition suggests, on the one hand, the public duties of the prophetic role: Nathan's job was precisely to "badger" King David after the latter had committed adultery with Bathsheba and arranged for her husband's death. On the other hand, it also suggests the intensity with which Smart desired to shelter a sense of privacy that would be, like the badger's cozy burrow, maintained or breached only on his own terms.

A third and perhaps even bolder challenge to the growing reification of "madness" appears in Smart's recreation of the non-linear rhetorical techniques found everywhere in the matrix of enthusiastic rhetoric. Well-known attacks by John Locke (on the abusive obscurantism caused by equivocal meanings), Joseph Addison (on the "false wit" of puns), and Samuel Johnson (on Shakespeare's unfortunate seduction by trivial quibbles) were confirming that a more rational relation between subjectivity and language would be constitutive of the newly sanitized eighteenth-century public sphere.[75] Different epistemologies require different rhetorical priorities. Locke, who elegantly analyzed the arbitrariness of linguistic signs, went on to redefine madness as an "associational disorder": that is, the accidental or merely idiosyncratic association of wrong ideas.[76] Given Smart's engagement with scientific ideas and nomenclature in the *Jubilate Agno*, it also seems relevant that the philosopher Paul Ricoeur has described science as a strategy of discourse whose leading feature is a defensive stance toward ambiguity.[77]

It is thus against the backdrop of this historical development – the marginalization of certain paralogical rhetorical techniques as private and even pathological – that Smart reasserts several features of an earlier enthusiastic and hermetic style. These include his several exercises on the alphabet, all of which are framed by his expansive version of the "Alpha-and-Omega" *topos*: "For Christ being A and Ω is all the intermediate letters without doubt."[78] They also include, with an elaboration of the Orphic

---

[72] *Ibid.*, A 44.

[73] *Ibid.*, B 733.

[74] *Ibid.*, A 45.

[75] For a useful account of this sanitizing process, see Peter Stallybrass and Allon White, *The Politics and Poetics of Transgression* (Ithaca: Cornell University Press, 1986), pp. 80–124.

[76] John Locke, *An Essay Concerning Human Understanding*, ed. Peter H. Nidditch (Oxford: Clarendon Press, 1975), p. 395.

[77] Paul Ricoeur, "Word, polysemy, metaphor," in *A Ricoeur Reader: Reflection and Imagination*, ed. Mario J. Valdés (Toronto: University of Toronto Press, 1991), p. 74.

[78] Smart, *Jubilate*, C 18. For a full-length study of Smart's alphabetic exercises, see Adelaide Katz,

"signatures" *topos*, an exploration of the hieroglyphic connotations of letters. Above all, Smart consistently opens his poem to the sort of associational logic as that which produced this line: "Let Jona rejoice with the Wilk – Wilks, Wilkie, and Wilkinson bless the name of the Lord Jesus."[79] Such "clanging" reaches its height in a catalogue of the "organ-stops," or orchestral timbres, of the English language.[80] Taking inventory of what he calls the "spiritual musick," Smart produces the following remarkable list:

> For the spiritual musick is as follows.
> For there is the thunder-stop, which is the voice of God direct.
> For the rest of the stops are by their rhimes.
> For the trumpet rhimes are sound bound soar more and the like.
> For the Shawm [a double-reed instrument] rhimes are lawn fawn
> moon boon and the like.
> For the harp rhimes are sing ring string and the like.
> For the cymbal rhimes are bell well toll soul and the like.
> For the flute rhimes are tooth youth suit mute and the like.
> For the dulcimer rhimes are grace place beat heat and the like.
> For the Clarinet rhimes are clean seen and the like.
> For the Bassoon rhimes are pass, class and the like. God be
> gracious to Baumgarden.
> For the dulcimer are rather van fan and the like and grace place
> &c are of the bassoon.
> For beat heat, weep peep &c are of the pipe.[81]

Jeanne Murray Walker argues that this passage elaborates on Smart's investment, through such figures as David and Orpheus, in the ordering powers of music and of the poet-musician.[82] It must be added, however, that the order thus created is distinctly syncopated and offbeat.[83] Its improvisational and capricious spirit is expressed in Smart's earlier assertion that "there is nothing but it may be played upon in delight."[84] And indeed, a line such as "For beat heat, weep peep &c are of the pipe" is perhaps only a step or two away from Thomas Tany's inscrutable and yet sonorous riff on the "Alpha-and-Omega" *topos*: "*Arki, vea, arni, ophiat, al sabi, arni, ary, alpha, am, O Threarpha, alba army anat.*"[85]

"The alphabet of redemption in Christopher Smart's *Jubilate Agno*" (Ph.D. Diss., Columbia University, 1984).

[79] Smart, *Jubilate*, B 173.

[80] It should come as little surprise that this passage has been quoted to illustrate Smart's "manic flight of ideas." See "The powers of night: Christopher Smart," in Gordon Claridge, Ruth Pryor, and Gwen Watkins, *Sounds from the Belljar: Ten Psychotic Authors* (New York: St. Martin's Press, 1990), p. 87.

[81] Smart, *Jubilate*, B 583–594.

[82] Walker, "Psalm," pp. 450–451.

[83] Lance Bertelsen has described a "doo-wop effect" in the *Jubilate*. See Lance Bertelsen, "Journalism, carnival, and *Jubilate Agno*," *English Literary History* 59 (1992), p. 372.

[84] Smart, *Jubilate*, B 255.

[85] Thomas Tany, *Theauraujohn, His Epitah* (1653). Cited in Jerome Friedman, *Blasphemy, Immorality,*

The combinatory and massively overdetermined quality of Smart's patterns of reference, though it has possible sources in such esoteric traditions as the Kabbala, also evokes the philosemitic Hebraicizing of English in seventeenth-century enthusiasm. And indeed, Smart's sense of the immanence of God in language evidently leads him, like Thomas Tany, Henry Walker, Abiezer Coppe, and other such macaronic writers, to a rejection of mere left-to-right linear reading. Smart can thus be said to have raised anew, albeit in a very different context, the millennial language politics of translation.[86] To translate, to bear across, to bear a cross, to bear witness to Christ – such are the manifold analogies that Christopher ("Christ-bearing") Smart – the translator of Horace and David – finds in his project of "translation." The crucial point, however, is that translation, as an act of linguistic crossing, prefigures the greater "translation" of the millennium itself: that "decisive troping," as William Kumbier puts it, when, in the twinkling of an eye, the last trump shall sound, and we shall all be changed.[87]

Like Emanuel Swedenborg, Smart thus provides an eighteenth-century rewriting of the old doctrine of "signatures."[88] Ralph Waldo Emerson described Swedenborg as "a translator of nature into thought,"[89] and we may similarly describe Smart as a translator of nature into writing, script, alphabets. Finding the shape of the Hebrew letter *lamed* in various natural vein-systems, Smart produces a "translation" of this "signature" involving something like hieroglyphs or ideographs. Correctly transliterating *lamed* as the equivalent of English *L*, Smart then *retranslates* it, punningly, as Hebrew "el," or God.[90]

> For the letter ל which signifies GOD by himself is on the
>   fibre of some leaf in every Tree.
> For ל is the grain of the human heart and on the network
>   of the skin.
> For ל is in the veins of all stones both precious and
>   common.[91]

and Anarchy: The Ranters and the English Revolution (Athens, Ohio: Ohio University Press, 1987), p. 173.

[86] See Nigel Smith, "The uses of Hebrew in the English Revolution," in *Language, Self, and Society: A Social History of Language*, eds. Peter Burke and Roy Porter (Cambridge: Polity Press, 1991), p. 55.

[87] William Kumbier, "Sound and signification in Christopher Smart's *Jubilate Agno*," *Texas Studies in Literature and Language* 24:3 (1982), p. 307. For more about "translation," see also Patricia Meyer Spacks, "Smart: mystique of vision (II)," in *The Poetry of Vision: Five Eighteenth-Century Poets* (Cambridge, Mass.: Harvard University Press, 1967), pp. 147–148; and Alan Liu, "Christopher Smart's 'uncommunicated letters': translation and the ethics of literary history," *Boundary 2* 14:1/2 (1985–1986), pp. 115–146.

[88] See Elizabeth Sewell, *The Orphic Voice: Poetry and Natural History* (London: Routledge & Kegan Paul, 1961), pp. 184–190.

[89] *Ibid.*, p. 187.

[90] See William Force Stead's annotations to his edition of this poem, *Rejoice in the Lamb: A Song from Bedlam* (London: Jonathan Cape, 1939), p. 231; see also Kumbier, "Sound," p. 303.

[91] Smart, *Jubilate*, B 477–479.

The same sensitivity to the shape of letters leads him to find in Hebrew מ
(*mem*; equivalent to English *M*) "the direct figure of God's harp."[92] Such acts
of paralogical translation constantly reiterate the point, as Patricia Meyer
Spacks puts it, "that all creation is related, so that arbitrary connections are
as meaningful as superficially logical ones."[93] And though the *Jubilate* draws
everywhere on scientific nomenclature, Smart's recycling of the "signatures"
topos makes clear that he rejects the Enlightenment's purging of hieroglyphic
and emblematic lore from the domain of natural history.[94]

As in the rabbinic principle of Biblical "omnisignificance," one must
assume that nothing occurs in *Jubilate Agno* by mere chance.[95] Hence
Smart's use of the word "conjecture", which reveals its etymology ("to
throw together") and combines it with the idea that Jesus is a "fisher" of
men's souls. The apparently random is recuperated by divine serendipity:
"For an happy Conjecture is a miraculous cast by the Lord Jesus." This is,
in fact, Smart's commentary on the Wilk – Wilks – Wilkie – Wilkinson
sequence mentioned above.[96] And indeed, attempting to read the *Jubilate*
with a full awareness of its echoes and puns, its miraculous casts into
Scripture and other texts, induces something like a "reader's sublime,"[97] a
state of absolute metaphor in which anything can potentially stand for
anything else. Reading *Jubilate Agno* is a process, like Smart's gratitude, with
no necessary end.

It is noteworthy, moreover, that Smart himself digresses in one passage
about such arresting semiotic infinitude, playing on the mystical empty-
fullness of alphabetic concatenation. The lines play in particular, as Stead has
noted, on a reading of the infinity sign, or "∞," as a chain of noughts:[98]

> For Cipher is a note of augmentation very good.
> For innumerable ciphers will amount to something.
> For the mind of man cannot bear a tedious accumulation of
>   nothings without effect.
> For infinite upon infinite they make a chain.
> For the last link is from man very nothing ascending to the
>   first Christ the Lord of All.[99]

---

92 *Ibid.*, B 524.
93 Spacks, *Vision*, p. 144.
94 Thomas, *Natural*, pp. 66–68.
95 See James Kugel, *The Idea of Biblical Poetry: Parallelism and Its History* (New Haven: Yale University Press, 1981), pp. 104–109. For a more skeptical analysis of "overinterpretation" as a practice licensed by the framing of texts as sacred, see Umberto Eco, "Overinterpreting texts," in *Interpretation and Overinterpretation*, ed. Stefan Collini (Cambridge: Cambridge University Press, 1992), pp. 45–66.
96 Smart, *Jubilate*, B 173.
97 As Thomas Weiskel observes, "Such a state is apocalyptic: it abrogates temporality, which is the necessary dimension of the syntagmatic flow." Thomas Weiskel, *The Romantic Sublime: Studies in the Structure and Psychology of Transcendence* (Baltimore: The Johns Hopkins University Press, 1976), p. 26.
98 Stead, *Rejoice*, p. 253 (note).
99 Smart, *Jubilate*, C 34–38.

The absent vowels in unpointed Hebrew texts join this "nothingness," which is a "feminine" negativity: "For the vowell is the female spirit in the Hebrew consonant."[100] Given the rich development in various speculative mysticisms of the "Alpha-and-Omega" *topos*, Smart's elaboration of it here cannot be traced to any one source. It is interesting to recall, nevertheless, that some seventeenth-century women prophets played, in a similarly gendered way, on the possible homology between mystically empty vessels and women's identity as a cipher to authorize their own texts.[101]

Some closely related lines make clear how involved Smart's wordplay is in a considered renegotiation of the gulf between the incommensurable realms of the private and idiosyncratic, on the one hand, and the universal, on the other. For Smart's "Alpha-and-Omega" passage shortly goes on to make reference to the ineffable language – in his phrase, the "uncommunicated letters"[102] – mentioned by Paul in his "third heaven" *topos*. Alan Liu has usefully juxtaposed the problem of translating such a divine language, as Smart proposes to do through his sacred poetics, with the following verse-pair:[103]

> Let Libni rejoice with the Redshank, who migrates not but
>   is translated to the upper regions.
> For I have translated in the charity, which makes things
>   better and I shall be translated myself at the last.[104]

The "Let" line simultaneously alludes to contemporary debates about bird migration and puns on the root sense of "translate." The "For" line, as unpacked by Spacks, suggests that "charity is singular and universal ('*the* charity')" and that literary translation is "a religious activity."[105] Liu further argues that the verse-pair establishes an ethic of charity in acts of translation – more broadly, interpretation – whereby a text is generously forgiven for its particular failings and hence, like the Redshank or St. Paul, translated into the "upper regions."[106] Taken together, therefore, these passages simultaneously validate Smart's claims to a sublime and ineffable experience and ask for generosity as regards his particular attempt to render the "incommunicable letters" of that experience.

Given his penchant for "translating" animals, moreover, it is hardly surprising that Smart goes on to finds cats in the Greek preposition *kata*, mice

---

[100] *Ibid.*, C 39.
[101] Sue Wiseman, "Unsilent instruments and the devil's cushions: authority in seventeenth-century women's prophetic discourse," in *New Feminist Discourses: Critical Essays on Theories and Texts*, ed. Isobel Armstrong (London: Routledge, 1992), p. 185.
[102] Smart, *Jubilate*, C 44.
[103] Liu, "Letters," p. 119.
[104] Smart, *Jubilate*, B 11.
[105] Spacks, *Vision*, p. 148.
[106] Liu, "Letters," p. 119.

in the Latin phoneme *mus*, and so on, until he has catalogued the "animal spirits" lurking in Latin, Greek, and, of course, English:

> For two creatures the Bull and the Dog prevail in the English.
> For all the words ending in -ble are in the creature. Invisi-ble,
>   Incomprehensi-ble, ineffa-ble, A-ble.[107]

A few lines later, the "Bull" theme resumes for some twenty more lines. Possibly punning on Greek *boule*, meaning "will," because God's will is the first manifestation of creation; possibly alluding to the Christian allegorizing of the sacrificed bull in Virgil's fourth Georgic;[108] and almost certainly alluding as well to the bull as one of the four cherubim of Ezekiel's vision, Smart assigns to the word "bull" a great importance:

> For BULL in the first place is of the word of Almighty God.
> For he is a creature of infinite magnitude in the height.[109]

> For there are many words under Bull.
> For Bul [the Hebraic Month] is under it.
> For Sea is under Bull [as the sea-bull, or horned fish].
> For Brooke is under Bull. God be gracious to Lord
>   ["Bully"] Bolingbroke.[110]

This long passage of "clang associations" constitutes what Smart refers to elsewhere as *sound* reasoning: "For there is a sound reasoning upon all flowers."[111] Smart, who wrote five odes (in competition for the Seatonian Prize at Cambridge) celebrating various of God's attributes, resurrects those same attributes here – invisibility, ineffability, incomprehensibility, and so on – as generative expressions of the "Bulldog spirit" of English.[112]

Smart's associational exercise on "bull," indeed, uncannily resembles Swift's manic set-piece about Lord Peter's "bulls." This resemblance, however, does not confirm the Augustan equation of enthusiasm with madness; on the contrary, it invites us to read Swift the manic punster as verging on authentic enthusiasm. As seen through the lens provided by Smart's achievement, Swift thus appears as a writer whose virtuoso parodies of enthusiasm sometimes carry him to a point where, in the words of Susan L. Manning, "satiric impersonation becomes itself a kind of celebration."[113] Both Smart and Swift "use language with a vigour

---

[107] Smart, *Jubilate*, B 643–644.
[108] Katz, "Alphabet," pp. 67–69.
[109] Smart, *Jubilate*, B 674–675.
[110] *Ibid.*, B 678–681. My bracketed interpolations are indebted to Williamson's annotations.
[111] *Ibid.*, B 504.
[112] Moira Dearnley, *The Poetry of Christopher Smart* (London: Routledge & Kegan Paul, 1968), p. 165.
[113] Susan L. Manning, "Mirth and melancholy: the generative language of fantasy in Swift and Smart," *Swift Studies* 7 (1992), p. 57.

which overflows distinctions between public and private, secular and sacred."[114]

The word B-U-L-L emerges from the morpheme -B-L-E: what had been attributed to God is now found to inhere in language itself, specifically the language of John Bull. Indeed, the importance in Smart's period of John Bull as a national symbol for the stubborn, corpulent, freeborn, beef-eating Englishman[115] suggests that his bullish exercise is motivated in part by his fervent patriotism. That Smart is willing to give "Bull" a founding significance in the "word of Almighty God," however, demonstrates again just how giddy his language is, just how close to blasphemy he is willing to come.[116] Such "sound reasoning" defies syntax, exchanging one part of speech for another, and shatters even individual words into morphemic fragments. It depends on the radical detachment of individual utterances from their context and a playful reframing of them in a domain well beyond the pale of a newly rationalized sphere of "common sense."

Smart's remarkable wordplay, indeed, which seems to saturate almost every syllable of *Jubilate Agno*, gives urgency to a much-vexed question in Smart studies: the editorial arrangement of *Jubilate Agno*. In the older standard edition by Bond, the poem can sometimes be read in two directions at once, something like a crossword puzzle. Reading horizontally across two facing pages, one sees connections between "antiphonally" related lines beginning with the words "Let" and "For." Reading vertically down the verso, one likewise sees the powerful formal and thematic parallelism connecting one "Let" line to the next. In Williamson's more recent edition for the Clarendon Press, one reads downward only, from one vertically paired doublet of "Let:For" lines to the next. In thus seeking to make the bicolumnar and "acrostic" reading experience of *Jubilate Agno* more accessible, Williamson has combined "Let" and "For" sections of the poem that in the manuscript are on discrete folio pages. This arrangement has obvious advantages in its clarity of presentation; however, as Guest points out, it does tend to eclipse the parallelism between the "Let" lines, thus minimizing an important dimension of the poem.[117] Also partly eclipsed is that sense of divinity as immanent in language – that effort, as James Holstun puts it, "to fabricate a new way of reading"[118] – that Smart appropriates from enthusiasm and rearticulates as a

---

[114] *Ibid.*, p. 54.

[115] See Jeannine Surel, "John Bull," trans. Kathy Hodgkin, in *Patriotism: The Making and Unmaking of British National Identity*, 3 vols., ed. Raphael Samuel (London: Routledge, 1989), III: *National Fictions*, pp. 3–25.

[116] Given that Smart was a Freemason, the pun may also refer, as Marie Roberts points out, to Papal Bulls condemning freemasonry. See Marie Roberts, *British Poets and Secret Societies* (Totowa, New Jersey: Barnes & Noble Books, 1986), p. 20.

[117] See Guest, *Form*, pp. 123–132. I have adapted and paraphrased some of my observations in this paragraph from my review of Guest's book in *Criticism* 33:3 (1991), p. 406.

[118] James Holstun, "Ranting at the New Historicism," *English Literary Renaissance* 19:2 (1989), p. 216.

challenge to the eighteenth-century's relegation of paralogical signification to the realm of private pathology.

Smart's most radical intervention, however, lies in the way his juxtaposition of liturgical forms with journal-keeping completely defamiliarizes the boundaries between private and public. Although Guest proposes to read the poem so as to keep each aspect discrete, *Jubilate Agno* is precisely that place, above all, where they are put into dialogue. It is Smart's contribution, indeed, simultaneously to "publicize" his spiritual journal and to "privatize" the liturgy. To be more precise: Smart's antiphonal form in *Jubilate Agno* is constituted in its modes of address by constant and abrupt "translations" between the public and private spheres. This is both his most manic rhetorical strategy and his most profound challenge to the privatization of madness.

Smart does indeed claim a public significance for the private dimension of his obscure existence. Moreover, the instability of the private "I" in *Jubilate Agno* would seem to belie the poem's apparent affinities with such humble and fugitive genres as the diary, journal, and notebook. For the *Jubilate* often subverts the self-grounding purpose by which a modern French author proposes to define a writer's journal. A journal, in Maurice Blanchot's words, is "a series of reference points that a writer establishes as a way of recognizing himself, when he recognizes the dangerous metamorphosis that he is vulnerable to."[119] *Jubilate Agno*, in contrast, itself constitutes a "dangerous metamorphosis," a veritable sea-change in which Smart is made new: "For I have adventured myself in the name of the Lord," he writes, "and he hath mark'd me for his own."[120] There is a very likely echo here of Milton's prayer at the opening of *Paradise Lost* for the heavenly muse to aid his "advent'rous Song / That with no middle flight intends to soar / Above th' *Aonian* Mount ..."[121] This Miltonic echo underscores the soaring ambitions toward a public voice that inform Smart's far-from-pedestrian diary.

Smart's refusal to write in terms of a merely empirical self contributes to another conspicuous feature of his manic style: the disjunctive "flightiness," or "lark-jump of joy,"[122] by which he proceeds from one thought to another. Neither such disjunctiveness, however, nor such disdain for the merely empirical self are unique to Smart's mode of journal-keeping. For enthusiastic spiritual autobiography is founded by a constitutive paradox. John R. Knott formulates this well, in considering George Fox's *Journal*: it is, he writes, "the autobiography of a man for whom a spiritual quest required an emptying of

[119] Maurice Blanchot, "The essential solitude," in *The Gaze of Orpheus*, trans. Lydia Davis (Barrytown, New York: Station Hill Press, 1981), p. 71.

[120] Smart, *Jubilate*, B 21.

[121] John Milton, *Paradise Lost*, in *John Milton: Complete Poems and Major Prose*, ed. Merritt Y. Hughes (New York: The Odyssey Press, 1957), pp. 211–212.

[122] Attributed to the English author John Fowles by Emily Coleman. Liner notes for LP recording of Benjamin Britten's choral setting of Smart's poem, *Rejoice in the Lamb*, RCA Victor, 1964.

the self."[123] And formal descriptions of Fox's *Journal* stress precisely its paratactic syntax, its additive and non-linear process of narration: "Everything that the Fox of the *Journal* is and knows," writes James Olney, "is based on isolated and transcendent moments, each complete in itself but otherwise unrelated to what goes before and after."[124] One is reminded as well of Abiezer Coppe's deliberately fractured evocations of his ineffable spiritual experience: "But perhaps I now speak," as he confesses, "with a stammering tongue."[125] Though Swift mocked such disjunctiveness by introducing nonsensical lacunae in *A Tale of a Tub*, Smart renews the potential of such form-breaking for creating a language that can gesture toward ineffable sublimity.

There are many curious circuits by which Smart translates between private and public. For despite his wistful praise of the retiring badger, Smart's supposedly private spiritual diary in fact constantly evokes a public context of meaning and imagined reception. Through his poetic vocation, Smart hopes, despite his stigmatization, to become acceptable, even beautiful. The harmonious beauty of a swan, Olor, and its punning link to the Latin for "to smell of," *olere*, thus become the site of an identification for Smart, who pairs Olor with a priest whose sacrificial offerings unto the Lord (Numbers 7:36) are of a sort the Bible describes as sweet and savoury:

> Let Shelumiel rejoice with Olor, who is of a goodly savour,
>   and the very look of him harmonizes the mind.
> For my existimation is good even amongst the slanderers
>   and my memory shall arise for a sweet savour unto the
>   Lord.[126]

His blending of sight and olfaction combines a sense sometimes associated with physical and emotional distance, vision, with the very close and intimate sense of smell: a synaesthesia that prefigures, as we shall see, more dramatic fusions.

The complexity of Smart's rhetoric at this point depends on the extraordinary extent to which he identifies himself with the words of his own text. What he calls his "existimation," borrowing from Latin *existimatio* and combining "existence" and "estimation," means a self, an "I," considered entirely as an object of discourse: something viewed, judged, estimated, esteemed.[127] Smart's "existimation" thus anticipates his

---

[123] John R. Knott, Jr., "The Acts of George Fox: a reading of the *Journal*," *Prose Studies: History, Theory, Criticism* 6:3 (1983), p. 229.

[124] James Olney, *Metaphors of Self: The Meaning of Autobiography* (Princeton, New Jersey: Princeton University Press, 1972), p. 177. See also Dean Ebner, *Autobiography in Seventeenth-Century England: Theology and the Self* (The Hague: Mouton, 1971), pp. 131–132.

[125] Abiezer Coppe, *Some Sweet Sips, of Some Spirituall Wine* (1649), in *A Collection of Ranter Writings from the 17th Century*, ed. Nigel Smith (London: Junction Books, 1983), p. 70.

[126] Smart, *Jubilate*, B 3.

[127] Bond, *Jubilate*, p. 41 (note).

posthumous "translation" into a *name*, a specular or mirrored identity, associated with praise.[128] Smart thus becomes, at the moment of his writing, what he imagines he will have been to his readers in the future. The private life is effectively nullified: Smart "existimates" already as an object of public remembrance. Such "existimation," as it turned out, was far in the future. For *Jubilate Agno* was to be unpublished for some 170 years – privately preserved as a medical curiosity, a case study in "poetic mania," rather than as a poem.

There is a further complexity, however, to be noted as regards the implications of Smart's juxtaposition of journal-keeping with liturgical forms: for just as the public mode in *Jubilate Agno* tends to rewrite Smart's private reality, so the converse is true. This formulation, indeed, permits us to see the poem's antiphonal structure as Smart's version of the manic rhetoric of enunciation. This fusional rhetoric entails a sublime transgression of the pronominal positions established in the very process of writing. As we have seen, the manic style formally transgresses the relations between text and reader, intrinsic and extrinsic, producing slippages between the positions constituted by pronouns and prepositions. It is through this manic pronominalization that the enthusiastic mode attempts to enact the transfigured subjectivity necessary to any realization of its apocalyptic desires.

Smart's remarkable poem does incorporate us, the readers, into its universal chorus of praise. Yet our place, or places, in this chorus of praise must be specified with care: for there is an implied *fusion of the first and second persons* in Smart's structures of address. In the imperative mode of his "Let" lines, "I" can also mean "you"; "you," moreover, can also mean "God." When Smart commands "Let so-and-so rejoice," it means both "(I) let" and "(You, O God) let." Thus, scandalous as it may seem, both Smart and the implied reader are, in some sense, *in God*: occupying, that is to say, God's discursive position. The fusion is enacted formally: Smart's position in his own devotional discourse, as the triumphant orchestrator of cosmic praise, echoes God's divine fiat in Genesis with its incantatory "Let ... Let ... Let."

This scriptural *topos*, a touchstone of the sublime, is widely echoed throughout English literature in the eighteenth century.[129] Smart himself twice remarks in the *Jubilate* on the sublime velocity of God's first creation: "For the propagation of light is quick as the divine Conception."[130] Yet critical discussion of the "Let:For" structure, which tends to trace it to sources

---

[128] See Geoffrey Hartman, *Saving the Text: Literature/Derrida/Philosophy* (Baltimore: The Johns Hopkins University Press, 1981), pp. 127–128.

[129] Alexander Pope echoes this *topos* in many of his major poems, including "Windsor Forest," "The Rape of the Lock," and "The Dunciad." And in his Lecture XVI, "Sublimity of sentiment," Bishop Lowth discusses the sublimity of the divine fiat at length. Robert Lowth, *Lectures on the Sacred Poetry of the Hebrews*, trans. G. Gregory (Andover, Massachusetts: Flagg and Gould, 1829), pp. 130–133.

[130] Smart, *Jubilate*, C 325.

in the Psalms,[131] generally neglects the remarkable logic of his poetic fiat.
Smart's use of the imperative "Let" is of course well within the enthusiastic
constellation. His positional fusion with God both recalls and refashions the
enthusiastic ventriloquism by which Abiezer Coppe and Mary Cary/Rand,
among others, wrote as the chosen instruments of God's voice.

The transgressive nature of Smart's structural logic becomes even clearer
when one considers the reversal of ordinary causal relationships that occurs
between the lines that begin with "Let" and those that, answering
antiphonally, begin with "For." The "Let" lines, which invoke a public realm
of rejoicing creatures, are, despite their serial priority to the "For" lines,
made to depend on them logically. Since the "For" lines usually refer to
Smart's private circumstances, the public world is omnipotently referred to
him: Shelumiel must rejoice with Olor *because* Smart's "existimation" is good
even amongst the slanderers. This logic, however, is disguised by the
metaleptic reversal by which Smart invokes the consequent effect, the
rejoicing, before the antecedent cause.

It must also be observed that Smart's antiphonal form is self-referential: it
makes a Borgesian "strange loop" or "tangled hierarchy" that mingles
different logical levels, as when an author becomes a character in his own
novel.[132] Specifically, there is a recursive loop in that Smart (as maker of the
poetic utterance) *invokes* the scene of rejoicing in which Smart (the "I," the
subject of the enunciation) is imaginatively positioned as the suffering or
rejoicing cynosure of the public events. I cannot agree with Guest's argument,
therefore, that the "Let" verses neither depend on, nor respond to, the "For"
lines.[133] Each type of verse depends on the other: but the true scandal of
Jubilate Agno is precisely the extent to which the poem threatens to subvert its
public dimension by "translating" acts of liturgical rejoicing into so many
contingent consequences of the "private" author's existence. It is here, in
Smart's defamiliarization of the public sphere's boundaries, that *Jubilate Agno*
is perhaps most radical, most an event in literary history.

Literary history itself, as Liu's analysis makes clear, can also be seen as a
process of "translation."[134] The reception of Smart's most daring poem says
a great deal about that process, and, especially, about the sheer strength of
the ideology that has assigned a recurrent "manic" rhetoric to the private

---

[131] A. D. Hope, for instance, mentions verses 34 and 35 of Psalm 69 as a possible model: "Let the
Heaven and earth praise Him, the seas, and everything that moveth therein; for God will save
Zion, and will build the cities of Judah; that they may dwell there and have possession." Harriet
Guest, however, also proposes comparisons with the Book of Job and the Apocryphal Wisdom of
Solomon. See Hope, "Apocalypse," p. 272; and Guest, *Form*, pp. 128–131.

[132] These terms for self-referentiality I have borrowed from Douglas Hofstadter's *Gödel, Escher, Bach:
An Eternal Golden Braid* (New York: Vintage Books, 1980). See Chapter XX, "Strange loops, or
tangled hierarchies," pp. 684–742.

[133] Guest, *Form*, p. 142.

[134] Liu, "Letters," pp. 132–140.

realm. It is thus not surprising that the "translation" of *Jubilate Agno*, in all possible senses of the word, has proven to be a gradual and uneven process. Though one critic suggests that the "literary Bedlam" of the twentieth century at last permits us to view it as a poem,[135] even this task has not been fully realized. W. F. Stead, who in 1939 brought forth the first edition of Smart's poem under the title *Rejoice in the Lamb: A Song from Bedlam*, constituted it through his editorially assigned subtitle as a specifically *mad* text. We have read it ever since, whether explicitly or implicitly, under the shadow of private pathology.

I hope that reframing both *Jubilate Agno* and the history of its critical reception will contribute further to the ongoing emancipation of Smart from the interpretative confinement in which he has long languished. It would be too tedious to inventory the references to "madness," and especially to "mania," in twentieth-century discussions of Smart. It must be said, nevertheless, that literary criticism has produced the second and longest of Smart's "jeopardies." From the beginning, the critical reception of Smart's work has established the centrality of madness as a means of understanding it. Even the myth that grew up around the initial publication of "A Song to David" – that Smart frantically scratched all 516 lines of it on the wainscot of his madhouse cell with a key – was not too absurd to be circulated by the *Monthly Review* in Smart's own time, or revived by Robert Browning, or further repeated by several twentieth-century critics.[136] And indeed, almost all later critics sooner or later invoke psychiatric terminology. The effect of such reifying language, however subtle, is yet another round of ahistorical privatization.

To be sure, a conspicuous pattern in the criticism of *Jubilate Agno* has been the progressive discovery of more and more order in the poem, more and more "reason" in the "madness." Yet to call the *Jubilate* a logbook, calendar, or unpublishable spiritual diary implies that it is pre-literary, like a rough draft, if not subliterary. The poem's originality, however, lies precisely in its way of putting into dialogue the homely and the transcendent, the spontaneous and the formal, the devotional and the congregational. Our translation of its achievement needs to find a vocabulary that faithfully observes the historical process by which religious "enthusiasm" was stripped of its collective resonance and relegated to the realm of private madness.

The madness that has been widely seen in Smart is decisively over-determined, as a particular rhetorical mode, by the history of the manic style. *Jubilate Agno* is thus not a one-of-a-kind freak or sport, trapped in the singularity of a merely private or autistic language. The *Jubilate* in fact has strong affiliations with the ethos of enthusiastic rhetoric, with its own peculiar

[135] John Hollander, "Romantic verse form and the metrical contract," in *Vision and Resonance: Two Senses of Poetic Form* (New York: Oxford University Press, 1975), p. 203.
[136] Sherbo, *Scholar*, p. 169.

constitutive elements, structures, and *topoi*, that we have studied here. The *Jubilate* is, moreover, as much a response to Smart's situation as evidence for how he arrived at that situation. And finally, the notion of a manic rhetorical *style* – a collectively defined mode handed down culturally rather than merely genetically – should encourage at least a measure of humility among those who purport to practice psychiatric diagnosis on a text written over 200 years ago. The manic tradition, after all, is precisely one of the silences – the historical abscesses, as it were – on which the psychiatric discourse *about* madness, however well-intentioned, has been founded.

When we do succeed in "translating" Christopher Smart, we may find that he has been waiting for us all along. In line B 15, he writes as follows:

> Let Ephah rejoice with Buprestis, the Lord endue us with
> temperance and humanity, till every cow have her mate.
> For I am come home again, but there is nobody to kill the
> calf or to pay the musick.

Smart's editors have noted both the allusion to the parable of the Prodigal Son and the possibility that Smart had been allowed a temporary release from the asylum. I find it more likely, however, that this is Smart's defiant response to the perplexities of his situation: a spooky and bittersweet version, indeed, of the enthusiastic "homecoming" *topos*, in which "home" is an entirely figurative state of being. So Abiezer Coppe had argued that "Some are at *Home*, and within; Some *Abroad*, and without. They that are at *Home*, are such as know their union *in* God, and live upon, and *in*, and not upon any thing below, or beside him."[137] As reworked by Smart, it is a *topos* that turns our ideas of dwelling, and of asylums, inside out.

---

[137] Coppe, *Some Sweet Sips*, in Smith, *Ranter*, p. 49.

7

Smart's bawdy politic: misogyny and the Second Age of Horn in *Jubilate Agno*

For when men get their horns again, they will delight to go uncovered.

Christopher Smart, *Jubilate Agno*, C 132

Enthusiastic rhetoric in the Cromwellian era was by no means free of the misogyny prevailing in seventeenth-century Britain. Nevertheless, the somewhat more egalitarian cultural space that female prophets were able to negotiate within the enthusiastic constellation made enthusiasm itself vulnerable to misogynist attacks. The female enthusiast thus looms very large in anti-enthusiastic invective. *A Tale of a Tub*, in its parodic representation of inspiration from below, typifies this anti-enthusiastic misogyny. Parodying the Quaker practice of permitting women to preach, the *Tale* transfers the imagery of anality and flatulence to the female genitals, which organs "were understood to be better disposed for the Admission of those Oracular *Gusts*, as entring and passing up thro' a Receptacle of greater Capacity, and causing also a Pruriency by the Way, such as with due Management, hath been refined from a Carnal, into a Spiritual Extasie."[1] A certain "emasculation" of plebeian authors is likewise implied here: for to indicate once again their "nothingness," Swift also draws on the venerable equation of the feminine genitalia with absence.[2] This vein of anti-enthusiastic misogyny has roots that can be traced back at least to the pointedly symbolic disguise – women's apparel – used by the male assailants in a brutal attack carried out against the Diggers' colony in Surrey in 1649, which left four male Diggers beaten senseless.[3]

It is symptomatic of this tendency to feminize enthusiasm that Joseph Addison – in response to the "French prophets" or Camisards, whose inspired

---

[1] Jonathan Swift, *A Tale of a Tub*, ed. A. C. Guthkelch and D. Nichol Smith, 2nd ed. (Oxford: Clarendon Press, 1958), p. 157.

[2] Shakespeare, as is well known, often plays on this sense of *nothing*, as when Hamlet replies to Ophelia's "I think nothing" with "That's a fair thought to lie between maids' legs" (*Hamlet*, III. ii. 117–119). See also John Wilmot, "Upon Nothing," in *The Complete Poems of John Wilmot, Earl of Rochester*, ed. David M. Vieth (New Haven: Yale University Press, 1968), p. 119.

[3] Gerrard Winstanley, *A Declaration of the Bloody and Unchristian Acting of William Star, and John Taylor of Walton*, in *The Works of Gerrard Winstanley*, ed. George H. Sabine (Ithaca: Cornell University Press, 1941), pp. 295–298. This episode is further discussed in the Introduction.

agitations and prophetic pranks provoked a backlash in the early decades of the eighteenth century – likewise enlarges upon the theme.[4] Addison's *Spectator* 201 (1711) is a characteristic attempt to define a middle way between the superstition of Catholicism and the enthusiasm of radical dissent. The enthusiastic mind appears in this essay as a feminized consciousness whose weakness threatens to cause the "degeneration" of "masculine" reason: "Devotion, when it does not lie under the check of reason, is very apt to degenerate into enthusiasm. When the mind finds herself very much inflamed with her devotions, she is too much inclined to think they are not of her own kindling, but blown up by something divine within her."[5] "Nothing is so glorious in the eyes of mankind," according to Addison's closing development of this gendered imagery, "...as a strong, steady, masculine piety; but enthusiasm and superstition are the weaknesses of human reason, that expose us to the scorn and derision of infidels, and sink us even below the beasts that perish."[6]

Smart's key symbol of horns in the *Jubilate*, given the context of this intensely gendered cultural terrain, absorbs a remarkable range of meanings. The fear of being slandered as a cuckold that Smart expresses in *Jubilate Agno* – "they throw my horns in my face"[7] – becomes, in a later prophetic passage, the triumphant "realization" that his supposed cuckoldry is yet another sign of his own prophetic election. In a lengthy fantasia on the theme of the "Second Coming of the Horn," which assumes that his male ancestors had potent horns on their foreheads, Smart goes on to make a predictable connection between sexual potency and male domination. Although cuckoldry is traditionally a signifier of castration,[8] Smart reverses this normative meaning into its opposite. Playing with the tradition of the "Horned Moses," he invests the cuckold's horns with a highly honorific meaning: "For in the day of David Man as yet had a glorious horn upon his forehead."[9] This reversal of his supposed cuckoldry, as Alan Liu points out, invests horns with

---

4   See Hillel Schwartz, *Knaves, Fools, Madmen, and that Subtile Effluvium: A study of the Opposition to the French Prophets in England, 1706–1710* (Gainesville: The University Presses of Florida, 1978), p. 62. I am indebted to Schwartz for the reference to Addison.

5   Joseph Addison, *Spectator* 201 (Saturday, October 20, 1711), *The Spectator*, 5 vols., ed. Donald F. Bond (Oxford: Clarendon Press, 1965), II, p. 289.

6   *Ibid.*, p. 290.

7   Christopher Smart, *The Poetical Works of Christopher Smart*, 4 vols., eds. Karina Williamson and Marcus Walsh (Oxford: Clarendon Press, 1980–1987) I: *Jubilate Agno*, B 115.

8   According to the OED's discussion of "cuckold," the metaphor of "giving horns" to a cuckold refers to the practice of planting or engrafting the spurs of a castrated cock on the root of its excised comb, where they grew and became horns, sometimes several inches in length. Although this is only one theory among several for the association between horns and cuckoldry, further support for it has recently been adduced. See Robert Bates Graber and Gregory C. Richter, "The capon theory of the cuckold's horns: confirmation or conjecture," *Journal of American Folklore* 100:395 (1987), pp. 58–63. As Graber and Richter point out, the German word for cuckold, *Hahnrei*, originally meant "capon."

9   Smart, *Jubilate*, C 119.

the ambivalence of a Freudian "primal word."[10] It is through this reversal that Smart links concerns about his domestic authority to broader claims about his literary and spiritual authority.

Smart's millennial symbol of horns thus gathers in a conspicuous political contradiction. On the one hand, the "horn of plenty," developed in the context of an agricultural harvest motif,[11] removes barriers between thee and me, mine and thine. It ushers in a better time, a more merciful time: "For I prophecy that there will be more mercy for criminals."[12] The Age of Horn, indeed, promises a time of financial mercy that would arrive too late for Smart himself: "For I prophecy that they will not dare to imprison a brother or sister for debt."[13] And yet, on the other hand, it also prophesies a new age of heightened male supremacy: "For I prophecy that there will be less mischief concerning women."[14] And indeed, Smart takes the cultural ideal of feminine self-negation to its logical conclusion: "For I pray God for a reformation amongst the women and the restoration of the veil."[15]

Although Smart's sexual politics has been discussed before, it has seldom been seen as integral to his millennial reimagining of the body politic. On the one hand, Christopher Devlin, for example, condemns the "extravagant misogyny" of Smart's views and describes Smart's "Second Age of Horn" prophecy as "one of the most shockingly crazy of his passages."[16] On the other hand, Lance Bertelsen argues that misogyny – given the extent to which Smart's textual practice affirms flux, paradox, and fluidity – cannot be seen as any sort of final word.[17] What needs further development in studies of the *Jubilate*, however, is a way of thinking Smart's millennium and his peculiar sexual politics simultaneously. For it is not enough to see the gendering of the "horn" symbol in *Jubilate Agno* as merely a residual misogyny: a trivial pocket of backwardness or pathology, as it were, in Smart's otherwise millennial vision.

As a strikingly liminal symbol, Smart's jubilee horn illustrates, first of all,

---

[10]   Alan Liu, "Christopher Smart's 'uncommunicated letters': translation and the ethics of literary history," *Boundary 2* 14:1/2 (1985/1986), p. 120.

[11]   *Ibid.*, p. 121.

[12]   Smart, *Jubilate*, C 65.

[13]   *Ibid.*, C 72. After his release from the asylum in January, 1763, Smart enjoyed the most productive half-dozen years of his literary career. He lived beyond his means, however, and was ultimately confined for debt in King's Bench Prison, where (though given the limited freedom of the "Rules," a small area around the prison) he spent the last thirteen months of his life. See Christopher Devlin, *Poor Kit Smart* (London: Rupert Hart-Davis, 1961), pp. 182–193; and Arthur Sherbo, *Christopher Smart: Scholar of the University* (East Lansing: Michigan State University Press, 1967), pp. 255–265.

[14]   Smart, *Jubilate*, C 66.

[15]   *Ibid.*, B 103. The Oxford edition of *Jubilate Agno* reads "amonst" for this line. I am grateful to Karina Williamson for pointing out to me that this is a misprint for "amongst."

[16]   Devlin, *Kit*, pp. 87, 122.

[17]   Lance Bertelsen, "Journalism, carnival, and *Jubilate Agno*," *English Literary History* 59 (1992), p. 379.

the transitional nature of the eighteenth century: "one of the key periods of emergence," as Julia Epstein and Kristina Straub point out, "for modern forms of sexuality, institutionalized sexual subcultures, and gender identity in the West."[18] The emergent blueprint of the sexual universe consisted of *two* sexed bodies, sharply defined by their polar opposition, and – given the dawning recognition of men who exclusively desired other men – *three* genders; the fourth or lesbian gender would visibly emerge by the late eighteenth century.[19] And it is indeed the shaming force of this "modern" agenda – this pressure to define himself in terms of a normative masculine identity grounded in a straight sexual orientation – that animates Smart's gendered symbolism. The embattled terrain of enthusiasm in the eighteenth century, however, provides a more focused and illuminating context in which to understand the remarkable complexity of Smart's jubilee horn: a symbol that tends to glide out from under the yoke of a stable masculine/feminine binary. Smart's affiliation with enthusiastic rhetoric in fact accounts both for the pressure to reaffirm his masculinity in *Jubilate Agno* and his ability to recast that masculinity in unexpected ways.

It must be granted that some of Smart's misogyny looks very like that found within seventeenth-century enthusiasm itself. To illustrate: a strong parallel between Smart, on the one hand, and Abiezer Coppe and Anna Trapnel, on the other, can be found as regards the interpretation of Queen Michal. Consider a verse-pair in which Smart, preoccupied as he was with King David, boasts of his scorn for the haughty "Michals" of the world. Echoing Proverbs 3:34, Smart returns scorn to the scorners of religious enthusiasm:

> Let Michal rejoice with Leucocreuta, who is a mixture of beauty
>   and magnanimity.
> For he that scorneth the scorner hath condescended to my low
>   estate.[20]

Coppe, it will be recalled, boasted that he was "confounding, plaguing, tormenting nice, demure Michal by skipping, leaping, dancing, like one of the fools..."[21] Trapnel likewise writes that she could not refuse to dance

[18]   Julia Epstein and Kristina Straub, "Introduction: The Guarded Body," in *Body Guards: The Cultural Politics of Gender Ambiguity*, eds. Julia Epstein and Kristina Straub (New York: Routledge, 1991), p. 6.

[19]   See Randolph Trumbach, "London's Sapphists: from three sexes to four genders in the making of modern culture," in Epstein and Straub, *Body Guards*, pp. 112–141. For a further mapping of the male homosexual landscape in this period, see G. S. Rousseau, "The pursuit of homosexuality in the eighteenth century: 'utterly confused category' and/or rich repository?" in *'Tis Nature's Fault: Unauthorized Sexuality during the Enlightenment*, ed. Robert Purks Maccubin (Cambridge: Cambridge University Press, 1985), pp. 132–168.

[20]   Smart, *Jubilate*, B 61.

[21]   Abiezer Coppe, *A Second Fiery Flying Roule* (1649), in *A Collection of Ranter Writings from the 17th Century*, ed. Nigel Smith (London: Junction Books, 1983), p. 106.

before the Ark of Christ's redemption, "though *Michols* mocked..."[22] Coppe, Trapnel, and Smart all seize upon the same passage of Scripture as an emblem of their defiant marginality as enthusiasts. The allusion to the scornful gaze of Michal, who dislikes David's extravagant leaping and dancing before the maidservants, targets the respectable *woman* for a dose of defiant scorn. In all three authors this vein of "anti-respectable" misogyny must be seen as overdetermined by the interaction, within the larger culture, of class and gender ideology. Even this parallel, however, demonstrates the need for the sort of analysis to be pursued here: for it makes a subtle difference that Smart uses this *topos* in response to a cultural climate far more saturated with anti-enthusiastic misogyny.

It is indeed the enemies of enthusiasm, among those tributaries of misogyny that fed into *Jubilate Agno*, that are most significant for our analysis. And though Smart's misogyny does have a biographical dimension, it is crucial to recognize that even this personal experience is filtered through such themes of a systemic sexual ideology as cuckoldry and female virtue.[23] These themes inform Smart's reaction to the traumatic breakup of his family. After he had been confined a second time, with no prospects of providing for his family, his wife Anna Maria and their two daughters moved to Dublin. Smart's various responses to the end of his marriage, which include the wish that Anna Maria would return,[24] finally resulted in the groundless belief that he was being slandered as a cuckold. The lens of the "cuckoldry" motif thus began to distort the way Smart reconstructed the events of his life. Believing that he had been "feminized" as a cuckold, Smart uses millennial prophecy as a way of reversing its meaning.

The familial context also includes Smart's renunciation, while in the asylum, of his claims to an inheritance. Evidently Smart felt that he had been manipulated into surrendering, for his mother's sake, his rights to a small entailed estate. The best guess is that Smart agreed to renounce his somewhat doubtful claims on the family's estate to a cousin, Richard Smart, on the condition that his mother was looked after.[25] "For my brethren have dealt deceitfully as a brook," he writes about this scene, "and as the stream of brooks that pass away."[26] Since he was involuntarily committed to Potter's

---

[22] Anna Trapnel, *A Legacy for Saints: Being Several Experiences of the Dealing of God with Anna Trapnel* (London, 1654), p. 14.

[23] For a useful survey of the varieties of eighteenth-century misogyny, see Felicity A. Nussbaum, *The Brink of All We Hate: English Satires on Women 1660–1750* (Lexington: The University Press of Kentucky), 1984. For a discussion of the shift in the meaning of female "virtue" between the middle and late eighteenth century, see Julie Shaffer, "The high cost of female virtue: the sexualization of female agency in late eighteenth- and early nineteenth-century texts," in *Misogyny in Literature*, ed. Katherine Anne Ackley (New York: Garland Publishers, Inc., 1992), pp. 105–142.

[24] Smart, *Jubilate*, B 324.

[25] Devlin, *Kit*, pp. 111, 178–181.

[26] Smart, *Jubilate*, B 74.

madhouse by his stepfather, and since that confinement broke up his marriage and wrecked his chances of producing a male heir, Smart's bitterness at the supposed disinheritance is not incomprehensible. What is intriguing, however, is the gathering, in the cluster of lines dealing with this disinheritance,[27] of animals known either for their horns or for their gullibility. These range from Platycerotes, a stag,[28] to the Gull,[29] to Musimon, a ram-goat hybrid.[30] The very name of the Wittal,[31] indeed, connotes "a knowing and complaisant cuckold." What Smart is both lamenting and celebrating is the economic loss of his opportunity to play the role of landed patriarch. It is a position that condenses a confluence of name, person, and land such that female sexuality – as one especially lively form of property – is supposed to guarantee the "legitimate" descent of the rest. Thus Smart, in surrendering his "flocks," implies that he himself has become a sort of ram-goat hybrid:

> Let Ezbon rejoice with Musimon, who is from the ram and she-goat.
> For I lent my flocks and my herds and my lands at once unto the Lord.[32]

As Kenneth Fraser Easton points out, the effect of these conjunctions is to constitute the economic threat to Smart's patriarchal status as a specifically sexual problem: "The 'Platycerotes' and 'Musimon' of the first and last 'Let' verses of the passage mark the sexual stakes: Smart's loss of inheritance is placed between the horns of cuckoldry he feared in his wife as he makes over his claim to his uncle's estate to his mother, another woman who abandoned him."[33] Smart's solution to this threat, then, is to conflate cuckoldry with the enthusiastic *topos* of "wise folly": "Let Sered rejoice with the Wittall – a silly bird is wise unto his own preservation."[34] Or again: "For I bless the thirteenth of August, in which I was willing to be called a fool for the sake of Christ."[35]

To be sure, the tension between honorable patronymic and disgraceful cuckoldry persists. It seems to resurface in line B 58, where Smart depicts himself as a modern St. George, slaying, according to Karina Williamson's annotation, "the *Dragon* of false philosophy and atheism":

> Let Manoah rejoice with Cerastes, who is a Dragon with horns.
> For CHRISTOPHER must slay the Dragon with a PHEON's head.

[27] *Ibid.*, B 46–52.
[28] *Ibid.*, B 46.
[29] *Ibid.*, B 51.
[30] *Ibid.*, B 52.
[31] *Ibid.*, B 48.
[32] *Ibid.*, B 52.
[33] Kenneth Fraser Easton, "'Hum-buggers-bougres': Christopher Smart, Mrs. Midnight, and *Jubilate Agno*," in "Bad habits: cross-dressing and the regulation of gender in eighteenth-century British literature and society" (Ph.D. Diss., Princeton University, 1990), p. 256.
[34] Smart, *Jubilate*, B 48.
[35] *Ibid.*, B 51.

"Pheon" in heraldic terms is a broad arrow: it looks like four barbed arrowheads arranged point-to-point, so that the barbs radiate outward into a star. The Smart coat of arms, as Williamson notes, was a chevron between three pheons. Smart's heraldic claim to genteel origins thus makes a spiritual weapon of his supposed ancestral distinction.[36] It is notable, however, that the dragon in question is horned. The counterpointing of heraldic pheons against horns suggests an unstable opposition in which each pole mirrors, and thus closely resembles, the other. It is, in any case, an opposition that will be overcome: for Smart himself soon begins to "magnify" horns.

Indeed, what is salvational for Smart about horns is precisely their supposed link to mighty ancestors like David. Smart's idol – the great Hebraic king, warrior, and poet, a tamer of evil melancholic spirits, a man after God's own heart – such as David supposedly had horns on his forehead. Thus Othello's "horn-madness" is disavowed: Smart, indeed, reclaims horns as an entirely positive symbol. The symbol of horns, nevertheless, remains entangled with themes of sexual domination:

> For the horn on the forehead is a tower upon an arch.
> For it is a strong munition against the adversary, who is sickness & death.
> For it is instrumental in subjecting the woman.
> For the insolence of the woman has increased ever since Man has been
>   crest-fallen.
> For they have turned the horn into scoff and derision without ceasing.
> For we are amerced of God, who has his horn.[37]

Smart has just previously lamented the punitive "amercement" of the glorious ancestral horn by God, performed in the "divine contempt of a general pusillanimity."[38] And he prophesies that the "Second Coming of the Horn" will reverse the current degeneracy of the English male and bring better mental health: "For the head will be liable to less disorders on the recovery of its horn."[39] Smart thus seems to arrive at a poetic knowledge that the very process by which the genitals of men become abstract symbols of political dominance also creates distortion and turmoil.

It is thus precisely in their engagement with the masculinist theme of cuckoldry that Smart's prophecies go beyond the merely personal and biographical. It is crucial, moreover, that the cuckoldry theme itself had been inflected in specifically anti-enthusiastic ways. For what Smart does, in effect, is to weave an irreverent anti-enthusiastic joke back into the texture of millennial prophecy. It will be recalled that one of Swift's more wildly

---

[36] Smart's ancestor, Sir John Smart, was apparently knighted in the time of Henry VI. See Albert J. Kuhn, "Christopher Smart: the poet as patriot of the Lord," *ELH* 30 (1963), p. 126 (note).
[37] Smart, *Jubilate*, C, 138–143. I have omitted the corresponding "Let" lines in this section.
[38] *Ibid.*, C 125.
[39] *Ibid.*, C 137.

transgressive moments in *A Tale of a Tub* is a quotation of the mistranslation in the Vulgate that spawned the "Horned Moses" tradition. This quotation is the means by which Swift's mad Hack intimates that a hypothetical inmate of Bedlam, an enthusiast who talks much of the *Whore of Babylon*, is also a cuckold: "You will find a Third [inmate], gravely taking the Dimensions of his Kennel; a Person of Foresight and Insight, tho' kept quite in the Dark; for why, like *Moses, Ecce cornuta erat ejus facies*" [Behold, his face was horned].[40] The logic of this joke, aside from the flirtation with blasphemy it permits, probably depends on its convergence with a vein of classic propaganda against enthusiasts: the accusation that they practiced "community of women."[41] Swift himself recycles this old charge in *A Discourse Concerning the Mechanical Operation of the Spirit.*[42]

The *topos* of the "Cuckolded Moses," indeed, appears to have become an irreverent weapon in the arsenal of anti-enthusiastic satire. A slightly later anti-enthusiastic text jabs with heavy-handed irony at the Camisards. This work, published anonymously in 1722, likewise plays on the "Horned Moses" theme; indeed, like *Jubilate Agno*, it juxtaposes horns of potency and plenty with the horns of a cuckold. Excavated by Philip Stevick,[43] it is entitled *A Sermon Preached by a French Hugonot Teacher to his Congregation, in 1689, in Praise of Cuckoldom: Printed at Cologne in French, and now translated into English, for the Consolation of all English Cuckolds*. In his dedication, the anonymous author, apparently referring to the "Horned Moses" tradition, writes as follows: "The chosen People were promised to have their Horns exalted; let us lift up our Heads boldly, which are thus arm'd, and defy our Enemies." And a few pages later, he writes, "How many cuckolds, Bretheren, are there? ah! how great a Number, whose Horns are the Horns of Plenty, who have no other Means but their Wives Kindness to live on, no other Rents or Revenues, but the Liberties gain'd by laborious Wives..."[44]

Smart's personal preoccupation with cuckoldry, then, merges with his need to defend enthusiasm from such ribald *topoi* as the above. Given that the entire trope of cuckold's horns is intrinsically ironic, figuring a conspicuous sexual lack as a mocking and displaced presence,[45] there is a double layer of irony in the equation of cuckold's horns with Biblical horns of plenty and salvation. One would not want to praise this passage as "saved" by such obvious ironies. What is striking, however, is that the *Jubilate* in some ways

40 Swift, *Tub*, p. 177.
41 See J. C. Davis, *Fear, Myth, and History: The Ranters and the Historians* (Cambridge: Cambridge University Press, 1986), pp. 103–107; Schwartz, *Prophets* pp. 61–65; and Hugh Ormsby-Lennon, "Swift and the Quakers (I)," *Swift Studies* 4 (1989), pp. 55–56.
42 Jonathan Swift, *A Discourse Concerning the Mechanical Operation of the Spirit*, in Swift, *Tub*, p. 286.
43 Philip Stevick, "The cuckold's horns," *Southern Folklore Quarterly*, 28: 3 (1964), p. 221. I am grateful to Jaya Mehta for this reference.
44 Published anonymously in London, 1722, pp. 6, 16. Cited in Stevick, "Horns," p. 221.
45 Stevick, "Horns," p. 221.

approximates this facetious "cuckoldry" *topos*, but with no irony. Smart's figuration, his defensive intervention, is precisely to literalize. *Jubilate Agno* thus eventually creates a context in which the potentially ironic tension between horns of plenty and horns of cuckoldry is minimized.

It is precisely this peculiar literalness, as a comparison with one of Smart's earlier poems shows, that so complicates Smart's relation to the dominant style of misogyny. A few years before he penned his prophecy of the "Second Coming of the Horn," Smart wrote the following little epigram on cuckoldry. "Apollo and Daphne" was published in 1750 under Smart's *Midwife* pseudonym of Ebenezer Pentweazle:

> When Phoebus was amorous and long'd to be rude,
> Miss Daphne cry'd pish! and ran swift to the Wood;
> And rather than do such a naughty Affair,
> She became a fine Laurel to deck the God's Hair.
> The Nymph was (no Doubt) of a cold Constitution,
> For sure to turn Tree was an odd Resolution:
> Yet in this she behav'd like a true modern Spouse,
> For she fled from his Arms to distinguish his Brows.[46]

As with so much misogyny, this passage has a certain *cited* quality: it is offered, in a typical mode of bad faith, as if in scare quotes.[47] The jocularity of it all, indeed, is enhanced by Mrs. Midnight's prefatory remarks: she complains that Pentweazle "is too apt to throw out Invectives against our Sex," but nevertheless elects to publish the piece as proof of her own impartiality.[48]

When Smart rewrites these same ideas in *Jubilate Agno*, he does produce a notably alternative rearticulation of the masculine. For it is not only his smirking tone, but the entire mode of discourse, and of subjectivity, that has changed. Moreover, though Devlin condemns the *Jubilate*'s misogyny as pathological, there is a sense in which it may be preferable to the quotidian misogyny of "Apollo and Daphne." For precisely by refusing the alibi of "saving ironies" in *Jubilate Agno*, Smart might be said to defamiliarize those same trite conventions of eighteenth-century misogyny he himself circulated in "Apollo and Daphne." The sheer literalism of *Jubilate Agno* unmasks, that is to say, the constitutive role of irony in mainstream misogyny: those disarming strategies of fraternal nudging and winking by which serious objections are preempted, are positioned as "humorless," with a mask of joky complicity. Such literalism is all the more striking in a poem that is otherwise profoundly saturated with tropes and wordplay.

[46] Christopher Smart, "Apollo and Daphne: An Epigram," in *The Midwife* III (1750), p. 137. (From the private collection in Yale's Beinecke Rare Book and Manuscript Library.) "Apollo and Daphne" is easily available in *Christopher Smart: Selected Poems*, eds. Karina Williamson and Marcus Walsh (Penguin Books, 1990), pp. 9–10.

[47] See R. Howard Bloch, "Medieval misogyny," *Representations* 20 (1987), p. 1.

[48] Smart, *Midwife*, p. 137.

So literal, indeed, is Smart's visionary recuperation of the "Horned Moses" *topos* – so tied is it to the letter of Scripture – that it apparently intersects with his alphabetic mysticism. In this context, the invisible "marking" of the forehead by the horns, of the male by the female, seems highly pertinent to his theory that "the vowell is the female spirit in the Hebrew consonant."[49] For it is worth remembering that the entire "Horned Moses" tradition depends precisely on the ambiguity of the unmarked vowels or "female spirits" that differentiate the identical roots in Hebrew of "shining" and "horned." The Hebraic words for "horn" (*qeren*) and "to shine" (*qaran*) are identical in an unpointed Hebrew text. (They have a common root in the concept of *radiance*: this leads in the one case to the shooting out of horns, and, in the other, to the emission of rays.) In Jerome's Vulgate, this potential confusion is realized in a mistranslation of Exodus 34:29. Moses is described in this passage as descending from Mount Sinai, marked by his contact with God by a shining face. A literal rendering of Jerome's translation into English would read: "When Moses came down from Mount Sinai...he knew not that his face was *horned*" (in Latin, *cornuta*). From this misprision, of which medieval scholars were well aware, a tradition arose in liturgical drama and in religious iconography of representing Moses with horns. Michelangelo's statue of Moses is perhaps the most famous instance of this long tradition.

Smart himself, moreover, as the following lines about the lost horn's "brightness" demonstrate, is well aware of this ambiguity:

> For this horn was a bright substance in colour and consistence as the
> nail of the hand.
> For it was broad, thick and strong so as to serve for defense as well as
> ornament.
> For it brighten'd to the Glory of God, which came upon the human
> face at morning prayer.
> For it was largest and brightest in the best men.[50]

Moses was both horned and radiant; his horn, indeed, was itself a shining ornament: such, apparently, is Smart's resolution of the interpretative crux. His interpretation, moreover, has a strangely self-reflexive quality. For the temporal presence and absence of the horn, which was "amerced" after the Babylonish captivity,[51] can be read as an allegory about "translating" the mysterious being/non-being of Hebrew vowels.[52]

If there is one sense in which Smart literalizes the "Horned Moses" *topos*, however, there is another in which he is the great "translator" of horns in

[49]   Smart, *Jubilate*, C 39.
[50]   Smart, *Jubilate*, C 120–123. I have omitted the corresponding "Let" lines.
[51]   *Ibid.*, C 126.
[52]   See the related discussion of Smart's attitudes toward "accents" or diacritical marks that translate writing into voice in Liu, "Letters," pp. 121–122.

general. For no one elaborates more imaginative figurations on horns than Smart. The following verse-pair, anticipating the themes of defense and ornamentation developed in the passage above, seems close to the heart of the reversals that Smart operates in *Jubilate Agno*:

> Let Chesed rejoice with Strepsiceros, whose weapons are the
> ornaments of his peace
> For I preach the very GOSPEL of CHRIST without comment & with
> this weapon shall I slay envy.[53]

Strepsiceros, as W. M. Merchant observes, is an African antelope whose horns, according to Pliny, are suitable for lyres: its "weapons," then, metonymically suggest David's harp and his poetic and musical gifts.[54] Smart thus translates the antelope's carnal weapons into an analogue for his own spiritual and artistic weaponry against envy. The connections, however, given that "Chesed" is a Hebrew word connoting kindness or special favor, go deeper still. For it is Smart himself, according to *Jubilate Agno*, who is marked as a "horned" cuckold, and yet who makes a state of peculiar grace out of that very fact.

Though at least one critic describes Smart's prophecy of de-and re-horned Man as "patently a generalized version of Smart,"[55] the broader context of eighteenth-century anti-enthusiastic rhetoric serves to redefine what is merely private in *Jubilate Agno*. Horns, like almost everything else in *Jubilate Agno*, are "translated" so as to rearticulate the boundaries of the merely personal. Personal shame, indeed, is precisely what horns promise to overcome: "For when men get their horns again, they will delight to go uncovered."[56] The line, part of a cluster dealing with hat-wearing, seems to suggest that hats are a symptom of shame, an attempt to conceal the lack of horns. The recovery of the horn, then, will soon permit a new-found delight in baring the head. The enthusiastic recuperation of a misogynist theme thus produces a paradoxical masculinity – simultaneously abject and exuberant, exposed to all and yet unashamed – that is significantly at odds with a dominant ideal of masculine control and spectatorship.[57]

A second eighteenth-century context for Smart's masculinist revanchism, along with the *topoi* of "cuckoldry," has to do with his own immersion in popular writing. It is worth remarking again that Smart attributed most of his own commercial writing to the female pseudonym "Mother Mary Midnight,"

---

[53] Smart, *Jubilate*, B 9.
[54] W. M. Merchant, "Patterns of reference in Smart's *Jubilate Agno*," *Harvard Library Bulletin* 14 (1960), p. 25.
[55] Morris Golden, *The Self Observed: Swift, Johnson, Wordsworth* (Baltimore: The Johns Hopkins Press, 1972), p. 26.
[56] Smart, *Jubilate*, C 132.
[57] See Kristina Straub, *Sexual Suspects: Eighteenth-Century Plays and Sexual Ideology* (Princeton, New Jersey: Princeton University Press, 1992), for a related discussion of spectatorship and gazing in the context of the theatre (Ch. 1) and of Colley Cibber's autobiographical strategies of rhetorical abjection and exhibitionism (Ch. 2).

a midwife. The patterns of gender ventriloquism at work are ambiguous. Smart, on the one hand, ventriloquized across gender lines, claiming to write, sermonize, and occasionally protest in the name of a gossipy old woman. On the other hand, Smart may well have felt himself "ventriloquized," and thus "emasculated," by economic pressures. It is thus fitting that his evocation of an old midwife serves to conjure up various images of harsh necessity: midwives were richly liminal figures, traditionally seen, as Robert Erickson demonstrates, as akin to the Greek Fates or *Moirai*, Lady Luck, and Dame Fortune.[58] It is as if Smart himself impersonates, or personifies, his economic fate: "By creating a midwife who is simultaneously a Grub Street author," as Lance Bertelsen writes, "Smart engages a multiply over-determined voice for expressing his response to his own protean role as Cambridge scholar and poet turned hack author turned tavern performer."[59]

The name "Midnight," moreover, connotes more than the nocturnal witching hour of transitions and transformations.[60] In alluding to Pope's *Dulness*, the name Mother Mary Midnight taps a broader misogynist "emasculation" of popular writing. This imagery involved, first of all, a tremendous backlash against the actual historical ascendance of female popular writers – novelists, journalists, chapbook writers – whose presence had become impossible to ignore.[61] Thus eighteenth-century opposition to the popular novel as a genre often focused on the fact that both novel-reading and novel-writing were dominated numerically by women. This mode of opposition, as Terry Lovell points out, belongs to a much larger pattern in the construction of the literary canon, of "singling out. . .female writers and. . .genres popular with women for special scorn."[62]

The fact that Smart himself cross-dressed in the "Old Woman's Oratory," moreover, suggests another dimension in which his personal experience overdetermined his response.[63] This is all the more true insofar as the traditional Puritan diatribe against the theater – William Prynne's *Histrio-mastix* (1633) is the classic instance – focused with special ferocity on the emasculating effects of cross-dressing.[64] Smart does not seem to have

58   Robert Erickson, *Mother Midnight: Birth, Sex, and Fate in Eighteenth-Century Fiction (Defoe, Richardson, Sterne)* (New York: AMS Press, 1986), p. 7.
59   Bertelsen, "Journalism," p. 365.
60   Erickson, *Mother*, pp. 40–41.
61   Bertelsen, "Journalism," pp. 364–365.
62   Terry Lovell, *Consuming Fiction* (London: Verso, 1987), p. 54.
63   For a study of this dimension of Smart's work that situates it in a broader context of cross-dressing and gender ideology, see Easton, "Habits," pp. 226–270.
64   See David Leverenz, "Why did Puritans hate stage plays?" in his *The Language of Puritan Feeling: An Exploration in Literature, Psychology, and Social History* (New Brunswick, New Jersey: Rutgers University Press, 1980), pp. 23–40; Laura Levine, "Men in women's clothing: anti-theatricality and effeminization from 1579 to 1642," *Criticism* 28:2 (1986), pp. 121–143; Colin McCabe, "Abusing self and others: Puritan accounts of the Shakespearian stage," *Critical Quarterly* 30:3 (1988), pp. 13–15.

responded to such sentiments – what Straub terms "the homophobic exclusion of ambiguous masculinity" – with the readily available reply that actors transgress gender codes for professional reasons rather than sexual ones.[65] Indeed, Smart himself takes up the traditional anti-theatrical polemic in *Jubilate Agno*: a fact that suggests a special susceptibility to this line of attack. Smart, moreover, was inevitably attacked on precisely the vulnerable point of his cross-dressing. John "Orator" Henley, the eccentric orator whose sermonizing in Clare Market Mother Midnight mimicked and parodied, replied in kind. As Easton points out, Henley retorted "with remarks about Smart's size ('Dr. Small Smart'), played with an effeminized form of his name ('Kitty Smart'), and made accusations of homosexuality: 'Ah Molly Smart! [...] Pimlico Molly Midnight translated to Rump Castle: Hum-buggers-bougres.' "[66] "This accusation would have hit home," Easton concludes, "not only because of the cultural association of sodomy with male cross-dressing, but because of the continual evocation of effeminate fops, castrati, and hermaphrodites in the context of *The Midwife*, *The Drury-Lane Journal*, and the Oratory."[67] Small wonder, then, that Smart claims in line B 129 of the *Jubilate* to have "the blessing of God in the three POINTS of manhood, of the pen, of the sword, and of chivalry." As a wielder of the phallic pen, Smart implicitly defines himself over and against the compromised masculinity of actors.

As Smart's insistence on the manliness of the pen suggests, his preoccupation with a trend of supposed degeneration relates in particular to the degenerate state of literary culture. He goes on in *Jubilate Agno* to work up considerable fervor around the conviction that men have become too much like women. Indeed, his prophecy of the "Second Coming of the Horn" can be seen as another version of the "degeneration" *topos* parodied in Swift's digression about the "decline of ears" among Englishmen. Smart, however, goes on to forecast a countervailing regeneration, a millennium that will, among other things, rid the nation of theatrical players:

> For I prophecy that men will live to a much greater age, this ripens
>   apace God be praised
> For I prophecy that they will grow taller and stronger.
> For degeneracy has done a great deal more than is imagined.
> For men in David's time were ten feet high in general.
> For they had degenerated also from the strength of their fathers.
> For I prophecy that players and mimes will not be named amongst us.[68]

---

[65] Straub, *Sexual Suspects*, p. 34, pp. 36–46.

[66] Easton, "Habits," p. 249. For further discussion of the necessarily protective subculture of eighteenth-century "mollies" or "sodomites," see Randolph Trumbach, "London's sodomites," *Journal of Social History* (Fall, 1977), pp. 1–33 and "Sodomitical subcultures, sodomitical roles, and the gender revolution of the eighteenth century: the recent historiography," *Eighteenth Century Life* 9:3, n.s. (1985), pp. 109–121.

[67] Easton, "Habits," p. 249.

[68] Smart, *Jubilate*, C 88–93. I have omitted the corresponding "Let" lines.

It seems likely that this passage figures, among other conflicting indices of decline and regeneration, shifts in literary history. The gigantic "stature" of the antediluvian Biblical patriarchs very possibly includes reference to the poetic skills of such literary fathers as David and Solomon.

Indeed, the strength and virile power of Smart's own "voice" establishes a strong link between regenerated writing and recovered "horns." As Smart's editors and critics have noted, the raised or exalted ram's horn is a common image of triumph and strength in the Hebrew Bible: the Psalms, moreover, refer to God himself as "my horn of salvation" (Psalms 18:2, KJV). What Smart adds to this is the notion that Christ's *kenosis*, the emptying out of his divinity entailed by human incarnation, involved a loss of his horn. Smart's vocal virility, then, prefigures the millennial recovery of the lost horn:

> For our Blessed Saviour had not his horn upon the face of the earth.
> For this was in meekness and condescension to the infirmities of
>   human nature at that time.
> For at his second coming his horn will be exalted in glory.
> For Christ Jesus has exalted my voice to his own glory.
> For he has answered me in the air as with a horn from Heaven to the
>   ears of many people.[69]

This link here between writing and voice reinforces Smart's punning celebration in B 80 of his sonorous voice and strong loins: for "lines" and "loins" are homophones in the eighteenth century.

Smart's sonorous and virile "horn-book," then, itself prefigures, like a warning blast of the trumpet, the millennium which it foretells. The theme of horns, moreover, around which Smart's prophecy is organized, also has a more specific millennial resonance: for it recalls certain *topoi* belonging to the enthusiastic repertoire. This strain of enthusiasm often focused its millennial expectations on the vision in the Book of Daniel of the ferocious fourth "beast," which is to make war against those "saints" who will ultimately usher in the millennium. This "beast," or kingdom, is described as having ten horns (Daniel 7:7). These horns – ten kings, as Scripture explains – are themselves to be subjected by another "little horn" prior to the millennium (Daniel 7:8). Prophecies applying this "little horn" to current events were, as Nigel Smith points out, widespread among the radicals, especially the Fifth Monarchists.[70]

An especially well-developed instance of such Fifth Monarchist symbolism

[69]　*Ibid.*, C 147–152.
[70]　Nigel Smith, *Perfection Proclaimed: Language and Literature in English Radical Religion 1640–1660* (Oxford: Clarendon Press, 1989), p. 94. See also B. S. Capp, *The Fifth Monarchy Men: A Study in Seventeenth-century English Millenarianism* (Totowa, New Jersey: Rowman and Littlefield, 1972), pp. 193–194. For the persistence into the late eighteenth century of millennial prophecy based on the Book of Daniel, see Jack Fruchtman, Jr., "Politics and the apocalypse: the republic and the millennium in late-eighteenth-century English thought," *Studies in Eighteenth-Century Culture* X, ed. Harvey Payne (Madison: University of Wisconsin Press, 1987), pp. 153–164.

can be found in *The Little Horns Doom and Downfall* by Mary Cary/Rand, which, along with its companion tract *A Description of the New Jerusalems Glory*, was published in 1651. The two tracts together defend the execution of Charles I, as well as further uses of the "material sword," as the fulfillment of Biblical prophecy against the oppressive and vaunting "little horn."[71] Against such a background, Smart's "magnification" of horns works to redeem the potentially oppressive symbol. Although Smart swerves sharply away from such sinister imagery for horns, he does go on to prophesy, with just the faintest echo of Fifth Monarchist subversions in civil affairs, the reign of "King Jesus": "For I prophecy that the name of king in England will be given to Christ alone."[72] And indeed, there are precedents among Fifth Monarchists as well for Smart's association of the millennium with improvements in longevity[73] and for strictures against the "effeminacy" of shaving.[74] Cary/Rand, for example, predicts that those blessed to live in the reign of King Jesus "shall live till they come to a good old age."[75] And Thomas Tillam mocks the Cavalier culture of hair in *The Temple of Lively Stones* (1660), attacking as "effeminate" men who shaved off their beards and wore long hair.[76]

It would seem to be through a poetic reawakening that Smart hopes to revive adoration and reverse the trend of literary and cultural degeneration. Exactly what, then, does his "Second Age of Horn" entail? Horns permit one to go shamelessly "uncovered"; they are cornucopian, a restoration of plenitude; they are most certainly weapons; yet they are perhaps first and foremost musical instruments associated with festivity and millennial change. It is highly relevant here that early in Christian tradition etymological vicissitudes, naturalizing a pun, conflated the Latin roots of "jubilation" and the Hebraic roots of "jubilee." Ushered in by a blast of a ram's horn (Hebrew *yobel*, whence the word), the "jubilee," an idea whose residual revolutionary force survived redaction in the post-exilic period, was conceived as a sort of legally mandated super-sabbath in which slaves were to be emancipated and all monopolized land was to revert to its former owners.[77] The connection of the word "jubilee" to the Hebrew for "ram's horn" points to the fact, as Peter Linebaugh says, that jubilee is first of all heard and proclaimed.[78]

---

[71] Mary Cary/Rand, *The Little Horns Doom and Downfall* (London: 1651), p. 41; *A Description of the New Jerusalems Glory* (London: 1651), pp. 122–131. For the Biblical prophecy against the "little horn," see Dan. 7:8–28.

[72] Smart, *Jubilate*, C 87.

[73] *Ibid.*, C 88.

[74] *Ibid.*, B 419; C 130–131. Capp, *Fifth* pp. 141, 155.

[75] Cary/Rand, "Horn," p. 71.

[76] Capp, *Fifth*, p. 141.

[77] See Malcolm Chase, "From millennium to anniversary: the concept of jubilee in late eighteenth- and nineteenth-century England," *Past and Present* 129 (1990), pp. 132–147; see also Peter Linebaugh, "Jubilating; or, how the Atlantic working class used the Bible Jubilee against capitalism, with some success," *Radical History Review* 50 (1991), pp. 143–180.

[78] *Ibid.*, p. 144.

Scattered references to the land-sharing "jubilee" *topos* can be found in such seventeenth-century Puritans as John Bunyan, who equates it in *The Advocateship of Jesus Christ* (1688) with Christian redemption through grace.[79] The concept, however, seems to have become much more popular in the following century. Peter Linebaugh thus points out that the Biblical jubilee was used throughout the eighteenth and nineteenth centuries as a justification for counter-hegemonic political resistance. Among slaves, Black Jacobins, and white abolitionists, the target of the jubilee was slavery; among radical agrarians, it justified resistance to land enclosures. Indeed, Spencian socialists, so called after the radical agrarian Thomas Spence (1750–1814), continued to use the jubilee idea for a secular socialism well into the Victorian period.[80] Thus the term 'jubilee' developed, as Malcolm Chase observes, "as part of popular political and religious vocabularies."[81] In the later eighteenth century, as Chase points out, "millenarians combined Leviticus 25 with the apocalyptic books of the Bible – Daniel and Revelation – to produce a reading of the year of jubilee as a prefiguration of the millennium."[82] Charles Wesley's hymn, "Sing to the Great Jehovah's Praise," thus combines the ideas of jubilee and the Second Coming – the time when

> Jesus in the clouds appears
> To saints on earth forgiven,
> And brings the great sabbatic year
> The Jubilee of Heaven.[83]

This jubilee theme, given Smart's sensitivity to verbal correspondences, enters his poem with the title inscribed at the top of the first page of the holograph manuscript: *Jubilate Agno*.

Arriving every fiftieth year – seven times seven plus one – the jubilee is an obvious figure for millennial renewal. The Bible's jubilee program (Leviticus 25:8–17, 29–31) was, as Arthur Waskow says, "rooted in the conception of sacred time that inspires the Sabbath tradition of rest, contemplation, and sharing on the seventh day of every week."[84] The sharing seems to be a periodic levelling device designed to prevent domination by material accumulation. Smart strikes a related anti-miserly note in line B 386: "For Tully says to be generous you must first be just, but the voice of Christ is distribute at all events." These ideals give additional resonance to such lines as the following:

---

[79]   John Bunyan, *The Miscellaneous Works of John Bunyan*, 13 vols., ed. Richard L. Greaves (Oxford: Clarendon Press, 1985), I: *Good News for the Vilest of Men/ The Advocateship of Jesus Christ*, p. 183.

[80]   See Malcolm Chase, '*The People's Farm': English Radical Agrarianism 1775–1840* (Oxford: Clarendon Press, 1988).

[81]   Chase, "Millennium," p. 133.

[82]   *Ibid.*, p. 136.

[83]   Cited in *ibid.*, p. 137.

[84]   Arthur Waskow, "From compassion to Jubilee: ecology and social meaning," *Tikkun* 5:2 (1990), p. 78.

For I am ready for the trumpet and alarm to fight, to die and to rise again.[85]

Let Matthat rejoice with the Trumpet-fish – God revive the blowing of the TRUMPETS.[86]

The jubilee theme, moreover, also informs one of the most discussed verse-pairs in *Jubilate Agno*:

Let Jubal rejoice with Caecilia, the woman and the slow-worm praise the name of the Lord.

For I pray the Lord Jesus to translate my MAGNIFICAT into verse and represent it.[87]

The pun on Jubal plus the musical overtones of both Jubal, the inventor of music, and St. Cecilia, patron saint of music, combine here to emphasize further the millennial meaning which Smart gives to "translation."[88] At the same time, the punning on "translation" itself, as Patricia Meyer Spacks points out, "foregrounds the role of literature as the medium of millennial change": it "provides a way of expressing the power of language."[89] One feels very near the center of Smart's millennium in these dense lines.

The theme of magnification seems to open the way to a more androgynous sense of "jubilee": one not marked, that is to say, by the sharp definition of a normative masculinity over and against either an "abnormal" masculinity or a demonized "feminine." Geoffrey Hartman shows by what chain of associative links Smart manages to connect Mary's Magnificat with woman and worm, "caecilia" being the name of the slow-worm.[90] This link is made by identifying Jesus, the mediator and translator, as the serpent-bruising offspring promised to Eve in Genesis 3:11: thus the pairing of the slow-worm with St. Cecilia suggests the archetypal conjunction of the serpent with Eve.[91] Like the archetypes of Eve and Mary, the reference to "woman" thus encompasses all women. In evoking the apocalyptic moment when God's promise to Eve will be fulfilled, then, the poem implicitly defines a certain outer limit to its misogyny.[92] For *Jubilate Agno* can at least foresee a time when women will be

85   Smart, *Jubilate*, B 38.
86   *Ibid.*, B 202.
87   *Ibid.*, B 43.
88   See William A. Kumbier, "Sound and signification in Christopher Smart's *Jubilate Agno*," *Texas Studies in Literature and Language* 24:3 (1982), p. 307.
89   Patricia Meyer Spacks, *The Poetry of Vision: Five Eighteenth-Century Poets* (Cambridge: Harvard University Press, 1967), p. 142.
90   Geoffrey H. Hartman, "Christopher Smart's *Magnificat*: toward a theory of representation," in *The Fate of Reading* (Chicago: University of Chicago Press, 1975), p. 92.
91   *Ibid.*
92   It is interesting to note that it is precisely by means of this passage ("my soul doth magnify the Lord") that George Fox refuted the belief, encountered in one group during his travels, that women have no souls. See George Fox, *The Works of George Fox*, 8 vols. (1831; rpt. New York: AMS Press, 1975), I: *A Journal or Historical Account of the Life, Travels, Sufferings, Christian Experiences, and Labour of Love in the Work of the Ministry of that Ancient, Eminent, and Faithful Servant of Jesus Christ, George Fox*, p. 72.

"translated" from beneath the shadow of Eve's supposed transgression. And indeed, Smart takes directly from Mary, who cancels out Eve's sin, the model for his entire poetic project of jubilating and "magnifying": a subtle echo, one could argue, of his "Mother Mary Midnight" shenanigans, and further evidence that his enthusiastic affiliations can lead him to a more complex, fluid, and liminal rearticulation of masculinity than might first appear. Even as he arguably displaces the figure of woman,[93] Smart himself thus assumes a nondominant position of "feminine" dislocation.

Nowhere is the impact of enthusiasm on Smart's rewriting of masculinity more apparent than in the domain of wordplay. It should come as no great surprise that a dominant eighteenth-century discourse about punning, like the manifest hostility toward enthusiasm and popular writing against which Smart also struggled, tended to position such verbal play as "female." Smart's enthusiastic reversal of this mainstream stigmatization of wordplay – this time through a bawdy subversion of the "celibacy" themes undergirding much of his own misogyny – enables his most thoroughly counter-hegemonic recasting of masculinity.

The backlash against punning is a phenomenon specific to the Enlightenment's cultural program of linguistic and orthographic standardization: that rationalization of discourse which Peter Stallybrass and Allon White describe as a systematic decathexis of the public sphere.[94] Consider the implications in this context of Samuel Johnson's well-known complaint about William Shakespeare's "irresistible" fascination with puns. About the same time as Smart wrote the *Jubilate*, Johnson penned his famous attack on carnivalesque linguistic play. A pun, Johnson says, like the luminous vapors in a swamp, is sure to "engulf" Shakespeare "in the mire." Johnson's judgment that a quibble was to Shakespeare, "the fatal Cleopatra for which he lost the world, and was content to lose it,"[95] epitomizes a tendency to feminize, and eroticize, non-rational discourse.[96] Although Johnson does not dwell on it, moreover, he is clearly aware that Shakespeare's wordplay is overwhelmingly bawdy. (It was left to a later lexicographer to clinch the point in a book-length study entitled *Shakespeare's Bawdy*.)[97]

It is not accidental, then, but rather the predictable precipitate of this

---

[93]   I am indebted here to the notion of "double displacement" explored, in a very different context, by Gayatri Chakravorty Spivak. See her "Displacement and the Discourse of Woman," in *Displacement: Derrida and After*, ed. Mark Krupnick (Bloomington: Indiana University Press, 1983), p. 171.

[94]   Peter Stallybrass and Allon White, *The Politics and Poetics of Transgression* (Ithaca: Cornell University Press, 1986), p. 97.

[95]   Samuel Johnson, "Preface," *The Plays of William Shakespeare* in *The Oxford Authors: Samuel Johnson*, ed. Donald Greene (New York: Oxford University Press, 1984), p. 429.

[96]   A useful description of this tendency can be found in Ruth Salvaggio's *Enlightened Absence: Neoclassical Configurations of the Feminine* (Urbana: University of Illinois Press, 1988), pp. 12–28.

[97]   Eric Partridge, *Shakespeare's Bawdy: A Literary and Psychological Essay and a Comprehensive Glossary*, rev. ed. (New York: E. P. Dutton & Co., 1969).

cultural moment, that the use of (or surrender to) something like a Freudian "primary process" or Kristevan "semiotic" would evoke from Johnson imagery physically threatening to the self-possession of the (implicitly male) intellect: mire, engulfment, and exotic *femmes fatales*. Hence the familiar notion that men too can be "feminized" by the irresistible passion/passivity of heterosexual desire, which tempts them – shades of Eve! – and thus threatens their self-mastery. And hence a mutual implication of images of femininity with particular formal practices stigmatized because they subordinate signified to signifier, enounced to enunciation, the "sons of heaven" (things) to the "daughters of earth" (words).[98]

Few authors are "seduced" into more puns per line than Christopher Smart. Indeed, *Jubilate Agno* deserves to be better known for its peculiar mode of oblique and punning bawdiness. Smart's overt treatment of sexuality in *Jubilate Agno*, especially female sexuality, assumes the besieged attitude of male chastity surrounded by dangerous temptresses. In thus equating chastity with misogyny, as Devlin points out,[99] Smart swerves away from the cheerful lustiness that informs several of his earlier poems, from "To Ethelinda" to "Lovely Harriote" to "The Pretty Bar-Keeper of the Mitre." For the poems of Smart's pre-confinement period, as Arthur Sherbo observes, return "often and lovingly" to the theme of the female bosom, and frequently insinuate Smart's "readiness and capacity for amorous encounter".[100] Among the most charming of these is a poem to his wife-to-be, "The Lass with the Golden Locks," which promises to sing exclusively to her despite masculine raillery.[101]

Jubilate Agno, however, seems to be very different. As a revision of the Noah's Ark myth, indeed, Smart's practice of coupling human beings and animals, unmatable species, leaves unclear the status in his new covenant even of procreative sexuality. As Hartman observes, "In the opening scene of the *Jubilate*, when Abraham presents a ram and Jacob his speckled drove, we cannot tell whether sexual generation is being sacrificed or consecrated."[102] Nevertheless, Smart's manic wordplay in the *Jubilate* is in several ways quite "bodily." Not only is his attitude towards language itself precisely sensuous and erotic, a tremendous love of the material medium, but his puns are frequently supercharged with erotic and bodily implications. It is above all this peculiar bawdiness that disrupts – and to some extent eventually subverts – Smart's attacks on women and female sexuality.

---

[98] Samuel Johnson, "Preface," *Dictionary of the English Language*, in *The Oxford Authors*, p. 310.

[99] Devlin, *Kit*, p. 122.

[100] Sherbo, *Scholar*, p. 135.

[101] Christopher Smart, "The Lass with the Golden Locks," in *Smart*, IV: *Miscellaneous Poems, English and Latin*, p. 193.

[102] Hartman, "Magnificat," p. 96.

A striking example of how Smart's bawdy punning can lead to a certain blurring of gender differentiation appears in line B 139, which invokes the doctrine of the "Immaculate Conception" – that is, the exemption of Mary from birth onward from the taint of original sin – and seems to make a common conflation of it with Christ's virgin birth:

> Let Mary rejoice with the Maid – blessed be the name of the immaculate
>   CONCEPTION.
> For I am in twelve HARDSHIPS, but he that was born of a virgin shall
>   deliver me out of all.

As Williamson explains, "Maid" is both a virgin and the name given to a young skate; "Twelve Hardships" suggests the Twelve Labors of Hercules, and thus may allude to a Hercules/Christ typology used elsewhere in the poem. The likelihood, however, of a phallic pun in "HARDSHIPS" makes the tone of these lines very strange indeed. To be "delivered," in this dense context, means to be redeemed, born again, as Christ was born outside the cycle of natural sexuality. It would also seem to mean "delivered" from his own desire, as if the masculine "hardships" of his carnal impulses were personified as a woman. In fact, we encounter here again the manic *topos* of gender-reversal. Smart "labors" – like Hercules, like a woman – to give birth to a purified and immaculate self. As in Coppe's elaborate description of being "pregnant" with the "child" of sexual desire, the androgyny in Smart's figurative language here pushes metaphor to the point of dissociating gender from the sexed body.

Smart connects the "impurity" of his formal techniques – from bawdy puns to disjunctiveness – to an explicit desire for carnal purity. Carnal knowledge, according to the poem's treatment of chastity, seems to hinder knowledge in its "purer" forms. Early in the poem Smart declares his preference of chastity to beauty: "Let Susanna bless with the Butterfly – beauty hath wings, but chastity is the Cherub."[103] In a similar spirit, he later makes a Pauline virtue out of his own enforced chastity: "For beauty is better to look on than to meddle with and tis good for a man not to know a woman."[104] Continuing this theme, he groups himself with Esdras (Ezra, the scribe who rediscovered the Jewish Law) and Sir Isaac Newton. Newton appears here, it seems likely, not on the basis of his scientific achievements, but, rather, on the basis of his self-proclaimed virginity and his interpretations of Revelation:

> Let Candace rejoice with the Craw-fish – How hath the Christian
>   minister renowned the Queen.
> For CHASTITY is the key of knowledge as in Esdras, Sr Isaac Newton and
>   now, God be praised, in me.

---

[103] Smart, *Jubilate*, A 92.
[104] *Ibid.*, B 104.

Let the Eunuch rejoice with the Thorn-Back – It is good to be discovered
   reading the BIBLE.
For Newton nevertheless is more of error than of the truth, but I am of
   the WORD of GOD.[105]

As Williamson explains, Candace, whose name means "pure possession," is
an Ethiopian queen mentioned in Acts 8:26–39. She was "renowned"
because her treasurer, the "Eunuch," was discovered reading Isaiah and
subsequently converted to Christianity. A disembodied intimacy of the gaze
substitutes here for a more overt sexuality: it is good to be discovered, seen,
"known," while performing a pious act.

As this last versicle suggests, there are subterranean connections in
Smart's poem between castration and chastity. The fear of being somehow
"cut off," in fact pervades the *Jubilate*, often in connection with female
sexuality. It is worth noting in this context that the Christian tradition of the
"Three Eunuchs" distinguishes between men who lack genitals because of
castration or congenital defects and "men who have made themselves
eunuchs for the kingdom of heaven's sake" (Matthew 19:12).[106] This
tradition was taken by John Wesley, among others, as recommending the
single life – lay celibacy – as a higher state than marriage.[107] Despite the
generally pro-matrimonial stance of Protestantism as a whole, then, one
need not follow Devlin in looking to Catholic heresies such as Catharism to
explain Smart's ascetic logic.[108] Eighteenth-century evangelical Protestantism provides a handier context. It is quite possibly from Wesley that the
famously celibate pietistic community, known after their emigration to
United States as the Shakers, derived their sexual doctrines.[109] The majority
of Wesley's followers, to be sure, tended to resist his call to the life of single
celibacy. Indeed – and this point also seems relevant to Smart – the overall
effect of his decentering of marriage seems to have been, among those tied
into close-knit Methodist fellowships, merely a more diffuse and free-floating
eroticism.[110]

In one example of the "castration" motif, Smart cites the evil fate of
John the Baptist at the hands of Salome, the more to rejoice in his own
safety:

---

[105] *Ibid.*, B 194–195.
[106] This is a revision of Deut. 23:1, where those "wounded in the stones" are excluded from the
   "congregation of the Lord" – doubly "amerced," so to speak.
[107] Henry Abelove, *The Evangelist of Desire: John Wesley and the Methodists* (Stanford: Stanford University
   Press, 1990), pp. 49–59.
[108] Devlin, *Kit*, p. 122.
[109] Abelove, *Evangelist*, p. 59.
[110] *Ibid.*, pp. 63–73. I find this analysis more convincing than E. P. Thompson's discussion of
   "sadomasochism" in Methodist imagery for Christ's wounds. See E. P. Thompson, *The Making of
   the English Working Class* (New York: Vintage Books, 1966), pp. 369–374.

> Let John the Baptist rejoice with the Salmon – blessed be the name of
>   the Lord Jesus for infant baptism
> For I am safe, as to my head, from the female dancer.[111]

John the Baptist rejoices here with the Salmon, near-anagram of S-A-L-O-
M-E, because Smart, locked up in the madhouse, is exempt from the deadly
influence of female sexuality.[112] One scarcely needs Sigmund Freud's notes
on Medusa's head to infer a link between decapitation and castration. The
more interesting point, perhaps, is the implied connection of baptism with
Smart's anagrammatic re-christening of Salome: he re-names her, implicitly
rewriting her story so that she and John the Baptist can rejoice together.
Despite Smart's affirmation of the Anglican position on infant baptism, it
seems questionable whether such enthusiastic revisionism – based on Smart's
punning "translations" – strengthens or subverts orthodoxy.

   In a similarly charged versicle, Smart expresses anxiety about his throat
and voice in terms of "things stranggled," probably a reference to the Biblical
dietary taboo on eating strangled animals, and, hence, a reference to
impurity. Punning on the Hebrew *ruach*, meaning breath or spirit, he invokes
Jorim to rejoice with the Roach:

> Let Jorim rejoice with the Roach – God bless my throat and keep
>   me from things stranggled
> For the power of the Shears is direct as the life.[113]

Hartman, noting that Smart's editors W. F. Stead and W. H. Bond have
tentatively explained "the power of the Shears" as referring to ancient
methods of divination, offers – tactfully, in a footnote – a supplementary
explication in terms of a misogynist pun on Shears/She-arse.[114] This
explanation is all the more persuasive because of its immediate context. Two
lines above Smart defines the "Shears" as "the first of the mechanical powers,
and to be used on the knees"[115] – a line that can be read polysemously as
describing practices in the realm of divination, tailoring, or sexuality. What
follows next, moreover, seems to be an implicit reference to Eve's sexuality as
a kind of dangerous "bait":

> Let Elmodam rejoice with the Chubb, who is wary of the bait and
>   thrives in his circumspection.
> For if Adam had used this instrument right, he would not have
>   fallen.[116]

The pun on She-arse may be compared in its rawness to Swift's cloacal image
of female "Aeolists" being inspired from below.

---

[111] Smart, *Jubilate*, B 140.
[112] See Merchant, "Patterns," p. 21.
[113] Smart, *Jubilate*, B 179.
[114] Hartman, "Magnificat," p. 322.
[115] Smart, *Jubilate*, B 177.
[116] *Ibid.*, B 178.

This outrageous pun, moreover, nicely joins a cluster of related images, such as Smart's notion that an "effeminate" form of pronunciation, the "clipping" of syllables, had something to do with the downfall of the Romans.[117] Shaving, too, can be seen as a plot against proper masculinity: "For shaving of the beard was an invention of the people of Sodom to make men look like women."[118] There is possibly a similar reference in "the power of the Shears" to Atropos, the "blind Fury" described in "Lycidas" as cutting off the "thin-spun life" of Edward King with her "abhorr'd shears."[119] The bawdy cutting of the word or *coupure* necessary to reveal the pun mirrors formally the "cut" that represents, for Smart, both the body and the threat of castration. Strangling, having one's wind or inspiration cut off, is another version of this threat. Smart's prayer, "keep me from things strangled," thus combines both impurity, in reference to dietary laws, and the idea of punishment. Chastity, as a sort of spiritual or figurative castration, seems to protect one against the more literal dangers of "impure" female sexuality.

This line of analysis sheds new light on what seems to be an instance of disjunction between the "Let" and "For" lines:

> Let Bartholomew rejoice with the Eel, who is pure in proportion
>   to where he is found and how he is used.
> For I pray Almighty CHRIST to bless the MAGDALEN HOUSE and to
>   forward a National Purification.[120]

The Magdalen House, as Williamson explains, was an asylum for prostitutes opened in 1758. Eel was regarded, she notes, as potentially "dangerous meat," requiring careful cooking.[121] St. Bartholomew, one of the twelve original disciples, was martyred, according to tradition, in Armenia. He was in fact flayed alive; his symbol, hence, is the knife. These facts permit us to see by what chain of associations he is joined with an eel and an asylum for prostitutes. Juxtaposed, knife and eel suggest at least the threat of castration. The pure and impure "use" of the eel generates the thought of prostitution, sexual impurity, as well as the hope for a "national purification" through such projects as the Magdalen House. In thus linking the sexual purity of women to the purity of the nation, Smart illustrates Michel Foucault's historical account of "modern" sexuality: a sexuality which shifts from an older politics of alliance, based on a "symbolics of blood" ("symbolique du

---

[117] *Ibid.*, B 417.
[118] *Ibid.*, B 420.
[119] John Milton, "Lycidas," in *John Milton: Complete Poems and Major Prose*, ed. Merritt Y. Hughes (New York: The Odyssey Press, 1957), p. 122.
[120] Smart, *Jubilate*, B 128.
[121] This idea appears also in the traditional ballad "Lord Randall," in which a young man's false love poisons him by feeding him fried eel.

sang") toward an increasingly racialized "analytics of sexuality" ("analytique de la sexualité").[122]

The phallic eel reappears to rejoice with the chaste Susanna, falsely slandered as an adulteress, in another disjunctive verse-pair concerned with sexuality and purity:

> Let Susanna rejoice with the Lamprey, who is an eel with a title.
> For the Wedding Garments of all women are prepared in the
>   Moon against the day of their purification.[123]

Perhaps the most charming aspect of these lines, once one has grasped their disjunctive logic, is their irreverence towards social ranks and titles. But to ask what creates connections across in the gaps in Smart's poem is to find oneself confronting rhizome-like associations – an underground root-system of erotic ramifications. The symbols embedded in this dense network of significance are thus entangled in an apparent fear of castration and, by way of self-protection, a countervailing longing for purification.

Submerged references to sexuality sometimes provide the link, otherwise apparently missing, between Smart's references to scientific experiments and his paired creatures. In another of his most apparently disjunctive verse-pairs, Smart appropriates technical terms from science (and an obsolete scholasticism) in order to figure the social "rising" that an honoring of the Lord's jubilee would represent. The surrounding "Let" and "For" lines, in this case, are concerned with the Sabbath and various scientific experiments respectively. What joins the two realms is the flesh:

> Let Tryphosa rejoice with Acarne – With such preparation the
>   Lord's Jubile is better kept
> For the rising in the BAROMETER is not effected by pressure but by
>   sympathy.[124]

Smart's phrase "such preparation," not clarified by the larger context, may refer to the fish's name, "Acarne," as meaning to Smart something like "abstinence from the flesh." ("Carnival," we recall, means "farewell to the flesh.") If that is the case, there are in fact three "risings" being associated here: the rising of the barometer, the "rising" of the dispossessed during the jubilee, and the "horniness" of sexual erection. To refrain ("A-carne") from the carnal rising better prepares one for the jubilant social rising, which itself is figured by the barometer's movements. The barometer, a sort of scientific wind or air instrument, measures atmospheric pressure, a good predictor of

---

[122] Michel Foucault, *Histoire de la sexualité*, 3 vols., (Paris: Editions Gallimard, 1976–1984), I: *La volonté de savoir*, p. 195. Trans. by Robert Hurley into English as *The History of Sexuality*, I: *An Introduction* (New York: Vintage Books, 1980), p. 148. The nexus of sexuality and nationalism is explored in depth in the essays collected in *Nationalisms and Sexualities*, eds. Andrew Parker, Mary Russo, Doris Sommer, and Patricia Yeager (New York: Routledge, 1992).

[123] Smart, *Jubilate*, B 193.

[124] *Ibid.*, B 213.

changes in the weather. The social rising, then, according to Smart, will occur not by "pressure," perhaps implying political violence, but by "sympathy": a word whose quasi-scientific meaning is here given a millennial twist.

One disjunctive verse-pair in *Jubilate Agno*, verging on the uncanny in tone, speaks impurely about a central myth of pure origins, Christ's virgin birth. In this penultimate versicle of the poem as we have it, Smart gives a benediction on strangeness and singularity. These lines, which insist that to be *odd* is in some sense to be *well*, subvert through a sexual pun the purity of the idea of maidenhood:

> Let Odwell, house of Odwell, rejoice with Lappago Maiden Lips.
> Blessed be the name of Jesus in singularities and singular
>   mercies.[125]

There is surely a self-reflexive reference here to odd speech. One critic has described this emphasis on strangeness as "basic to the Christian outlook" and sees Smart as having reinvented a religious sublimity that achieves its effects "through a paradoxical emphasis on the singular, the small, the meek, the odd, and the ridiculous."[126] This description, however, fails to exhaust interpretation of the lines. For given the importance of "coupling" in the poem, "odd" may specifically mean alone or sexually uncoupled: one rather than two. "Oddness" and "singularity" may figure literary originality here also: "originality" understood, indeed, as nothing less than the total anomaly of virgin birth. As such, it is Smart's defiant answer to Swift's joke about "modern pygmies" and their manic inventiveness on the single subject of the lower body. Most crucial, however, is the vernacular name for the flower: for "Lappago Maiden Lips" would seem to be among those old-fashioned popular terms for plants – Keith Thomas lists such examples as "black maidenhair," "naked ladies," "pissabed," "mares fart," and "priest's ballocks" – that would begin to be bowdlerized as indecent by the late eighteenth century.[127] The likely associative links between the "singularity" of Christ's virgin birth and "Lappago Maiden Lips" hints, in a manner typical of the *Jubilate*, at a shocking reference to Mary's lap and labia. However one defines a sublimity such as this, its leading feature is the "unmanly" refusal to subordinate signifier to signified. What is most sublime, surely, is the serenity with which the pairing seems to level, once and for all, the purity/impurity distinction.

Smart's bawdy punning thus has a certain levelling tendency that finally seems to work against his misogyny. Even Smart's fantasia on the horn,

---

[125] *Ibid.*, D 236.
[126] David Morris, *The Religious Sublime: Christian Poetry and Critical Tradition in 18th-Century England* (Lexington: The University Press of Kentucky, 1972), pp. 179–180.
[127] Keith Thomas, *Man and the Natural World: A History of the Modern Sensibility* (New York: Pantheon Books, 1983), p. 85.

indeed – which Devlin describes as "extravagant misogyny" and "one of the most shockingly crazy of his passages"[128] – concludes on a more conciliatory note. Around verse C 153, as both Liu and Easton point out, Smart begins a punning transmutation of the phallic horn into a cornucopian female principle.[129] A mellower agricultural theme, highlighting generativity and fertility, undergirds this last movement of Smart's prophecy.[130] The "horn of plenty"[131] thus gathers in a whole range of references to flowers, fruits, earth, milk, honey, bees, and so on.[132] Easton describes this shift most provocatively: "Under the sign of the masculine Smart unearths an omphalos – the earth as a generative power – and the horn here comes to cross-dress itself, as it were, like Hercules and Omphale exchanging clothes. . ."[133]

By means of the traditional equation of plowing and impregnation, Smart finally seems to redeem the image of sexual generation in *Jubilate Agno*. As Easton points out, the horn in the following lines refers to the ancient use of horns as plows:[134] "For when Man was amerced of his horn, earth lost part of her fertility."[135] Still more interesting is the sequel to this idea:

> Let Nebai rejoice with the Wild Cucumber.
> For earth will get it up again by the blessing of God on the
>   industry of man.[136]

Nebai comes from a Hebrew root signifying "produce" or "fruit." The notion that earth will "get it up again" certainly does suggest female erection, as Easton points out; that idea, however, is not so much an "oxymoron"[137] as a *clitoral image* that is mirrored in the "Wild Cucumber." I submit that it is precisely in this homely trope that Smart seems to move toward some sort of acceptance of an "undomesticated" female sexuality, of a "wild" excess beyond the control or "industry" of man, and, most interestingly, beyond the merely complementary image of the uterine cornucopia.[138] One should not be entirely surprised, then, that it is in the "Second Age of Horn" prophecy that Smart finally seems to find his way back to memories of domestic

128   Devlin, *Kit*, pp. 87, 122.
129   Liu, "Letters," p. 121; Easton, "Habits," p. 267.
130   *Ibid.*
131   Smart, *Jubilate*, C 153.
132   Liu, "Letters," p. 121; Easton, "Habits," p. 267.
133   *Ibid.*
134   *Ibid.*
135   Smart, *Jubilate*, C 156.
136   *Ibid.*, C 161.
137   Easton, "Habits," p. 268.
138   For a discussion of clitoral symbolism and its relative lack of theorization, see Paula Bennett, "Critical clitoridectomy: female sexual imagery and feminist psychoanalytic theory," *Signs* 18:2 (1993), pp. 235–259. For more about the eighteenth-century shift in models of sexuality (between what Thomas Laqueur has called the "one-sex" and the "two sex" models), see Cath Sharrock, "Hermaphroditism; or, 'the erection of a new doctrine': theories of female sexuality in eighteenth-century England," *Paragraph* 17: 1 (1994), pp. 38–48.

affection: "Let Tabbaoth rejoice with Goldy Locks," he writes in C 128: "God be merciful to my wife."

Smart's remarkable wordplay deserves to be compared to the seductive quibbling found in the whole range of authors, from Gertrude Stein to James Joyce, for whom wordplay is central. The more crucial issue, however, is to what extent Smart's broader affiliations with enthusiastic rhetoric tend to subvert, or at least tame, the misogynist import of his millennial prophecies. The subversive effect of enthusiastic rhetorical modes implies the need for a more nuanced account of their potential contribution to our reading of seventeenth- and eighteenth-century literature. It is not enough to register the contribution made by enthusiasm, by way of its vernacular energies and radical ideas, to an oppositional politics based on resistance to class stratification. More complex and fraught, and perhaps more unexpectedly interesting, is the imaginative energy dedicated in enthusiastic rhetoric to reinventing – one is tempted to say *revamping* – the body politic as a whole.

8

Smart's poetics of place: myth versus utopia in *Jubilate Agno*

For there is a traveling for the Glory of God without going to Italy or France.   Christopher Smart, *Jubilate Agno*, B 35

The criticism of Christopher Smart's religious poems, especially *Jubilate Agno*, has been recurrently preoccupied with questions of vertical scale. What does it mean for Smart to link the gambols of his pet, Jeoffry the Cat, to Mary's Magnificat? And how shall we understand the interplay of smallness and sublimity in Smart, himself a diminutive man and self-proclaimed second "David"?[1] Though these investigations have been crucial to the understanding, say, of *Jubilate Agno*'s daring subversions of the Great Chain of Being – honored by Smart, as Geoffrey Hartman observes, only insofar as it continues to "electrify the tongue"[2] – they have not adequately explored the poem's horizontal spatiality. Such an exploration, indeed, permits us to rethink the notion of Smart's supposed mania in a new context. It allows us to enter *Jubilate Agno* through the poem's utopian and millenarian dimension, which necessarily concerns place, and, more generally, through the politics of spatial location.

The topic of socially organized space serves to remind us again that the biographical Smart, in being confined to an asylum, suffered a dramatic contraction of his own horizons. His infamous assertion in the *Jubilate* that he is divinely appointed to be, as he claims, "the Reviver of ADORATION amongst ENGLISH-MEN,"[3] can be seen in this view as an attempt to vault outward on a map of concentrically nested geographical scales – or kinds of places, from neighborhoods to nations – that reaches from the body to the cosmos. It

---

[1]   This question is addressed in different ways in David Morris' *The Religious Sublime: Christian Poetry and Critical Tradition in 18th-Century England* (Lexington: University Press of Kentucky, 1972), pp. 170–180; and Alan Liu's "Christopher Smart's 'uncommunicated letters': translation and the ethics of literary history," *Boundary* 2 14: 1–2 (1985–1986), pp. 115–146.

[2]   Geoffrey H. Hartman, "Christopher Smart's Magnificat: toward a theory of representation," in *The Fate of Reading* (Chicago: University of Chicago Press, 1975), p. 87.

[3]   Christopher Smart, *The Poetical Works of Christopher Smart*, 4 vols. eds. Karina Williamson and Marcus Walsh (Clarendon Press, 1980–1987), I: *Jubilate Agno*, B 332.

expresses, above all, a transgressive desire to "jump scales" from a severely narrowed to a greatly expanded horizon.[4]

I shall argue in this chapter that the imaginative redrawing of boundaries, both marking and transgressing the multi-levelled and concentric spaces of "inside" and "outside," is the activity above all others that motivates *Jubilate Agno*. The most interesting and yet most neglected domain of this frequently utopian activity, however, appears in the tension between Smart's militant patriotism and his attempt in *Jubilate Agno* to create a cosmic and universal vision. Though written from the extremest margin of British society, Smart's visionary poem is in fact strongly marked by Britain's global position, in the seventh decade of the eighteenth century, as an ascendant center of naval and economic power. Far from being an idiosyncratic transmission from celestial spheres, *Jubilate Agno* is fundamentally shaped by the various nationalist discourses of its own moment. *Jubilate Agno*, indeed, can be plausibly read as the rearticulation of an older class-based enthusiasm within the terms of emergent nationalist discourses.[5] Any searching analysis of this nationalism, moreover, must come to terms with the way Smart's envisioning of England's global role is embedded in expansionist ideologies. Such an analysis, however, though necessary as a supplement to seeing Smart merely as a "patriot of the Lord,"[6] does not exhaust the kinds of spaces found in the *Jubilate*. For it is precisely by working through the broader spatial politics of *Jubilate Agno* that one can specify the particular achievement of Smart's vision. Although Smart's feat in *Jubilate Agno* is often taken to be the visionary approach to another world, it can better be seen as the neutralization, in this world, of a multi-levelled and politically charged opposition between "inside" and "outside." Indeed, the truly visionary achievement of *Jubilate Agno* is not its much-praised "otherworldliness" so much as its particular way of negotiating with some very worldly limits.

Jubilate Agno frames various contemporary events in millennial terms, finding in their outcome the predestined triumph of a militant English Protestantism. Moreover, it is precisely the rootedness of Smart's visionary poetics in contemporary conditions that galvanizes his imagination. The local and situated nature of this imagining is sufficiently evident in a verse-pair that

---

[4] Neil Smith, "Contours of a spatialized politics: homeless vehicles and the production of geographic scale," *Social Text* 33 (1992), p. 60.

[5] For more about the centrality of Protestantism to eighteenth-century nation-building, see Linda Colley, *Britons: Forging the Nation 1707–1837* (New Haven: Yale University Press, 1992), pp. 11–54.

[6] See Albert J. Kuhn, "Christopher Smart: the poet as patriot of the Lord," *English Literary History* 30 (1963), pp. 122–129. Both Paul Gilroy and Gauri Viswanathan warn against the theoretical conflation of nationalism with imperialism. See Paul Gilroy, *'There Ain't No Black in the Union Jack': The Cultural Politics of Race and Nation* (Chicago: University of Chicago Press, 1991), pp. 154ff; and Gauri Viswanathan, "Raymond Williams and British colonialism," *The Yale Journal of Criticism* 4:2 (1991), pp. 47–65.

touches on contemporary events in the international scene. Smart, who had
been involuntarily confined to an asylum by his in-laws, establishes early in
the poem an analogy between military developments on the global scale and
his own sense of personal abandonment and betrayal:

> Let Zurishaddai with the Polish Cock rejoice – The Lord restore
>   peace to Europe.
> For I meditate the peace of Europe amongst family bickerings and
>   domestic jars.[7]

Here Smart draws an analogy, deliberately unheroic and deflating, between
contemporary warfare and family bickering. This is a reinforcement of
pacifist sentiments also expressed in a prayer "that all the guns may be nail'd
up, save such as are for the rejoicing days."[8] There is a notable ambiguity,
however, in Smart's attitudes. On the one hand, Smart provides a critique of
belligerent nationalism in his fable "The English Bull Dog, Dutch Mastiff,
and Quail" (1755), in which he urges a cosmopolitan tolerance: "Give
prejudices to the wind, / And let's be patriots of mankind."[9] On the other
hand, he himself goes on to wax patriotic in time of war. In Hymn XVII,
probably written between 1762 and 1763, Smart offers thanks for "the naval
sway / Which o'er the subject seas we claim."[10] It seems likely, therefore,
that the peace on which Smart meditates in *Jubilate Agno* is a *Pax Britannica*.

Consider, as another example, an image whose ambiguity is typical of
Jubilate Agno. The *Jubilate* looks forward, among other millennial phenomena,
to the return of a sacred city-garden: "For I pray God to bless improvements
in gardening," Smart writes, "till London be a city of palm-trees."[11] This
could be merely a further example of Smart's reinvention, via Robert
Lowth's lectures on Hebrew poetry, of an earlier sacred poetics and
"Oriental" imagery. One wonders, however, given Smart's attitude toward
England's glory at this historical moment, if it refers as well to palm trees as
imperial spoils of the "exotic" east. It is precisely the disturbing ambiguity of
the image that is intriguing: the push and pull between an older sacred
language – the Biblical *topos* of the "Promised Land" – and the far-reaching
language of an emerging British empire.

It is not inevitably debunking, however, to bring together, within the same
field of analysis, the poem's otherworldly and this-worldly dimensions.
Indeed, to speak of otherworldliness alone, while ignoring Smart's engagement with the conditions of his moment, would badly skew our grasp of the
nature of his visionary achievement in *Jubilate Agno*. The two dimensions

---

[7] Smart, *Jubilate*, B 7.
[8] *Ibid.*, B 4.
[9] "The English Bull Dog, Dutch Mastiff, and Quail," in *Smart*, IV: *Miscellaneous Poems, English and
Latin*, p. 299.
[10] Hymn XVII, in *Smart*, II: *Religious Poetry 1763–1771*, p. 65.
[11] Smart, *Jubilate*, B 28.

simply cannot be separated. It is just such a liminal status, moreover, that Louis Marin and Fredric Jameson have ascribed to utopian texts in general.[12] Like Wallace Stevens' palm tree, poised at the "end of the mind," the utopian text marks a historical limit, a stalling point, even as it points toward a transcendence of such limits.[13] Thus Jameson has suggested, in an early and immensely suggestive article, that the deepest subject of utopian discourse is precisely its own inability to escape history. In this seemingly paradoxical view, the very points at which utopian visions fail to transcend the historical conditions of their own possibility – fail to lift themselves, by their own bootstraps, as it were, beyond "what is" – are the genre's most "authentic" and most "vibrantly political" moments.[14]

It is thus precisely in the contest between this world and another still striving to emerge – that is to say, in Smart's peculiarly fraught poetics of place – that the true interest of *Jubilate Agno* lies. It is important to remember, in this context, that the *Jubilate* was written in a period coinciding with England's Seven Years' War with France (1756–1763). As a struggle for colonial possessions and markets on such varied fronts as Canada, India, coastal Africa, and the West Indies, this may have been the first true world war. It also marks the first age of major English imperial expansion. An intoxicating series of British military successes enabled England to despoil France, its chief colonial rival, of colonial territories from Montreal to Calcutta. This geopolitical violence, which induced a wave of crass jingoism in Britain, polarized human communities into competing nation-states. What may be less obvious is the extent to which British national identity was ultimately being shaped by the supra-national context of a burgeoning imperial social formation. Populations were beginning to be divided according to the developing logic of a hemispheric "global rift" – as yet not fully consolidated – between "East/South" and "West/North."[15] For western Europe's intercontinental economic order had by this time managed to subordinate

---

[12] See Louis Marin, *Utopiques: Jeux d'espaces* (Paris: Les Editions de Minuit, 1973). Available in English as *Utopics: Spatial Play*, trans. Robert A. Vollrath (New Jersey: Humanities Press Inc., 1984). See also Fredric Jameson, "Of islands and trenches: neutralization and the production of utopian discourse," in *The Ideologies of Theory: Essays 1971–1986*, Theory and History of Literature Series, 2 vols. (Minneapolis: University of Minnesota Press, 1988), II: *Syntax of History*, p. 101. "Of islands and trenches" was originally published in *Diacritics* 7:2 (1977), pp. 2–21. For another return to Marin's work on utopia, see Richard Halpern's *The Poetics of Primitive Accumulation: English Renaissance Culture and the Genealogy of Capital* (Ithaca: Cornell University Press, 1991).

[13] See Wallace Stevens, "Of Mere Being," in *The Palm at the End of the Mind*, ed. Holly Stevens (New York: Vintage, 1967), p. 398. Stevens' palm tree, in fact, belongs to an imaginary geopolitics in which a mundane and wintry "north" is opposed to a lush, tropical, and exotic "south" (including portions of the American south and west). This structure, something like a Connecticut tourist's experience of the neocolonial world-system, determines many of the symbols in Stevens' poetry. See Fredric Jameson's "Periodizing the 60s," in *The 60s without Apology*, eds. Sohnya Sayres, Anders Stephanson *et al.* (Minneapolis: University of Minnesota Press, 1984), pp. 198–199.

[14] Jameson, "Utopian," p. 101.

[15] See L. S. Stavrianos, *Global Rift: The Third World Comes of Age* (New York: Morrow Press, 1981).

large regions of eastern Europe and Latin America to a global capitalist economy, to establish a vast trans-Atlantic traffic in enslaved Africans, and to fortify an ever-expanding beachhead in the Indian subcontinent. Western Europe had, moreover, imposed on the geographically adjacent Ottoman Empire, through capitulatory treaties, the foundation for a system of grossly unequal trade.[16]

Because *Jubilate Agno* is not disengaged from this history, the poem's true interest lies in the particular way Smart negotiates resolutions within it. The poem struggles with a deeply felt contradiction between a merciful inclusiveness (which resonates with cosmopolitan or universalist values) and exclusion (which registers, among other things, the closure enforced by an imperial nationalism). The kind of reading needed to grasp Smart's utopian negotiation of this conflict in the *Jubilate* must attend to a deeper structural logic. Smart himself tells us that "the Circle may be SQUARED by swelling and flattening,"[17] and in that wry spirit I hope to map the poem's central preoccupation with reimagining spatial boundaries onto the semiotic square.[18] From the initial antinomy between inclusive and exclusive space, the poem's logic generates two further negations (not inclusion and not exclusion), and, finally, two distinct attempts to resolve the conflict. Of these latter, the "mythic" resolution attempts merely to combine or bridge inclusion and exclusion. The "utopian" resolution, however, effects a sort of double cancellation, or neutralization, by combining the two negative terms. Although both of these mediations work to resolve, in some sense, the original antinomy, it is the great strength of Marin and Jameson's work to highlight the general distinction between a merely "mythic" and a truly "utopian" resolution.

It is not only that such an approach enables us to perceive crucial patterns in a text that is poorly understood, I would argue, when taken as the very textbook specimen of the anti-systematic;[19] but that, even more crucially, it permits us to foreground the truly visionary process of resolution operating in that text. In the following analysis, I will demonstrate to what extent the *Jubilate* operates within and against, rather than totally outside, the world of logical antinomies. In so doing, I hope to show that the real achievement of

---

[16] *Ibid.*, pp. 122–140.

[17] Smart, *Jubilate*, B 374.

[18] I have in mind Jameson's use of the Greimassian semiotic square. For Jameson, the semiotic square is a heuristic "discovery principle" for modeling the process of meaning itself as a terrain of social conflict. The "vocation" of the square, for Jameson, is to map the possible positions available within a given conceptual framework: the limits, in effect, of the thinkable. In exposing these limits, the square provides a model for analyzing the process by which thought is ideologically contained. See Fredric Jameson, Foreword to A. J. Greimas, *On Meaning: Selected Writings in Semiotic Theory*, trans. Paul J. Perron and Frank H. Collins, Theory and History of Literature Series (Minneapolis: University Press of Minnesota, 1987), p. xv.

[19] See Raman Selden, *Practicing Theory and Reading Literature: An Introduction* (Lexington: University Press of Kentucky, 1989), pp. 51–54.

Jubilate Agno lies in its struggle to neutralize the conflict between inclusive and exclusive space.

The situation, above all, to which *Jubilate Agno* responds is exclusion. In the lexicon of the *Jubilate*, "amercement" is the most compelling synonym for this initial term of our analysis. To be "amerced," in Smart's usage, is to be cut off, excluded, as Cain was by God's curse.[20] On the cosmic scale, for instance, Smart's prophecy that a lost "masculine" horn will be recovered proclaims humanity's "amercement" of God and the angels, who still possess the horn that we have lost.[21] Christ's human incarnation, moreover, which necessitated the emptying out of his divine nature, specifically required the "amercement" of his horn. At the Second Coming, then, "his horn will be exalted in glory."[22] Amercement, in this perspective, is, like original sin, a universal plight.

More personal overtones, however, emerge early in the poem's musings about bodily and domestic amercement. In the following reference to the sterile sex-life of mules, sexual deprivation figures as a mode of amercement:

> Let Anah, the son of Zibion, lead a Mule to the temple, and bless
> God, who amerces the consolation of the creature for the
> service of man.[23]

And in B 70, we find a poignant development of the abandonment theme in terms that seem applicable to someone involuntarily confined by his in-laws to an asylum: "For the Fatherless Children and widows are never deserted of the Lord." From Smart's need to assert this faith amidst great adversity, one may speculate, the utopian poem springs.

The general motif of *inclusion*, belying Smart's own apparent solitude, then provides the exact contrary to *amercement*. *Jubilate Agno* redraws the boundaries of a cosmos now imagined as rejoicing in its diversity. One of Smart's names for this inclusivity is *mercy*, which he defines as infinitely superior to justice.[24] Thus *Jubilate Agno* begins by invoking a scene of collective worship that is to include all of creation. Through a pun on "tongues," Smart sets up its polylinguistic diction:

> Rejoice in God, O ye tongues; give the glory to the Lord, and the Lamb.
> Nations, and languages, and every Creature, in which is the breath of
> life.[25]

---

[20] Smart's usage is probably influenced by Milton's line from *Paradise Lost* describing the results of Satan's rebellion among the angels: "Millions of spirits for his fault amerced / Of Heav'n" (Book I, ll. 609–610). See John Milton, *Paradise Lost*, in *John Milton: Complete Poems and Major Prose*, ed. Merritt Hughes (New York: The Odyssey Press, 1957), p. 227. The original sense of the word, according to the OED, is to be fined arbitrarily, at the mercy of another.

[21] Smart, *Jubilate*, C 143–144.

[22] *Ibid.*, C 149.

[23] *Ibid.*, A 12.

[24] *Ibid.*, B 320.

[25] *Ibid.*, A 1.

"Tongues" in these lines means both "the organs of speech" and "languages": this opening pun thus announces Smart's plan to engage in a generously cosmopolitan mingling of languages. And indeed, Smart creates a space in the *Jubilate* where jaw-breaking exotics such as *Omphalacarpa* and *Lithizontes* coexist with such exuberantly home-grown coinages as "the Great Flabber Dabber Flat Clapping Fish with Hands."[26]

Smart's most crucial image for this globally inclusive project is Noah's Ark:

> Let man and beast appear before him, and magnify his name together.
> Let Noah and his company approach the throne of Grace, and do
>   homage to the Ark of their Salvation.[27]

This Ark, soon to be daringly conflated with the Ark of the Covenant, is intended to include, and save, every living creature.[28] Unclean beasts, as well as clean, are invited into Smart's "Ark," as are small and obscure creatures. So expansive is Smart's revision of the Christian covenant, indeed, that he defies many features of human anthropocentrism. The flea, the roach, and even an intestinal worm are included; so too is the humble toad, though the latter goes unmentioned in the Bible.[29] For Smart, confined in an eighteenth-century madhouse with "neither money nor human friends,"[30] no creature seems beneath his notice. It is especially this dimension of the poem that has frequently been seen as "otherworldly" and "Franciscan."[31]

Inclusion generates, as its answering complement within the poem's exploratory logic, the implied category of *not inclusion* or (in the poem's preferred language) *purification*. Through loud prayers of praise and gratitude, Smart intends his poem to exorcise the cosmos of linguistic pollution: lies, blasphemy, slander, cursing. Much of the poem's formal relentlessness, its ritualistic and incantatory flavor, belongs to this exorcising motive. This is a mode that implicitly *comes after* transgressive inclusions, almost as if the cleansing flood of Genesis, no less than the new covenant with Noah, needs to be recapitulated. In terms of religious history, this will be something like a second Reformation. Its scope and scale, moreover, are often seen as specifically national. Thus Smart blesses a recently opened asylum for former prostitutes in national terms: "For I pray

---

[26] *Ibid.*, D 11.
[27] *Ibid.*, A 3–4.
[28] See Christopher Devlin, *Poor Kit Smart* (London: Rupert Hart-Davis, 1961), p. 107. Harriet Guest points out that Smart may be telescoping *three* "arks" here: the two arks mentioned above plus Christ as the "ark" or vessel of God on earth. See her *A Form of Sound Words: The Religious Poetry of Christopher Smart* (Oxford: Clarendon Press, 1989), p. 139.
[29] Smart, *Jubilate*, A 29.
[30] *Ibid.*, B 283.
[31] See John Middleton Murry, "A note on the madness of Christopher Smart," in *Discoveries: Essays in Literary Criticism* (London: W. Collins Sons & Co. Ltd., 1924), p. 185; Devlin, *Kit*, p. 17; and Morris, *Sublime*, p. 171.

Almighty CHRIST to bless the MAGDALEN HOUSE and to forward a National purification."[32]

Much of *Jubilate Agno* is indeed a ritual act of purification. Many of the poem's key verbs belong under this performative rubric: "bless," "rejoice," "praise." Smart believes that through his praising activities, as A. D. Hope observes, "the fallen creation is gradually purified and restored."[33] And literary notions of purity, no less than any other, bear out the conclusions of Mary Douglas' *Purity and Danger*, where impurity (or "dirt") is shown to be, contextually, the anomalous and disorderly. Dirt, viewed through the lens of social anthropology, is that which symbolically violates taxonomic categories: it is "matter out of place."[34] For Smart, such demonized disorder has to do with "dirty" or transgressive language. Before the millennium can be properly ushered in, a thorough-going linguistic purgation must occur:

> For the AIR is contaminated by curses and evil language.[35]
>
> For the AIR is purified by prayer which is made aloud and with all
> our might.
> For poysonous creatures catch some of it and retain it ere it goes
> to the adversary.[36]

The Satanic "adversary" is later described as the source of "all whispers and unmusical sounds,"[37] of cant,[38] and of nightmares.[39] *Jubilate Agno* also imagines purification as a fiery judgment:

> For all the filth of wicked men shall be done away by fire in eternity.
> For the furnace itself shall come up at the last according to
> Abraham's vision.[40]

The newness of Smart's song, then, involves recovering a lost purity, a militant repristination of language. Smart's appropriation of scriptural language, indeed, is a weapon: "For the word of God," he says, "is a sword on my side."[41]

The poem's restless logic, however, does not abide here: for Smart is determined to explore all the positions and possibilities that emerge from his

[32] Smart, *Jubilate*, B 128.
[33] A. D. Hope, "The apocalypse of Christopher Smart," in *Studies in the Eighteenth Century*, ed. R. F. Brissenden (Toronto: University of Toronto Press, 1967), p. 280.
[34] Mary Douglas, *Purity and Danger: An Analysis of the Concepts of Pollution and Taboo* (London: Routledge & Kegan Paul, 1966), p. 40. See also Geoffrey H. Hartman, *Criticism in the Wilderness: The Study of Literature Today* (New Haven: Yale University Press, 1980), pp. 115–157; and Peter Stallybrass and Allon White, *The Politics and Poetics of Transgression* (Ithaca: Cornell University Press, 1986).
[35] Smart, *Jubilate*, B 221.
[36] *Ibid.*, B 224–225.
[37] *Ibid.*, B 231.
[38] *Ibid.*, B 237.
[39] *Ibid.*, B 370.
[40] *Ibid.*, B 292–293.
[41] *Ibid.*, B 20.

initial problematic. The theme answering to *amercement*, then, is *not amercement*, for which the poem's most resonant synonyms are hyperboles of abundance, limitless variety, and *extravagance*: "For GOD," as Smart says, "is an extravagant BEING and generous unto loss."[42] And again: "For the names and numbers of animals are as the name and number of the stars. – "[43] The creation, in a way that again seems to come after some prior purification, is seen as sublimely infinite and generative. Hence Smart's use of the harvest image of cornucopia in his prophecy of the lost horn recovered: "For the horn is of plenty," he writes, "because of milk and honey."[44] And hence the poem's other key verb, "magnify," which undergirds his description of the entire poem as a "Magnificat."[45] This magnifying activity Smart compares in B 251 to Jesus' multiplication of the loaves.

The formal corollary of such infinitude is polylingual diction and polysemous wordplay. Such "prankish" wordplay, as the pun on "Ark" indicates, is often exuberant and daring. Thus Smart works out in one versicle a claim for his sonorous voice in terms of his sexual endowment:

> Let Japhia rejoice with Buteo who hath three testicles.
> For I bless God in the strength of my loins and for the voice
> which he hath made sonorous.[46]

That Smart is also celebrating his *poetic* voice is obvious in the pun on lines/loins, homophones in the eighteenth century.[47] His hyperbolic poetic virility – not two, but three testicles – stands for the triumph of plenty over purity, sexuality over sterility. Smart's incessant wordplay, which often induces a sense of infinite semiotic regress, works against any possible petrification of his exuberant work into dogma.

Most interesting is what this structural analysis throws into relief: the poem's attempts, through both "complex" (mythic) and "neutral" (utopian) terms, to mediate the tensions between inclusion and exclusion. The "complex" term, according to Jameson, is the site of mythological resolution or mediation *à la* Lévi-Strauss, with myth here assuming all the "bad" senses of mystification, hegemonic containment, and so on. "Mythic" closure, in this view, tends to produce an ideological mirage of social harmony that screens out the social totality. From Jameson's hint that utopian resolutions are "authentic" and "politically vibrant," moreover, we can infer that they are

---

[42] *Ibid.*, C 380.
[43] *Ibid.*, B 42.
[44] *Ibid.*, C 161.
[45] *Ibid.*, B 43.
[46] *Ibid.*, B 80.
[47] William Collins's "Ode on the Poetical Character," as Manuel Schonhorn pointed out to me, makes the same pun in the phrase "blest prophetic loins." See William Collins, "Ode on the Poetical Character," in *The Poems of Thomas Gray, William Collins, and Oliver Goldsmith*, ed. Roger Lonsdale (London: Longman's, 1969), p. 429.

generally more interesting than mythic ones. Such will be my contention here: that Smart's utopian term, "sincerity," produces a far more persuasive resolution than his merely mythic catalogues of rejoicing creatures.

What, then, is the "complex term" that attempts to synthesize the poles of this poem's conflict between exclusion and inclusion? For the complex term I have adopted a pun made explicit by Geoffrey Hartman: "ADD-oration."[48] This term, while evoking Smart's great incantation to "ADORATION" in "A Song to David," refers here to Smart's relentless practice of listing names, which combines, as any listing must, elements of inclusion and exclusion. Such an attempt to synthesize through the mere addition and accumulation of names does not convincingly solve, even within the poem's own terms, the problem it addresses. For the "mythic" resolution repeatedly lapses into a practice of appropriation and possession on the one hand, or of hierarchical ordering, on the other. The political limits of Smart's "ADD-oration" are precisely those one associates with pluralistic gestures of token inclusion.

The joy of enumeration is indeed an extremely conspicuous feature of Smart's style in the *Jubilate*. There are many catalogues in *Jubilate Agno*. These range from lists of writers for whom Smart gives thanks – Swift, Pope, and Gay – to lists of contemporary obituaries, to lists of minerals, flowers, colors, and creatures, to playful punning sequences on lists of alphabetic characters, to a meditative list of the attributes of his cat Jeoffry. The "consideration" of Jeoffry is widely known and justly celebrated. Many of the other listing exercises, such as the catalogue of various "rhymes" as if each had a specific orchestral timbre in the great pipe organ of language, also have great charm.

Because the range and variety of Smart's lists is so remarkable, it is tempting to read Smart's inventories, like his diction, as entirely inclusive and "democratic." In fact, however, Smart incorporates at least two different sorts of lists into the *Jubilate Agno*. One is indeed radically inclusive, reminiscent of the grand tradition of democratically levelling catalogues from the Ranters to Walt Whitman. Like their deliberately provocative juxtapositions of tent-makers and scholars, presidents and whores,[49] Smart's juxtapositions of, say, Boaz with the Rat,[50] Joseph with the Crocodile,[51] Job with the Worm,[52] Candace with the Crawfish,[53] and Alexander with the

---

[48] Hartman, "Magnificat," pp. 87–88.
[49] Coppe's levelling list, also discussed in Ch. 2, makes the point that unlearned sectarians are the spiritual equals of their supposed betters in the university. See Abiezer Coppe, *Some Sweet Sips, of Some Spirituall Wine* (1649), in *A Collection of Ranter Writings from the 17th Century*, ed. Nigel Smith (London: Junction Books, 1983), p. 60. In his "Song of Myself," Whitman juxtaposes a prostitute with the president and his cabinet in a list that also includes a peddler, a bride, and an opium-eater. See Walt Whitman, "Song of Myself," in *Leaves of Grass and Selected Prose*, ed. Sculley Bradley (New York: Holt, Rinehart and Winston, Inc., 1949), p. 36.
[50] Smart, *Jubilate*, A 33.
[51] *Ibid.*, A 46.
[52] *Ibid.*, A 51.
[53] *Ibid.*, B 194.

Sea-Urchin[54] seem calculated to obliterate distinctions. Lance Bertelsen thus stresses the connection of this "levelling" quality with Smart's other contributions – as "Mother Mary Midnight," for instance – to the burlesque productions of eighteenth-century popular written and theatrical culture.[55]

Jubilate Agno, however, also comprises another sort of catalogue, the levelling tendency of which pertains more to commodification than social equality. A considerable portion of section D, in which the catalogues pair familial "houses" with precious stones and tropical exotica, marks a point in Smart at which the various listing rhetorics of natural history, European voyage literature, commercial merchandising, and colonial exploitation converge.[56] So the House of Beacon is invoked to rejoice with Amadavad, "a fine bird in the East Indies" (D 201) and the House of Crockatt likewise rejoices with Emboline, "an Asiatic shrub."[57] So too in an earlier verse-pair, probably deriving from a contemporary pharmacopia, Smart meticulously tabulates "the five varieties of the Indian Myrobolan tree, whose fruit was used for purges".[58]

> Let Col-hozeh rejoice with Myrobalans, Bellerica, Chebula, Citrina,
>   Emblica, and Indica.
> For I prophecy that players and mimes will not be named amongst us.[59]

The Hebrew roots of "Col-hozeh" evoke the notion of a seer or prophet, and so set up the prophesying gesture that follows.[60] The "Let" line promotes a sense of happy abundance inseparable from colonial appropriation. The

---

54 *Ibid.*, B 233.
55 Lance Bertelsen, "Journalism, carnival, and *Jubilate Agno*," *English Literary History* 59 (1992), p. 370.
56 The catalogue of imported luxury items is a favorite eighteenth-century commonplace. Louis Landa is among the earliest critics to explore this *topos*. See his "Of silkworms and farthingales and the will of God," in *Studies in the Eighteenth Century*, ed. R. F. Brissenden (Toronto: University of Toronto Press, 1973), II, pp. 259–277. See also Laura Brown's *Alexander Pope* (Oxford: Basil Blackwell, 1985), pp. 8–45. For a feminist critique of the *blazon* tradition, see Nancy Vickers' "Diana described: scattered woman and scattered rhyme," *Critical Inquiry* 8 (1981), pp. 265–79. An impressive synthesis of these insights can be found in Patricia Parker's "Rhetoric of property: exploration, inventory, blazon," in *Literary Fat Ladies: Rhetoric, Gender, Property* (London: Methuen, 1987), pp. 126–154. For more about the colonial overtones of botanical science, see Deepak Kumar, "The evolution of colonial science in India: natural history and the East India Company," in *Imperialism and the Natural World*, ed. John M. Mackenzie (Manchester: Manchester University Press, 1990), pp. 51–66. For the imperial aspirations and affiliations of natural history more generally, see Mary Louise Pratt, *Imperial Eyes: Travel Writing and Transculturation* (London: Routledge, 1992), pp. 15–37. George Anson's *A Voyage Round the World* (1748), from which Smart derives his fantastic allusion to the Sea Lion – "The Great Flabber Dabber Flat Clapping Fish with Hands" (D 11) – is aggressively expansionist. See George Anson, *A Voyage Round the World*, ed. Glyndwr Williams (London: Oxford University Press, 1974), p. 96.
57 Smart, *Jubilate*, D 210.
58 Williamson's note, *Jubilate*, p. 100.
59 Smart, *Jubilate*, C 93.
60 Col-hozeh appears only in genealogical lists in Nehemiah: as the father of Shallun, who helped to rebuild the walls of Jerusalem after a fire (Neh. 3:15); and of Baruch, who dwelled inside the rebuilt walls (Neh. 11:5).

"For" line here, like others in the *Jubilate*, seems to revive the seventeenth-century Puritan polemic against the theater. Thus internal "purification," in a combination perfected during the Cromwellian era,[61] seems here to go hand in hand with external expansionism.

Moreover, though Smart imagines his poem as a Noachian ark, a chambered refuge from the terrible flood of human history, *Jubilate Agno* also tallies the imaginary dominions of a greatly expanded British empire. In a passage of prophecy just preceding his prediction of the lost horn found, he comes up with an international version of the "body politic":

> For the Liturgy will obtain in all languages.
> For England is the head and not the tail.
> For England is the head of Europe in the spirit.
> For Spain, Portugal and France are the heart.
> For Holland and Germany are the middle.
> For Italy is one of the legs.[62]

This is too playful to be harshly judged; however, it does in fact mark a participation by Smart in a populist mode of aggressive nationalism. He envisions, in Albert Kuhn's words, "a spiritually transformed map of Europe, perhaps even a Holy Anglican Empire, and certainly a millennium."[63] England, the "head" of the various members, is understood as the origin of spiritual renewal and thus sets the standard, religious and linguistic, to which the others must be assimilated.

Smart's scriptural rhetoric tracing the descent of peoples is still more problematic in its political implications. This phase of his mythic resolution, simultaneously levelling and hierarchical, results in something like an anthology of ethnic and cultural lore. Smart's text, like many examples of "early ethnography" as practiced in the sixteenth and seventeenth centuries, seeks to explain cultural diversity in ancestral terms that can be traced back to Noah's sons.[64] This obsession with origins is of a piece with the more

---

[61] Cromwell pursued a vigorously imperialistic foreign policy, the fruits of which included the conquest of Ireland, the acquisition of Jamaica, Nova Scotia, and Surinam, the strengthening of the East India Company, and the refurbishing of British naval power. His "Western Design" involved, above all, the establishment of a permanent British base in the West Indies. As Christopher Hill points out, Cromwell's "Western Design" policy "for the first time made the Caribbean the theatre of European power politics which it was to remain for 150 years." Christopher Hill, *The Century of Revolution 1603–1714* (1961; rpt. New York: W. W. Norton & Co., 1982), p. 135. As Karina Williamson observes in her annotation, it is immediately after Smart has mentioned Jamaica that he goes on to make his one direct (and very negative) reference to Cromwell (see Smart, *Jubilate*, B 273–274 and Williamson's note).

[62] Smart, *Jubilate*, C 100–105. For the sake of argumentative clarity, I have omitted in this passage, as well as several others, the corresponding "Let" lines.

[63] Kuhn, "Patriot," p. 122.

[64] See Margaret T. Hodgen, "The ark of Noah and the problem of cultural diversity," in *Early Anthropology in the Sixteenth and Seventeenth Centuries* (Philadelphia: University of Philadelphia Press, 1964), pp. 207–253.

general fascination with antiquities that inspired Gray's "The Bard,"
Macpherson's Ossianic "fakelore," and Bishop Percy's collection of
ballads.[65] Like the various antiquarian and primitivist speculators of his own
time, then – William Stukeley's *Stonehenge* (1740) is one of his sources –
Smart is at pains to establish factitious cultural and religious continuities
across vast gulfs of historical time. Just as the "arch-Druid" Stukeley argued
for a prehistoric colonization of Britain by pious Phoenicians, implausibly
attempting to derive Welsh from Hebrew,[66] so Smart traces "Englishness,"
by way of the Romans and the Chinese, back to Abraham. Smart was not
particularly idiosyncratic, as Howard Weinbrot argues, either in so doing,
or in finding "Eastern" origins for most of Europe.[67] Nevertheless, it is
precisely Smart's troubled preoccupation with origins and ancestry that
pushes his genealogical tendencies toward a vaguely ominous ethnic
taxonomizing.

Smart's text comes just prior to, and thus just barely avoids, what Margaret
T. Hodgen calls "racialism" in the "familiar nineteenth- and twentieth-
century sense of the term."[68] It does not attempt, according to the distinction
argued by Hodgen, to reclassify some members of the human race as "among
the beasts."[69] Indeed, the theocentric perspective of the Hebrew Bible, as
Kwame Anthony Appiah points out, tends to emphasize not "race," as a
matter of biological heredity, but, rather, the shifting relation of distinct
peoples to God's covenants, blessings, and curses.[70] Given the accelerating
momentum of imperialism, however, certain contradictions inevitably arise as
Smart undertakes – in addition to his personal quest for ancestral validation –
a geographical quest to prove the "spiritual credentials" of the English
people.

Smart announces a "British-Israelite" passage by reaffirming in line B 62
that the English can be traced back to Abraham through David and Joab.
His next genealogy touches on his own ancestry, for his mother was Welsh:
"For the WELCH are the children of Mephibosheth and Ziba with a mixture
of David in the Jones's."[71] Smart claims to be *like* David because he is actually

---

[65]	See Ian Haywood, *The Making of History: A Study of the Literary Forgeries of James Macpherson and Thomas Chatterton in Relation to Eighteenth-Century Ideas of History and Fiction* (London: Associated University Presses, 1986). For a discussion of "metalepsis" as *the* trope for the retrospective fabrication of origins in this period, see Clement Hawes, "Leading history by the nose: the turn to the eighteenth century in *Midnight's Children,*" *Modern Fiction Studies* 39:1, pp. 147–168.

[66]	See Stuart Piggott, *William Stukeley: An Eighteenth-Century Antiquary* (Oxford: The Clarendon Press, 1950), pp. 119–129 and *Ancient Britons and the Antiquarian Imagination: Ideas from the Renaissance to the Regency* (New York: Thames and Hudson, 1989), pp. 143–146.

[67]	Howard Weinbrot, *Britannia's Issue: The Rise of British Literature from Dryden to Ossian* (Cambridge: Cambridge University Press, 1993), p. 418.

[68]	Hodgen, *Anthropology*, p. 213.

[69]	*Ibid.*, p. 13.

[70]	Kwame Anthony Appiah, *In My Father's House: Africa in the Philosophy of Culture* (New York: Oxford University Press, 1992), p. 12.

[71]	Smart, *Jubilate*, C 435.

descended *from* him.[72] The next few lines describe antipathies within the British Isles, revealing Smart's standard English view of the first victims of British imperialism, the "low" Irish:

> For the Scotch are the children of Doeg with a mixture of Cush
> the Benjamite, whence their innate antipathy to the English.
> For the IRISH are the children of Shimei and Cush with a mixture
> of something lower – the Lord raise them![73]

The next lines, then, begin to list the peoples of Europe and parts of Asia. Unsurprisingly, the Roman Catholic French, current and traditional military enemies, get hit with a double humiliation: they are pegged both with an odiously incestuous origin (as the children of Lot) and a dire fate (as Moab, the tribal name of a kingdom conquered and subjugated by King David).[74] Exactly what Smart has in mind for them becomes clear in line C 97: "For I prophecy that the Reformation will make way in France when Moab is made meek by being well drubbed by the English."

And indeed, though it enacts a cosmopolitan listing of mingled tongues, the *Jubilate* also prophesies the triumphant international hegemony of Smart's mother tongue. English will replace Hebrew, Smart says, as the sacred language of the West. The prophecy made in the following verse-pair celebrates an unpalatable linguistic imperialism. More than that, it seems to imply a division of the world along the now-familiar lines of "the West and the Rest":

> Let Philip rejoice with Boca, which is a fish that can speak.
> For the ENGLISH TONGUE shall be the language of the WEST.[75]

And Smart makes a similarly imperial vaunt elsewhere, alluding through "Guinea Hen," as Williamson notes, to English military victories in 1758 on the Guinea coast of West Africa:

> Let Zuar rejoice with the Guinea Hen – The Lord add to his
> mercies in the WEST!
> For the HOST is in the WEST[76] – the Lord make us thankful unto
> salvation.[77]

---

[72] For more about the "Celtophilia" that may be behind this passage, see Weinbrot, *Britannia*, pp. 485–507.

[73] Smart, *Jubilate*, C 436–437.

[74] For more about "Moabite" as war-time Protestant jargon in 1763, see Colley, *Britons*, p. 31. For the speculation that the term reflects Smart's anxieties about having married a (covertly) Catholic woman, see also Devlin, *Kit*, pp. 66–67.

[75] Smart, *Jubilate*, B 127.

[76] I am grateful to Charles T. Hatten for calling my attention to the striking polysemousness of "West" in these lines. In the first line, it may mean nothing more than West Africa; in the second, it may mean any of the following: the British Isles, as the western-most part of Europe; the British troops in Canada and the Americas; or western Europe as a whole, as opposed to Asia. In the latter case, the very name of the "West" would suggest a certain international solidarity, war or no war, among the European colonial powers.

[77] Smart, *Jubilate*, B 8.

Zuar is mentioned in Numbers 1:8 in a genealogical catalogue of soldiers available to Israel. A quibble on "host," meaning both the English troops and the Eucharistic sacrament, adds a perverse pun to the colonial enthusiasm. These are colonizing sentiments, imperial claims to be the exporter and producer, rather than the importer, of language and religion. They mark a point at which a truly cosmopolitan perspective – annexed by, for, and to a narrower Eurocentric horizon – suffers a silent "amercement."

A final example of the political limits of "ADD-oration" is manifest in the way that mere listing, the mere gesture of inclusion, elides the historical realities attached to Smart's different names. Consider, for our first exhibit, that the capaciousness of Smart's new "Ark" leads him to refute a hoary old *topos* associated precisely with the Noah story.[78] Smart, knowing that advocates of slavery defend it by claiming that Africans are the cursed descendants of Noah's son Ham and/or Cain,[79] easily answers this rationalization in its own terms:

> Let Ebed-Melech bless with the Mantiger, the blood of the Lord is
>   sufficient to do away the offence of Cain, and reinstate the
>   creature which is amerced.[80]

Ebed-Melech is recorded in Jeremiah 38–39 as an Ethiopian servant in the court of Zedekiah who interceded to save the prophet's life, and thus is promised God's deliverance. The Mantiger, better known as the Manticore, is a legendary Plinian monster from Ethiopia, supposed to have a triple row of teeth, the face and ears of a man, the body of a lion, and the stinging tail of a scorpion. The Manticore is also supposed to relish human flesh, and there is doubtless in "Man/Tiger" a punning reference to this trait, as well as to the ferocity of the first murderer, Cain. Smart's line is an elaborate way of saying that Africans, though descended from Cain, are nevertheless entirely redeemed through Christ's sacrifice. The "curse," if it ever was operative, has been cancelled by Christ.

Now consider the sheer erasure of enslaved Africans implied in the following verse-pair:

> Let Toi rejoice with Percnopteros which haunteth the sugar-fens.[81]
> For I bless God in the honey of the sugar-cane and the milk of the cocoa.[82]

[78] See Winthrop D. Jordan, *The White Man's Burden: Historical Origins of Racism in the United States* (London: Oxford University Press, 1974), pp. 9–10.

[79] In line B 216, Smart asserts that "Some of Cain's seed was preserved in the loins of Ham at the flood." It is Ham's son Canaan that is actually doomed to be "a servant of servants" in Noah's curse of Gen. 8:25. As Williamson explains, though Ham was descended from Cain's brother Seth, Smart may have identified Canaan and Cain.

[80] Smart, *Jubilate*, A 89.

[81] Percnopteros is an Eagle in Pliny, possibly confused here, as Williamson informs us, with a second, fen-haunting eagle. Toi, a very minor Biblical figure, made a treaty with King David.

[82] Smart, *Jubilate*, B 78.

These lines seem to be Smart's version of one of the commonplaces of the eighteenth-century "progress" tradition: the imagining, in the course of the westward progress of civilization, an Edenic "promised land" in the Americas.[83] The references to sugar plantations, however, mark a super-charged moment when the very attempt to imagine the Biblical "promised land" of milk and honey unwittingly conjures up instead the violent history of the colonial sugar trade.[84] Here the mere enumeration of creatures and people, in declining to articulate the social relations between them, fails utterly to synthesize or "straddle" them persuasively. That failure, moreover, is symptomatic of the systematic inattention to colonial violence and exploitation by which metropolitan consciousness preserved its political "innocence." Such ignorance, in this case, is not so much otherworldly as profoundly sanctioned by the powers of this world.[85]

One must grant that sometimes the levelling momentum of Smart's catalogues produces surprising illuminations. The Dutch, including colonial settlers in South Africa – some of whose descendants have rationalized a viciously racist economic system into the late twentieth century with a version of "Dutch-Israelitism" – are lumped in by Smart as "children of Gog" with the very "Hottentots" (Khoikhoi and San peoples) they have so oppressed and disdained:

> For the DUTCH are the children of Gog.[86]

> For the Hottentots are the children of Gog with a Black mixture.[87]

The formal egalitarianism of this list is matched here by Smart's pointed insistence on common origins.[88]

Intriguing as such moments are, however, they do not fully subvert the disquieting logic at work here: the partition of humanity into ethnically named peoples. The tenth edition of Linnaeus' *Systema Naturae* (1758) provides a major

---

[83] See George Berkeley's "On the prospect of planting arts and learning in America" (1752), which equates the westward progress of empire with a new golden age. See also Raymond C. Cochrane, "Bishop Berkeley and the progress of arts and learning: notes on a literary convention," *Huntington Library Quarterly* 17:3 (1954), pp. 229–249.

[84] See Sidney Mintz, *Sweetness and Power: The Place of Sugar in Modern History* (New York: Viking Press, 1985).

[85] It is instructive to compare these lines with a famous episode from Voltaire's *Candide*, published precisely as Smart was writing his *Jubilate* (1759). Among the examples of human misery Candide encounters is a paraplegic slave in Dutch Surinam. The enslaved Black man uses the occasion to inform Candide that his own mutilations – the amputation of his left leg and his right hand – are the price he pays so that Europeans can eat sugar. Candide, having lost just a bit more of his tattered innocence, weeps in response. See M. de Voltaire, *Candide, or Optimism*, trans. and ed. Robert M. Adams (New York: Norton, 1966), pp. 41–42.

[86] Smart, *Jubilate*, B 438.

[87] *Ibid.*, B 444.

[88] As Hannah Arendt points out, the Boers, through the peculiar theology of the Dutch Reformed Church, "simply denied the Christian doctrine of the common origin of men ..." Hannah Arendt, *Imperialism* (New York: Harcourt/Brace/Jovanovich, 1951), p. 75.

instance of such classifying logic, which had by this time expanded from traditional natural history into the naming, the ordering, and (implicitly) the hierarchical ranking of a half-dozen human populations.[89] It is in their flirtation with this discourse that Smart's ethnic catalogues seem troubling. Although so-called scientific racism should not be read backwards into a theocentric text, it is fair to recognize in such taxonomic activities a transitional quality: Smart's "early anthropology," as a peculiar mixture of theocentric narrative and quasi-scientific classification, does indeed mark a historical crossroads. Such systems of classification can usefully be seen as, in David Theo Goldberg's phrase, "the preconceptual grounds of racist discourse."[90]

If we were to end our analysis here, with Smart bogged down in the contradictions of his time, we would have many examples of the "mythic" resolution of antinomies. However, we would have found no sign of what Marin calls the "historically empty" ("historiquement vide") place of a future yet to be conceived.[91] The discovery of what is truly utopian in *Jubilate Agno* requires that we complete our structural analysis of the poem's deep logic. The reward for such an analysis is a final paradox of place. For the utopian in *Jubilate Agno* is most persuasively exemplified by "sincerity," by the notion of an ideally unconstrained and unbuttoned discourse. To be sure, the ideal of sincerity, a widespread *topos* in British literature by 1750, can be traced back to seventeenth-century radical Puritans.[92] The quest for immediacy among enthusiasts, as we have seen, went so far as to dislocate ordinary language and subjectivity. The zeal and beauty of Smart's utopian project, however, enable him to put his own stamp on the theme. Given Smart's difficulties in figuring the millennium, moreover, "sincerity" constitutes both a *koan*-like conundrum and a sort of breakthrough.[93] The very difficulty of placing "sincerity" illustrates perfectly Marin's remark about the double sense of "place" in utopian figuration: "Utopia develops its 'utopics' as spatial figures, but within discourse, its sole means of bringing them about. Utopics are discursive spatial figures: discursive places or *topics*."[94] ("Elle développe ses

[89] See P. J. Marshall and Glyndwr Williams, *The Great Map of Mankind: Perceptions of New Worlds in the Age of Enlightenment* (Cambridge, Mass.: Harvard University Press, 1982), pp. 244–245; see also Pratt, *Eyes*, p. 32.

[90] See David Theo Goldberg, "The social formation of racist discourse," in *Anatomy of Racism* (Minneapolis: University of Minnesota Press, 1990), especially pp. 301–305. See also Gareth Cornwell, "Race as science, race as language: a preliminary enquiry into origins," *Pretexts* 1:1 (1989), pp. 3–17.

[91] Marin, *Utopics*, p. 11; *Utopiques*, p. 26.

[92] See Leon Guilhamet, *The Sincere Ideal: Studies on Sincerity in Eighteenth-Century English Literature* (Montreal: McGill-Queen's University Press, 1974).

[93] According to Jameson, utopian neutralization may be seen, at best, as a sort of riddle or *koan*: a vehicle, as he writes, for "bring[ing] the mind up short before its own ideological limits, in a stunned and puzzled arrest of thought before the double-bind in which it suddenly finds itself paralyzed" (Jameson, "Utopian," p. 89). Marin likewise emphasizes that utopia is "preconceptual": a discourse of the figure rather than of the theoretical concept (Marin, *Utopics*, p. 8).

[94] *Ibid.*, p. 9; *Utopiques*, p. 23.

'utopiques' comme des figures d'espace et cependant dans le discours qui est son unique moyen d'effectuation: *utopiques*, figures discursives d'espace, *lieux* de discours, *topiques*.") Smart's invocation of "sincerity," rather like the Christian notion that the Kingdom of God is within, marks a decisive limit, a stalling point. And yet it is precisely through the *topos* of "sincerity" that Smart most effectively neutralizes the inside/outside split and provides a utopian space.

Smart's "sincerity" *topos* remains liminal: for "sincerity" is neither fully part of, nor entirely removed from, the realm of particular actions and their consequences. "Sincerity" emphasizes instead a quality of attitude, a general manner, that informs each individual act. It would seem that such "sincerity" entails a suspiciously metaphysical notion of an authentic or unmediated "inside," currently vulnerable to deconstruction from any number of angles. Such is not the case, however, with Smart. For Smart's notion of "sincerity" entails a rigorous refusal to make a vigilant and wary consistency, as a function of "normal" identity, an end in itself. Whether Smart writes as a poet, as a Protestant, as a patriot, or even as the "Reviver of ADORATION amongst ENGLISH-MEN," he does not speak consistently from any single fixed and authoritative position. Thus Smart's images for interior space, for the "place" from which he speaks, sometimes turn out in *Jubilate Agno* to be surprisingly empty. One indication of this is his subtly startling alignment of "soul" with "echo" – surely the most secondary, mediated, and derivative discourse possible: "For ECHO is the soul of the voice exerting itself in hollow places."[95] And indeed, a larger pattern of "hollow-place" imagery, as Alan Liu demonstrates, eventually enables Smart to imagine his role in literary translation as the construction of himself as a "special hollowness" or "empty place."[96]

It is thus quite appropriate that the theme of "sincerity" emerges first in *Jubilate Agno* with an arresting image of immutable transparency:

> Let Hamul rejoice with the Crystal, who is pure and translucent.
> For sincerity is a jewel which is pure and transparent, eternal
>   and inestimable.[97]

"Hamul," a nondescript personage in several Biblical genealogies, may appear here with the Crystal because the name's Hebrew root is connected with compassion. The image, then, has multiple valences: for the crystal's lapidary "hardness"[98] also represents Smart's unyielding commitment to a

---

[95] Smart, *Jubilate*, B 235.
[96] Liu, "Letters," p. 122.
[97] Smart, *Jubilate*, B 40.
[98] Although Mary Douglas observes that an overly rigid quest for purity can lead to a "petrified" or "lapidary" sense of one's own unchanging existence and uncompromised identity, Smart's "crystalline" purity strikes me as contextually very different from such a phenomenon. See Douglas, *Purity*, p. 162.

spiritual practice. Because a crystal is a medium of light rather than a radiant center and source, however – neither mirror nor lamp – it cannot stand for the illusion of a plenary and centered self. Indeed, Smart here transmutes his involuntary condition of public surveillance and exposure into a figuration of preemptively chosen openness, into a willed challenge, as it were, to the verbal boundaries separating "inside" and "outside." Given the possibility of a pantheistic pun on "Christ-All" that was also exploited by Abiezer Coppe, the crystal is indeed an apt image for Smart's strangely "empty" notion of personal sincerity.

By emphasizing "sincerity," moreover, Smart insists that his individual actions, however fallible or misguided, are informed by an enthusiasm that transcends and exceeds all such particulars. Thus, despite his recognition that his utterance is grounded in nothing but "sincerity," he does not withdraw into a guarded and circumspect quiescence. The construction of his metaphysical ground as emptiness and transparency is, for Smart, no reason not to speak and act. On the contrary, he is forever rejoicing, forever speaking, forever reinventing himself. In so doing, he risks being terribly wrong both about who he is and what he says. Even so, "sincerity" is precisely that one place from which Smart can be neither mercilessly exclusive nor blasphemously impure. Under the rubric of sincerity, therefore, *Jubilate Agno* appropriately celebrates both a roaring lion and the idea of a full-bodied, all-inclusive human voice:

> For a man speaks HIMSELF from the crown of his head to the sole of
> his feet.
> For a LION roars HIMSELF compleat from head to tail.[99]

The juxtaposed images are an apt epitome of the poem's project of vocal inclusion and strength. If and when Smart is wrong, he will be entirely wrong, roaringly wrong, *sincerely* wrong.

The greatest social risk that Smart assumes in the name of "sincerity," however, is the sheer refusal to identify with a fixed and secure position. Smart instead associates himself with a "rare" sincerity, thus finding himself, as he willingly admits, a greater prodigy than the exhibits of a freak-show:

> Let Eli rejoice with Leucon – he is an honest fellow, which is a rarity.
> For I have seen the White Raven and Thomas Hall of Willingham
> and am myself a greater curiosity than both.[100]

Thomas Hall was a contemporary gigantic boy. Smart links his parallel and self-conscious "rarity" to honesty and purity in the colors of the White Raven and Leucon, the white heron. Thus Smart insists that his "sincerity," though verging on a confessional exhibitionism, entails no impurity. Neither puffed

[99] Smart, *Jubilate*, B 228–229.
[100] *Ibid.*, B 25.

up with disdain for oddness nor tainted by hypocrisy, he embraces "freak" as an acceptable name for the extravagant place from which he speaks.

Indeed, the proof of sincere adoration for Smart is precisely a willingness to refuse the social conventions associated with a recognition of one's fixed place and position. Hence his willingness to ignore social decorum, just as King David, despite the scornful glance of his wife Michal, danced uninhibitedly, uncovered before handmaids, when the Israelites recovered the Ark of the Covenant. To worship properly, one must be unguarded. Smart believes he is persecuted for being, as he writes elsewhere, "more unguarded than the others."[101] "Sincerity" is a manner free of "acting," moreover, in the further sense of role-playing and hypocrisy, which Smart elsewhere links to the professional theater.[102] "Sincerity" thus refuses and rebukes a merely theatrical performance of good deeds for the wrong reasons, as in the following attack on the hypocritical politics of "Charity": "For Charity is cold in the multitude of possessions," as Smart writes, "and the rich are covetous of their crumbs."[103] Smart's "sincerity" entails a refusal to be boxed in by the conventions of place and position – the phrase "a good family" comes to mind – that permit an insidious conflation of morality with social privilege.

Smart's radically different poetics of place emerges most vividly when he rewrites, by way of a double cancellation, our understanding of lying. Observing that he mentions in one verse a "foundation on slander,"[104] Geoffrey Hartman alerts us to Smart's anxiety about slander and lying, describing it as "an anxiety about the foundation, about origins, and so about the truth issuing from his own tongue."[105] Perhaps the most crucial genealogical claim Smart stakes, then, is the one in which he honors his maternal ancestry as a legacy of truth-telling. Through a figurative sense of his mother's native Welsh, mother tongue of bards, he claims to inherit sincerity:

> Let Ziba rejoice with Glottis whose tongue is wreathed in his throat.
> For I am the seed of the WELCH WOMAN and speak the truth from
>   my heart.[106]

Karina Williamson annotates these lines by explaining that Ziba won favor by telling lies (2 Samuel 16:1–4), that "Glottis" (the quail) takes its name from its longer tongue, and that Smart's mother, Winifred Griffiths, came from Wales. The "For" and "Let" lines thus juxtapose Smart's claim to sincerity with a liar (Ziba) and a creature (Glottis) whose long tongue "wreathes" in his throat.

[101] *Ibid.*, B 124.
[102] *Ibid.*, B 345.
[103] *Ibid.*, B 154.
[104] *Ibid.*, B 170.
[105] Hartman, "Magnificat," p. 89.
[106] Smart, *Jubilate*, B 91.

Hartman remarks elsewhere that this same line, full of anxiety about ritual purity and language, "implies a disturbance touching at once the mother and the mother tongue."[107] This interpretation evidently assumes that Smart intends a contrast between himself, as a "pure" speaker of truth, and the "impure" pair of lying, tongue-twisting creatures invoked to rejoice in the "Let" line. It seems more likely, however, that the juxtaposition works in precisely the opposite direction. For Smart's "sincerity" is a matter, strictly speaking, neither of a lying façade nor a revealed interior depth. Because Smart's notion of "sincerity" does not and cannot preclude all sort of misrepresentations, he links himself with Ziba and Glottis precisely on the basis of similarity rather than contrast. Indeed, as W. M. Merchant points out, "Ziba" means "plant" ("twig" in Aramaic), and so is linked to Smart as the "seed" of the Welch Woman.[108] Thus nothing so fully authenticates Smart's claim to "speak the truth from [his] heart" as his implied acknowledgment in these lines that in the very activities of naming and placing he himself inevitably risks "lying": the sort of verbal action, that is, that he feels has victimized him personally, and, more generally, has polluted the verbal cosmos. This awareness, though it cannot "transcend" discourse, does nevertheless persuasively figure an ideal place at once within, and yet insistently beyond, complicity with the lies of the powerful.

A closely related moment, which seems to empty out the distinction between truth and vanity, appears in the following sequence of "For" lines.

> For Solomon said vanity of vanities, vanity of vanities all is vanity.
> For Jesus says verity of verities, verity of verities all is verity.[109]

The "extraordinarily tense parallelism" that William Kumbier observes in these lines – precariously separated, as he points out, only by the placing of Jesus' words in the present tense[110] – comes dangerously close to blurring any distinction between sacred truth and vain falsehood. The formal repetition has an inescapable levelling implication, as do the sloganized sayings themselves: for it comes to pretty much the same thing to say that "all is vanity" and that "all is truth." To be sure, Solomon is subsequently blamed for castigating folly,[111] whereas Jesus is praised for not reviling even in hardship.[112] Taken as a whole, however, the passage serves again to locate the grounds of Smart's own "folly," his sincerity, in a neutral zone defined neither by verity nor vanity.

---

[107] Hartman, *Wilderness*, p. 143.

[108] W. M. Merchant, "Patterns of reference in Smart's *Jubilate Agno*," *Harvard Library Bulletin* 14 (1960), p. 23.

[109] Smart, *Jubilate*, B 287–288.

[110] William Kumbier, "Sound and signification in Christopher Smart's *Jubilate Agno*," *Texas Studies in Literature and Language* 24:3 (1982), p. 296.

[111] Smart, *Jubilate*, B 289.

[112] *Ibid.*, B 290.

My emphasis on the neutralizing force of Smart's "crystalline" sincerity, as opposed to his merely additive listing activities, foregrounds its achieved utopian resolution – and thus, as Jameson would say, its political vibrancy. Ironically, it is this very vibrancy, as constituted by the distinction between "myth" and "utopia," that seems to disappear in Jameson's later attempt to think "utopia" and "ideology" simultaneously.[113] The utopian, in Jameson's later and far more sweeping notion, seems to lose any specificity beyond a collective desire for solidarity. Insofar as such a gregarious yearning can prefigure a universal community, utopia is a dimension of all cultural productions.[114] Thus, according to the view advanced in *The Political Unconscious* and elsewhere, utopia is as ubiquitous as the desire to belong to a group. Jameson goes on to argue that marxist critics should perform a qualified recuperation of the utopian moments in even the most glaringly reactionary texts.[115] The concept of utopia becomes so elastic that the textual celebration of any conceivable historical force whatsoever – say, the solidarity of the most brutal oppressors – can be read, allegorically, as the (manipulative and reified) expression of a more universal desire for a classless society.[116] The interpretative violence required, in the allegorical passage from partisan to universal, would necessarily be in direct proportion to the historical violence and exploitation associated with the particular solidarity under consideration.[117] It is not clear, moreover, that this sweeping notion of utopia-cum-ideology explains, any more adequately than the concept of myth, the insidiously seductive appeal to the political unconscious achieved by oppressive textual resolutions.

[113] Hence, in an otherwise fascinating reprise of his extensive work with the semiotic square, Jameson's rather startling reference to the "complex or utopian term." See his foreword to Greimas, *Meaning*, p. xiv. The "complex or utopian term" remains distinct from the neutral term; the latter, however, receives little emphasis as a point of special interest. It seems relevant that Jameson nowhere cites Marin in this later reprise of his work.

[114] Larysa Mykta has observed that Jameson, perhaps in a strategic effort to accelerate the historical reckoning by which utopian desires can be gratified, seems at times to confuse their expression with their realization. Larysa Mykta, "Jameson's utopias," *New Orleans Review* 11:1 (1984), p. 51.

[115] Versions of this position appear in a whole succession of Jameson's texts, including the following: the chapter on Ernst Bloch in *Marxism and Form* (Princeton, New Jersey: Princeton University Press, 1971); "Reification and utopia in mass culture," *Social Text* 1, 1979; "Religion and ideology: a political reading of *Paradise Lost*," in *1642: Proceedings of 1980 Essex Sociology of Literature Conference*, ed. R. Barker (Colchester: University of Essex Press, 1981); and, most definitively, in the conclusion to *The Political Unconscious: Narrative as a Socially Symbolic Act* (Ithaca: Cornell University Press, 1981).

[116] *Ibid.*, pp. 290–291.

[117] Cornel West thus argues that Jameson's "utopianism gone mad" reflects the naiveté of a particular historical experience: "Given the barbarous atrocities and large-scale horrors inflicted by hegemonic ruling classes in Europe, Africa, Asia, and Latin America, only a Marxist thinker entrenched in the North American experience could even posit the possibility of ruling-class consciousness figuratively being 'in its very nature Utopian.'" Cornel West, "Ethics and action in Fredric Jameson's hermeneutics," in *Postmodernism and Politics*, ed. Jonathan Arac (Minneapolis: University of Minnesota Press, 1986), p. 140.

To be sure, no one doubts the strategic value of balancing debunking interpretations, which often seem predictable and overly programmatic, with a more positive hermeneutics. Insofar as literary critics are also concerned with nuances of genre and figurative process, however, there is a severe cost if utopia, because it is everywhere, turns out to be nowhere in particular. What Jameson seems to renounce in his later work is a refined critical tool for distinguishing between qualitatively different sorts of textual resolution.

The earlier and more suggestive distinction between myth and utopia provides a finer optic for reading Smart's *Jubilate Agno*. It permits us to see that Smart's vibrancy in the *Jubilate* is based, paradoxically, precisely on a certain kind of tremendously ambitious failure. For "sincerity" names precisely Smart's inability to imagine fully, even in the symbolic space of a poem, an all-inclusive and cosmopolitan "Ark": a horizontal space untainted by motives of domination. "Sincerity," however, does not imply self-critical reflection in the usual sense. Its force, indeed, depends precisely on its being both more and less than such critical reflexivity: more effervescent and less inhibited than the workaday ego, more pure and less indirect in its negativity than ordinary self-consciousness. "Sincerity" thus also names and foregrounds a certain crisis, a prolonged state of liminality, in Smart's own ebullient subjectivity. If this "sincerity" is "madness," such madness nevertheless partly takes its form as the hard-won utopian thought of its particular moment. Such a poignant and costly achievement deserves to be, in Smart's lovely phrase, "translated in the charity."[118] For such "sincerity," though it remains "preconceptual," does nevertheless succeed in designating Marin's "historically empty" place of a future yet to be adequately conceived in social theory, much less realized in social practice.

It is only by distinguishing between "ADD-ORATION" and "sincerity" as qualitatively different sorts of textual resolution that one can get beyond the cliché of Smart's "vertical" orientation to a celestial world. In unduly emphasizing the otherworldliness of *Jubilate Agno*, some critics have gotten stuck in a potentially reductive confusion of a merely additive "ADD-ORATION" with the essence of Smart's achievement. In recognizing that Smart's "mythic" and "utopian" resolutions involve quite different orders of figurative mediation, we bring into sharp relief those dimensions of his text that engage most strenuously and creatively in wrestling with things as they are. Such a secular reading of Smart's enthusiasm does not so much diminish its spirituality as restore its vitality: for "sincerity" is not otherworldly, but, rather, a particular stance for negotiating with the limits of this world. It is a stance of playful self-displacement that reveals, above all, the special potential of "manic" or enthusiastic discourse.

Smart's unique contribution, given a more homogenizing view of symbolic

---

[118] Smart, *Jubilate*, B 11.

mediations, could easily be eclipsed. For the special "manic" project of Smart's poem, and what is authentically challenging about *Jubilate Agno*, is simply not to be found in every text whatsoever. We cannot afford to overlook, in our own efforts to break through narrow horizons, such an unusual text. We still need a critical language that can recognize and use the cutting edge of such a text as a wedge through and beyond the present. And we still need a political practice that will begin to translate the piercing zeal – ultimately neither normal nor merely pathological – of Smart's utopian "sincerity."

Epilogue

Beyond pathology

In heaven, too
You'd be institutionalized.
But that's all right...
Theodore Roethke "Heard in a Violent Ward," from
The Collected Poems of Theodore Roethke

Mania and Literary Style has shown the historical frequency with which a vocabulary of psychomedical pathologization serves the interests of the political *status quo*: the normalizing, disciplining mechanisms, that is to say, of cultural subjection. The clearest implication of this book is that literary and cultural criticism, far too often an anti-enthusiastic enterprise, should not use the vocabulary of individual pathology without full awareness of its historical resonance. In the case of enthusiasm, at any rate, the "pathological" is precisely that collective and oppositional phenomenon which, though surprisingly influential in literary history, has barely begun to be integrated, as a significant and enduring mode, into our shared narrative of literary history.

Mania and Literary Style should thus serve to foreground the unhistorical assumptions that frequently license psychiatric diagnoses of literary figures working in this style. A historical reckoning with "mania" as a rhetorical mode brings into view, for example, the homogenizing and reductive force of the "private" model of mania used in Kay Redfield Jamison's *Touched with Fire: Manic-Depressive Illness and the Artistic Temperament*. The book's biological essentialism – its reduction of all causality to the single level of genetic inheritance – is foretold by the emblem on its title page: a double helix, signifier of "the genetic," adjacent to a sketch of Byron. *Touched with Fire* gathers a lengthy list of artistic case histories, including those of Byron and Smart, under the rubric of manic-depressive illness. Manic-depressive illness is a strictly biological disease, according to Jamison's speculations; but it is a disease, in its less extreme manifestations, with certain artistic compensations.[1] Jamison's disciplinary raid on art and literature serves to amass very

[1]   Kay Redfield Jamison, *Touched with Fire: Manic-Depressive Illness and the Artistic Temperament* (New York: The Free Press, 1993).

230

heterogeneous kinds of evidence under the rubric of science: family trees, poems, graphs which purport to quantify data based on hearsay or self-reporting, and biographical and literary anecdotes. Thus a realm of historically bound meanings is stripped of all history except the genetic inheritance of "tainted blood." It scarcely seems to occur to Jamison that her own discipline, the "artistic temperament," or even "mania" itself, might have complex histories. Because her own canned version of the eighteenth century (as an age of moderation and reason) does not suit her argument, for instance, she passes over it perfunctorily, as a "comparatively brief period,"[2] and hurries on to friendlier ground: an equally predigested account of the "fiery" Romantics.

Touched with Fire is best read as a cautionary tale about the reduction, in the context of a neuropsychiatric disciplinary imperialism, of one level of reality to a supposedly more elementary, more real level. Thus for Jamison the neurobiological level is understood as prior to, and far more important than, the psychological or social levels. Consider, however, the following example of an "event": one's garbage, because of a strike, is not picked up. It is true that this event, as with any other, involves mechanisms best describable in the language of physics: the operation of the engines in garbage trucks, the rotting of uncollected garbage, and so on. However, a physical description alone could never predict nor fully explain the workers' decision to strike. There are causal mechanisms of such an action at the social level that necessarily elude a purely physical description.[3]

A manic text is exactly such an event as a strike. Although the creation of a manic text very likely involves, in some cases, specific neurobiological factors, such factors can go only so far in explaining such a text. Christopher Smart himself recognizes in *Jubilate Agno* that he has, as he says, "a greater compass both of mirth and melancholy than another."[4] This reflection, indeed, is one of the pieces of evidence used to buttress Sir Russell Brain's diagnosis of Smart's "cyclothymia" in 1961.[5] It is difficult to say, however, whether Smart's "cyclothymic" temperament, which Brain admits that he shares with such very different writers as James Boswell and Samuel Johnson, correlates with anything very specific about either his vocation as a poet or his writing style. His "temperament," in any case, manifested itself quite differently in

[2]   *Ibid.*, p. 52.
[3]   This example is adapted from Andrew Collier, *Scientific Realism and Socialist Thought* (Hertfordshire: Harvester Wheatsheaf, 1989), pp. 47–48.
[4]   Christopher Smart, *The Poetical Works of Christopher Smart*, 4 vols., eds. Karina Williamson and Marcus Walsh (Oxford: Clarendon Press, 1980–1987), I: *Jubilate Agno*, B 132.
[5]   Sir Russell Brain, "Christopher Smart: the flea that became an eagle," in *Some Reflections on Genius* (Philadelphia: J. B. Lippincott Co., 1961), pp. 113–122. This line is also quoted in a recent psychiatrically oriented essay that recapitulates Brain's diagnosis. See "The powers of night: Christopher Smart," in Gordon Claridge, Ruth Pryor, and Gwen Watkins *Sounds from the Bell Jar: Ten Psychotic Authors* (New York: St. Martin's Press, 1990), p. 87.

other texts written at roughly the same time as *Jubilate Agno*. If a neurobiological pathology is the common substrate of such different texts by Smart as the *Jubilate*, "A Song to David," and the *Hymns and Spiritual Songs*, we still have no adequate account of how and why these texts – not to mention writings by Boswell and Johnson – manifest it so differently.

The restoration of historical depth to the concept of mania permits a similarly skeptical scrutiny of the terminology more recently applied by a medical doctor to Smart. William Ober's terse diagnosis of Smart's condition – "a religious monomania without intellectual deterioration"[6] – illustrates again the nonchalance with which modern psychiatry, supposedly dealing in timeless entities, often absorbs rival discourses. Are we to understand by this incoherent concept – "a religious monomania" – that medical science has finally settled the question of what critical attitude one ought to take toward the specifically spiritual dimensions of Smart's poetics?

Ober's attempted hedgings of his labeling only serve, in the end, to incite more questions. It would seem to be to his credit, for example, that he also acknowledges that "Smart's 'estrangement'…merely took him back a century in terms of religious feeling, and in *Jubilate Agno* to a Hebraic rather than an English rhetoric."[7] In fact, however, Ober simply leaves unresolved the relationship between this point and his medical diagnosis. Is the religiosity of a given period or people then to be seen, in a scientific age, as intrinsically pathological? Or is it only certain subcultural phenomena – often a badge of group membership and radical political identity – that must be construed in terms of abnormality? If we situate Smart in the context of an enthusiastic constellation, we know that he was not alone in taking inspiration from the rhetoric of Biblical Hebrew.

Is the pathological element in Smart a question, perhaps, of intensity, of the enthusiastic tone? For Ober, the word "control" seems to condense the crucial social and aesthetic values at stake in Smart's poetry: "In *Jubilate Agno* the experiment with enthusism and the Hebraic antiphonal mode was uncontrolled, and it is not to Smart's discredit that he abandoned the experiment."[8] One wonders in exactly what sense an aesthetic "experiment," even an uncontrolled one, can be pathological. In any case, it is difficult not to hear in Ober's diagnosis the echo, centuries later, of seventeenth- and eighteenth-century Anglican pamphleteers. And indeed, as Ober's example makes especially clear, in declaring enthusiastic religious attitudes "mad" or "discreditable," one implicitly forecloses the possibility that there could be any sort of political or spiritual legacy to be reclaimed from the democratic religious traditions spawned in the seventeenth century. Such a question-

---

[6]   William Ober, "Madness and poetry," in *Boswell's Clap and Other Essays: Medical Analyses of Literary Men's Afflictions* (1979; New York: Perennial Library, 1988), p. 192.

[7]   *Ibid.*, p. 187.

[8]   *Ibid.*, p. 188.

begging judgment, while couched in the authoritative language of medical science, is not politically neutral. To biologize the transgressive energy of a text in the manic style is to risk sealing off any treatment of the relation between the irreducibly symbolic features of its subjectivity and their related context of social practices.

It must be said that more fruitful encounters between literary criticism and contemporary neurobiological psychiatry are beginning to appear. *The Flight of the Mind*, Thomas Carramagno's interdisciplinary "neurobiography" of Virginia Woolf, largely succeeds in emphasizing the biological substrate of manic-depressive illness without reducing Woolf's writing to its effects.[9] Carramagno, a literary critic, discusses Woolf's fiction as an adaptive and creative response to bodily vicissitudes – swings in the chemistry of her brain – that were beyond her control. She shaped her fiction to express what those biological vicissitudes, the disjunctive ups and down of manic-depressive illness, had taught her about consciousness: the radical ambiguities of interpretation, the fluidity of subject-object transactions, the blurriness of the line between sanity and madness, the flux of identity, the transience of reality. Though he devotes considerable space to clearing the ground of psychoanalytic interpretations, Carramagno depends throughout on a dialogue with the theorists of object-relations, from Melanie Klein to D. W. Winnicott. Carramagno's interpretations, therefore, though strongly biographical, are open to the level of existence in which subjectivity constitutes itself through intersubjectively meaningful images and symbols. The book's subtlety is thus achieved, above all, by a willingness to respect multiple levels of reality.

In presenting Woolf's fiction as a creative transformation of the experience of illness, Carramagno largely avoids diagnosing the texts themselves as pathological. The lesson of his relative success is that one should be wary of an unmediated reduction of a text to the epiphenomena of disease: for texts are indeed heavily mediated and overdetermined creations. Although the body is certainly one textual mediation among others, history courses through channels other than chromosomes alone. Carramagno's interpretation of Woolf, though it does not engage with the possibility of a manic literary mode, is open to the critical exploration of textual determinants operating at the cultural level.

In tracing the contours of a manic style in the seventeenth and mid-eighteenth centuries, *Mania and Literary Style* also points toward further developments in the history and transmission of manic rhetoric. Each of these, of course, would need to be seen as a new transformation of the mode according to its particular historical circumstances. Some well-known texts that might be reconsidered in this regard include, among others,

---

[9] See Thomas Carramagno, *The Flight of the Mind: Virginia Woolf's Art and Manic-Depressive Illness* (Berkeley: University of California Press, 1992).

Laurence Sterne's *Tristram Shandy*, William Blake's *The Marriage of Heaven and Hell*,[10] and Thomas Carlyle's *Sartor Resartus*: the final hypertrophy of the manic "clothes philosophy." Moving across the Atlantic, one finds the American manic in such texts as Herman Melville's *Moby Dick*, Walt Whitman's "Song of Myself," Gertrude Stein's "Patriarchal Poetry," James Agee's *Let Us Now Praise Famous Men*, Allen Ginsberg's "Howl,"[11] and Ishmael Reed's *Mumbo Jumbo* (the latter deliberately exploiting manic wordplay as a counter-Enlightenment motif). Certain essays of Ralph Waldo Emerson, such as "Nature," also might be seen as verging on this incantatory mode. And the well-known listing propensities of such figures as Vladimir Nabokov and William Gass certainly pay homage to the manic. Most intriguing of all, perhaps, is David Simpson's recent suggestion that literary theory itself – especially insofar as it seeks to be programmatic, systematic, and "methodical" – owes a certain kind of intellectual debt to the makers of the English Revolution and to the eighteenth-century Methodists.[12]

Other examples will doubtless come to mind. I would further insist, however, that the fact that the manic has become an influential literary mode does not merely illustrate the predominance of manic-depressive illness among poets, as Kay Redfield Jamison claims. Be that as it may, it also illustrates, more crucially, the way that literature can serve as a kind of specialized aesthetic haven or ghetto for alternative and marginalized elements that otherwise resist ready incorporation.[13] For this is the true paradox of the manic style: even as enthusiasm has entered deeply into the fabric of literary tradition, its political affiliations, as a collective and enduring counter-discourse, have been largely overlooked.

It should no longer be adequate, moreover, merely to gesture by way of context toward Biblical models. For the point of enthusiasm, as we have seen, is a highly selective appropriation of particular Biblical *topoi*, from King David's scandalous dancing to Mary's Magnificat to prophetically levelling catalogues to symbolic "pranks." It is a literary style in confrontational dialogue with a more conservative appropriation of Scripture. As Keith Thomas has shown, utopian thought in the mid-seventeenth century, deeply entangled with millenarianism, arose in reaction to a profoundly conservative, pessimistic, and anti-utopian religious teaching that rationalized the

---

[10] For a recent study situating Blake more generally within the revived enthusiasm of the 1790s, see Jon Mee, *Dangerous Enthusiasm: William Blake and the Culture of Radicalism in the 1790s* (Oxford: Clarendon Press, 1992).

[11] Bruce Hunsberger makes a case for the direct influence of *Jubilate Agno* on "Howl" in his "Kit Smart's howl," in *On the Poetry of Allen Ginsberg*, ed. Lewis Hyde (Ann Arbor: The University of Michigan Press, 1984), pp. 158–170.

[12] See David Simpson, *Romanticism, Nationalism, and the Revolt against Theory* (Chicago: The University of Chicago Press, 1993).

[13] See Raymond Williams, *Marxism and Literature* (Oxford: Oxford University Press, 1977), p. 125.

political *status quo* through reference to original sin.[14] What remains essential to the manic mode is what Cornel West emphasizes in the liberation struggle of African-Americans in the United States: the prophetic and revolutionary use of the hope, *against all odds*, that God sides with the oppressed.[15]

[14] Keith Thomas, "The utopian impulse in seventeenth-century England," in *Between Dream and Nature: Essays on Utopia and Dystopia*, eds. Dominic Baker-Smith and C. C. Barfoot (Amsterdam: Rodopi, 1987), pp. 20–46.

[15] Cornel West, *Prophesy Deliverance: An Afro-American Revolutionary Christianity* (Philadelphia: The Westminster Press, 1982). There are of course many parallels to be explored in other traditions rooted in Biblical prophesying. These adjacent traditions, however, need to be studied in their own historical contexts; they are mostly outside the historical scope of this study. See, for instance, *The Apocalypse in English Renaissance Thought and Literature*, eds. C. A. Patrides and Joseph Wittreich (Ithaca: Cornell University Press, 1984); Sacvan Bercovitch's *The American Jeremiad* (Madison, Wisconsin: The University of Wisconsin Press, 1978); Donald Weber's *Rhetoric and History in Revolutionary New England* (New York: Oxford University Press, 1988); Elizabeth A. Petroff's *Medieval Women's Visionary Literature* (New York: Oxford University Press, 1986); Joseph Owen's *Dread: The Rastafarians of Jamaica* (London: Sangster's Book Stores Ltd., 1976); Deane William Ferne's anthology, *Third World Liberation Theologies: A Reader* (Maryknoll, New York: Orbis Books, 1986); and Michael Adas' *Prophets of Rebellion: Millenarian Protest Movements against the European Colonial Order* (Chapel Hill: The University of North Carolina Press, 1979).

Index

Abelove, Henry, 129n, 142, 199n
Addison, Joseph, 166, 179–80
Althusser, Louis
  interpellation, 21, 29–31, 64
  overdetermination, 10, 21, 28, 33, 39, 116,
    168, 190, 231–5
anagrams; see wordplay
Anglican Church, Anglicanism
  Book of Common Prayer, 157
  and evangelical revival, 129–31
  and high-church reading of Smart's poetry,
    133–4
  interpellative address of, 31
  and liturgical form, 157–8, 173
  pamphleteers for, 4–5, 16, 104
  Smart's liminality within, 131–4
animals
  as emblems of madness, 104, 161–2
  as featured in poetry of sensibility, 162
  as included in expanded covenant, 163
  in pantheistic thought, 84–6
  as spirits in language, 170–2
  seen as persecuted, 161
  torture of, 162
  and zoological defense mechanisms,
    164–6
annihilationism, 85, 163
anti-theatrical discourse, 150, 190–1,
  225
Appiah, Kwame Anthony, 218
Astell, Mary, 66
Aylmer, G. E., 48

Bauman, Richard, 40–1, 52n
Bauthumley, Jacob, 85–6, 96
Behn, Aphra, 66
Bernard, Saint, 71–2
Bertelsen, Lance, 138, 190–1, 216
Blake, William, 162, 163, 234
Blasphemy Act (1650), 35, 97
Blome, Richard, 45, 92
body-politic topos, 51, 59, 63, 68, 119–20
Boehme, Jacob, 12n, 13

Bond, W. H., 157–8
Brain, Sir Russell, 231–2
Browning, Robert, 15, 177
Bunyan, John
  The Advocateship of Jesus Christ, 194
  Grace Abounding to the Chief of Sinners, 29, 30
  The Holy War, 164
  Pilgrim's Progress, 3
  bipolar world-view of, 29
  despair of, 44
  incarceration of, 9, 161
  lay preaching of, 31
Burton, Robert, 5
Butler, Samuel, 35

Calvinism, see Stachniewski
Camisards see Huguenots
Carramagno, Thomas, 233
Cary/Rand, Mary, 73, 112, 193
catalogues
  as element of manic style, 9
  as imperial inventories, 216
  as levelling device, 53–4
  variety of in Smart, 215
Clarkson, Laurence, 85
class
  defined, 2–3
  as class struggle without class, 2–3
  as element of manic style, 9; see also
    magnification
  formation of and identity, 9–10
  formation of and gender, 11–12
  as constitutive of manic rhetoric, 28, 43
  as constitutive of the irony in A Tale of a Tub,
    106–7
  and popular/elite cultural divide, 108–9
  as constitutive of Smart's project in Jubilate
    Agno, 144
Cohen, Alfred, 14, 96
Cohn, Norman, 13, 45
Collins, William, 132, 214n
community-of-wives topos, 49, 50, 186
Conventicle Act (1664), 160

CAMBRIDGE STUDIES IN EIGHTEENTH-CENTURY ENGLISH LITERATURE
AND THOUGHT